TIM RENTON entered the House of Commons as MP for Mid Sussex in 1974, served as Minister in the Foreign Office and the Home Office, and was Government Chief Whip from 1989 to 1990. He subsequently became Minister for the Arts and remained in the Commons until 1997, when he was moved to the House of Lords as Lord Renton of Mount Harry, the Sussex Down where he lives. He is the author of two novels, *The Dangerous Edge* (1994) and *Hostage to Fortune* (1997).

Opposite: Tim Renton in Downing Street on his first day as Government Chief Whip, 27 October 1989.

To Alice,
with whom I have shared
so many adventures

Chief Whip

PEOPLE, POWER AND PATRONAGE

IN WESTMINSTER

Tim Renton

POLITICO'S

First published in Great Britain 2004

This paperback edition published in Great Britain 2005 by
Politico's Publishing, an imprint of
Methuen Publishing Limited
215 Vauxhall Bridge Road
London SW1V 1EJ

1 3 5 7 9 10 8 6 4 2

A CIP catalogue record for this book is available from the British Library

ISBN 1 84275 129 8

Printed and bound in Great Britain by
Bookmarque Ltd, Croydon, Surrey

CONTENTS

Die Politik ist keine exakte Wissenschaft. *

OTTO VON BISMARCK, 1863

* Politics is not an exact science.

PREFACE

Now in the popular mind the office of whip is one with which many strange fancies and doubts are associated and one, too, which all combine to a suspicion to render mysterious.

Northern Star

The concept of a freely elected politician being whipped to make him forget his principles and vote instead for a measure that he does not agree with strikes at the heart of representative democracy. It disillusions those voters, a diminishing number, who still listen to or read about Westminster politics. Yet, without whipping and the organisation of parliamentary business that goes with it, the Commons would be a shambles.

This is the paradox that I explore in this book. For thirteen months I was Margaret Thatcher's last Chief Whip. The first part is the story of those months which embraced the rebellions over the Poll Tax and ended with Margaret leaving No. 10 – the only Prime Minister in our history to have been effectively voted out of office by her own parliamentary party.

I found the role of Chief Whip so extraordinary, so pivotal, that I decided to research the history of parliamentary whipping – how it began and, particularly, the increasing influence of the Government Chief Whip, who started by infrequently attending Cabinet at the bidding of the Prime Minister and who is now a full member. It is a story that has never been told before and I am grateful for the help that many ex-Chief Whips and parliamentary colleagues offered me in researching and suggesting archives and sources. In the second part of the book, I go into detail about a number of Chief Whips who, as in my case, found themselves at the centre in a crucial moment in history.

One of these was Henry Brand, the Liberal Government Chief Whip from 1859 to 1866, about whom I write in Chapter 7. When he resigned as the party's Whip in 1868, the *Northern Star* continued the quote on the previous page with these words:

> It would be impossible to describe the exact feeling with which it [the office of whip] is vulgarly regarded, because, as it has no formally prescribed duties attached to it and no visible routine connected with it, it is a subject of that fertile speculation which ranges between all possible extremes. Without attempting to solve the doubts or explain the mysteries, we may state that the office of whip is perhaps the most important one connected with the government... It requires tact, discretion, prudence, ability, knowledge of men's character as well as men's actions – affability never descending to mistaken familiarity. Few can be found to possess the rare gifts required for the discharge of such arduous duties; but it must be conceded to Mr Brand that he exhibited them in the highest degree and succeeded in usefully exercising them, not only for his party but his country.
>
> No one knew better the temper of the times and the temper of the House than the quiet unobtrusive man who seemed to observe nothing, and care for nothing, that was passing around him. In the heat of ardent discussion, in the rush and tumult of division, he alone was calm and imperturbable; yet he had weighed every circumstance, calculated every chance, used every effect, and employed every resource that could contribute to success.

This is a description to which, of course, any of us ex-Chief Whips would gladly aspire, but it has to be put into the context of the time. The mid and late nineteenth century was a period when Chief Whips were the constant subject of articles and comment. In his Palliser novels Anthony Trollope made the reporting of Parliament and the detailed description of the Chamber and its occupants a fashionable subject. *The Times* was full of parliamentary debates. Political parties had become established, but being in Parliament was very much a part-time activity. So messages were regularly sent to the Opera House, the theatres and the Pall Mall clubs urging members in white tie and tails to hurry back to the Commons to vote. The Government Chief Whip was not only the source of these messages. He was the main conduit for jobs in the growing Civil Service, later for governing parts of New Zealand, Australia, Canada and India and, finally, for knighthoods, baronetcies, membership of the Privy Council and peerages. In at least one case he chose the future Prime Minister.

During the nineteenth and early twentieth centuries more and more people were given the right to vote and Members of Parliament came from much more varied backgrounds. The power of the whips, as organisers and controllers of the parliamentary process, increased alongside the growth in the electorate, leading to Enoch Powell's remark in the 1960s that whips in parliament were as inevitable as rats in sewers.

But times change, and so do pressures in Parliament, especially when the government has a large majority. The popular saying is now 'Don't rebel on more than one subject at a time, it only confuses the whips.' Whips from the government party have come to be seen as an extension of over-powerful government, diminishing the ability of the Commons to restrain the executive. Today's Government Chief Whip is an emasculated version of Henry Brand. The final two chapters deal with the current Parliament and make some suggestions for the future.

ACKNOWLEDGEMENTS

I am particularly grateful to P. M. Gurowich for sight of his doctoral thesis on 'Party and Independence in the early and mid Victorian House of Commons'; to Anthony Hampden for the loan of correspondence to and from Henry Brand, 1st Viscount Hampden; to Lord Chilston and the publishers Routledge & Kegan Paul for quotations from *Chief Whip*, the biography of Aretas Akers-Douglas, 1st Viscount Chilston; to Cameron Hazelhurst and Christine Woodland and the publishers The Historians' Press, for quotations from *A Liberal Chronicle: J. A. Pease 1908-1910*; to Gay Charteris and Mary Pearson for hospitality and sight of David Margesson's papers; to Jamie Crathorne for the loan of Nancy Dugdale's diary on the Constitutional Crisis, November-December 1936; to Nancy Joan Seligman for reminiscences about Ted Heath; to Francis Pym for wise counsel and permission to publish his minute to Ted Heath of 5 October 1971; to Paul Bryan for the loan of his book *Wool, War and Westminster*; to the Librarians and Archivists at the Bodleian, the House of Commons and the House of Lords libraries, the Churchill Archives Centre, and the National Library of Scotland; to Raymond Hylton for loan of a book of letters to Sir William Jolliffe; to Diana Cavendish for extensive and enthusiastic research work; to John Sainty for an admirable list of Government Chief Whips' potted biographies; and to Kenneth Baker for assistance in finding cartoons of past Chief Whips. I am very grateful for the time and advice I was given by Geoffrey Howe, Ted Heath, Murdo Maclean, Michael Jopling, Ann Taylor, Hilary Armstrong, James Arbuthnot, Denis Carter, Bertie Denham, Andrew Mackay, David MacLean and Richard Ottaway. I thank Robert Skidelsky, Asa Briggs, and Anthony Seldon for allowing me to pick their brains, and John Sainty for his invaluable potted biographies of parliamentary secretaries. I would like to thank my agent Gill Coleridge and my publishers Iain Dale and Sean Magee for their enthusiasm and support, and my especial thanks for their hard work and patience go to my secretary of the last few years, Clare Kennard, and my House of Commons secretary, Ann Harvey, both of whom will recognise parts of the text all too well.

PART
ONE

ONE

Up the greasy pole, 1989

My first brush with the Government Chief Whip happened in 1981. Margaret Thatcher had been Prime Minister and Geoffrey Howe Chancellor of the Exchequer for two years. One evening, rather than voting with the government on one element in Geoffrey Howe's budget, a retrospective tax on the banks, I decided to go home. I had made too many speeches against retrospective taxes when we were in opposition. An old friend, Jock Bruce Gardyne, then a junior minister at the Treasury, told me it was too small an issue to make a fuss about, but my wife, Alice, a loyal supporter, agreed with me. I was John Biffen's parliamentary private secretary, an unpaid job but one that included me in the list of the supposedly faithful and obedient. The Liberals forced a vote while I was away, and my absence was noted by the whips.

The next evening, I was summoned by the Government Chief Whip, Michael Jopling, to his Commons office. This is a small, poky and dark room but it lies at the heart of the Commons between the Members' lobby and the central lobby. Next door is the large room in which most government whips have their individual desks. I could say, Jopling kindly told me, that I had left the Commons early because I was ill, and then I would be forgiven. Otherwise, I would have to resign. John Biffen fought to defend me but to no avail. I resigned.

A year later, Jopling even more generously asked me to join the office as a junior whip. I refused for personal and selfish reasons: I was earning good money from consultancies and business directorships that helped us pay the school bills; and I wanted, whenever possible, to get to our home in Sussex in the evening to see Alice and those of our five children who were still living at home. The thought of staying in the Commons until midnight, or later, to

3

watch over and cajole weary colleagues to remain until the final adjournment debate did not appeal to me.

In 1983, yet more magnanimously, Geoffrey Howe, still Chancellor of the Exchequer, asked me to join him at the Treasury as his Parliamentary Private Secretary. This was irresistible. Despite my resignation two years earlier, I had great admiration for Geoffrey as a politician and as a liberally minded individual. I accepted and, after the election later that year, I joined him again when he became Foreign Secretary. A year later, I became a junior Foreign Office minister and spent the next three years circulating the globe, from Beijing to Berlin, from La Paz to Manila, sampling the expertise of British diplomacy, listening to Shevardnadze utter the words 'perestroika' and 'glasnost' when they were new in our vocabulary, and appalled by the horrors of Gaza.

By 1989 I had got as far as being a Minister of State at the Home Office, reporting to Douglas Hurd and responsible for a large mixed bag that included asylum seekers, open government and broadcasting. I was working on a draft Broadcasting Bill when a late July reshuffle of the Cabinet took place. The major upheaval was the mistaken removal of Geoffrey Howe from the Foreign Office to the role of Leader of the Commons. The fact that the title of Deputy Prime Minister was added to his post made little difference.

I wrote a contemporary note about the day of the reshuffle that read:

The days before a reshuffle have an unreal quality about them. There seems little point putting down your wise thoughts on whether the government or the Independent Television Commission should appoint the members of the new Channel 4 Trust when you do not know if you're going to be there, in a few days' time, to argue your point of view.

I got two red boxes over the weekend, one of them full with 250 letters for me to sign and a note attached from Jane Harrison, the head of my private office, saying that the typing office had been hard at work and we were now nearly up to date for the recess. I dutifully signed them all whilst Alice took photographs of me working on what we presumed might be my last boxes. At fifty-seven, I knew that the Prime Minister had to get rid of some of her older ministers in order to make way for younger blood, and I had no illusions that I was likely to be promoted to the Cabinet. The next day, with its leaks and

4

rumours and changes and bad blood, was like a whole Palliser novel crammed into twenty-four hours. My own timetable ran as follows:

Monday 24 July
7.00 a.m., as I dress, the BBC news tells me that there is to be such a large reshuffle that Monday is reserved for changes in the Cabinet, Tuesday will be for smaller fry.

8.50 a.m. Kevin Kitchener, my driver for the last five years, meets me at London Bridge Station.

'Well,' I say, 'I'm still with you for today.'

Kevin does not reply but I then ask him whether he's going to take any holiday in August.

'I haven't finalised my August holiday plans yet,' says Kevin. 'I'm waiting to hear who my minister is.' A typical Kevin reply, I think. Civil, but not very tactful.

9.15 a.m. In the Home Office. I told Jane Harrison I understood why they gave me 250 letters to sign over the weekend. There was no question of catching up before the recess. It's simply that they all had my name typed at the bottom and they didn't want to have to re-type them. Jane grins and does not deny it.

9.30 a.m. A typical morning Prayers meeting with ministers, press secretary, parliamentary private secretaries and a few senior civil servants present. (Prayers is the traditional name given to these briefing 'what's up today?' meetings although direct requests to the Almighty are rare.) Douglas Hurd is in relaxed form. He is to make a statement this afternoon, at 3.30, in the House of Commons on war crimes. Clearly he expects to be in post to make it. I ask a question about the next stages of our reorganisation of the Passport Office. Douglas says to Clive Whitmore, our permanent secretary, 'See that the papers about this are passed to me through Tim Renton.' Evidently he expects me to be around. John Patten is not present. Has he already been summoned to No. 10? As we walk out of the private office, I see Douglas Hogg brandishing a thick, short leather whip. I don't know where he has got it from. 'Are you demob happy?' I ask.

'No,' says Clive Whitmore. 'He's getting ready for transfer to the Department of the Environment. Hence the whip.' Why? I wonder. Something to do with the Poll Tax?

10.30 a.m. I meet Tim Yeo, Douglas Hurd's parliamentary private secretary, and David Lidington, his senior political adviser, in the Home Office corridor. Yeo tells me that John Patten is at a conference at Esher, but has his hotline ready in case he has to rush up to London. Peter Brooke has already been summoned to No. 10. He kindly adds, 'It would be crazy to move you from broadcasting. You know so much about it.' It seems to me to be a likely reason for being moved. He adds, 'Last week at the 1922 meeting the PM said that the Broadcasting Bill next session would be a difficult one. That's the only one she gave that description to.' The Broadcasting Bill more difficult than the reform of the NHS? I wonder to myself.

11.15 a.m. I ring Alice with a sit. rep. Not much to tell her yet but I'm still in place behind my desk.

1.15 p.m. Kevin drives me round to the House of Commons and tells me that both Peter Brooke and Chris Patten have been round to No. 10.

1.30 p.m. I take lunch out on a tray to the sunlit terrace of the House. I see Alan Clark there. At sixty-one he's even older than me and I go and sit beside him.

'Have you heard anything?' asks Clark. 'Peter Morrison has rung me twice this morning.'

'No. Nothing,' I reply.

'No gossip?'

'No.'

'I hear John Patten is going to Education,' says Clark, 'Gummer into the Cabinet because of promises made when he ceased being party chairman, together with Chris Patten and Peter Brooke. John Moore, David Young and Paul Channon are all out and Kenneth Baker is going to Conservative Central Office.'

'That's a very quick exit for John Moore,' say I. 'Only two years ago he was darling of the party conference.'

'That's the fascination of politics,' says Clark, 'that's why we can't any of us give it up. It's the cruellest blood sport of them all.'

'It's terribly public,' I comment. 'Going to Downing Street with all the press reporters there, it's like going to the Place de la Révolution, with a guillotine sitting there.'

'Exactly,' replies Clark. 'You sit at your desk expecting a phone call. When it comes, it's like getting into a tumbril. I think we should all be put in Downing Street, Cabinet ministers and junior ministers alike, on a day like this. The street should be fenced off and the whips would be there armed with electric prods, Sir Bernard Ingham (Margaret Thatcher's press secretary) would stand on the steps of No. 10 in a white suit, calling out our names.'

'Don't go to Glyndebourne this afternoon,' I suggest.

'I hate Glyndebourne,' Clark replies.

2.40 p.m. I am back in my room at the Home Office. Jane Harrison enters and comments that she's a better messenger today than Kevin. 'Peter has just rung from the Home Secretary's office. You're staying with us. We're very pleased.'

I ring Alice and tell her and she, kindly, sounds very pleased too.

3.00 p.m. The Labour MP, Jack Straw, comes to a meeting on an immigration case. He tells me that he's just written a farewell letter to Kenneth Baker. 'You can perm for his successor,' he adds, 'out of a short list of four: Brooke, Chris Patten, Gummer or Fowler.'

3.25 p.m. In the voting lobby at the House of Commons, I congratulate Chris Patten. I ask him where he is going to. He looks embarrassed as it is not yet officially announced and mumbles, 'somewhere very sensitive.' (He went to the Department of the Environment, responsible for the Poll Tax.)

4.30 p.m. Still in the House of Commons following Douglas's statement on War Criminals, I see my PPS, Humphrey Malins. 'I hear from Tim Yeo,' he says, 'that you're staying. Quite right. No one else knows about broadcasting. John Patten is staying too.'

'Yes. Hogg has been promoted to Minister of State elsewhere.'

On my way I ran into Elinor Goodman of *Channel Four News*. She tells me that George Younger is going from the Ministry of Defence to be chairman of the Royal Bank of Scotland. This really surprises me, though it makes a lot of sense. She continues, 'I gather there've been difficulties with Geoffrey Howe. He has been put in charge of a new department concerned only with the European Community.'

In Speaker's Court I see Peter, Geoffrey's driver, whom I have known for many years. He's leaning on the mudguard of his car. 'Is that your Jaguar, Peter?' I ask him.

'Well,' he replies, 'it is for today.'

5.00 p.m. Back at the Home Office, I bump into the lady who is in charge of the Correspondence Section of Douglas Hurd's office. 'You're staying,' she says, 'I'm so glad. But Mr Hogg is going and that makes me very sad.'

'Oh, are you sure?'

'Oh,' she continues, 'he has been very briefly at Number Ten. He came back looking very sad and said he was out.'

'Perhaps he just meant,' I say, 'that he had been promoted to another department.'

'Perhaps,' says the Correspondence lady in a tone of voice implying total disbelief.

5.40 p.m. After another division in the House of Commons, I see Geoffrey Parkhouse of the Glasgow *Herald*. He confirms that George Younger is going to the Royal Bank of Scotland and then adds, 'Geoffrey is staying at the FCO. He is determined to keep Chevening. I had lunch with him there yesterday.'

I ask who is going to Defence in the place of George Younger and Parkhouse tells me that it is Tom King.

7.10 p.m. Back in the House for another vote. I meet Michael Mates MP and Murdo Maclean, the eminence at our whips' office. They tell me that Tony Newton is going to Social Security and Parkinson to Transport. We agree that the latter is a surprising turn-up for the books. Mates adds that he hears Geoffrey is to be Deputy Prime Minister and Leader of the House while John Major goes to the FCO. 'What?' I exclaim. 'Talk about choosing your heir apparent.'

Murdo says comfortingly to me, 'It's quite right, you're staying to do the Broadcasting Bill. All this stuff about young people. You need some safe hands who get on with colleagues.'

I ask about Lynda Chalker and Douglas Hogg.

'I don't know,' says Murdo. 'There have been so many changes since I first saw the list.' We were joined in our huddle by Alan Clark. I had just heard that he was taking David Trefgarne's job at Defence and 'there you were,' I chide him, 'looking so gloomy at lunch.'

'I knew all the time,' says Alan, 'but I didn't know what was happening to anyone else. I didn't like to say.'

'She couldn't send Currie to Central Office,' says Mates.

'She could,' I add. 'It wouldn't be such a bad idea.'

'Anything could happen today,' says Mates. He adds that he thinks Major's appointment is a mistake. 'The heir apparent has been declared too early. Look what happened to Parkinson.'

Around 8.00 p.m. the official announcement of the changes is made.

8.45 p.m. again in the division lobby. John Moore walks towards me and greets me with a very brave smile. He shrugs off the sympathy that I express to him and we talk about the bad performance of *The Magic Flute* that we both saw at Covent Garden last week. He apologises for the fact that he wanted to buy me a drink at the bar but he had no money in his pocket. I am impressed by his courage.

Various friends, Bowen Wells, Bernard Braine and others, asked me, 'Are you all right?' The most asked question during the day. I assure them that I am and that my deepest desire is to bring in the Broadcasting Bill.

9.15 p.m. On my way to the tea room I meet a Labour MP with a full list of our appointments in his hand.

'Where did you get that?' I ask.

'From the doorman.' I hurry to our whips' office. They have only one copy of the appointments, from which many MPs are trying to make their own copy.

I go to the tea room. I am joined there by Humphrey Malins and we discuss whether he should continue as my PPS in the next session. I hope that he will.

'We'd better have dinner once a week in the dining room,' says Malins, 'during the Bill. We will have to do a great deal of canvassing of our back-benchers.'

We are joined by Tristan Garel-Jones. I learn later that he has become Deputy Chief Whip but he does not mention this. He discusses at great and amusing length the amazing party he and his wife went to near Dijon last weekend. It was full of members of the House of Orléans. We are joined by David Harris, Geoffrey Howe's PPS. 'Was Geoffrey very upset?' I ask.

'Very,' says Harris. 'He didn't know it was coming.'

'But surely a month or two ago he expected to go. That was the impression I had from Elspeth when we were staying at Chevening.'

'But not in the last month,' says Harris. 'When he turned up for the meeting this morning he simply didn't know. He was unprepared and very upset.'

'He could have refused,' I say. 'That would have caused a stir.'

'Yes, but then Mrs T. could have said that she offered him a job; that she had discharged her responsibility by doing that. Geoffrey wouldn't accept until he had worked out his status as Deputy Leader, Chairman of H&L Committees and Head of the Star Chamber. When I went round to the Foreign Office at lunchtime, his private office was virtually in tears.'

Our little table in the tea room was completed by the arrival of Edwina Currie bearing a tray. She asks if a list of the appointments is available. And I joke about only Labour MPs having the list.

'It doesn't matter,' says Currie. 'I've been far too busy to look at it anyway.' What an amazing capacity she has to irritate and I strongly hope that she did not get an appointment at Conservative Central Office.

9.45 p.m. I go to the library and get a list of our appointments there. They have plenty of copies. I see that Douglas Hogg has indeed got a job as Minister of State at the DTI. I am sorry to see that Simon Glenarthur has gone. He made some mistakes over Hong Kong. But that was easy enough to do. He was a nice guy.

10.00 p.m. On my way to my office in the bowels of the House of Commons I see Ian Stewart. We have the two rooms next door to each other and I have noticed him walking stiffly with a stick for the past six months. He tells me that he is taking honourable retirement. 'I have got to do this if I'm not permanently to damage my back.' I say how sorry I am, and Ian adds, 'I shall watch the progress of my colleagues with great interest.' I think to myself what a decent man he is.

And so I go to bed, once again with a red box.

It was out of the tension that arose from Margaret Thatcher's removal of Geoffrey Howe from the Foreign Office that I found myself Chief Whip four months later.

TWO

No. 12, 1989–1990

October 1989 was not a happy time for the Conservative Party. Margaret Thatcher had been Prime Minister for ten years and, despite the entreaties of her husband, Denis, showed no sign of relinquishing No. 10. Although she and Nigel Lawson, as Chancellor of the Exchequer, had managed to rein in the expenditure of Whitehall departments, the same was not true of local authority spending and the Community Charge had been put forward as a means of making householders more aware of their Council's spending. It was seen as a regressive tax, a tax that would hit the less well-off harder than the rich, and thirty-eight Conservative MPs had already voted against the detail of the Poll Tax, as the Community Charge was always disparagingly called. This reduced the government majority to twenty-five.

Even more important, though, was the continuing rift between Margaret Thatcher on one side and Geoffrey Howe and Nigel Lawson, Chancellor of the Exchequer since 1983, on the other over exchange-rate policy and Britain's relations with the European Union. In the summer reshuffle of 1989 Margaret Thatcher's removal of Geoffrey Howe from the position of Foreign Secretary to that of Leader of the House of Commons was a sideways step that made him deeply unhappy. The fact that he was also Deputy Prime Minister did not make up for his disappointment after having been either Chancellor of the Exchequer or Foreign Secretary for ten years, and during all that time successfully responsible for one of the great departments of state. Geoffrey was not particularly comfortable with the minutiae of House of Commons procedure and, in any event, he strongly disagreed with the Prime Minister's hostility to closer union in Europe. After just two years as Chief Secretary, the second-ranking post at the Treasury, John

Major moved into Geoffrey Howe's place at the Foreign Office. A lacklustre campaign in the summer had seen the Conservatives lose thirteen European Parliament seats to Labour. Michael Heseltine, out of the Cabinet since 1986, hovered enigmatically in the background, regularly making speeches in which he put forward his own policy and strategic ideas without any actual disloyalty to the leadership. His was a clever balancing act between rebellion and oblivion.

The final bust-up came on 26 October when Nigel Lawson resigned as Chancellor of the Exchequer. The reason he gave was the Prime Minister's insistence on consulting and being guided by Alan Walters, who for three years had been her personal economic adviser and who was strongly opposed to European integration. Underneath it all lay a fundamental split on whether and when we should join the European Exchange Rate Mechanism.

Since joining Douglas Hurd's team at the Home Office at the June 1987 election, I had remained in close touch with Geoffrey Howe and friends from the Foreign Office. My responsibilities for immigration saw to that. Asylum seekers were already a problem that worried me greatly and I had, with Foreign Office briefs in my case, visited Sri Lanka and gone north to Jaffna in a little aeroplane full of well-armed soldiers in order to find out whether there were genuine causes for Tamils to seek refuge in England. The pressure of work at the Home Office prevented me from following the European debate closely but my interest in it was deeply felt perhaps because of having a German grandmother and of having hitchhiked across France at the age of fourteen. I was asked to join the One Nation Club, of which Ted Heath was a founder, soon after I became an MP – our primary purpose was to meet on Wednesday evenings for a good meal and a little debate in the Commons dining room C – and the first speech I ever made at a Conservative party conference was in 1973 in support of our entry into the Common Market.

On the evening of 26 October Alice and I were at the BBC's Bear Ball raising money for Children in Need. I had recently had a hip replacement operation and I was particularly pleased with myself for dancing a vigorous charleston without my new metallic hip coming out of joint. During the course of the evening, in between dancing and the cabaret, we learned that

John Major was moving, after only four months at the Foreign Office, to take Lawson's place at the Treasury. Douglas Hurd, my boss at the Home Office, would replace him as Foreign Secretary and David Waddington would move from Government Chief Whip to Home Secretary. Waddington had succeeded John Wakeham as Government Chief Whip in 1987 and both of them were rightly regarded as close allies of the Prime Minister.

Our host, David Hatch, the managing director of BBC Radio, told me that he had listened anxiously to hear if I was being reshuffled too, and he kindly added that he was glad I was not. I gently pooh-poohed the idea. I knew quite well that I was staying at the Home Office in order to do the Broadcasting Bill in the coming session. We left the BBC Ball around midnight.

As we were driving along the Embankment, my car phone rang. At the other end was Jane Harrison, my senior private secretary, telling me that Downing Street were looking for me. My heart fluttered a bit. I told Jane we would be back at our little house in Eaton Row in fifteen minutes. When we got there, I found a message that Geoffrey Howe had rung around 10.30 p.m. I wondered whether he would ring again. At about a quarter to one Geoffrey telephoned and, after a few formalities as to where I had been wasting my evening, said that he had been asked to get in touch to see if I would take on the job of Chief Whip. 'Cor,' I said. Then, more appropriately, I added that I would like to talk to Alice about it and ring him back. The thought of becoming Chief Whip had never occurred to me.

My talk with Alice was a formality. We both knew this would plunge me right into the middle of Downing Street, party politics and the heart of government. I had little idea of the precise job specifications but it was irresistible. I rang Geoffrey back and said that I would take it on. 'Well, that's firm then,' said Geoffrey. 'I will tell the Prime Minister and she will be in touch with you in the morning.'

Kenneth Baker, then chairman of the party and very much in Margaret's confidence, told me later that he had put my name forward to be Chief Whip at a meeting at No. 10 that evening when only he, Andrew Turnbull, Margaret's principal private secretary, Charles Powell, her foreign affairs adviser, and Bernard Ingham, her chief press secretary, had been present. It was reckoned that I would be good at knitting the different sides of the party together and, particularly, at acting as a bridge between Margaret Thatcher and Geoffrey Howe. Geoffrey told me subsequently that he had enthusiastically endorsed the idea.

The next morning the telephone rang shortly before nine o'clock. A familiar flat voice from the other end said, 'Number Ten Downing Street here. Will you hold on a moment for the Prime Minister?' A pause ensued and I wondered whether Margaret and Denis were finishing their eggs and bacon. In the end, she came on the line, her voice clear as a bell, and told me that she was glad I was taking on the job of Chief Whip. I said I was delighted to do so. I thanked her for asking me and added that I was sorry about the circumstances.

'I have to face the facts as they are,' she said, as she asked me to meet her at No. 10 later that morning. My world changed.

When I walked down Downing Street two hours later, there was a horde of photographers and pressmen on the Foreign Office side of the road. I gave them a wave and entered the door of No. 10. We met at the far end of the suite of rooms on the first floor overlooking Horse Guards Parade. Geoffrey and Kenneth Baker were there along with Mark Lennox-Boyd, Margaret's parliamentary private secretary. She shook my hand quite formally as she came into the room. Then we started talking about who should succeed me at the Home Office.

The Prime Minister was looking white-faced and, not surprisingly, strained. There was a good deal of talk about what should be said to the press and whether John Major, as the new Chancellor, should make an announcement during the morning that would head off any sterling crises when the New York market opened. We learned as we talked that he was going to be interviewed on the *One O'clock News*, and this was considered sufficient. We broke up after about half an hour. I walked out of Downing Street feeling, I confess, about seven storeys high. I gave an even cheerier wave to the press and cameramen. One of them shouted at me, 'Are you resigning your job?' 'That's not my style,' I shouted back.

In 1989, apart from the small rooms off the Members' lobby at the heart of the Commons, the whips' offices consisted of the ground floor and basement of No. 12 Downing Street. Generally, from Monday to Thursday when full Commons business did not start until 2.30 p.m., the whips were at No. 12 in the morning and in the Commons in the afternoon and evening. No. 12, rebuilt in the twentieth century, faces up Downing Street towards Whitehall; the big windows inside look north on to Horse Guards Parade and west on to St James's Park. The offices are few: three rooms, hall and loo, and a big L-shaped room called the whips' room. This was dominated by a long table at which lengthy Wednesday morning meetings were held to discuss the state of the party and the business for the following week. Champagne was served at around 11.30 a.m. in small silver mugs and in modest quantities. At the far end of the room were sofas and armchairs. We moved the photographs of previous teams of whips into the hall and, with the support of government funds, Alice bought a range of bright new cushions. We regularly asked Conservative backbenchers to come over for an evening drink where we were often joined by the Prime Minister for whom Doris, the lady in charge of the worldly side of our life, kept a special bottle of whisky. We borrowed pictures from the government art collection and a good landscape by Winston Churchill looked down on the long conference table.

Below, in the basement, was a warren of small offices for secretaries and assistants. The substantial rooms on the floors upstairs had already been taken either by the Chancellor, the Cabinet Office or the Prime Minister's own policy units. Today the whips' offices on the ground floor and in the basement have also been confiscated by the various press and spin units of No. 10 and the whips have been moved to the Cabinet offices, between No. 10 and Whitehall. Conservative leaders have vowed that, once re-elected, they will return No. 12 to the whips.

There is a ground floor corridor that runs through the buildings from No. 12 into No. 11, the Chancellor's home, on into No. 10 and then through a warren of passages to the Cabinet offices. As an alternative, the Chief, as the Chief Whip is always called, can go up the stairs in No. 11 and come out on the first floor of No. 10, close to the room that Margaret used as her study.

Like the Delphic oracle, much is made of the obscurity of the whips. The hidden access from No. 12 to No. 10, out of the view of the press waiting with the cameras in Downing Street, was one of those carefully nurtured mysteries. But speed of access was very important. At our first meeting, the Prime Minister said that I could ask to see her at any time and, in moments of pressure, this might happen two or three times a day, with the demand coming either way. A quick corridor between the offices was essential.

In my office, just off the hall and looking down on the garden of No. 10 and then over to Horse Guards Parade, was a mahogany desk used by both Gladstone and Disraeli and a battered deep chair in which Winston Churchill was reputed to have sat. The tattered condition of the imitation leather made this a possibility. Below a picture by Romney of Lady Eliza Kerr was a reader at which Disraeli was said to have stood as he perused government documents.

I had thirteen whips below me. Tristan Garel-Jones was deputy and treasurer of Her Majesty's Household. David Lightbown, the next most senior, was comptroller of Her Majesty's Household, and next in the pecking order came Kenneth Carlisle, the pairing whip and vice chamberlain of Her Majesty's Household.

These three offices are called, in the royal encyclopaedia, the white staves. They are of huge antiquity. The treasurer and vice chamberlain date back to the reign of Edward III, the comptroller to that of Edward IV. Each carries a white staff as his wand of office which he can keep when he ceases to be a whip.

The treasurer is never asked to do any practical work but he can go to lunch in the royal household mess. The comptroller, too, has little officially to do except travel with the treasurer and his white stave in the carriage procession at the State Opening of Parliament. When they pass St Stephen's entrance to the House of Commons, they traditionally wave their staves at their colleagues on the pavement, and a loud cheer goes forth from the Members of Parliament, all totally incomprehensible to the public standing by.

The vice chamberlain, on the other hand, remains at Buckingham Palace with the Lord Chamberlain who has seen the monarch into her carriage and then handed responsibility for her over to the Master of the Horse. He, in turn, rides beside the carriage until they reach Westminster where horses are dismounted and monarch and responsibility are handed over to the Lord Great Chamberlain.

Meanwhile, the Lord Chamberlain stays at Buckingham Palace, protecting the throne from any usurper during the sovereign's absence and the vice chamberlain stays with him. This is redolent of seventeenth-century history. The vice chamberlain can be held hostage in the event of Parliament detaining the sovereign and stopping the monarch's return from Westminster back to the royal household. I asked Kenneth Carlisle what he and the Lord Chamberlain did in the Queen's absence and he said, hesitatingly, 'Well, there is a bottle of whisky…'

But, having seen the monarch safely back into Buckingham Palace, the vice chamberlain is the one that has permanent serious duties. It is he who delivers to the monarch a loyal address relating to the Queen's speech with which the session is opened in the House of Lords, and in turn he relays back to the House the sovereign's reply. Then, every day, he writes the Queen's Telegram. This is a summary of the day's proceedings, traditionally written on two sheets of A4 paper, finished by 6.00 p.m. and then delivered by special messenger to Buckingham Palace. A brisk style is appreciated. When the Conservatives came into government in 1979, Spencer Le Marchant was vice chamberlain and pairing whip. His summary was particularly appreciated at Buckingham Palace; he was a keen follower of the horses and often managed to slip racing tips into the day's proceedings. I understand, though, that e-mails are now taking the place of the special messenger.

At garden parties, the 'royal title' whips walk with their white staves down the 'Queen's passage' and, with the help of the royal equerries, find suitable visitors and guests and arrange for them to be introduced to the monarch by the Lord Chamberlain. The aim, of course, is to do this in a slick and competent manner, and thus the senior whips have a chance to impress their family and friends. For the rest of the working year they do not see much green grass and sunlight.

Although I had refused Michael Jopling's offer to become a whip in 1982, I found the thirteen months during which I was Chief Whip the most exciting of my working life, and not just exciting but surprisingly enjoyable. Other former Chief Whips – Humphrey Atkins, Willie Whitelaw, Michael Jopling, Michael Cocks – told me the same thing: that, of all their parliamentary lives, they looked back at their years as Chief Whip as being the most fun, despite the extraordinary strains and difficulties in which the Chief inevitably finds himself.

My deputy, Tristan Garel-Jones, had an unlimited knowledge of the strengths and weaknesses of our colleagues. He was a born conspirator but hated rebellious MPs, even though as a backbencher he would certainly have been one himself.

Not since Lesley Wilson in 1921 had a Conservative MP been Government Chief Whip without previous experience of the office, but I had no feeling that this was held against me either by the other whips or by my fellow MPs. Rather the opposite. I received kindly, congratulatory letters from colleagues, emphasising that it was time for a change of mood and tactics, particularly about the Poll Tax, and hoping that I could achieve this. In the year ahead I never felt that lack of experience of the office hindered me. Tristan, David Lightbown and Kenneth Carlisle steered me through the quicksands. They showed me in which seat I was, according to tradition, to sit during our daily conferences at 2.35 p.m. in our Commons offices and, if I happened to mention any MP of whom I thought particularly highly, I was always told that he was an Old Etonian, corrupt, in debt and probably gay, with a penchant for black boyfriends. Tristan's standard phrase about a colleague was that 'he was as mad as a ferret', and sometimes this was collectively enlarged to 'they are all behaving like a sackful of ferrets.'

Tristan's acquaintance with the wiles of our parliamentary colleagues was supplemented by the extraordinary skills of Murdo Maclean. He had already held the position of private secretary to the Government Chief Whip for ten years and knew every detail of how you crammed a quart of parliamentary business into a pint pot. He was an expert on guillotines, procedure, select committees, standing orders and the idiosyncrasies of MPs. His was an extraordinary career: the Mr Fix-It of the House of Commons, he had started life in the Outer Hebrides, worked for a year as a clerk in an employment exchange in Glasgow and then moved to the Board of Trade and the Prime Minister's office before coming to No. 12 at the age of thirty-six. He was now in a situation at the heart of government where not only was Machiavellian cunning needed but also a command of the trust and respect of every political party in the House. If Murdo said to me, 'The Opposition won't play ball if you insist on having that Bill on Wednesday, but they will finish it at ten if you change it to Thursday,' I knew it was wise to follow his advice.

With Murdo on one side of me, Tristan on the other and an experienced team of whips in the office, I was well supported for the parliamentary battles, the intrigue and sheer cussedness that dominated the last year of Margaret's long prime ministerial reign.

But a good whip is not just a sergeant major. He is also a counsellor and a nanny. Giving tea to some and gin and tonic to others, the Chief Whip has an overall responsibility for the health and sanity of his flock. I received a constant but unsurprising stream of worries about marriage, illness and debt. A few of our colleagues were extraordinarily generous in bailing out those whose private businesses were failing or whose overdraft did not, temporarily, permit them to pay the school fees. But by tradition if not by law, it is not permissible for an MP to go bankrupt. Sometimes the pairing whip, Kenneth Carlisle, would tell me that so-and-so had asked to be 'slipped' – away from the Commons – on such or such a day ahead because he wanted to be celebrating his wedding anniversary with his wife. We knew well enough that he had been separated from his wife for some time but he would be slipped all the same. Some were anxious to talk about their personal problems, others, understandably, wished to remain silent.

From the very outset of my term at No. 12, I felt that our whips' office had to remain impartial in any election for our parliamentary leadership. Although I, as Chief, had had the hands lain on me in blessing by the Prime Minister, it was not my duty to use the whips to canvass support for her. Our job was, above all, to take the best route which would help the parliamentary party to stay together and in government. As a result, when within a few weeks Anthony Meyer announced that he would run against the Prime Minister, I extended a hand of moderate friendship to him, tried to persuade him to desist but did not threaten him with expulsion from the party or attempt to bully him into submission.

It was often said – doubtless apocryphally – that Jack Straw, as a young MP, announced his intention of rebelling against the Labour whip on a particular issue. Michael Cocks, the Opposition Chief Whip of the day, summoned him and put over the official party line. Jack Straw listened and said that he did not find the argument particularly convincing. At this point, Michael Cocks seized Jack by the genitals, held on to them tight while Jack turned white in the face and finally released him with the comment, 'Are you convinced now?' I never tried anything comparable.

I had, though, a heavy Victorian mahogany ruler, a present from my brother-in-law, Adam Fergusson. It looked like an elongated policeman's truncheon. It lived on my desk in the Chief Whip's Office in the House of Commons. When miscreants came to see me, and they were booked in at any time between 4.00 p.m. and 10.00 p.m., I sometimes used to bang this heavy ruler into my hand. It gave me a sense of comfort and sometimes I saw a rebellious MP flinch.

If a particular MP was falling out of line, the whips, in their daily notes, used to say, 'It's time the Chief saw so and so.' The suggestion would be discussed at our 2.30 p.m. meeting and, if there was general agreement that this was a necessity, a message would go out to the offender and an appointment would be made. Some were frightened, others were not. I remember a particular occasion when a parliamentary colleague had behaved very badly in business dealings with the son of another Conservative Member of Parliament. Reports of this reached me and I summoned the MP to see me. Before he even sat down in the chair on the other side of my desk, I let fly and told him that he had behaved like a total shit. He was surprised. We argued. He told me I was too emotionally involved as the other MP was seriously ill. I raised my voice, he raised his and the door between my room and the whips' office was not soundproof. We got nowhere, other than that we never spoke a friendly word to each other again, but Tristan Garel-Jones, who had overheard our conversation, gave me his unstinting approval. Trying to decide what treatment was appropriate and would be effective for each of our colleagues was a particularly difficult task. It inevitably meant a thorough knowledge of their circumstances, their ambitions and their likely reaction. Persuading a colleague not to rebel when he had intended to do so, or to take part in a Friday debate on a strange subject that would be of little interest either to his constituents or to the press, made amateur psychologists of all of us in the whips' office.

I swapped drivers on my first full day at No. 12, Monday 30 October. In a way this was symbolic. Kevin Kitchener had driven me, faithfully but slowly, ever since I became a junior minister at the Foreign Office in September 1984. But I had learnt from my predecessor, David Waddington, in my short period of instruction the previous Friday that he had always stayed in the House every night until the bitter end. I did not want Kevin staying night after night until two or three in the morning and then driving back all the way to Kent to a young and ambitious wife. In addition, No. 12 had an old faithful, Joe Bergin, who had been driving Chief Whips since cars were invented. He had one of the coveted plaques that permitted him to drive directly from St James's Park across Horse Guards Parade, under the arch and into Whitehall, and he then had a habit of driving very fast down the middle of Whitehall, from the Admiralty to Downing Street, between the advancing and retreating traffic. On one occasion, a policeman stopped us at the Downing Street gates, picked a red cone off our front bumper and said, 'I think you've forgotten this, Joe.'

The staff at No. 12 knew Joe well and obviously wanted to keep him. That I should change drivers was my first decision as Chief Whip. But I persuaded David Heathcoat-Amory, who had gone from the whips' office to take Virginia Bottomley's job at the Department of the Environment, to adopt Kevin instead, so at least he was only back in the limbo of the general drivers' pool for about twenty minutes.

Arriving daily at No. 12 was like arriving at a tiny embassy. The glossy black door was opened as I walked towards it by John, the messenger. By the time I had walked across the hall to my room and settled myself down at the desk that Disraeli and Gladstone had used, the indefatigable Doris would arrive with a cup of coffee. No question of my ringing my private office after some minutes and asking tentatively, as I always used to at the Home Office, whether the kettle was boiling. That was not the way the Chief was looked after.

Douglas Hurd was an excellent and conscientious Home Secretary but a bad delegator. He found it difficult even to delegate to me the decision about the wording of a pamphlet persuading people to apply out of season, in early winter or early spring, for their passports; he had to look at it himself. Now, the decisions regarding the parliamentary treatment of government business, the cajoling of ministers to think not only of their departments but also of the reaction of MPs to what they had planned, and the persuading of one's colleagues to attend or not to rebel lay with me.

I saw more of the Prime Minister in my first week at No. 12 than I had in all the previous five years as a minister. I saw her elated and immensely cheerful and a born leader, and also depressed, querulous and so tired at dinner in the Commons that I thought she was going to fall asleep between courses. I also saw an immense amount of Geoffrey Howe, since, as Lord President and Leader of the House, it was his job to decide, with the relevant Secretary of State, on the final shape of legislation, mine to squeeze it into the parliamentary schedule.

The whips, like the spies that kept Philip II's enormous empire together, listen everywhere in the House of Commons – in the tea room, in the dining room, in the bars and on the front bench while ministers are speaking and questions are being asked and answered. They report back via notes or word of mouth on everything, and all of this information is assessed by the whips collectively every day while the House is sitting. The Chief Whip joins the junior whips at 2.35 p.m. on Mondays, Tuesdays and Thursdays and important scraps of information are discussed.

My years of dealing with backbenchers and their constituency immigration cases at the Home Office were a good prior training, but the whips' office could not be more different from a government department. Gone were the lengthy submissions from officials setting out the background, discussing the various options and then asking the minister for a decision.

I sat on a number of the most important committees, known only by initials – H and L and QL and others – all chaired by Cabinet ministers or the Prime Minister. If I was asked in Cabinet or committee whether I thought the Bill we were discussing would get through Parliament by Easter, in the way that the Secretary of State presenting the legislation wanted, I only had to say that I thought it would be very difficult to achieve such a target date, and that was the last word. No one else had, or was meant to have, such a feel of what was or was not possible in parliamentary terms.

Sometimes in the Home Office I was almost overwhelmed by the amount of paper that crossed my desk. Every night I would take home three red boxes to be read before breakfast the following morning, four boxes at the weekend. The whips' office was different.

At first I suffered from paper starvation. I used to complain to my small team of four key officials – Murdo Maclean, Robina Finlay, my 'political' adviser, Miss Straight, my Civil Service assistant private secretary, or Stan Colley, ex-navy and very good on any part of the routine that Murdo forgot

– that I had little in my red box every night. That's the good part of the job, they said to me. And, after a few weeks of wondering and worrying, I got used to the haphazard nature of the way in which information reached us from other departments.

As Chief Whip, responsible 'for government discipline' in the words of the Spanish newspaper, *El Pais*, I inherited an extraordinary position. Nigel Lawson had just resigned with utmost acrimony. Two days after I was appointed, Margaret appeared on television. Questioned by the influential journalist and former MP, Brian Walden, she said that she really could not understand why he had left. A week later, Nigel answered with the utmost clarity that he had made clear that either the Prime Minister sacked her adviser, Alan Walters, or he would leave.

Geoffrey Howe was still bitterly hurt about the manner of his removal from the Foreign Office, and Elspeth Howe went round the dining rooms of power making no secret of her fury at the manner in which her man had been treated. The Tory Party was riven by the argument of whether we should concur with faster and greater European integration or whether we should do our utmost to delay and hinder it. The tactical argument was about joining the Exchange Rate Mechanism; that was the preliminary wind that heralded the hurricane. The strategic argument was about having one European Central Bank and one European currency and the steady removal of power from national Parliaments to Strasbourg and Brussels.

Then there was the possibility, which rapidly turned into a probability, of elections for the chairmanship of the 1922 Committee (the all-important Conservative backbench committee), the first election since Edward du Cann had been ousted by Cranley Onslow five years earlier, and elections for the leadership of the party. Add to this a newspaper story that Cecil Parkinson would be accused in a Channel Four documentary of insider trading in shares (the documentary was never broadcast, nor was the story substantiated by the newspaper) and a tremendous procedural row in the House of Commons about Private Bills – such a row that I had to get the Speaker out of bed in his pyjamas after midnight in order to get his help in sorting out Harold Walker, the chairman of Ways and Means, who had given up all attempts to control the business – and I could not have had a more hectic baptism. It was exciting from the start.

My personal and enduring problem was the question of the relations between Margaret Thatcher and Geoffrey and Elspeth Howe. The day after my appointment as Chief Whip, Geoffrey gave a speech to an Anglo-Spanish gathering in Bath. The part of the speech regarding our future relations with the European Community was written about in the press the next day as being yet another airing of disagreement on the European Community between Geoffrey and the Prime Minister. More fundamentally, the speech was seen by a number of commentators as a sign of Geoffrey flexing his muscles as Deputy Prime Minister and exercising his right to talk from commanding heights about a wide range of matters and the problems ahead of us. On the following Wednesday, 1 November, I exercised for the first time my right of asking for a private meeting with the Prime Minister and I saw her around 6.00 p.m. in her little drawing room upstairs with only Andrew Turnbull present.

The ostensible purpose of my visit was to say that we, the whips' college, wanted to appoint Nicholas Baker as the next whip. I then got on to the subject of unanimity at the top of the party. I said I was certain that the parliamentary party wanted to see members of the Cabinet under her leadership not only singing the same tune but singing it in harmony and in the same key. This, not surprisingly, touched a raw nerve in her. She pointed out to me that in the previous day's economic debate the challenging remarks quoted back at her by the opposition had all come from senior figures on her own side – notably Geoffrey and Nigel Lawson. She regarded their discordant voices as treachery.

Alice and I decided to ask Geoffrey and Elspeth to lunch at Mount Harry, our home in Sussex, the following Sunday. Despite the old friendship between us it was not a happy occasion. I took Geoffrey for a walk along the South Downs and we were followed at twenty yards' distance by his bodyguard. Although I had earlier suggested we might go for a walk, Geoffrey had brought neither boots nor any sort of outdoor coat; he had to borrow some of ours. Not so his bodyguard who, looking exactly like Sherlock Holmes' Watson, was accoutred with tweed stalking hat, Barber coat, gumboots and pipe. He even had a heavy watch chain with a medallion hanging from it, but, at least, he remembered to shut the gates behind us.

Geoffrey and I, on a lovely autumn day, walked in gathering gloom. The woes of Madrid and Nassau and other international meetings came pouring out – why did she always have to have the last word on every subject? Why did she adopt such a 'triumphalist' approach so that she was always right and others were always wrong? Did she not understand that we were losing friends everywhere because of her evident reluctance about progress in the Common Market, and that soon the Japanese would start reconsidering their investments in the UK if we came to be judged as an excessively reluctant partner in greater European integration?

Geoffrey complained that there was no longer any such confidential forum at which he and the Prime Minister and one or two other key ministers could exchange views as had existed with the Thursday morning breakfasts in 1979 and 1980. Why was he not a member of ODE, the key committee that, under the Foreign Secretary's chairmanship, discussed the basic economic details regarding our overseas position? Why had he not been consulted at all after Nigel Lawson's resignation about who should succeed him? The list of woes and grievances was almost endless and at one stage Geoffrey said that there was a limit of tolerance beyond which his continuing as Deputy Prime Minister really was not worth it.

I knew that Geoffrey was going back to London to have a meeting with the Prime Minister. What I did not expect, sitting rather gloomily at my desk at home around 6.00 p.m., was for the telephone to ring and a voice at the other end to say, 'Number Ten Downing Street here. The Prime Minister wishes to speak to you,' and then the Prime Minister came on the line with the opening words, 'I wanted to know how your meeting with Geoffrey had gone, Tim.' She knew about it from her friend and confidant, Ian Gow, to whom I had mentioned our lunch appointment two days earlier.

'Not very well,' I replied and I tried to tell her as honestly as I could the sources of Geoffrey's main worries and anguish.

I was, as I had expected, hit by a gale. When I said that Geoffrey wanted to be a member of ODE, I was told that this was not an important committee, that it dealt only with minor economic details and that Geoffrey sat, of course, on the main OD Committee under her chairmanship. When I mentioned Geoffrey hankering for the working breakfasts of 1979 on a Thursday morning, the Prime Minister promptly said, 'But the trouble with those breakfasts was that five or six people came to them and one of them leaked who was present and everything we said. So I stopped the breakfasts.'

But I persevered. I ended up by suggesting as strongly as I could that the Prime Minister should find time to have half an hour alone each week with Geoffrey so that they could simply talk out problems of any sort. I purposely did not mention anything to do with the European Community, the ERM and EMU as that would just fan the flames. I stressed, knowing how sensitive the Prime Minister was now to thoughts of Geoffrey being disloyal, that all these problems were soluble but that Geoffrey, with his vast experience and so many years at the heart of government, must be consulted as a senior and most experienced member of her team.

At around ten o'clock the telephone rang and it was Downing Street and the Prime Minister again. 'It wasn't at all as you told me it would be, Tim,' said the Prime Minister. 'You got it quite wrong. I've spoken to Geoffrey and he went on and on about the ERM and the European Community. He wanted to make me change my mind and said that, if I didn't, he wondered whether it was worthwhile his going on and staying in government.'

The words poured out. The Prime Minister sounded tired, cross and worried. I prayed for guidance to put the right words into my mouth. I repeated what I had said earlier, that I felt the essential thing for Geoffrey was to know that his experience was being well used, even though, of course, I understood that he and the Prime Minister had different views about the pace of movement in the European Community. I stressed how loyal Geoffrey was at heart. Then, to my surprise, the Prime Minister said that she had agreed to see him for half an hour each week. The conversation went on, not getting much further, until I suggested that we might meet the following evening over a glass of whisky, after a vote in the House, and talk this out further. She paused and then said, 'All right, good night.' And to my surprise she added, 'God bless you, Tim,' and rang off.

I went to see Willie Whitelaw in his room in the House of Lords three days later. I explained, as I saw it, the need for the Prime Minister to accept Geoffrey's role as deputy premier, and to share her thinking on more subjects with him. Willie promised me that he would look for an opportunity to have a word with the Prime Minister. He told me that he did not think his own relationship with the Prime Minister would have survived if he had continued as Home Secretary. But the fact of his going to the House of Lords after the 1983 election and then being Leader of the Lords as well as Deputy Prime Minister put new life into their *entente* as he ceased to have a department, whose policies he had to defend with the Prime Minister. He was detached from all of that and could simply give her his advice without being thought to be biased in pushing his own department's case.

The days were crowded. I attended a meeting of the Privy Council on 1 November, kissed hands with the Queen (the Clerk to the Council told the four of us at his training session beforehand that the advice of his office was that your lips should certainly touch the Queen's hand; you should not just kiss the air) and I swore the formidable oath that if I found any secrets that were likely to be damaging to Her Majesty's person or her possessions at home or abroad I would divulge them only to Her Majesty or to other members of the Most Honourable Council. No more leaks about broadcasting to Ray Snoddy at the *Financial Times*.

The next day I attended my first Cabinet meeting and sat at the far end of the table looking down at the Prime Minister and her twenty-two Cabinet colleagues. Under Margaret Thatcher, the Chief Whip was not a member of the Cabinet but was always asked to attend, primarily to speak on parliamentary matters and business in the Commons in the days ahead. The following week, after my second Cabinet meeting, Tom King, now the Secretary of State for Defence, told me that he had thought, during Cabinet, that I was beginning to look like a Chief Whip. Tim Rathbone, our close friend and neighbouring MP in Sussex, said rather the same thing. He had noticed that I had a good 'Chief Whip' expression on my face in the Commons – a determination not to show any emotion at all except to laugh occasionally.

A few days before the opening of the 1989–90 parliamentary session Anthony Bevins, then political editor of the *Independent*, rang me at home. He said that his soundings seemed to indicate that there would be an election for the leadership of the party in the new session and that there might well be a pro-EEC candidate from the left and an anti-EEC candidate from the right, plus Sir Anthony Meyer, a likeable pro-European well to the liberal side of the Tory Party. Bevins added that he found an atmosphere of carelessness around, his precise words, among those who were disillusioned with the leadership of Margaret, even one of desperation.

Two weeks later on 5 December, Anthony Meyer announced his candidacy against Margaret for the leadership of the party. His role was that of a pilot fish which the bigger fish would watch and possibly follow. He was a bizarre character whom it was difficult to meet without his wife and his dog being present as well. I was determined to put into practice my view that the whips should not take sides in any election for the leadership, and I said as much to my colleagues in the office. I had always been on good terms with Anthony and I invited him to come to see me in my House of Commons office two days before nominations closed. I did not anticipate that Anthony would reveal to the Press Association that morning that he had been 'summoned' to see me, and press speculation ran high as to what was the ultimate torture that I could use – urge his constituency association to deselect him, remove the Conservative whip from him, blackball him from the Carlton Club: these and other instruments of persuasion were mentioned. In fact, I decided in advance that any attempt to browbeat Meyer would lose Margaret votes rather than the opposite. I wished us to have a good-humoured election that would make it easier to continue running the parliamentary party afterwards. So, when Anthony came to see me I offered him a cup of tea, made the inevitable suggestion that he should stand down as any leadership election might be divisive for the party and, when this was refused, talked about the need for keeping the whole process as calm and even-tempered as possible.

What I did not anticipate was that, after leaving my office, Meyer would say to the press that he had 'a jolly nice cup of tea' with me, rhapsodising on the *entente cordiale* that existed between us. This caused a good deal of understandable mirth in the press and I thought Margaret might consider that I was erring too close to the enemy camp. When I next saw her, I told her that I was sure, after my meeting, that Anthony would stand but that he had promised to put out a helpful statement after the election was over the following Tuesday. She looked doubtful and said that she did not trust him. She herself held up remarkably well under what was more of a strain than she allowed to appear. She had one or two television interviews in which she appeared to contradict herself regarding her future intentions. First, she said she did not intend to continue as leader long after the next election. Then, because of the uproar that caused, she implied that she would be quite happy to fight a fourth and a fifth election as leader, thus prolonging her reign almost to the year 2000. Only when she realised that this was not a very good theme either did she start refusing to be drawn.

There was no question that Margaret was not going to win the absolute majority required in the first ballot. The sole matter for dispute and speculation lay in what would be the number of those who did not support her, either by abstaining, spoiling their ballot papers or voting for Meyer. The common view was that if the total, out of 374 MPs, of those who did not support her was around forty to fifty that was perfectly containable and satisfactory. If, however, that total rose to eighty, she would be in trouble. If it was above one hundred, although winning on the first ballot, she might well have to decide that this was insufficient support and retire very quickly.

On Sunday evening, two days before the ballot, Tristan Garel-Jones told me that the unofficial committee organising Margaret's support reckoned that they had forty-five 'hopeless' MPs who were certain not to vote for Margaret, together with twenty-five who were at the best doubtful. These figures were too high for comfort, given that certainly some who had promised loyalty to the Prime Minister would, when they got to the ballot box, vote for the other way. The missing factor was the liar factor.

I wrote in my diary:

On the day, Tuesday 5 December, the voting started at 10.00 a.m. in one of the large committee rooms. I voted at around 2.00 p.m. and found Cranley (Onslow) and two members of the 1922 Executive Committee, Tony Grant and Charlie Morrison, presiding. There was certainly no great secrecy in that there was no booth in which to stand and make a hidden cross. I marked my ballot paper more or less in public for Margaret, dropped it in the black ballot box and then asked Cranley and his colleagues whether they would like a cup of coffee. They all said they would, so I went down to the tea room. On my way back with the cups, I was waylaid by a number of newspapermen in the corridor outside the committee room. 'How's it going?' they asked. 'How many people have voted for the Prime Minister so far?' At this final stage in the election I felt I could show great confidence in Margaret's success. So I said that it was going very well and more than 400 MPs had already voted. This was promptly written down in a number of shorthand notebooks, and then one or two reporters realised that it must be wrong – we only had 374

MPs – and laughed with me. Andrew Rawnsley in the *Guardian* the next day did not find it very funny.

A few minutes after 6.00 p.m., when the ballot closed, I went to my office in the House and told Tristan that I thought the overall vote of the non-Thatcher supporters would be fifty-four. The minutes passed tensely. Finally, around 6.27 p.m. there was a knock on my door and in came Greg Shepherd (Murdo Maclean's assistant in the Commons) rather flushed and carrying a little bit of paper. This said: Meyer 33, Prime Minister 314, spoilt 24. A total of 371. Margaret had 84 per cent of the votes.

I knew that by now Margaret would be on her way to Buckingham Palace for her weekly audience with the Queen which was due to start at 6.30 p.m. I decided to ring Margaret's car myself. Typically, I was informed by No. 10 that the Prime Minister's car telephone was not working. So I asked to be put through to the Palace and was connected with Andrew Turnbull seconds after the Prime Minister had disappeared into the royal audience. I told him the figures and added that I thought that it was the best result that could have been hoped for. He said he was surprised at the number that had actually voted for Meyer. I was too but did not admit it. I then rang Bernard Ingham (Margaret's press secretary, a proto-Alastair Campbell) who was pleased to be told the news directly – the relations between him and Charles Powell (seconded from the FCO to be Margaret's private secretary in 1984 and by now a close confidant) were not such as to make him want to hear the news from Charles's lips. I then telephoned Willie Whitelaw. He also commented that he thought that the figure for Meyer was too high for comfort and I concurred with Willie.

I went on to a large party being given at the Travellers Club. On my way up the staircase I met Paul Fox, then managing director of BBC Television. He immediately launched into the argument that the Prime Minister had too many votes against her for comfort. I asked Paul, if he stood for election as managing director of BBC Television, whether he thought 84 per cent of the staff would vote for him. Clearly he did not, and he had the grace to admit that with a smile.

That evening, after the ten o'clock vote, Margaret came into the whips' office at my invitation for a celebration drink. I had been anxious that she should come in order that she and the junior whips should mutually feel that they were associated with her victory, after the impartiality and abstinence from campaigning that I had forced on them. Mark Lennox-Boyd accompanied her. We opened bottles of champagne, Margaret drank her usual glass of whisky and we toasted her. It was a very good-humoured occasion, with Margaret sitting in a chair by Tristan Garel-Jones's desk and all the whips seated around her talking freely. But she looked tired.

Although the following day the papers tried to make something of the fact that sixty of our parliamentary party had not supported her and, adding that figure to the total of the opposition parties, then said that she did not have the support of a majority in the House, that argument did not run for more than a day. What the papers never fastened on to, nor did the Prime Minister ever know, was that Cranley Onslow and his officers of the 1922 Committee succeeded in losing one vote. They issued 372 ballot papers, they counted 372 names as recording their votes, either directly or by proxy, but the total only came to 371. Everyone was in too much of a hurry to announce the result for a recount to be in order. So, when the newspapers speculated on Wednesday 6 December on who were the two absentees besides Michael Heseltine, I chuckled silently at the knowledge that in fact there was only one.

Denis Thatcher would have said that loyalty won the day. Ten days earlier, when we went to No. 10 for a marvellous evening in which Rostropovich played his cello to a small audience, headed by the Prince and Princess of Wales, Denis had said to Alice, 'How are things in your patch? Is everyone all right? I was not far from you recently – Peter Hordern's patch. I thought they were absolutely whizz. Very loyal. Loyalty is the name of the game and that's what it's all about.'

He then turned to me and reaffirmed the point, 'Loyalty's the name of the game, isn't it?'

But the real message for me was that the Tory parliamentary party could have a disputed contest against a sitting Prime Minister and leader of the party without evidently tearing itself apart.

Obviously, changes would have to be made in the rules. When we got a Christmas card from an unknown gentleman called Kenneth Walsingham from the Midlands, enclosing a short letter in which he said that he would like to stand for the leadership of our party, we realised, for instance, that, had he obtained two Tory MPs as his proposer and seconder, there was no reason why he should not have stood. There was nothing in the rules to state that all candidates had to be Tory MPs or peers. The period between announcing a date for nominations and the date of the first round of balloting was too long – nearly two weeks – and it was questionable whether someone should be able to stand with just one proposer and a seconder. There was discussion that any candidate should be supported by at least fifteen MPs as proof of his seriousness, just as any parliamentary candidate has to have twenty or thirty electors publicly supporting him. But these were all for the future. The immediate point was that we had got through the election; and we were not backbiting about it.

I also thought that my own relations with the Prime Minister were slowly improving. Whenever she could, she came to our small weekly drinks parties at No. 12 where the special bottle of whisky was produced and she relaxed and gossiped with our backbenchers as if she was one of them. But, despite the early promises, access to her at No. 10 was never an easy matter. She was jealously guarded either by Mark Lennox-Boyd or by Andrew Turnbull or by Charles Powell. If I said that I wanted a quick word with her, one or other of them wanted to know in some detail why and usually managed to turn up at the meeting as well. I was at times reminded of a book about the court of Haile Selassie. The author, who had served at the court for many years, pointed out that access to the King was everything. If a new person approached the King and was allowed to bear a sword or hold a cup or be given an audience that lasted a minute or two, everyone noticed, wondered why, and schemed either to make use of this new avenue of approach or to plot its downfall. I remembered too the importance of Ladies of the Bed Chamber and Gentlemen of the Household in that they obtained the ear of the King or Queen at vital moments, when royalty were off their guard. Getting Margaret's ear was not wholly different.

We met a lot in the days before Christmas to discuss Norman Fowler's forthcoming resignation and who should replace him, passports for Chinese in Hong Kong, and the growing difficulties about the level of the Community Charge in England. I followed John Wakeham's advice and, if I wanted to say something in a Cabinet committee that she chaired or at Cabinet itself, I warned Andrew Turnbull in advance and made it clear what it was that I would like to say and my reasons for it. This seemed to work. At least, a day or two before the Christmas recess, Margaret suddenly said to me that I had done a great deal since my appointment and I must be looking forward to the holidays.

The good times did not last long. Hardly had we finished the leadership election campaign than the whips' office was sniffing trouble about the Community Charge. In the fastness of the Home Office I had barely been aware that in April 1988 our majority had fallen to twenty-five when we voted on what was called the Mates' Amendment to the Local Government Finance Bill. This said, in essence, that the level of the Community Charge should be related to the individual's liability to pay income tax. It was a rough and ready amendment but it drew the positive support of thirty-seven of our Conservative colleagues and a number of others abstained.

The first five Orders on the specific grants for the financial year 1990–91, which would have a direct effect on the levels of Community Charge, were to be debated in the House soon after we returned from the Christmas recess. In the last week before the holiday the whips did a first trawl of the party, not pressing colleagues too much but trying to get a general impression of whether they would support us on the Orders or not. The answer we came up with was that forty-one would vote against us and forty-two would abstain. On this basis, as we had an overall majority of ninety-nine, we would lose by twenty-five votes.

I asked to see the Prime Minister on Wednesday 20 December. As soon as I mentioned to her that I wanted to talk about the Community Charge, she said, 'I know. You are going to tell me that we will lose.'

'Yes,' I said. I went into the preliminary nature of our trawl and said that it was bound to be superficial because we had not been asking very detailed questions. We did not want to do so as we had no wish to arouse colleagues' suspicions that we might be in real trouble. Nonetheless, the figures were ominous. I mentioned no specific number to the Prime Minister – some instinct told me that it was better not to do so – nor did she ask me any questions about exact numbers, but I said that our present indications were that we would not win.

The Prime Minister asked me to go and see both the Chancellor of the Exchequer, John Major, and the Secretary of State for the Environment,

Chris Patten, to tell them about this. Her wish was that they should do some emergency planning during the Christmas recess to see if there was any means of offering more subsidy and thus bringing back a number of colleagues on our side. She stressed that I was to see them alone without civil servant officials nor was I to mention this to any other ministers. She was particularly anxious that news of what we were talking about should not reach Kenneth Baker. He had sent her a number of memoranda speaking gloomily of our prospects in the local elections of May 1990 if we went ahead with the Community Charge on the existing basis. The Prime Minister feared that, if he got wind of what I was saying about the voting figures, he might leak this and thus force her and the Chancellor's hand into making more money available.

That morning I went to see John Major at the Treasury. I had not been there since my days as Geoffrey Howe's parliamentary private secretary. I wandered around the circular corridors in the Treasury looking for the Chancellor's office, having come in through the car park. I was struck by the routine incompetence. I was not met by anyone at the entrance to the building, nor did anyone I asked seem to know the way to the Chancellor's office. Eventually I found him in his long-panelled room and I explained our problem. John Major, an experienced ex-whip himself, did not like it. He said he certainly could not give away much money without ruining his Budget strategy; already the revenue from VAT and Corporation Tax on company profits was coming in at a considerably lower rate than forecast. He had had to make money available for haemophiliacs and war widows' pensions. If he was required to make yet more money available for the Revenue Support Grant Orders which subsidise local authorities, he would get the reputation of being an easy touch. This would do nothing for sterling. A Budget that raised taxes, rather than one that kept them static, would be in prospect.

Nonetheless, I told him that the Prime Minister had asked me to come and see him in order to ask both him and Chris Patten to do some work on an emergency scheme during the holidays. This would be used only if we felt in the days, or even hours, before the debate on the Orders that it was absolutely necessary to introduce this in order to win a majority.

Later that day, Chris Patten came to my office in the House of Commons and he brought David Hunt, the Minister for Local Government who was in charge of the detailed negotiations on the Community Charge, with him. I went over the same ground with them. They agreed that their department would work with the Treasury on this over the holidays.

The day before we left for Christmas in Scotland the telephone rang at home and one of the Downing Street secretaries asked Alice if we could go to Chequers for lunch on New Year's Day. We could not make it, but I hoped it was all a step in the right direction of a better bridge between Margaret and myself. After all, it was the absence of that bridge that had been my main worry when I was asked if I would be Chief Whip.

THREE

Spring 1990

I came back from holiday early. On Wednesday 3 January, we had the mini reshuffle in which Norman Fowler resigned as Secretary of State for Employment, Michael Howard was promoted to his job and Michael Spicer was moved up to Minister of State at the Department of the Environment with Tony Baldry taking his place in turn at the Department of Energy. All went smoothly. I wanted to be in London as it was the first shuffle of any sort in which I had been involved as Chief Whip. Before Christmas I had gone over the permutations of promotion with the Prime Minister, once it was clear that Norman wished to resign immediately. Michael Spicer and Tony Baldry had both been on my shortlist for promotion and I was pleased that she had gone along with those I recommended. We tried out names on each other but, with the help of the other whips, I made sure in advance that I knew who I would like to see promoted.

The House reassembled on Monday 8 January. Those led by Michael Mates, the MP for East Hampshire and close ally of Michael Heseltine, who had regularly attacked the principle of the Community Charge were now joined by a miscellaneous group of Conservative MPs. They felt very strongly that the new tax was going to be introduced at too high a level in the months ahead either because the Treasury grant was too low or because it would bear particularly unfairly and unjustly on their individual constituency. This group was headed by Rhodes Boyson who had been, as Minister at the Department of the Environment, one of the original architects of the scheme but was now an opponent. David Wilshire, in Conservative Spelthorne on the edge of London, could not understand why his District Council's Community Charge was going to be around

£500 while in neighbouring Slough, a marginal seat held by John Watts, it was to be as low as £200.

The whips were therefore faced with an unholy alliance of the left wing of the party – George Young, Charlie Morrison, Tim Rathbone, Hugh Dykes – joining with the right wing of the party – Rhodes Boyson, Jim Pawsey, Elizabeth Peacock. We did a much more detailed trawl of our parliamentary colleagues on the Community Charge Orders. This meant that every whip went around the thirty or so regional MPs for whom he was personally responsible. Our new list showed twenty-seven against and fifty-two doubtful. Counting those against as two because they might go into the opposition lobby and the doubtfuls as one because they would abstain, we now had 106 against us on 12 January as opposed to 124 on 20 December. On this basis we would lose by seven, assuming a total turnout of the opposition.

Alice and I had been asked to lunch with the Prime Minister at Chequers on Sunday 14 January. Chequers has a particular charm in that it is not a pretentious house. Set in ordinary countryside not many miles north of Heathrow, it is not approached by large double gates or surrounded by an eight-foot-high stone wall. The gates are modest, the gravel drive is short, the front door of medium size, and the interior is warm and welcoming. We had not been there for some years and I was struck again by the beauty of the panelling in the house, particularly in the dining room. The Prime Minister and Denis obviously loved the place and were very proud of it. There were few things the Prime Minister enjoyed more than being asked about the pictures and led on to talk about them. However, from the Community Charge point of view, it was a strange lunch. There were about fourteen of us. Among the guests were both George Young and his wife and George Gardiner and his wife. Both these Georges were committed to being difficult in the vote on the Orders, which was now fixed for four days ahead, Thursday 18 January. Their reasons were totally different, Young because of his opposition to the Community Charge in principle, Gardiner because of the baleful effects of our proposals on Surrey County Council who, it seemed, had been cheerfully overspending for years without ever informing their MPs about it.

About 3.45 p.m. the last of the other guests were gone. The Prime Minister suggested we went back from the large hall, with its big open fire, to the smaller room where we had had sherry before lunch. We walked in there, Alice joining us as the Prime Minister had said to her, 'Do come as well. You must know a lot about this now.'

I told the Prime Minister that, on the basis of our present calculations, we might still lose the vote.

'Lose,' she repeated in a tone of quiet distaste.

'Yes,' I replied but I explained that our figures had got better since December, and the loss was predicated upon all the opposition parties turning out in full force and this was unlikely. 'In short,' I said, 'we think we can win but it may be very close indeed.'

'It will be very bad if we don't,' the Prime Minister said. We talked about the consequences of that and the fact that the opposition would then table a no confidence motion which would have to be debated within the following days.

The Prime Minister was quiet and thoughtful. She did not try to ask me to be specific about our figures nor did she quarrel with any of my reasoning. There was no interruption from her, rather a careful listening to what I had to say.

Our conversation did not last more than ten minutes. We walked to the front door, all three of us thinking about the consequence of a defeat the coming Thursday.

'The job you do, Tim, is a very important one,' said the Prime Minister on the doorstep.

We got into our car, driven by the admirable Joe Bergin. As we wheeled round the patch of gravel in front of Chequers, Alice and I both looked back at the open front door and the Prime Minister waved to us. She looked a rather small and lonely figure.

The whips worked hard in the intervening days. We were helped by a number of things. There was no sign of any public division between the Treasury and the Department of the Environment. There were no informal press leakings by Environment ministers saying that, if we got in trouble on Thursday, it was because the Treasury had not given them all the money they had asked for; nor did we have Treasury ministers saying quietly, at a lunch in the Garrick, that of course the Department of the Environment had misallocated their Community Charge money and had got their priorities wrong. All of this was helpful in keeping the issue surprisingly quiet. The press did not cotton on to the fact of how worried we all were, with careful plans being made as to who should say precisely what in the event of us losing a vote on Thursday 18 January, when we would have to take the no confidence debate and so on.

On Wednesday the Prime Minister called another meeting. Beforehand, I went over the figures again with the whips. We had by now, we thought, reduced the rebels in our own party to twenty-seven against and thirty-three doubtful. On this basis, assuming all the opposition were present, we would win by twelve votes. But we already knew that Dafydd Wigley was ill, and that at least one Ulsterman would not be present. We were becoming more confident every hour. At the meeting, I said that the whips were unanimous in suggesting that we should let the current Rate Support Grant proposals stand and that we should not seek any last minute addition of public money. I added that there was, in the words of Chris Patten's note to the Prime Minister of the previous day, 'no neat, simple and cheap solution' that would necessarily secure the support of, say, two dozen of our rebels.

Chris had circulated a week earlier a paper which showed the possible effect in reducing the Community Charge by the expenditure of another £200 million. He assumed that this was the maximum extra sum available from the Treasury and he demonstrated that it was not enough to help substantially the local authorities of a number of our aggrieved colleagues. The Treasury ministers were enormously relieved to hear this, and this view won the day.

Thursday afternoon came. For me, it was like the day of the Boat Race for which the crews have prepared for weeks with tremendous attention to detail. We all had our lists of parliamentary colleagues whom we were to see, and to try and persuade, during the course of the afternoon. I was kept, like heavy artillery, for the final salvo. I started seeing rebellious colleagues at 5.15 p.m. and then saw them at quarter-hour intervals through until 8.00 p.m. Three I passed on to the Prime Minister herself.

In the debate we were helped by the excellent, patient and humorous speeches of Chris Patten and David Hunt and by the fact that both these ministers had a fund of goodwill stemming from their past reputations. This greatly reduced the number of abstentions, even if it did not much alter the number of those who actually voted against us. As someone said to me the following day, 'What a different result we would have had if Nick Ridley had opened the debate and David Mellor had wound it up.'

Having seen, and argued and talked with, colleagues for three hours, I dined quickly in the Members' dining room and came back into the Chamber to listen to David Hunt. He was persuasive and charming and spoke, as Chris Patten had done, without a note. The vote came and shortly before it Tristan handed me a card in which he had worked out that our majority would be twenty-eight. But he had written underneath, 'I reckon we will pick up a few absentees on the other side so I predict our majority will be between thirty-five and forty.' In fact there were fourteen absentees on the other side, divided between Liberals, Labour and the Ulster Unionists.

The Prime Minister came and sat on the Treasury bench as we waited for the vote to be announced. I leaned over Chris Patten and said to her, 'I think it will be about thirty-five.'

'Thirty-five?' she said, looking delighted. 'I was told it would be about twenty.'

A few seconds later the whips announced the result. We had a majority of forty-six, twenty-one more than on the Mates' Amendment two years before. Looking back on all the discussions and worries of the past month it seemed almost impossible.

Earlier in the afternoon, Mark Lennox-Boyd had told Kenneth Carlisle that the Prime Minister would be delighted to come back to the whips' office to have the traditional drink with us, if we won. We asked Chris Patten and David Hunt as well. The moment the second vote was over and it was clear that Labour was not going to force a vote on the remaining reports, the Prime Minister looked at me, smiled and said, 'Is that it?' 'Yes,' said I, 'let's go and have a drink.' We walked round the lobby and back through the Members' lobby together. As she entered our whips' office, a small cheer went up. We put her in the big chair in the centre of the room and the whips gathered around her. Everyone talked happily and excitedly for twenty minutes or so, and we were joined by Chris and David and by Andrew Turnbull. The mood was festive, rather like a Christmas evening after a long day of looking after the family. We were tired but happy and drank periodic toasts to the ministers at the Department of the Environment, to the Prime Minister and to ourselves.

There were pleasant things said in the press about the whips' office over the next few days. Even Robin Butler, the head of the Civil Service, and Charles Powell congratulated me when I saw them at the beginning of the following week and on Monday 22 January, at one of our regular meetings with Geoffrey Howe, John Belstead (Leader of the House of Lords) and Kenneth Baker, the Prime Minister looked at me and said, 'You must have done some remarkable organising.' At least I felt that Tristan, also new in his job as Deputy Chief Whip, and I had come through our first real parliamentary test unexpectedly well.

I wrote in my diary:

> Had we overemphasised the dangers? I don't believe so. If all the opposition had turned up and had voted against us our majority on the second vote would have been down to two. If Chris Patten and David Hunt had not made such good speeches on the night and had not used to the extent they did their own reputations and patience in dealing with colleagues, our majority could have been paper thin or non-existent.

For me, the personal irony was that, if I had not been a minister, I would have voted for any amendment tying the Community Charge to ability to pay. I always thought of the Charge as a dangerously regressive tax. But, as Chief Whip, I allowed ministerial obligations to take precedence over my own doubts.

The elation soon appeared naïvely optimistic. We went all too quickly from the January victory into ten weeks of constant battering, in Parliament and out. The nadir was reached on the first weekend of the Easter recess, 7–8 April, when opinion polls showed Conservatives with only 24 per cent support, more than twenty points behind Labour, and the Prime Minister also with a personal rating of 24 per cent – the lowest figure for a Prime Minister, the *Daily Telegraph* pointed out cheerfully, since poll ratings had started. Problems with the discipline of the party were still growing.

As we lost the mid-Staffs by-election in early March, on a swing of over 20 per cent and as the anomalies of the Community Charge piled up, the impression was that the government was failing. The newspapers, who had for so many years bolstered and admired the Prime Minister, now did an about-turn and joined in foretelling her downfall and another leadership election during the course of 1990 of which Michael Heseltine would be the certain victor. The press were like lemmings. If the *Guardian* wrote a serious piece about Tory dissent, *The Times* felt duty-bound to write an even more detailed analysis of rebellion in the parliamentary party, which was at best based on discussions with ten or twenty of our MPs, but was often founded on odd remarks from a few rabid souls like the Wintertons, Nicholas and Anne, Tony Beaumont-Dark and Tony Marlow. The *Independent* then picked up the story and even George Jones of the *Daily Telegraph* found himself writing long and deep projections of disaster ahead.

The *Daily Telegraph* in a long piece by Simon Heffer on 29 March chided me as being too approachable, and accused me of not putting my stamp of authority on the parliamentary party. But the traditional hierarchy of the Conservative Party had disappeared as Margaret Thatcher had wanted it to; respect for authority within the party had gone with it. I did my damnedest with tea for some in my room in the House of Commons and a G&T for others at 12 Downing Street. But when John Cole wrote in a *Listener* article that the Tory Party had become virtually unwhippable I felt that perceptiveness was on his side rather than on Simon Heffer's.

Alice and I went to the Central Council Meeting, an annual rally for constituency bigwigs, at Cheltenham on 30 and 31 March. The Prime Minister made a good speech on the Saturday morning which stirred the party faithful. She began with the line 'To avoid any possible misunderstanding, and at the risk of disappointing a few gallant colonels, let me make one thing absolutely clear; I have not come to Cheltenham to retire.' Obviously I thought the reference to a few gallant colonels was not just directed at the military pensioners of Cheltenham but also at Michael Mates – Colonel Mates – a leading champion of the 'Heseltine for Prime Minister' campaign. But this was precisely the opening that the branch and association chairmen, treasurers and agents wanted to hear, and they roared their approval. The whole speech was delivered with great punch. The team leaders went back to their constituencies much happier. What they did not know was that there had been debates throughout the night on the content of the speech. The final draft, as a weary Mark Lennox-Boyd told me, had only been ready at 7.30 a.m.

John Major and Chris Patten had been charged with writing a section for her on the Community Charge. Margaret did not like what they produced and rang John Major at the EC Finance Ministers' Meeting in Ireland to tell him, reputedly, that he was 'as much use to her as the skin on a cold rice pudding'. Chris Patten said to me wearily on Saturday morning, 'We are very close to the precipice.' But then the Prime Minister went on the stage, sang her aria which included the lines 'But everyone has the right to look at government and Parliament to protect them as Community Charge payers from overpowering taxation. They will not look in vain' – lines that she told me later she had written herself – and the audience cheered and cheered. She was in many ways a prima donna, surprisingly nervous and tense before her public performance, giving everyone hell, and then singing her part marvellously, relaxed and smiling and accepting the bouquets with charming grace.

The part that particularly interested me at Cheltenham in my Chief Whip's role was the number of references from speakers from the floor to 'whingeing backbench MPs or faint-hearted elected representatives'. This tenor of criticism fitted in with action that we had decided in the whips' office we must take against some of our own parliamentary colleagues, those who were most often absent without leave, without telling us that they were going to be away, and that despite having been paired or allowed to slip away without a pair on many occasions. Needless to say, they included most of the government's regular and hostile critics.

Another disease had been with us for some months. On a number of occasions twenty or thirty of our colleagues had found that if they got together and publicly disagreed with the government over some good but expensive cause, they could encourage a sufficient backbench rebellion to persuade ministers that more money had to be found. Since I had arrived in No. 12 this had happened over war widows – £200 million – special treatment for those who had received HIV-infected blood transfusions – £26 million – and increased allowances for the elderly in residential care – £90 million.

It reached a climax on the night of 13 March. We lost a vote on a Labour amendment to the Social Security Bill, the aim of which was further to increase allowances for those in residential care. Only the day before we had thought that we would have around twenty-five to thirty rebels, but the debate dragged on forty minutes longer than intended. Tony Newton (Secretary of State for Social Security) spoke at length, answering every point made by our backbenchers but without giving anything away and in the end lost more votes than he gained. Towards the end of the debate we got a sense that we might be going to lose.

I sat in my usual seat at the despatch box end of the front bench. Tristan was next to me as the division lobbies closed and the tellers put their heads together about the vote and wrote out the voting slip to give to the Speaker. We got a message from the whip at the far end of the bench, the whip on duty : 'If we lose, should we vote against Labour's new clause being added to the Bill?'

This is normally an absolute formality. One just does not bother to vote on the Speaker's question 'Is the clause to be added to the Bill?' for if the House has just agreed to the contents of the new clause, there is little point in adding to one's humiliation, or wasting time, by voting against the formal addition of the clause to the Bill. That goes through on the nod. I sent a message back to the whip at the far end of the bench, 'No, do not bother to vote against it.' Then I thought again and said to Tristan, 'I've changed my mind. Some may have drifted off or gone home after the first vote. So let's say we will vote against the new clause being added to the Bill if we are beaten by ten votes or less. Tell the whip at the far end.'

The tellers came in carrying their bit of paper with the result on it. Traditionally, the paper is held by the whip whose side has won the vote. There were shouts of approval from the opposition benches as they saw a Labour whip clutching the result of the division, and he formed up to the despatch box, with the other three tellers by his side, and announced, 'The Ayes to the left 258, and Noes to the right 255.' A great cheer went up from the opposition, a sigh of disbelief from our side. My colleagues had suddenly realised that, if enough of them were bloody-minded and voted against the government or abstained, we could actually lose a vote.

The Speaker stood up and read out formally the result of the vote approving the content of the new clause. Then he shouted, 'Is the new clause to be added to the Bill?' 'No!' we roared from our end of the front bench. Others on our side picked up the cry quickly and joined in. 'Aye!' the opposition shouted. So we voted again.

The diary note that I made the following day reads:

I barge up to several of our MPs, including Geoffrey Johnson Smith (MP for Wealden) who had not supported us on the first division. 'You have made your point. Do not vote for the clause to be in the Bill,' I say, 'it will cost £250 million.' I see other whips doing the same. Rough stuff. We win by twenty-seven votes – 246 (?) to 219. I find out later that ten of our MPs had switched from voting No to abstaining. For the rest, Labour MPs had gone off, thinking that there was only one vote.

At 11.30 p.m., I go to see the PM in her room in the House. She is sitting at one end of a long sofa, Mark Lennox-Boyd at the other, in silence, like a couple from a Pinter play. They are clearly waiting for someone or something to turn up. I tell her what has happened, that we didn't foresee the size of the revolt and so on, and I explain about the second vote. The Prime Minister says, 'You whips saved the day by being quick-witted.' She is very kind but very tired. I explain our tactics for the rest of the night and tomorrow. We may let the business just drift on – Labour have some forty new clauses still to be debated – and thus we could lose Wednesday's business altogether, including DTI Questions. She likes the sound of that as these may otherwise concentrate on the report on the Al-Fayeds. She says as she leaves and goes down the stairs, 'Now be cheerful.' I tell the office this.

Wednesday 14 March

We meet again in the Prime Minister's office at 9.30 a.m. with Kenneth Clarke. I have had a little sleep on my sofa but no breakfast. I make a quick cup of tea on the kettle in my office, which I had installed. I explain our new tactics to the Prime Minister. We had spent the whole night debating five new clauses only with immensely long speeches by Robin Cook. We will therefore go for the guillotine motion shortly and end the debate during the course of the morning. She takes it all in very quickly. She is quickly angry about those who did not support us and reels off some favourite names – Gardiner, Bendall, Churchill, J Knight – why them...? 'Do they not realise the cost has gone up a hundred times in ten years? We are just writing blank cheques for the residential homes.' That night the gold pencil goes through Winston's name for a knighthood. Unforgiving.

The next week we started debating in the whips' office what steps we should take against the seventy malcontents in our parliamentary party who were becoming increasingly rebellious.

On the last day of the parliamentary term, 5 April, I had a forty-five-minute session alone with the Prime Minister and Andrew Turnbull. I told Margaret that I had just written to thirteen MPs about their rotten voting record and I went over the background of the hard core of our MPs who regularly failed to turn up. I thought she was tired and dispirited and in some measure distancing herself from parliamentary problems. Her attitude was friendly but that of a chairman saying to one of his executive directors, 'You are employed to sort that out; you get on with it and make as little a mess of it as possible.' I thought it wise to forewarn her that I might decide to send the voting records of our most difficult colleagues to their constituency chairmen. She made no comment. At the end, rather wearily, she wished me a good Easter holiday. I wished her the same and hoped that her visit to Bermuda and discussions with President Bush would go well.

'Ah,' she said. 'First, before that, we have got the International Drugs Conference.' Poor woman, I thought.

Five days later the Prime Minister flew to Bermuda for a day of discussions with President Bush. The American press picked up the theme of decline and fall from the British. The Trafalgar Square riots against the Community Charge two weeks earlier were painted as the backcloth to a violent, depressed Britain for which Thatcherism was no longer an effective political remedy. As one Bermuda commentator said, if Margaret had previously been an 'up' thing, she was now certainly a 'down' thing.

Yet, in her own mercurial temperament, she was certainly not always in a down mood despite the battering that she was getting daily from the press and in the television bulletins. I broke my holidays in order to spend a day in London concentrating on my constituency correspondence. Before I started I went along the passage through No. 11 to No. 10. I wanted to ask Charles Powell for tips about Henry Catto, the new American ambassador whom Alice and I were to meet at dinner that night. Standing, almost lounging, outside the office that Charles shared with Andrew Turnbull was the Prime Minister, sparkling in a pepper and salt suit with a large, showy brooch. If she had been firing on only two cylinders when I last saw her, the situation was now all changed.

'I am feeling much better, Tim,' she said. 'I have had time to think. That is often the way when Parliament is not sitting. One has time to do some long-term thinking.' She turned to one of her private secretaries. 'Have you found that note I sent yesterday to John Major about the Community Charge?' The secretary fumbled among papers on his desk. 'Has the Chief Whip seen a copy of it?' she asked. 'No,' she replied to her own question. 'Of course he has not. Not even Chris Patten has seen a copy of it. Make a copy of it and let us go into the Cabinet room and talk about it.' I guessed that Margaret had some spare time in her diary and was longing to have a good debate with a political colleague. I mentally said goodbye to Mrs Harvey, for many years my loyal constituency secretary, who had just arrived at No. 12 with her plastic bag packed with files full of unanswered constituency letters. I followed Margaret and sat across the long table from her. She was joined by a new private secretary. He handed me over the table a copy of a note written by Margaret to John Major the day before. 'Read that,' she said, 'and tell me what you think of it.'

The first page was all about the effect of the Community Charge on the RPI, and it contained a detailed argument as to why the RPI increases should reflect the net cost of the Community Charge, after Transitional Relief and other benefits, rather than the gross. The obvious wish was to keep down the rise in the RPI, flowing from the introduction of the Charge, to the greatest extent possible. This I could go along with, provided that the technicians at the Treasury and the Department of Employment would agree. On the second page, though, I got into the sticky part. The Prime Minister suggested to the Chancellor that there should be a surcharge on the incomes of all of those earning more than, say, £50,000 a year that would be equivalent to an average Community Charge throughout the country – that is, around £370. The purpose of this surcharge would be publicly stated to be to provide more funds either for Transitional Relief or for other Community Charge benefits directed at helping, particularly, those in the C2 class – the young families on average earnings or below average earnings who were finding the transition from rates to the Community Charge extremely hard to bear. The surcharge could be either temporary or permanent. It could be at a multiplier of the average Community Charge for those on yet higher incomes, for instance those earning £100,000 p.a. could pay a surcharge of twice the average Community Charge.

I read the minute quickly. Margaret asked me what I thought. I gulped mentally and said that I did not like the idea of the surcharge. It did not sound right. If we had to raise additional money, I would prefer to put up the top rates of tax. A surcharge, I thought, would be reminiscent of the worst days of Labour Budgets when we had surcharges on investment income. Such a measure would lose us political points on two grounds: first, we would be told that the Community Charge was in a mess; and secondly, we would be accused of getting our taxation policy into a mess in order to try and salvage the Community Charge.

Margaret looked at me across the table and started arguing.

'We cannot possibly put up direct taxation, Tim. That goes against the whole of our policy for the last ten years. I fought to get taxation down to the level at which it is now. But people on higher incomes, above £50 or £100,000, could not mind a surcharge put on them that would go to help out people on lower incomes, people who are having difficulty in paying the Community Charge. It would be seen to be fair.' The word fairness came up a number of times in her argument. At one moment she even said, 'It is not fair that Denis and I should be gaining so much on our house in Dulwich when others on £180 or £190 a week are having to find so much more to pay.'

I refrained from saying anything along the lines of 'I told you so' or 'why did you not think of this earlier?' I remembered a Monday lunch at No. 10, very soon after the June 1987 election, when we talked about the Community Charge and I had mentioned that I worried that the tax was regressive. 'What does that matter?' the Prime Minister had asked. Most of the cost of local government would still be paid out of income taxes which were progressive. 'And,' she had added ominously, 'remember, Tim, that we have all just fought a general election on the basis of introducing the Community Charge.'

Thirty months later we were stuck in the mire of the Community Charge and wondering how on earth to get out of it. The Prime Minister said, 'It will be no good, Tim, just tinkering at the edges. We have got to do something substantial or we shall lose the next election.' She quoted from a number of the letters she had received attacking the detail of the Community Charge and she added that she felt very depressed about it. I went on arguing against a specific surcharge on those with higher incomes. We debated in a friendly manner for an hour without convincing each other. I said I would mull it over and the Prime Minister replied, 'You mull. But we have got to do something.' To my surprise, as I left the room, she added, almost apologetically, 'I hope you did not mind my getting at you.'

'Not at all,' said I. 'We just had a good forceful argument with each other.' In the event, no more was heard of this extraordinary idea. It was one of the occasions when I felt that she was out of step even with her own philosophy.

The same ambivalence was visible in the Prime Minister's attitude to the issue of British passports for the Hong Kong Chinese, but this time for creditable reasons. It was a problem that had hung over us for months.

After the massacre in Tiananmen Square on 4 June 1989 a committee chaired by the Prime Minister had sat to consider whether, in the light of those awful events in Beijing, we should change the attitudes we had all firmly held until then and decide to allow some Chinese from Hong Kong to gain the right to settle in Britain or to travel on British passports without previous residence in the UK.

This went against the spirit and the principle of the Immigration and Nationality Acts that had been passed in 1971, 1981 and 1988. This committee was unable to reach firm conclusions and was usually bad-tempered. The Prime Minister wanted those allowed permission to reside here to be limited to young entrepreneurs who would set up successful factories in Milton Keynes or Basingstoke. The Foreign Office wanted the numbers to be high – a figure as high as 500,000 was mentioned at one time – and the legislation to be by way of substantial changes in either the 1971 or the 1981 Acts. The then Home Secretary, Douglas Hurd, wanted the number to be as low as possible and the legislation to be by way of changes in the immigration rules which would require the minimum amount of debate in the Commons and could be changed without primary legislation. As immigration minister, I sat in on these meetings and appreciated how different the attitudes of the Prime Minister, Geoffrey Howe and Douglas Hurd were.

Then came the reshuffle. Douglas Hurd went to the Foreign Office, David Waddington to the Home Office and I went to No. 12, where I quickly realised that this was going to be one of my immediate problems. Douglas Hurd, in his new role, wanted to visit Hong Kong during the Christmas holidays and wished to make an announcement about the package we were proposing for the Hong Kong Chinese before the Christmas recess so that the details would be out and available for debate when he was in the colony. In fairness to Douglas he did not press hard for higher totals, but he was anxious to come out with a reasonable, generous and comprehensive scheme. David Waddington, innately cautious, inherited all the Home Office scepticism and made it clear at committee meetings that, first, he did not want a scheme at all and that, second, he very much doubted whether any scheme could possibly work.

I knew from visits as a Foreign Office minister how worried many in Hong Kong were about what would happen after the handover to China in 1997. They were frightened that the free trading market and the low taxes that together had helped Hong Kong grow so rapidly would disappear and that China would stamp their single-party orthodoxy onto the Hong Kong Legislative and Executive Councils. On the other hand, I felt that the case for asylum seekers to find refuge in Britain was much more persuasive than that of the well-skilled Hong Kongers. The whips' view was that few of our colleagues felt a great moral obligation to help Hong Kong in the run-up to 1997, and this I reflected in our discussions.

This was not at all what the Prime Minister wanted to hear. Indeed, she nearly threw a tantrum as she insisted that we owed a debt of honour to help Hong Kong in the situation in which the colony now found itself post-Tiananmen Square. She refused to believe that our colleagues were so lacking in their sense of duty. I had to admire Margaret for her loyalty to Hong Kong, despite her inconsistency. What I was admiring was a paradox in her. When I was at the Home Office, she had been a most difficult person to deal with on immigration matters. I remembered a note that she had sent to Douglas Hurd written in fury at 2.00 a.m., when she discovered from the papers in her box that we had given leave to remain in this country to one of her constituents whom she felt we should have deported. Now she was arguing more passionately than anyone else in Cabinet about our duty to

Hong Kong, even if the issue would cause us to lose a lot of blood in the Commons and would anger her friends on the right wing of the party.

A scheme finally evolved after a lot of bargaining about numbers. Fifty thousand heads of households, one-third coming from the public sector and two-thirds from the private sector, would be awarded British passports, and these would also be available for their wives and children under the age of eighteen. The lucky ones, particularly those from the private sector, would be decided on a points system, unique in our immigration history, in which most points would go to those in their thirties and early forties whose professions showed a 'tendency to emigrate' from Hong Kong.

Douglas Hurd announced the scheme two days before we broke up for the Christmas recess, and he was immediately entangled in an argument with Norman Tebbit. Speaking from the front bench below the gangway, Norman said that we were going against the commitment in our manifesto to be the party that reduced immigration in this country. Douglas, his face in a rare flush of anger, said that in all his years as Home Secretary he had been well aware of the need to reduce the numbers of immigrants and he 'needed no lessons on this matter' from the Rt Hon. Member for Chingford. No sooner was Norman out of the Chamber and into the Members' lobby than he was approached by journalists to whom he announced that he would lead the campaign against the Bill. Within a few hours headlines were screaming that there would be a major rebellion in the Tory ranks and that as many as eighty of our own party might not support us. Obviously, with a majority of ninety-nine in the House, if eighty colleagues actually voted against us, our majority would be turned into a defeat by sixty-one.

I took comfort from the fact that, during the forty minutes of questions and answers that followed Douglas Hurd's statement in the Commons, representatives of the Liberal Party, the SNP and the Ulster Unionists indicated that they would either support us or at least not be in the lobbies with the Labour Party whose opposition, coming from a party that was committed to a much more generous approach to immigration, seemed wholly hypocritical. In addition, a number of Labour MPs such as Peter Shore and Diane Abbott indicated they would not follow their party whip.

Our junior whips felt particularly nervous about the Hong Kong Bill. A number of them felt that the measure was wrong. On 26 February 1990, as the details of the Bill were being finalised and we had to agree when to debate it in the House and whether to take it on the floor of the whole House or, as I wished, send it in the normal manner to a committee of sixteen or twenty MPs, I met the Prime Minister and told her that there would still be about eighty of our colleagues against us on the issues. These would include many of her personal friends, and to get the Bill through we would need the support of the minority parties. She smiled at me across the table in the Cabinet room and said almost apologetically: 'When I gave you the job of Chief Whip, you didn't think you'd have to take this on.'

'Oh, but he loves it,' Mark Lennox-Boyd chipped in.

'We can't resile from this,' the Prime Minister continued. 'I've made commitments internationally – to Lydia Dunn (Member of the Hong Kong Legislative and Executive Councils) and others.'

'I thought you'd say that,' said I. 'So I haven't tried to persuade you otherwise.'

'If it happens and we lose it,' said the Prime Minister, 'at least we will be able to say that we tried but could not deliver.' These were noble sentiments, although a little rumour started in the weeks ahead, and kept on coming down the passage between No. 10 and No. 12, that actually the Prime Minister was thinking of scrapping the Bill because of the fuss it was creating with the Tebbits in our own party.

When, just before the Easter recess, Geoffrey Howe and I learned from the great campaigner for women's rights on the Labour benches, Jo Richardson, that they did not want to have a day debating the Embryology Bill on the Thursday immediately after the Easter recess, 19 April, because so many Labour MPs would not come to the House at all that week, we promptly put on the second reading of the Hong Kong Bill for that day instead. This drew protests from all sides, including from a number of our own colleagues who said that we were not giving enough notice between the publication of the Bill and the second reading debate, but the biggest protest was from the Prime Minister in Cabinet who suddenly found herself committed to a specific date for this unpleasant issue.

Geoffrey Howe and I had only decided at 10.00 a.m. on Thursday 29 March to take advantage of the probable low attendance of Labour MPs and to put on the second reading for 19 April.

Cabinet was due to start half an hour later. The Prime Minister's private office was informed by telephone but Margaret had not had time to think about it. After Geoffrey had announced the business in Cabinet and I had told Cabinet of the whipping, the Prime Minister's anger emerged. She said that she wished we had not announced this just before the Easter recess. It would give two weeks for our opponents to marshal their troops and two weeks in which the newspapers would be full of articles about a further split in the Tory Party. Geoffrey left me to put forward the argument in favour of changing our previous plans and choosing the Thursday immediately after we came back from the Easter holidays.

John Wakeham, previously a very successful Chief Whip and at that time Secretary of State for Energy, sat on my left in Cabinet. He passed me a note saying, 'I would have considered reading out the wrong business and squaring her afterwards to change to what you want – which I think is right. But it is easier to sit on the sidelines!' At the end of Cabinet I went up and apologised to Margaret for not giving her more advanced notice.

'I only learned about it when a note was slipped in my hand as I was coming down the stairs to Cabinet,' she said.

This was a reminder for me of the advice Wakeham had earlier given me. The Prime Minister never liked to be taken by surprise in a Cabinet announcement and the Chief Whip, acting as one of the Prime Minister's right arms, should make certain that he knew the Prime Minister's thinking in advance and tried to fall in with it in any open debate, no matter what was said privately between them before or after.

Before the recess, I had talks with both Jim Molyneux of the Ulster Unionists and Paddy Ashdown and Jim Wallace of the Liberals, officially about the unusual manner in which we were going to handle the free votes on the clause on embryo research and any new clauses on abortion in the Embryology Bill, but also to sound them out about the Hong Kong Bill. Molyneux was a little evasive; he could not be certain how many Ulster Unionists would turn up and vote on the night but he was certain that any who were present would not support Labour. Paddy Ashdown and Jim Wallace were more clear. Their colleagues would be whipped to vote for the Hong Kong Bill, but also against all discussion of it being in a committee of the whole House. They agreed this would extend the arguing for far too long. In return, I promised that one of their numbers would be on the committee that decided the selection of amendments for the Embryology Bill and the order in which they were debated. Given their party's interest in this subject, with David Steel on one side of the argument and David Alton on the other, this was well deserved. It was also a clear case of mutual help between those who were usually in political conflict.

I worried as I waited for the debate on the Hong Kong Bill on 19 April. The thought of it weighed on me throughout the Easter holidays. One of the worst things whips have to do is to rely on winning a vote by virtue of support from the opposition. This is unpredictable; you cannot be certain that those who said they would support you will actually turn up on the night, nor can you chase them during the hours before the vote to see what they are going to do and to make certain that they have not changed their mind. I knew the junior whips were still very anxious about the result. Nonetheless, I felt confident. I thought the Labour Party would be split on the issue and all the forty-four votes of the opposition minority parties would either be with us or would abstain.

And so it turned out. There was a good debate, Peter Shore speaking particularly well from the opposition side and attacking the half-promises of more immigration put forward by Roy Hattersley, in between opposing our Bill. Hattersley himself seemed very uncomfortable in the first fifteen minutes of his speech, the paradox of being against the Bill while arguing for less control on immigration being one that he could not explain away. All the whips worked hard on our colleagues throughout the evening. We persuaded a number to abstain rather than to vote against us on the main Labour opposition to the second reading, but then to vote with us on the second procedural vote and thus defeat the motion that the whole of the Bill should be taken on the floor of the House.

Norman Tebbit's group had been particularly confident that they would win that second vote and thus defeat the Bill by hours of procedural wrangling late at night on the floor of the House when we would not be able to stop our troops from going home. Norman Tebbit got his eighty Tory supporters, divided between those who voted against us and those who abstained. Some thirty of the Labour Party also abstained but thirteen of the fourteen Liberal MPs voted with us and so did the Social Democratic Party and a number of the Ulstermen. In consequence, we won by high margins, winning the vote on the second reading by ninety-seven votes and defeating the procedural motion by 115 votes.

I went round to the Prime Minister's room at the House of Commons after the votes. She was pleased but, as far as she was concerned, it was already water under the bridge, another problem passed. She was busy discussing with Bernard Ingham how to handle the announcement of John Wakeham's appointment as the minister responsible for coordinating 'the development of presentation of government policies'. I was surprised and made the obvious point that it was essential for Geoffrey Howe and Kenneth Baker, the chairman of the party, to be told about this well in advance and their approval obtained; the press would love to have another opportunity of saying that this was another case of Geoffrey being bypassed. This was a foretaste of what lay ahead. John's official post was Secretary of State for Energy. He was greatly occupied with the privatisation of the electricity industry. There was no reason for him to take charge of the government's press and public relations other than that he stood out as one of the few Cabinet members whom Margaret totally trusted. She sensed this was the support she was going to need in the months immediately ahead.

FOUR

Summer 1990

The major debate on the Hong Kong Bill over, my attention focused on the continuing crisis of confidence in the parliamentary party. The media told us every day, and particularly the heavy newspapers on Saturday and Sunday, that the parliamentary party was in turmoil and that a large number wanted a change of leadership. Fed on this diet, questioned constantly by lobby correspondents as to whether they thought we had more chance of winning the next election if we had a change of leader, a growing number of Tory MPs showed their doubts. This was hardly surprising; our standing in the polls was low with Labour at one time gaining a 24 per cent lead over us; the Prime Minister's popularity was at the lowest ever recorded by opinion polls for a sitting Prime Minister; the argument about the Community Charge went on. But the Prime Minister showed her character. At no time, from my return from holiday on 18 April until we broke up again on 24 May, did I see her either rattled or self-doubting. I listened to her arguing passionately, particularly about the reform of the Community Charge. But never did I get any hint that the constant criticism of her in the newspapers was telling on her or that she was minded to give up.

During these difficult weeks we never did a headcount of those who might want to see her abandon the leadership. I felt that this could be a disastrous exercise, producing a result that it would be difficult for me not to act upon. I told the whips' office, the moment we came back from the Easter recess, that I did not want us to chew over the bones every day as to the size of the leadership revolt, but that, at some stage, we might have to sit down and have a very serious discussion about it. Obviously, I wondered about my own position as Chief Whip, honour-bound to advise the Prime

Minister if I felt that a majority of the parliamentary party was against her. But I came to the conclusion that, at least for the time being, a great deal was speculation, gossip and uncertainty, not hard facts. It would have been different if I had received a letter signed by, say, 200 Conservative MPs saying that they were convinced that it was time for a change of leadership. Then I would have had to act. But I received no such letter.

Instead, I received letters from the secretaries of the One Nation Club and of a group named Nick's Diner (after Nick Scott, MP for Chelsea, the majority of its members were not, in No. 10's terms, 'one of us'), each with about twenty-five MPs as members, and each telling me they had concluded at dinner the night before that the Prime Minister should go, but neither suggesting either an alternative leader or a firm course of action. I sat on these letters. I showed them to no one, although, under today's rules, put together they might have caused the chairman of the 1922 Committee to call for a vote of confidence in Margaret. Every day the whips' notes contained some reference or other to a tea-room conversation in which a member of our party had loudly proclaimed his opinion – it might have been Tony Marlow or Neil MacFarlane – that it was time for a change. The press argued Michael Heseltine's case harder than ever. The actual group around Michael seemed a very small one, but Michael Mates and Keith Hampson were the two who were constantly named as his lieutenants.

The local elections on 3 May brought matters to a head. Kenneth Baker, the chairman of the party, had consciously made the Community Charge the prime subject of the elections. He had also focused on Westminster, Wandsworth and Bradford as three 'flagship' councils, all of them with small Tory majorities, all with low Community Charges. The slogan for the campaign was 'Labour Councils cost you more'. If we lost the three flagships, then it was quite clear that we were not winning the argument. The Community Charge would be sunk and, with it, probably the Prime Minister.

The media had sensed this and there were a great number of Heseltine events planned for immediately after 3 May – appearances on key television programmes, an article to be published in *The Times* in which he would put forward his alternative to the Community Charge, to be followed by a speech at Harrogate in which he would elaborate on his politics and ideas.

The whips' notes on 2 May told me of the conference of Heseltine's supporters to discuss their next moves that was planned for the coming weekend, and we considered at our daily meeting how to infiltrate the conference. I was told in strict confidence that Michael Heseltine had consulted Michael Havers about the 'constitutional position' and I also learned that he had been in touch with his own moles at Conservative Central Office.

In the event the rocket that had gone up so far and so fast, increasingly aided by the speculation in the press, temporarily faltered. We lost one flagship – Bradford. We kept the other two, Westminster and Wandsworth, with increased majorities. We won Ealing from Labour and we savaged the Labour majority in Brent, all cases of voters rebelling against high Community Charges. We did not do well in other parts of the country but we lost fewer seats than we had feared and we proved that 'Labour Councils cost you more' was a potentially winning argument.

Michael Heseltine's article appeared in *The Times* a few days after the local election results. It made a reasonable argument, setting up the various ways of improving the Community Charge and adding one or two new touches of Michael's own – for instance, that the mayor or chairman of each authority should be the directly elected chief executive and that councils who wished to spend over the government's assessment of their spending needs should hold a referendum to see whether they had the support of their own electorate in raising additional revenue.

But the article was a damp squib simply because so much had been expected of it. Michael did not come out flatly against the Community Charge or unequivocally for it. He was caught in the dilemma of a swimmer trying to go with the tide but, nonetheless, to be faster than all the other swimmers. The mood in the parliamentary party changed perceptibly and very quickly. Tony Marlow, who had behaved badly over the Hong Kong Bill and had insulted his own colleagues by hinting that they might have taken freebies to Hong Kong, approached Tristan Garel-Jones and told him that he realised he had been behaving rather stupidly. The first swallow, we thought. Admittedly, Tony Marlow a week or two later said that he was convinced the party needed a change of leadership.

A number of parliamentary colleagues told me that they now thought that the Community Charge needed fine-tuning – on the question of the standard charge for second homes and such like – but they could live with the principle of it. Meetings of the 1922 Executive and of the full committee were sparsely attended. Cranley Onslow and his two vice-chairmen, Marcus Fox and Geoffrey Johnson Smith, did not have much to tell me when they came to see me on Thursday evenings after the 1922 meeting had ended. Bernard Ingham pronounced that the mood of the lobby correspondents had changed. From being a pack of jackals waiting for a dying body to be thrown them, they suddenly became more attentive, less carping and critical. 'We have turned the corner,' said the Prime Minister, 'but there are other corners ahead of us.'

Before the changes introduced by Robin Cook that arguably made the Commons timetable more user-friendly, whips' lore had it that July was by far the worst month. In the pressure to get business through before the long summer recess, debates went on until late in the night. Since many of the debates went on to a series of amendments to Bills, there was no set pattern as to when the votes would take place. So whips were constantly telling parliamentary colleagues, 'Yes, please, you must stay for another vote. No, I am afraid we do not know when the vote will be. Yes, we will try to see that it happens as soon as possible but that may not be until one or two in the morning,' etc. Consequently, MPs came to hate their whips, and in turn whips came to despise ministers who could not bring in a Bill without having hundreds of last minute amendments to it, and who then insisted on talking at far too great a length to those amendments.

Summer 1990 was no exception. By the end of July, I was so irritable that even a momentary delay at home – someone keeping me waiting for a minute by the car – made me unreasonably angry. I would keep my temper from 8.00 a.m. until midnight with parliamentary colleagues but then bite off the head of my wife or one of my children on Saturday morning. The pressure was due not to any exceptional rows over policy or the content of Bills but to a succession of wayward personalities. The Bill that got into real difficulties was the Scottish Law Reform Bill and this produced one of the worst of the personality clashes. The Bill was a package of measures that did not just allow solicitors greater opportunity to act as advocates in the Higher Courts but that also, for example, allowed police to enter clubs without a formal search warrant. It also changed the period after which divorce was permissible. We only had six Scottish backbenchers. Four of these were on the standing committee studying the Bill and three – Nicky Fairbairn, Bill Walker and Allan Stewart – decided to object to various parts of the Bill. This meant that we lost our majority on the committee.

Nicky had been objecting to a great deal of government legislation for years, partly out of pique that he had lost his job as a Scottish law officer, and he blamed the Lord Advocate for this. Bill Walker had a right wing on both shoulders. He was a vice-chairman of the Scottish Conservative Party, dedicated to Michael Forsyth, the new young Scottish Party chairman, and bitterly opposed to Malcolm Rifkind, the Secretary of State. Allan Stewart succeeded in giving the impression that he would simply follow leads given by Nicky and Bill.

Michael Forsyth, the most junior minister at the Scottish Office, in turn gave less than stalwart support to his boss, Malcolm Rifkind, who became progressively gloomier and more tetchy as the summer progressed.

The whip on the Bill, Michael Fallon, only managed to keep matters moving by clever manoeuvres. One week, for example, Malcolm had to go to Edinburgh to be in attendance on the Queen at Holyrood. There was no way that the Secretary of State could be absent from Scotland on this royal occasion; nonetheless, Michael got one of the Labour members to pair with Malcolm and thus covered his absence. The Bill got bogged down in committee with many of the delaying tactics coming from Nicky Fairbairn. In the whips' office we debated whether to introduce a guillotine on it on the Floor of the House but were told by Nicky, Bill and Allan that, if we did, they would vote against everything in the Bill when it went back to the committee for the remaining proceedings. In the end, we reached a compromise by which large chunks of the Bill were dropped. This was humiliating for Malcolm, and the Scottish newspapers revelled in this, talking every day about the rebellions within the ranks of Scottish Conservatives.

What quickly became clear was that the Bill was only a symptom of far deeper trouble. The Prime Minister had herself appointed Michael Forsyth as chairman of the party in Scotland a year before. It was said that she had not even consulted Malcolm about this but had merely informed him of the decision. Malcolm and Michael were as chalk and cheese. Malcolm was the educated lawyer leaning towards the left of the party, already perhaps rather tired after four years as Scottish Secretary and with no great prospect of a better Cabinet job under Margaret. Michael, on the other hand, younger and very ambitious, knew that the Prime Minister had blessed him. He belonged to the No Turning Back group of which Michael Fallon and Francis Maude were also members. I was soon being lobbied by the older Scots members in the House – George Younger, Hector Monro and Alec Buchanan-Smith – all of whom told me that the party was becoming irrevocably split in Scotland. Constituency chairmen, they said, had little confidence in the younger men and women whom Forsyth had put into key positions in the Central Office in Edinburgh, the older agents were leaving in droves, and communications between the constituency associations and Scottish Central Office had virtually ceased. Malcolm came to see me at the beginning of July and made plain his concern about Michael's loyalty as Scottish Party chairman. He pointed out that the first issue of the new monthly *Scottish Conservative Magazine*, of which Michael Forsyth had appointed the editor, had included many flattering references to Michael himself but no mention at all of the Scottish Secretary of State.

At the end of the first week of July I had my first discussions with the Prime Minister about the forthcoming major ministerial reshuffle. I suggested that Forsyth should leave the Scottish Office and be appointed instead to one of the Whitehall departments whose writ ran in Scotland. The two obvious examples were either Energy or the higher education job at Education; in both of these cases their remit covered the whole of the United Kingdom. I was not keen that Forsyth should be promoted from parliamentary under-secretary to Minister of State but was prepared to concede that promotion if, in return for him moving from the Scottish Office, he gave up his post as chairman of the party in Scotland. This was eventually agreed. Forsyth would go to the Department of Energy as Minister of State; Peter Morrison would give up his job there and, the Prime Minister suggested, become her parliamentary private secretary instead.

This was how matters stood until the weekend before the reshuffle, although Malcolm made me nervous by saying that he thought Forsyth could be more difficult as minister in another department than as a junior minister in the Scottish Office. I decided not to pay attention to that conclusion of Malcolm's. The argument about where Forsyth should be placed on the ministerial ladder continued when the House of Commons came back for the emergency debate on the Iraq invasion of Kuwait on 6 and 7 September.

On the strength of his support from the Prime Minister, Forsyth bargained that, in return for giving up the chairmanship of the party in Scotland, he would move up to Minister of State at the Scottish Office with responsibilities for health and education transferred to him from other ministers at the Scottish Office. Hours of negotiation went on while the Gulf war was taking place.

At one point, in the middle of the morning, the Prime Minister said, 'Should I see Michael again now? Straight away?' A pause, and then she added, 'But I have a telephone call from George Bush at 12.15 about the Gulf crisis, and really I must read my brief first.'

'I really think you should read your brief, Prime Minister,' I said. 'After all, you are in any case planning to see Michael for lunch at around 12.45.'

'Yes, all right, I will read my brief.'

This was an interesting insight into the Prime Minister's priorities. Forsyth duly moved up the ministerial ladder and received a much redrafted letter of support from the Prime Minister herself. Lord Sanderson took over the Scottish Central Office and within four weeks had dismissed three of the young directors appointed by his predecessor. The Prime Minister never understood Scotland and its particular ambitions. At times, she appeared to resent Scotland being part of the United Kingdom. The lack of harmony in our party organisation could only take us in the direction of losing us more of our few Scottish seats.

Six weeks earlier, towards the end of July, I was working on the details of the ministerial reshuffle when a *Spectator* article appeared, full of Nick Ridley's ramblings to the editor, Nigel Lawson's son Dominic, in which his dislike of the Common Market in general and of the Germans in particular was unsparingly revealed. Geoffrey Howe rang me as soon as he heard the details on the *Today* programme, hours before most of us had got our copy of the *Spectator*, and my telephone rang throughout the Thursday morning with anguished calls from MPs and from MEPs who were in session in Strasbourg.

I was not particularly surprised at Nick's outburst. It had become clear from his comments in Cabinet over the months that he was increasingly disenchanted, as Trade Secretary, with his experience with EC Commissioners, indeed with all the works of the European Community. This was a considerable change from his position in the 1970s when we were in opposition and when I regarded him as one of the most fervent supporters of our EC membership. The growing dislike of the Germans was, of course, a reflection of the Prime Minister's own attitude. She had a great fear of German unification which aroused in her folk-memories of the 1930s. I remember her saying at Cabinet on 8 February, 'They are going ahead totally selfishly. They have not consulted with us at all.' Douglas Hurd, in reply, commented that the West Germans were driven to act with speed by the 70,000 immigrants who had come from East to West Germany in the five weeks since 1 January. Most of these, he said, just wished to exchange their Trabant for a Golf.

Some time in June I had asked Nick whether he proposed to resign at the next election. He said that he did but he wished to inform the Prime Minister personally first. A week or two later he took me aside in No. 10 to tell me, in effect, to forget our previous conversation. He said that he had changed his mind as he saw himself as the Prime Minister's last firm supporter in Cabinet. Everyone else was being swept along on waves of Euro enthusiasm.

Nick, however, had now let himself get caught in an elementary tiger-trap. Both the things that he said and the manner in which he had said them, as quoted in the *Spectator*, were unacceptable in a government that was a willing and active member of the Community. Michael Heseltine rang me on the Thursday evening to say that the Prime Minister should sack Nick immediately and should not wait overnight for his return from Hungary where he was on government business.

I saw the Prime Minister on Friday morning in the House and tried to lead her, gently, into realising that it would be unacceptable for Nick to stay and that most of our colleagues realised this. I knew that she would find this very difficult. Temperamentally, she had enormous regard for Nick. He was one of the last of the faithful around her. We got on to the details of the reshuffle and I suggested that, if she were free, I would come over to

Chequers to discuss this with her during the weekend. 'What a good idea,' she said. 'You and Alice must come to supper on Saturday evening.'

In the meantime, the Ridley affair rumbled on. Steve Norris, Nick's parliamentary private secretary, and a headstrong individual, got the mistaken impression that most of the parliamentary party wanted Nick to stay on. He repeated this to Nick when he returned from Hungary late on Friday night, and this was reflected in a BBC News broadcast at 1 p.m. on Saturday which gave the firm impression that Nick was not going to resign but would leave it to the Prime Minister to take the decision. Peter Emery, a senior Tory MP, chairman of the Procedure Committee, and so forth, promptly rang me to say that he could not believe what he had just heard. Nick was throwing the ball back at the Prime Minister in a dishonourable manner. If Nick was not made to go he, Peter, would think of resigning the whip for three months.

Horrified by the broadcast, I rang Andrew Turnbull to say that the Prime Minister should not authorise Downing Street to say anything in support of Nick until we met for supper that evening. It would be disastrous if the Prime Minister put herself in a corner from which she could not extricate herself. Andrew, however, told me that the Prime Minister had now been speaking to Nick and would ring me in a matter of minutes. She duly did so. In a calm, clear but tired voice she said that she and Nick had talked and that Nick was coming to the conclusion 'that it would not be in his best interests for him to stay on in government'. She expected an announcement to that effect to be made later that afternoon. And so it was. The intervening hour or two were spent on the drafting of the appropriate letters between the Prime Minister and Nick. I heard the actual announcement that he was leaving the government on the 6.00 p.m. news as Alice and I were driving over from our home in Sussex to Buckinghamshire.

We arrived at Chequers on a lovely July evening. The Prime Minister was out in the rose garden and with her, toddling around, was her grandson. Denis was leaning over a wall, G&T in his hand, staring at the Buckinghamshire middle distance. The Prime Minister, like any grandmother, occasionally darted to prevent her grandson falling into the rose bushes.

Margaret tried to put a brave face on everything but she was depressed and low. She went into the house to fetch copies of the letters that she had exchanged with Nick and showed them to me, almost touchingly, emphasising the personal attachment to Nick that was clear in the letter she had written to him accepting his resignation. I felt very sorry for her and I kept on saying comfortable words along the well-worn lines: I know how much you will miss him and what a support he has been to you over the years but nonetheless, Prime Minister, he was quite right to resign. There was no way in which he could have stayed on.

Alice told me afterwards that Denis had been in a very gloomy mood and at one moment had said to her, 'All I am really waiting for is to get the hell out of here.' We kept up a show over dinner trying to jolly the Prime Minister and Denis along. I could not help thinking that it was like a sad family party, bemoaning the loss of a favourite cousin.

After dinner, the Prime Minister visibly pulled herself together and said, 'Come on, we are now going to talk about the reshuffle together,' and to Alice, 'Of course, you come along too.' We went into the drawing room by the hall. Margaret and I sat down on one of the large sofas. I had written out in the car as we drove over a draft of what I thought the various moves should be, taking into account Nick's departure. This had inevitably made the list of changes a good deal longer than it was before.

The Prime Minister took one look at the list, started off with the first on the list, Agriculture, and then promptly slipped away at a tangent. This was the hallmark of all conversations about reshuffles. One would start at a fixed place but find, within seconds, that she had darted all over the scenery, and pieces that had been elaborately woven into the tapestry a day or two before would fall apart in the most haphazard manner. I went through my suggestions, continually trying to bring her back to my draft list. She interrupted, jumped from one department to another and then – worst of all – occasionally leaned back and fell asleep for some seconds.

After a while, Alice, sitting on the opposite sofa and amazed at the confusion, suggested that she should act as secretary and make a list, a compilation of our various suggestions. 'What a good idea,' said the Prime Minister. 'I will get you some pens and paper.' She jumped up, left the room and came back within a few minutes with some paper and several different coloured pencils. Alice faithfully wrote down all the different computations and possibilities, occasionally observing that we were giving two people the same job.

After about an hour, Alice agreed that everyone had been placed, and I said I would pull together the lists and all the different ideas and have the draft ready on Monday. The Prime Minister came to the door of Chequers to wave us off and stood there as we went round the circular flowerbed in front of the house in our car, waving but looking, we both felt, small and isolated.

On Sunday, Alice set out on her word processor a precise scheme of how and where every existing minister either stayed where he was, left the government altogether or moved across to slot into a different department. This put everything in order in a number of different columns, but it took us much of the day. We corrected the mistakes where we had moved one parliamentary under-secretary into two departments at once or moved him or her out of a department but provided no other job.

I took our draft up to No. 10 the following day and gave Andrew Turnbull three copies of it. He was pleasantly surprised and, in the various revised drafts that followed over the next week before the reshuffle was completed, all followed the exact format that Alice had created.

As a result of Nick's departure, Peter Lilley moved over from the Treasury to become Secretary of State at the DTI, Francis Maude moved from Minister of State at the FCO to take Peter's job at the Treasury and this left the slot of Minister of State dealing especially with the European Community vacant at the Foreign Office. I was delighted about this as it enabled me to persuade the Prime Minister to move Tristan Garel-Jones over from being my deputy at the whips' office to a job at the Foreign Office for which he was eminently suited.

The following Monday, as he cleared his desk at No. 12 he told me that he intended to ring Joe Bassano, the parliamentary leader in Gibraltar. Bassano was an old friend of Tristan's, but he had, for years, been a thorn in the side of the British government. He was willing to provoke Britain into war with Spain in order to get matters changed in a manner that would ease the life of Gibraltar residents.

'I shall tell Bassano,' said Tristan, 'that we really must sort out the problems together, for example, this stupid problem about Gibraltar airport. But, in order to show that things are now different, I shall for the first time ever speak to him in English rather than in Spanish.'

I was a wet blanket. 'I think,' I said cautiously, 'that you'd better speak to your civil servants at the Foreign Office, Tristan, *before* you ring Bassano. Just to be on the safe side'. His ebullience was lovely to see.

Fortuitously, the move of Tristan to the FCO proved significant in the Prime Minister's fatal election campaign three months later. No longer my deputy, he could not act as the unofficial contact between the whips' office and the Prime Minister and her team as he had done nine months before when Anthony Meyer threw his hat into the ring. Now he followed his natural loyalties and acted as the firelighter of the opposition, as Alan Clark described him. Alastair Goodlad, a stalwart and much less conspiratorial character, moved up in the Office to become my deputy.

Another person I was anxious to place out of the whips' office into a department was Kenneth Carlisle. I had always liked Kenneth and I came greatly to admire and appreciate the quiet way in which he dealt with the problems of pairing. As the pairing whip it was always up to him, on nights when we did not have a three-line whip, to see how many people he could allow away in addition to those who had bisques. The term 'bisque' comes from croquet and gives you a free or an extra turn. It was typical of the Tory Party that we chose such an arcane word to indicate the night out, when backbenchers could leave the House on a two-line whip without being paired. Given the size of our notional majority, every backbencher got a bisque about once every three weeks.

Kenneth's was a horribly difficult job. Ministers, particularly, were always asking to be 'slipped' in order that they could go and make speeches or attend what they regarded as important dinner parties. Others came and said that it was their wedding anniversary or that they had tickets for the opera at Covent Garden and 'couldn't you possibly let me away for tonight?' Kenneth played his hand with an easy, insouciant air. He did not try, quite rightly, to have a large majority every night but was content if our majority was on most occasions around thirty or forty on a two-line whip. Only once did he get it wrong when he allowed too many people away and we lost the vote on the question of allowances for those in residential nursing homes, for which he wrote to me the following day apologising.

Kenneth was a quiet, thoughtful man. He did not have the brashness of Michael Fallon or of Tom Sackville, two other whips. He was already forty-nine and I reckoned that if I did not get him out of the whips' office now into a departmental ministry he might never have another chance.

Even on the Monday, 23 July, as No. 10 began making phone calls to all the ministers who were either going or coming or moving sideways, it looked as if the whole reshuffle might fall apart. The intention had been to move Michael Forsyth into the Department of Energy and Douglas Hogg to take Peter Lilley's job at the Treasury. However, John Wakeham, as Secretary of State for Energy, baulked at taking Forsyth. Douglas Hogg said he could not move over from the DTI to the Treasury because if he did so, Sarah, his wife, would have to give up a well-paid job as a financial editor of a national newspaper, and so on. By 10.30 a.m. I had already had to dash twice from No. 12 to the little drawing room on the first floor at No. 10 in order to put my finger in the hole in the dyke and stop everything going adrift.

At one moment the Prime Minister said tearfully, 'I really cannot go ahead with this reshuffle.' Andrew Turnbull and I calmed her, took her back to the beginning and moved the jigsaw pieces around. By the end of the day it was all done. The reshuffle was well received in the newspapers, and I felt a great sense of relief. The promotion of Tristan Garel-Jones tickled the fancy of some serious political writers like Bruce Anderson. Stories appeared of his methods in the whips' office: how, for example, one MP who had just voted against the government had met Tristan on the terrace of the House and 'I looked at his face and where his eyes should have been there were just two pits of hatred.'

On Wednesday we chose two new whips, and George Young came in to occupy the No. 3 slot in the office. Getting George to rejoin us in the whips' office where he had last been in 1979 was regarded as a stroke of genius in that he had been one of our leading opponents over the Community Charge. We were thus considered to have neutered the anti-Community Charge brigade by getting one of their brightest sparks to join the payroll vote. The idea came from Tristan; it was his farewell present to the whips' office. George was a popular choice and an effective whip.

The last days before the summer recess were enlivened by an exchange of correspondence between Nicholas Winterton, the MP for Macclesfield, and myself.

For a long time Winterton had been one of our most tiresome Members. I had sent him a letter at Easter pointing out how poor his voting record was and how many times he was away from the House when there were divisions, without giving us any notice. A similar letter had gone to ten other MPs. Winterton's reply had been less than contrite. He merely said that he thought I would have better and more important things to do than write him such letters.

The whips were longing to take some action against him, particularly Tom Sackville who was his area whip. I was finally stung into action by hearing him on two occasions in July being unnecessarily rude from the front bench below the gangway to Geoffrey Howe, both times to the utter delight of Labour MPs sitting opposite. He boomed insults as if they were pearls of wisdom. On 18 July I wrote him a letter that had been drafted and redrafted by Tom Sackville, Tristan Garel-Jones and myself. I did not rebuke him for voting against us. Nor did I threaten to remove the whip from him. But I reprimanded him for being away so often without letting us know, and also I objected to his rudeness to colleagues.

I did not send my letter to the press but I told Winterton I was sending copies to his constituency and area chairmen and to Peter Lane, the chairman of the National Executive. I got a six-page handwritten diatribe back from him which appeared on the television news before I even received it and included comments like 'I am not prepared to receive ill-considered lectures from you or any member of the whips' office' and 'as for your reference to my commitment and loyalty this criticism is beyond contempt.' The press loved it, and of course Winterton was written up as the champion of individual democratic rights and the true representative of the people of Macclesfield fighting against the party bureaucrat, myself. After a day, when the media were clearly going against me, I released my original letter to the Press Association and this prompted the headline in the *Daily Mail* of 25 July 'You are rude and show contempt, Renton tells maverick Tory.' All great fun, and just the way to end the summer term, but Winterton won on points and I knew I would have to take further action against him in the months ahead.

All that should indeed have been the end of term. But, after breakfast on Monday 30 July, the local paper, the *Evening Argus*, rang me and told me of

Ian Gow's murder by a car bomb at his house in Hankham twelve miles away from our house in Sussex. This tragedy had happened an hour before. Although we often disagreed on politics, Ian had been a good friend. We had entered the House on the same day, we were neighbours in Sussex, we had mutual friends in the two twin bishops, Peter and Michael Ball. I had great respect for his wife, Jane, and I admired the way in which he had resigned from the government rather than vote for the Anglo-Irish Agreement. This was particularly honourable since I knew very well how much he loved being in the government and how close he was to Margaret Thatcher. For him, resigning was like tearing off an arm, and it was the act of a brave and dedicated person.

I had asked him to propose the Address in November 1989 at the beginning of the last session of Parliament, and he had done this with typical wit and style.

As soon as I heard of Ian's murder, I rang No. 10 to say that Alice and I would drive over to be with Jane immediately. No. 10 got us clearance from the Sussex police. It was a horrible day, full of anguish. The Prime Minister herself arrived at Hankham sometime after 3.00 p.m. She came out of the car and up the steps into the garden looking a little lost, pale, not quite certain where to go. I felt enormously for her. Ian had been a very close friend. Without doubt he had been the parliamentary private secretary on whom she had most relied. As she said during the course of the day, 'If I was feeling low, Ian would often say to me, "Come back and have some supper just with me and Jane." And I often did.' I knew from past discussions just how fond she was of him, as someone she could confide in and relax with.

I took Margaret into the house, showed her the room where Jane was and then went out and spent some time discussing arrangements with Roger Birch, the chief constable, and with Father Jonathan, the local priest at their church. He was a lovely large man, in his late twenties or early thirties, wearing sandals, a sort of Sussex Don Camillo who hugged every woman in the room when he entered. Father Jonathan had intended to have an informal communion service at 7.00 p.m. I suggested that that was moved forward to 6.00 p.m, and then perhaps the Prime Minister could attend it as well. Father Jonathan agreed, and Margaret stayed on talking to Jane, talking to Alice, sitting on the staircase, drinking cups of tea. At one stage we drove down the lane and, standing opposite the Doghouse, as Ian had insisted on his house being named, we saw the remains of the car where it had been blown up. The chief constable asked whether we wanted to walk over and look at it more closely. Margaret refused and so did I. It was too personal, too violent.

At six o'clock the impromptu Mass took place in Father Jonathan's church. Jane was in the front row with her two sons. On the other side of the church was the Prime Minister, Peter Morrison, now her PPS, and Andrew Turnbull. Margaret looked withdrawn, not her usual dominating self, and quietly miserable. I have never known such a supportive congregation. It was not just that they came up to kiss Jane but their spirit was obviously and collectively wishing to sustain her. Led by Father Jonathan, they had all come to love and cherish her and her sons.

At the end of the service to which we had been brought by brutality and murder, the doors in the west of the church opened and there beyond the serried ranks of photographers and reporters were the rolling folds of the Sussex Downs, bathed in sun and looking typically peaceful. They were such a contrast to the violence that had taken place twelve hours before at the Doghouse. It was hard to consider them part of the same life.

Two days later Margaret flew to Aspen, Colorado, for an international conference and meetings with President Bush. That night Iraq invaded Kuwait and a day later the Prime Minister had the first of many discussions about the invasion with the President. She had already thought out what she intended to say – that Iraq must be resisted and Kuwait protected at all costs. When she met the President, she told him, in the words of her own autobiography, 'my conclusions in the clearest and most straightforward terms'. During August I periodically suggested to the Prime Minister over the telephone that Parliament should be recalled to discuss the Kuwaiti situation. She was not very keen on this and appeared not to want the Commons to become too closely involved, but Parliament finally met for an emergency session on 6 and 7 September. Members of Parliament listened to wise speeches from Douglas Hurd and Tom King on the progress in the Gulf while I spent some of my time in the argument about Michael Forsyth's future that I have described above.

FIVE

Autumn 1990

The days around the reshuffle of 1990 and of Ian Gow's brutal death marked the apex of my relationship with the Prime Minister. As the summer holidays passed, it went downhill with a speed that surprised me. This was partly due to the influence of Peter Morrison, her new parliamentary private secretary. After two years as her PPS, Mark Lennox-Boyd had been promoted and had become the junior minister at the Foreign and Commonwealth Office in the July reshuffle. Peter Morrison had always been a very strong admirer of Margaret's. He and I came into the House at the same time and he was a member of the Dining Club that we, the new Tory MPs of 1974, formed on our arrival in the Commons. With conscious obscurity, we named it the Alf Bates Club after a little known Labour MP. Thus we were not cast as a bunch either of prejudiced lefties or of hard right-wingers, a wise foresight. Peter was the only member of the club who was convinced in early 1975 that Margaret should and would win the battle for the party leadership.

The appointment of a new parliamentary private secretary for the Prime Minister coincided with Nick Ridley's unhappy resignation. The job of a PPS, who is an unpaid member of the government, is essentially to keep the minister to whom he is attached advised of how Parliament is moving, in terms not just of legislation but of goodwill and ill will. Conversely, the PPS keeps parliamentary colleagues informed of his minister's plans, reactions and hopes. He is a communicator, not an executive. Some ministers get very close to their PPS, others ignore them.

Margaret very much wanted a friend as her new PPS, someone she could feel easy with. Mark Lennox-Boyd had been a bit grand. When she said that

Peter Morrison was her choice for the job I was surprised. I wondered whether he was wise or firm enough and I was worried about his drinking habits. But, perhaps wrongly in retrospect, I did not try to insist on her changing her choice. I had argued for Nick Ridley's departure a few days before. Given her obvious feeling of loneliness, almost isolation, I did not think I could argue against Peter as well. He, in turn, although he had already been a Minister of State – second in the ministerial hierarchy – regarded being appointed her PPS not as a downgrading but as the pinnacle of his own career, a job of immense importance. The potential conflict that can always exist between the Government Chief Whip and the Prime Minister's PPS was present under the surface during all of his short reign. As he increasingly had Margaret's ear, I lost it. And he had it from the day that he was appointed.

Alice and I stayed with her brother, Adam Fergusson, and his wife, Poppet, in her family's house outside Aix-en-Provence. As Adam pushed a pastis in a floating glass over the pool to me, he made full use of his expertise as a past member of the European Parliament and now an adviser to Geoffrey Howe at the Foreign Office. He lectured me on the necessity of our accepting that a European single currency was inevitable and of our joining that bandwagon. We could not afford to be left out. If we were part of the bandwagon now, we would be able to influence the speed and the direction it took.

Later in September, I visited six European capitals to discuss the forthcoming intergovernmental conference on political union with party leaders and members of political committees. From all of them I got much the same message. They wanted to bind the newly united and larger Germany more firmly into the Community. Germany was willing to take this step then but might not be in ten years' time when she would be even more clearly the largest European economic force. Therefore, now was the moment at which to move towards greater union, however that be defined. I wrote in my diary, 'I gradually came to accept the argument myself but remained hopeful that, by throwing a good deal of dust into the air, the Tory Party might be able to avoid an internal collision before the next election. After all, there was no question of a new European Act being presented to Parliament for ratification before 1992.' My optimism was quickly to be shattered. Though I was silent in the Commons as by tradition the Chief Whip only speaks to announce by-elections and the result of votes, my support for the European cause inevitably damaged my relationship with No. 10.

The Conservative Party Conference in early October was a strange one. All the usual speeches were made, praising the work of the Prime Minister and of the government and furiously attacking the opposition, but there was an air of unreality about the proceedings. The conference seemed to be shadow-boxing, and we were waiting for bigger battles against a different backcloth. The only serious conversation I had with Margaret was about a Tory Member of Parliament who had been stopped on his way home from the conference and found to be over the alcohol limit. I debated with her whether he should be asked to give up his ministerial job. She was not very interested and he wisely pre-empted us by taking the initiative and immediately sending in a resignation letter.

Ten days before the Commons reassembled, John Major, the Chancellor of the Exchequer, rang me on Friday afternoon at my constituency office to tell me that sterling was going into the European Union's Exchange Rate Mechanism. I was pleased and congratulated him on finally winning the Prime Minister's approval for this step. The exchange rate, at 2.95 deutschmark to the pound, was high but John thought it was manageable. In this he was supported by the Governor of the Bank of England and the top Treasury official. *The Economist* summed up the generally favourable view in the press with the words: 'ERM offers Britain its best opportunity of lasting improvement in economic performance.' But the decision opened up the seismic rift in the parliamentary Tory Party.

Within a day of the Commons reassembling on 15 October, Tony Favell resigned as John Major's parliamentary private secretary. He said to me that the only reason for his decision was that he had been Major's PPS for four years, he had a marginal seat and he now wanted to spend more time in his constituency. But he told the BBC the following morning that his resignation was due to the fact that he did not agree with our drift into a more integrated Community. He was unhappy about our joining the ERM.

That evening I saw the Prime Minister in her room at the House of Commons at around 11.00 p.m. Her first comment to me was frankly unpleasant. 'Your master's speech on Europe last week was very unhelpful,' she said.

I was shaken. 'Geoffrey is not my master' I replied. 'You are, if I may say so, my mistress.'

'All right,' the Prime Minister retorted, 'your ex-master. The two worst things at Conference last week were Geoffrey Howe's speech about getting on to the European train and Ted's announcement that he was going to Iraq.'

She then launched into a passionately angry description of what had happened at the Madrid Summit fifteen months before. Geoffrey Howe and Nigel Lawson, in her words, had conspired to force her to accept possible entry into the Exchange Rate Mechanism. But she and Alan Walters had already worked out what she wanted to achieve – the 'Madrid Conditions for joining ERM but no firm date stated on which we would join'. She had heard David Hannay, our man in Brussels, saying at one stage in the corridor at the Madrid Summit to David Williamson, Delors' Chef de Cabinet, 'Has she agreed to a firm date? She must agree to a firm date.' A year later, David Hannay ended up as our man at the United Nations rather than as our ambassador in Washington, the top post that he might reasonably have expected.

Nigel Lawson and Geoffrey Howe, the Prime Minister continued, both said that if we agreed to enter ERM there would be no pressing on to a single currency, 'but that is the direction that Geoffrey is now taking,' she added. 'I am not prepared to give up all our hundreds of years of history. If necessary, I will ask every constituency association in the land to ask their MP or candidate whether he or she is in favour of a single currency.'

I heard this outpouring with a great deal of foreboding and thought that the Prime Minister, sadly, was looking backwards towards defending our sovereignty rather than forward as to how we could establish a European identity with which British pride and patriotism were compatible. I was also very annoyed by the reference to Geoffrey Howe as my 'master'. This must have shown because Peter Morrison came along to my room later that evening to apologise for the remark.

Sadly, moving Geoffrey Howe from the Foreign Office the previous July and making him leader of the House of Commons had not lessened the strain between Margaret and Geoffrey. Geoffrey was unhappy at leaving a post which he had greatly enjoyed and where he felt his skills were being fully used. Whatever the prestige attached to being Leader of the House of Commons and Deputy Prime Minister, I never thought that Geoffrey, after the Treasury and the Foreign Office, could settle down in this new position. Equally, Margaret did not forgive Geoffrey his pro-European stance nor the fact that he went on making speeches pressing for a more committed attitude to Europe. I was pig-in-the-middle between the two of them.

The Rome Summit took place ten days later. Andreotti, the Italian Prime Minister, refused to discuss the failure of EC agricultural ministers to agree on a general cut in EC farm subsidies although this was a precondition for the success of the GATT round. The EC terms were already a fortnight behind the final deadline. Instead, he pressed on with getting all his European colleagues, bar our Prime Minister, to agree to 1 January 1994 as a firm date for starting Stage 2 of Economic and Monetary Union (EMU). The Prime Minister fumed publicly in her press conferences and said that her European colleagues were 'living in cloud cuckoo land'.

Two days later she made a statement to the House on the Rome Summit. The prepared and written statement which she read out to the Commons was soberly correct and agreed that a single currency might eventually come into force as a follow-on to the common currency, but only if Parliament and the people so wished. This balanced language, though, was thrown away in the forty-five-minute exchange of Questions and Answers that followed. There, egged on by the encouragement of anti-Europeans on both Conservative and Labour benches, Margaret said that she did not believe that the proposals for a hard ECU were likely to work and that she did not think the hard ECU would ever be a very popular currency. In her view, she said, too many powers and rights had already been given away by the House of Commons to the Commission. She hoped no more of these would be conceded and that everyone would come to the House of Commons with that aim in mind.

As a bravura performance, the parliamentary session was a great success. But my heart sank as I listened to it, knowing that her essential opposition to any further moves towards European union – no matter whether this was called federation or integration or whatever – was coming out, and this was bound to ferment dissent among our MPs, and particularly between herself and Geoffrey.

Two days later the House rose for the short break before the new session. We just avoided a ping-pong battle with the House of Lords on the Dangerous Dogs Bill, and the associated Dog Registration Scheme which the Lords quite rightly wished to amend. The Commons had no time left before the end of the session in which to accommodate discussion of the Lords' amendments, and we typically avoided a contest by a last-minute compromise. Alice and I drove back to our Sussex home for the weekend. As I walked through our front door, just before 5.30 p.m., Geoffrey Howe rang me to tell me that he was going in to see the Prime Minister at No. 10 to tell her that he was resigning. I was more surprised than I should have been. I tried, a little half-heartedly and with some sense of hopelessness, to dissuade him but I recognised that at last, like Boxer in *Animal Farm*, Geoffrey had decided to make his stand. That morning the Prime Minister had rebuked him sharply in front of a full Cabinet when she learned that several parliamentary Bills, including a complicated parliamentary Pensions Bill, were not yet ready for the coming session. This was due to a combination of ministerial changes of heart on detail and a shortage of expert parliamentary draftsmen. Geoffrey, as Leader of the House, bore the responsibility but it was scarcely his fault. Margaret behaved in a manner that might possibly have suited her dealings with a wayward and very junior minister but not with her Deputy Prime Minister who was also an old ally. But I noticed that, on this occasion, Geoffrey had hardly bothered to defend himself.

From that moment to late in the night my telephone never stopped ringing. Geoffrey called me again around 6.15 p.m. to tell me that he had handed in his four pages of resignation letter – 'more like a manifesto,' said Andrew Turnbull when he rang me a few minutes later, asking me to talk to Cranley Onslow, Hurd, Major and Baker, giving them the 'line to take': the differences on the Community have been exaggerated; treat Geoffrey's resignation more in sorrow than in anger; for goodness sake do not kick him in the teeth, and so on.

The Prime Minister told me over the telephone that she wished to bring Tebbit back into the Cabinet. I was horrified and urged her not to, saying it would alienate the pro-Europeans and divide the party yet further. 'You are always on the wrong side,' the Prime Minister said. 'Look at the people you have been suggesting to me recently.'

'You mean in the July reshuffle?' said I. 'That's not fair. Several right-wingers got promotion then – Michael Fallon, Peter Lilley; and Neil Hamilton came into the whips' office.'

'No, the July reshuffle was all right, but the recent Honours List, your suggestions then were quite different.'

I protested, knowing that in some measure the Prime Minister was only saying this to taunt me and to test my reactions. Eventually, we agreed to meet on Friday morning at 10 a.m. and she finished with her usual cheery farewell – 'Cheer up, God bless.'

Alastair Goodlad, the Deputy Chief Whip, rang me at around 10.30 p.m. with news of what he described as a terrible drinks party at No. 10 – himself, Andrew Turnbull, Charles Powell, Denis Thatcher and the Prime Minister's political adviser, John Whittingdale. They were very gung-ho about bringing Norman Tebbit back as Secretary of State for Education. Goodlad pointed out that Tebbit had been extremely difficult to us about the Hong Kong Bill a few months before. 'He was quite right,' said Denis Thatcher. 'He was against immigration.'

My brother-in-law, Adam Fergusson, rang to say that Geoffrey, talking to him a few minutes earlier, had said, 'Tim has had less long than I have had to try and reconcile the irreconcilable.'

On Friday 2 November, I got to No. 12 at around 9.10 a.m. and waved at the photographers already gathered in the street. At around 9.30 a.m. a message came through from Andrew Turnbull that Margaret had cancelled a meeting and would like to see me straight away. I found her in the downstairs private secretaries' room where Turnbull and Powell normally worked. They were there, as well as Bernard Ingham. All three stayed throughout our conversation but did not say a word. The Prime Minister fired off about the advantages of bringing Norman into the Cabinet as Secretary for Education. I countered by arguing that, although this would show that she was firmly in charge and would please a part of our party, it would alienate others and would make the task of keeping the parliamentary party together that much harder.

'What do you mean – that it would show I am in charge?' said the Prime Minister. 'Who says that I am not in charge?'

I had chosen my words unwisely. I argued round that one and then got back to the point. Neither of us would give in. She said that she needed a friend in Cabinet and that I was always suggesting people who were opposed to her philosophy. She kept on pointing out that it was only by her strength and determination that she had got policies changed and driven through over the last ten years. John MacGregor, at Education, was failing to ram home the educational changes that were needed. There must be someone strong at the helm. Therefore MacGregor should take Geoffrey's place as Leader of the House and Tebbit could come in at Education. My point remained unchanged: I thought this would be seen by the pro-Europeans as a declaration of war and it would split the parliamentary party yet further. At one stage I said that it would make a leadership election more likely. I immediately got the answer I expected. 'I do not care about elections,' said the Prime Minister – exactly as she had a year ago – 'if they do not want me they can get rid of me.'

We had been at this dualogue for nearly an hour and I thought I was making a little progress. She, at least, seemed to be beginning to hesitate in her determination when the telephone rang on Powell's desk. It was Norman Tebbit answering an earlier message to let No. 10 know of his whereabouts. Powell asked Tebbit where he would be over the next hour or two in case he was wanted. I could see the Prime Minister edging nearer the phone and I thought to myself, a banal but true thought, that this was one of those historic moments which might change the course of political events. She took the phone away from Powell. I could only hear her side of the conversation.

'Norman, what do you think of the present difficulties?' Pause. 'Do you think there will be open war on the European situation?' (Norman's answer is clearly 'Yes'.) Pause. 'Do you think you could be more help to us outside or inside the government?'

My heart sank. I felt like grabbing the phone at that moment and trying to stop the conversation going any further.

'Yes, yes, I see. Well, I am wondering what you would think of helping us by doing the Education job. I really must move John MacGregor.' Long pause while Norman considered. 'You could help inside or outside the government?' Pause. 'All right, think about it. You ring back within the hour.'

On such discussions hangs the fate of governments, I thought. But I was wrong. Norman Tebbit rang again and said that he was only twenty minutes away in a car and would come to No. 10. We broke up and I went back to No. 12. There, Alastair Goodlad told me that John Major had rung to say that he too thought it would be disastrous if Norman rejoined the Cabinet but he did not want me to quote his name in saying that to the Prime Minister. Tebbit came in to see the Prime Minister and I learned that, because of the constant attention needed to look after Margaret, his wife who had been crippled in the Brighton bombing, he wisely stood firm on the point that he could not take on a Cabinet job.

At about 11.30 a.m. I went back to No. 10, this time to the upstairs study and we went round the course again.

'Norman will not take the job,' said the Prime Minister 'so who do you suggest?'

I argued for William Waldegrave or John Patten for the Health portfolio, MacGregor to be Leader of the House and Ken Clarke moving from Health to Education.

'All you do is offer me two left-wingers,' said the Prime Minister petulantly.

I disagreed and pointed out that they were the senior ministers of state and that all her favourite right-wing young Turks, such as Francis Maude, Michael Portillo and Peter Lilley, had recently been moved to other jobs which they should not give up so soon.

My preference was for William Waldegrave because, after a bad start, he had done well in acting as second string to Douglas Hurd on the Kuwait crisis, while John Patten at the Home Office had the long Criminal Justice Bill ahead of him on which he had worked for three and a half years.

'Waldegrave is too unbalanced,' she said. We argued on. 'He has done very well on the committee dealing with the Gulf,' she conceded. 'Indeed I think he is better on that committee than Douglas Hurd is.'

Eventually she gave in. 'All right, let it be William. But the rest must be right-wingers.'

What simplistic labels, I thought. I tried to get Peter Lloyd promoted from under-secretary at the Home Office dealing with immigration to Minister of State but that failed to find favour. Eventually we agreed that Douglas Hogg should move from the DTI to do William's job at the Foreign Office and John Redwood should be promoted from under-secretary to

Minister of State at the DTI, with Edward Leigh, who had done a great deal of work for the whips on the back benches, coming in as under-secretary in the same department.

'The DTI will be a really right-wing department,' said Margaret with evident satisfaction. 'Tim Sainsbury is the only left-winger there, a left-winger who has far more money than all the right-wingers put together.'

I knew Tim and his brothers well. 'He is not a left-winger,' I said. 'His family did not make all that money by being left-wingers.'

The conversation started to become quite light-hearted. The Prime Minister was far happier now that a plan was decided on. She had a gift for using her femininity and flattery to persuade males to do work they did not necessarily want to take on, and I admired her for the ruthless way in which she exploited this talent. John MacGregor did not want to leave Education with a job half-done, and Kenneth Clarke was very hesitant about taking another detailed and difficult brief when the reforms in the National Health Service were just ahead of him. She buttered them both up over the telephone, telling John MacGregor that he was being promoted and would do the job of Leader of the House 'brilliantly' because of his past experience as a whip and his knowledge of a number of government departments. To Kenneth Clarke she gave the assurance that his legal mind and training would enable him to master a brief very quickly, and that he was just the tough man needed to push through major changes in public education. She put behind her any hint of regret at Tebbit having refused the job an hour earlier.

Clarke asked for five minutes to think it over but in fact he took fifteen minutes. The tension mounted in the study and I tried to divert her by talking about other things. We got on to the reasons for Geoffrey's resignation and I found myself saying as bluntly as I could that she had roughed Geoffrey up without any justification about both the parliamentary Pensions Bill and the delay in legislation coming before the new session. He had been made the scapegoat, caught between the Chancellor of the Exchequer and the trustees of the Parliamentary Pension Fund in one case and the overworked parliamentary draftsmen in another. I urged her not to be as rough on John MacGregor. I added for good measure that, as she knew, her differences with Geoffrey over Europe were fundamental and of long standing and by no manner of means just about tone and comment, which was the story that was going out from No. 10. She listened patiently and apparently carefully but immediately changed the subject. I did not know whether in fact this meant she had listened but did not like what she heard, or that she had simply been pretending to listen.

Eventually Kenneth Clarke rang and accepted with continuing reluctance. William Waldegrave, who had been waiting in the nearby room with the dark green wallpaper, was called in and the Prime Minister told him to his evident and understandable pleasure that, at last, he was coming into the Cabinet as Health Secretary. He looked shaken and delighted in equal measure.

Once the initial exchange was over William added that, without being sycophantic, he wanted to say how much he had enjoyed being on the committee dealing with the Gulf crisis and how impressed he had been by the Prime Minister's leadership on that committee. 'I can say this now that you have offered me the Cabinet job, Prime Minister,' added William, 'it is you who have been the hub on which all the Western involvement in the Gulf has turned. You have pulled the whole thing together and, without you, it would not have worked.' The Prime Minister brushed his tribute aside with a smile.

After he left, Margaret, who earlier had been saying that there was really no excitement in this reshuffle, was more reconciled to the thought that it might all work out for the best. I argued that William's emollient and intelligent approach could be just what was needed to put over the NHS reforms that were planned for the following year.

I left the Prime Minister at around 2.20 p.m. This reshuffle had taken nearly five hours to put together. In the end the Prime Minister did not appear to hold against me my determined opposition to Tebbit but I reflected on the way we had ended up dividing people into simple categories of right-wing and left-wing, and I was aware again of her sense of isolation. 'I need a friend in the Cabinet' was the phrase that haunted me, both from the night before and from the opening round that morning.

The weekend press stirred the pot. Michael Heseltine issued a public letter to the chairman of his constituency saying that Britain must make its position on the European Union much clearer and then left for four days in Amman. Douglas Hurd effectively defended the government's position in a long interview with Brian Walden but even he, when Brian Walden asked him how the differences would be dealt with in the debate on the Queen's Speech that lay ahead, could only answer, 'I think it will be all right.'

The press were full of speculation that, if Geoffrey Howe threw his hat into the election ring, then Michael Heseltine certainly would too. In the background I felt a great sadness at Geoffrey's going. It was he who, with great generosity, had brought me back into front-line politics in 1983 as his parliamentary private secretary at the Treasury, although I had resigned over the retrospective tax in his 1981 Budget. I had been with him for four years at the Foreign Office and had worked with him very closely throughout the last year, as a Chief Whip must with the Leader of the House. Though I had become impatient at times, I respected his wisdom and good temper. I had always found him the most loyal of friends, one who would never let you down, or score a point off you, and who would never go behind your back to take a trick at your expense. There could not be a kinder and more friendly man. He had, rightly, satisfied his own honour by resigning but he had made the immediate future of the Prime Minister and the government totally uncertain.

The new session opened on Wednesday 7 November. In the course of the usual pre-session party at No. 10 the night before, Margaret, talking in front of me about the reshuffle of the previous Friday, said, 'I think I got the best of both worlds. I offered Norman Tebbit a job and he refused it.' I could not look at her, so I looked instead for the white-coated waiter with gin and tonics on his silver tray.

When I got home on Friday 9 November, the telephone was once again ringing. This time it was Alastair Goodlad telling me that the *Sunday Times* had just delivered a tape to the Northern Ireland Office of a conversation that had been illegally intercepted in Northern Ireland from the mobile car telephone of Richard Needham, the parliamentary under-secretary. The conversation was apparently with his wife, Sissy, and it included the comment from Richard that 'I wish that cow would resign.'

The female voice replied, 'Yeah, I know, she seems to be hanging on,' and then Richard said, 'I had a long [unintelligible] you would think, wouldn't you, I said to Seamus Mallon today you would think, frankly, wouldn't you, after so long she would be quite happy to go.'

There were political implications in this incident in that the Seamus Mallon to whom Richard had been speaking was an SDLP MP in Ulster, that is, a member of the opposition. One could imagine that the Unionist MPs, the allies of the Tory Party, would be furious at Richard discussing in this manner the future of the British Prime Minister with an opposition Ulster Member.

Later that evening I came back from my constituency advice surgery to find Andrew Turnbull on the telephone from No. 10. The authenticity of the voices on the tape had been checked and there was no reason to doubt that they were indeed Richard Needham and his wife. Andrew and I agreed that he would take the tape up to the Prime Minister who was in her flat at No. 10, and I would ring her five minutes later. Before the five minutes passed, my telephone rang and there was the Prime Minister on the line.

'Poor you, I am so sorry for you,' I said.

'You must not take it too seriously, Tim,' replied the Prime Minister. 'I have been called much worse things before. After all, this is only a three-letter word.'

'It's very good of you, Prime Minister,' I said, 'to take it like that. I'll ring Richard Needham immediately and tell him to call you and apologise to you.'

'Oh, I don't think that you need do that,' said the Prime Minister.

'Yes,' I said, 'I think he should apologise to you as a member of your team. Also, if he does apologise and this breaks in the press in a day or two, No. 10 can just say that he has made his apology and as far as you are concerned that is the end of the matter.'

'All right. If he wants to ring and apologise, he can, but you must make clear to him that he does not have to. Don't take it all too seriously.'

We said goodnight. I rang Richard who, after some hesitation about the authenticity of the tape as he doubted that he had ever referred to the Prime Minister as a cow, agreed to ring her and say he was sorry. This little incident showed a very good side of Margaret. Her resilience and her ability to laugh off this sort of silly rudeness was something I admired enormously.

But the clouds continued to gather. The day before, we had lost the Bradford by-election with a swing of approximately 21 per cent to Labour. The rats could be heard scuttling off the ship.

The previous week the president of Michael Heseltine's Henley constituency association had sent him a letter of rebuke about his pro-European, anti-Thatcher attitudes and statements. There were dark mutterings, and then some of Michael's constituency officers disowned the president's letter. This was steamy stuff. The press were hoping to get a comment out of me and told me that the Heseltine camp were feeling increasingly gung-ho. I was amused to hear someone on the radio on Sunday morning referring to 'Henleygate'.

Late on Sunday afternoon, Tony Bevins of the *Independent* rang me and I told him that the media were exaggerating the whole matter. They wanted a contest and they were making it seem inevitable that Heseltine would have to enter the fray and have a battle. If he did not, he would be unworthy of his reputation. Tony Bevins denied this, as I thought he would. He said that a very senior backbencher, 'someone well versed in the political arts', had told him that Heseltine already had 120 pledges of support for the first ballot. On that basis, he said, 'I bet my last dollar that Heseltine will come into the fight in the first round.' He would declare himself either on Wednesday or Thursday morning after hearing what Geoffrey had to say in his speech in the House. 'These are very fraught days,' he added. I could only agree with the sentiment.

Everyone was edgy at the Prime Minister's normal Monday meeting at 12.45 p.m. I told the story of the Prime Minister's reaction to Richard Needham's phone call – 'Don't worry too much, Tim, he only used a three-letter word' – in order to emphasise her courage and ability to dismiss trivialities. Those present laughed, and Margaret looked grateful. I felt there was a great tenseness in her.

I mentioned at the morning meeting that we had heard that Geoffrey Howe would be speaking the following afternoon.

'What will he talk about?' queried the Prime Minister.

I said I thought he would talk about the economy as well as the European Community.

'But he agrees that we should not go for a single currency and now we have joined the Exchange Rate Mechanism,' said the Prime Minister, implying that Geoffrey should be quite content.

Andrew Turnbull pointed out wisely that Geoffrey would say that, if we had joined ERM earlier, the economy would be in a better shape now. This was prophetic. I did not want to get into a slanging match about Geoffrey and I was glad that this didn't happen.

I stayed behind for a few minutes when the others left to go to the usual Monday lunch with ministers and found the Prime Minister really uncertain about what to do. She mentioned that she was making the speech at the Lord Mayor's Banquet that evening, but it was not easy to put a great rallying cry into that. 'It is only ten minutes,' she said. And then after a long pause, 'Ah well, we will have to see how it goes.'

Geoffrey Howe made his resignation speech at the beginning of Public Business the next day, before the debate on the Queen's Speech resumed. It was heard in silence and it was, as I said to him a day or two later, horribly good. The House was, of course, packed. I sat in the Chief Whip's usual seat, by the gangway on the front bench. The Prime Minister was one or two places away from me. Alice was seated in the Chief Whip's box underneath the gallery. Arabella, Geoffrey's faithful secretary, was next to her and in tears for some of the time. Alice told me later that for much of the speech the Prime Minister sat with her left leg crossed over her right, looking at them in the Chief Whip's box, not necessarily seeing them but contemplating them.

Geoffrey spoke with what sounded like quiet confidence. He had a very clear delivery and the content of the speech divided between economic argument, fierce criticism of the Prime Minister's stance on Europe and light-hearted comment: 'I have been told that I resigned only over differences of style. If so, I must be the only minister in history who resigned when he was in full agreement with the government on policy.' He kept the House deeply attentive and I have never heard a speech to which I listened more carefully and which made me feel more miserable.

I knew all the bitterness and the hurt feelings and resentment that were in Geoffrey's mind – the snubs from the Prime Minister, the failure to consult him, the comments that he would make to me about the fact that he was not sitting on the daily committee that was considering the Gulf crisis 'and yet I am Deputy Prime Minister' and so on. I had seen and heard this polite, gentle, wise man being humiliated so often by the Prime Minister in the past year, and I knew that this speech was the result of such misjudgement. It was terribly well done.

Afterwards I went to my room by the whips' office between Central Lobby and the Members' lobby and then, despite all my sympathy with what Geoffrey Howe had said, I felt I must go and say some comforting words to the Prime Minister. I went along the passage and found Margaret making remarks like, 'so he would give in to Europe on everything.' Bernard Ingham was sitting with pen poised, ready to put that sort of comment into an unofficial press briefing from No. 10.

I said, 'You must not say anything like that. You must not analyse Geoffrey's comments about Europe. Say that you are very sad to hear such a speech from a friend and colleague with whom you have worked for so many years. Do not say any more than that.'

Peter Morrison picked up my theme and repeated it, and in the end that was the only message that went out from No. 10. My predominant thoughts were still about holding the party together as an election for the leadership became more inevitable every minute.

An hour later as I was sitting talking to Rob Hayward, one of our backbench colleagues, about his recovery from illness, Bob Hughes, who acted as Ted Heath's unofficial parliamentary private secretary, came into my office and said that Ted would like to come and see me. Ted was in the smoking room and was available immediately. So the imaginary red carpet was rolled out, Rob Hayward disappeared and Ted came to pay a call on me for the first time in my year at the whips' office. He entered my room – the hallmark jowls shaking, his expression intense.

'I thought, as an older ex-Chief Whip, I would just come and remind you about the tradition of the impartiality of the whips' office on these occasions,' said Ted.

I thanked him but emphasised that I did not need any reminding. Indeed, the *Independent* that morning had repeated my instructions to the whips that they had to remain strictly and visibly impartial, taking no part in any campaign to support either the Prime Minister or, if he stood, Michael Heseltine.

'It was the same,' I said, 'in 1975, wasn't it, when Margaret Thatcher stood against you, Ted?'

Ted did not much like being reminded of that and said, 'Oh, the tradition though goes back much earlier. In 1940 it was the Chief Whip, David Margesson, who had to go and tell Chamberlain to stand down and not to have Halifax as his successor but Churchill instead. He had to do that even though Chamberlain had a majority of eighty.'

I could see the drift the conversation was taking. I reminded Ted of the story that Geoffrey Rippon, a long-time parliamentary colleague of Ted's, had told me the week before that, when Ted was Chief Whip in 1956 or 1957, he had told Geoffrey Rippon, 'If you go on supporting any more motions in favour of Europe, you will have to resign as a parliamentary private secretary.'

The jowls flapped. 'Did I say that?' said Ted doubtfully. 'If I did, it did not fit in with what I was doing behind the scenes.'

I let that pass and we parted on friendly enough terms A few minutes later I went to the Speaker's rooms for my weekly meeting with Jack Weatherill, the Speaker. Jack had been Deputy Chief Whip in 1975 during the Heath–Thatcher election contest. I told him of what Ted had just said to me and Jack grinned with pleasure.

'He is an old hypocrite,' he said. 'I remember it well. He was furious when Humphrey Atkins, his Chief Whip, told him that the whips had to be impartial. "I appointed you all," he said, with a clear implication that we should all be supporting him. In the end it was decided that the Deputy Chief Whip could be sacrificed. So I was the one who had to go along every day with messages about how we thought people were going to vote.'

The days ahead were like the minutes before the start of the Grand National, when horses parade in the ring with jockeys in their racing colours, sweating slightly. Every movement was commented on by press, radio and television. Tension in the camps was very high, and we did endless counts in the whips' office as to what we thought the result might be.

Would Michael Heseltine have challenged Margaret for the leadership even if Geoffrey Howe had not resigned? I am sure he would. He had been quietly laying the ground for over a year and he must have calculated that the autumn of 1990 represented his best chance. A year later would be too late, too near the date of the next general election. After that election, if Margaret had won, she would presumably have gone on for a year or two and then the torch would have been handed on to a younger successor. If she were to lose the election, and the odds were already very strong in favour of her losing, there was bound to be a race that included some of the forty- or fifty-year-olds in the Cabinet: Ken Clarke, John Major or Peter Lilley. The odds would by then be against Michael, just turning sixty, winning. If Michael was ever to win the leadership of the Tory Party, it had to happen soon.

Conscious of all this, I asked Cecil Parkinson, as a friend of Michael's, on the evening of Tuesday 13 November if he would put in a plea to Michael to avoid breaking up the party and decline to stand, even at that late stage. Cecil saw Michael that evening but told me later that Michael had said that, even twenty-four hours earlier, he might have agreed not to stand. But now, having heard Geoffrey's speech, he was determined to do so. I thanked Cecil for trying but doubted the accuracy of what I had been told. In the whips' office Alastair Goodlad had told us the day before that Michael had said during a shooting lunch on the previous Saturday that he would stand. It was interesting that a remark made in as casual a setting as a shooting lunch should reach the whips but I thought this was just the sort of relaxed, off-your-guard occasion on which truth slips out.

Sure enough, my telephone rang soon after nine the next morning. Michael was on the line and told me that he had decided to accept nomination for the leadership election. His nomination papers, though, were not to go in until the following morning. Clearly he was going to spend the next twenty-four hours trying to find as prominent a proposer and seconder as he could muster.

I thanked Michael for telling me and said that I very much hoped that there would be no personal mud-slinging on either side. The party had to be united after the election was over. 'I quite agree,' said Michael, 'and that is what I have told my associates.' I wondered. The *Sun* newspaper had had a terrible front page the day before, attacking Michael's supporters, accusing Michael Mates of being a philanderer and mentioning Keith Hampson's alleged pawing of the knee of a police constable in a night club. I told Michael that I had sent messages to the *Sun* protesting at this, and I hoped there would be as little muck-raking as possible.

The Prime Minister started Cabinet the next day by saying that she was very grateful to all the colleagues around the table for their public support and she hoped that everything would be over very soon and that we could get back to normal business.

Of course, although we had a normal Cabinet meeting, the only subject in everyone's mind was the election contest ahead. Later in the day I went to the meeting of the backbench 1922 Committee to announce that Cranley Onslow was returned unopposed as chairman of the committee. This was a relief for the Prime Minister's supporters as Cranley was felt to be both reliable and firmly on her side.

After a few minutes, I read out the business for the coming week. The atmosphere was excited and overcharged. During the meeting Cranley made some comment to me which made me realise that he did not understand the precise way in which the required majority of 15 per cent of those entitled to vote worked. He did not accept that the 15 per cent was an unchangeable figure of fifty-six votes but thought rather that it depended on how many people had voted either for Margaret or for Michael Heseltine. I wrote out on a piece of paper the precise figures that were needed – the winner had to get at least 187 votes (being one more than 50 per cent of 372, the number of our MPs) and at least fifty-six more votes (being 15 per cent of 372) than the nearest rival. Cranley reluctantly accepted my fiat. My interpretation favoured the challenger as it meant that the winner had to be ahead by a larger margin, but I had no doubt that I was right.

The next day, Friday 16 November, I spent an hour and a half with Robin Butler, the Secretary to the Cabinet, and Andrew Turnbull, going over the constitutional position. They were going to see Robert Fellowes, the Private Secretary to the Queen, that afternoon, and we discussed the various options. We agreed that, if the Prime Minister were beaten in the ballot next Tuesday, she would go to the Palace and offer her resignation to the Queen the following morning but she would preferably agree to stay on as Prime Minister until a new leader of the Conservative Party was chosen. This would follow the pattern of 1975 when Harold Wilson announced his intended resignation but said that he would stay on until his successor had been chosen, a process that took about three weeks.

If the Prime Minister wished to give up the job immediately, or at least not to appear in the House of Commons again – I thought this was very unlikely but the civil servants wanted to cover it – then John MacGregor should act as chairman of the necessary committees but not take over any formal prime ministerial powers. He would do this both because he was Leader of the House, a senior position, and also because he was not a contender in the leadership election. I would ring round the various members of the Cabinet after the ballot on Tuesday night or early Wednesday morning to make sure that they would be happy with John MacGregor taking on these temporary duties. At some stage in our long discussion Robin Butler and Andrew Turnbull tried to query what 'a majority of those entitled to vote' meant in our leadership rules, arguing that it did not embrace those who were sick or just absented themselves. I denied this, told them that they were being semantic and said that, in any event, I had given my interpretation to Cranley Onslow. I was determined that it should not be disputed and they accepted this.

An hour later, I saw Merlyn Rees in a passage in the House of Commons. He told me that he had been Callaghan's campaign manager in 1975. After the election was over, he had compared notes with Denis Healey's campaign manager and they had found that between 20 and 25 per cent of all Labour MPs had firmly promised their support to both campaigns. 'But I was high up in the government,' added Merlyn, 'and I made certain that none of them got jobs. If their word could not be trusted they did not deserve a job.'

Over the weekend difficulties started to emerge about the fact that the Prime Minister would be in Paris for the Conference on Security and Cooperation in Europe just when the leadership election would take place. It transpired that Peter Morrison, her parliamentary private secretary, had agreed with Kenneth Baker, John Wakeham and Norman Tebbit that the Prime Minister should hold a press conference in Paris immediately after the election result was known on Tuesday evening. They would telex her the following day, Monday 19 November, as to what they felt her reaction should be to the various options. I queried the wisdom of having a press conference straight away on the grounds that the Prime Minister might say something immediately after the result that she would regret an hour or two later after taking further advice. I thought the plan was an example of bad judgement on Peter Morrison's part or simply an excess of loyalty.

'But this is what we agreed yesterday,' said Peter, 'and we are going to have this meeting to discuss the options tomorrow.'

'In that case,' I said, 'I as Chief Whip must be at that meeting.'

'Of course,' said Peter, 'I will see that you are.'

I rang him back a few minutes later to say that I thought Cranley Onslow should be there as well. He had a constitutional position. Under the election rules he was having consultations with Conservative peers and with MEPs.

My suspicions were aroused. I could see a cabal forming of those who were particularly friendly and sympathetic to the Prime Minister and who might well give her advice on what to do in the event of an indecisive vote – one in which, for example, she got a clear majority but did not have a fifty-six-vote lead over Heseltine. This advice, I felt, might well not be the same as the advice that I would give in the interests of the party. As we drove to Sussex, I said to Alice that I very much doubted we would get through the week ahead without blood on the carpet. The factions were building up. There would certainly be those who would press Margaret to go on at all costs, provided she was the first in the first ballot, while others of us might well be saying that, if she did not have a decisive enough majority, she should stand down after the first ballot. Some of her advisers would have a self-interest in her decision, and Peter Morrison's job as parliamentary private secretary obviously depended on Margaret's survival.

The battle hotted up on Monday. In the morning I went to a meeting of the Prime Minister's campaign team with George Younger in the chair, Norman Tebbit, John Wakeham, Peter Morrison, John Moore, Cranley Onslow and Gerry Neale. The Prime Minister was now in Paris for the OSCE Conference and the signing of the Treaty on Troop Reductions in Europe. It was agreed that the only difficulty lay if the vote tomorrow fell in the 'grey area' – between 187 and 200 votes for the Prime Minister but no clear lead of fifty-six votes over Heseltine. The mood of the meeting was that, if that happened, the Prime Minister should immediately tell the press that she had 'every intention' of standing for the second ballot. She would go off to the ballet with President Mitterrand for two hours, and then fly back during the night for consultations with those of us around the table. My assumption was that if the consultations led to her being urged not to go into the second ballot, she would then be able to reconsider her 'every intention' to go on.

There were obvious traps in this scenario. But George Younger, as her campaign manager, supported it, saying that, if she did not take this positive and immediate stance, rats would start nibbling away at her position straight away. I did not like it but went with it as I trusted George's judgement.

The latest forecasts as I left the House around 11.00 p.m. that Monday evening were 320 for the Prime Minister from Peter Morrison and 120–130 for Heseltine from a number of sources. On this basis, the Prime Minister would win easily in the first ballot and the difficult scenario of her wondering whether or not to go forward for the second ballot would not develop at all.

The following day was election day. Unlike the year before, and the light-hearted contest with Anthony Meyer, I have no recollection of bantering with the press outside the committee room where we voted. It was a great deal grimmer. Peter Morrison came into my office at No. 12 on Tuesday morning to see me before flying off, as he put it, 'to hold the Prime Minister's hand in Paris' when the election result was announced.

From 6.20 p.m. onwards we had an open telephone line from my office in the House to the room in the Paris residence where Peter and the Prime Minister were sitting. Alastair Goodlad and Andrew Turnbull came to join me. I talked banalities down the line with Peter while we waited for the result to arrive. I told him to give the Prime Minister my good wishes. I noted that she had not come on the line to talk directly to me herself – and I heard Peter saying, 'Tim sends you a hug.' She replied, 'Tell him that I want his vote.' Was there a suspicion in her mind? I had agonised over how to vote. It was only in the last month that I had come painfully to the conclusion that I could not vote for the Prime Minister as I disagreed too profoundly with her attitude on the European Union, and I also felt that she was increasingly reliant on those like Norman Tebbit, Michael Forsyth and other members of the No Turning Back Group who were leading the party in the wrong direction. On the other hand, having fought for her for so long, I could not vote against her. So I abstained. I realised that, if this decision ever became public, I would face criticism or a lack of understanding but I could see no alternative that I could square with my conscience.

At 6.32 p.m. Greg Shepherd from the whips' office arrived with the card in his hand. The figures were: Heseltine 152, Thatcher 204, abstentions and spoiled papers 16, absent 0. Total 372. She had the absolute majority but was only fifty-two votes ahead, four short of what was needed and, to avoid doubt, the whip I had put in charge of supervising the vote, had written underneath, 'Second ballot necessary.'

I said to Peter, 'I have got the figures. Can I give them to the Prime Minister?'

'Let me take them down first,' he replied. I could not argue with him over the phone, so I gave them to him and I heard him passing them on to her.

She came on the line. 'Does this mean a second ballot, Tim?' in a voice with a perceptible catch in it.

'Yes, I am afraid so, Prime Minister,' I said. 'You got a good majority of the party but not quite enough. A second ballot will be necessary.'

'I will go and talk to the press straight away,' she said.

'Yes, but you will use the words that we agreed that you confirm that it is your intention to let your name go forward to the second ballot.' This was important.

'Yes,' she said. 'Intentions can always be withdrawn.'

That was the end of our conversation together. She hurried out down the stairs to address the press at the ambassador's residence. I watched on television as she came out on to the floodlit steps without hesitation and full of confidence, and announced to the world that she would fight on. My discussions over the next half-hour were all either with Charles Powell, who was in Paris too, or with Peter Morrison.

By Wednesday morning Margaret was back at No. 10.

The opposition had put down a No Confidence motion for the Thursday afternoon. I particularly tried to persuade Margaret not to make the statement in the Commons about the Conference on Security and Cooperation in Europe on Wednesday afternoon but to deal with that and answer the No Confidence debate on Thursday. I had severe misgivings that she would otherwise not have enough time on Wednesday afternoon for the individual consultations with Cabinet colleagues that they would expect, and on which her survival depended. But there was no curbing Charles Powell's enthusiasm for her to put on a bravura performance on both occasions.

This was, in the event, to prove fatal. If she had given herself time on that Wednesday to talk with each of the worried and potentially disaffected Cabinet ministers separately, over a cup of tea in the privacy of No. 10 Downing Street, she might have averted the ministerial crowd scene that occurred that evening around her office in the Commons, and in the upper ministerial corridor. This, with individual ministers emerging from her office in turn and egging each other on to be firm and not to pull their punches, was disastrous for her.

Anticipating something of this, I argued over the telephone with Charles Powell but he would have none of it. He was curt and dismissive of reflective advice. This attitude, though, was also a measure of his own profound confidence in the Prime Minister's ability to strong-arm her way through every situation and to win in the end. He had seen the tactic work so often over previous years, and, I think, had developed such a deep disdain for Westminster politicians that he did not believe it could not and would not continue to be successful. And so it came about that Margaret was not available to talk to Cabinet colleagues until Wednesday evening, after her statement on the OSCE and an audience with the Queen.

For the rest of that Tuesday evening, I had a succession of colleagues coming to see me to tell me that either she should stand down before the second ballot or she should go forward. Cranley Onslow dined with me in the House of Commons. I tried to cheer him up as he was deeply unhappy that he had announced the result of the first ballot in Room 12 while about 200 colleagues were waiting in Room 10 to hear it. They missed the news and eventually only heard it from other MPs or press reporters outside in the corridor. Some of them were more furious, I was told, than they had ever been in their political lives. They had been hit where it hurt – in their pride in their information-gathering abilities at a historic moment.

From 10.30 p.m. to midnight that evening we had a meeting in the whips' office to discuss the result of a partial trawl of colleagues. The purpose of this was to find out how many might change their voting intentions and switch from Margaret to Heseltine in the second ballot. We came up with a net figure of a possible loss of twelve for her. Michael Heseltine came to see me at my request and I asked him, more or less formally, whether he would consider giving up his challenge and serving in a Cabinet led either by Margaret or by Douglas Hurd. To the first he said that such a change would be needed in her style and ability to consult with colleagues that he did not think it was a possibility. For the second he said simply, 'No, because I am convinced that I am an election winner for the Conservatives and I do not think that Douglas is.' He was frank in discussing the Cabinet appointments he would make if he won. He said that he would like to keep Hurd as Foreign Secretary and Major as Chancellor. He would also certainly want to give Peter Lilley a job in the Cabinet as he thought a good deal of him, and he would bring Geoffrey Howe back. He said that he would wish to keep me as Chief Whip. The reason he gave me for keeping me on was that I had not leaked the fact that he had missed a three-line whip on the day of his putting in his nomination, and therefore he felt he could trust me. I merely said that I would certainly not hold him to this, since if he won he would surely want to think carefully about who he chose as Chief Whip.

My greatest surprise in our conversation was his insistence that Peter Tapsell, one of those who nominated him, was 'a man of great ability and distinction whose merits have simply not been noticed'. This was not my impression. I regarded him primarily as a successful stockbroker.

I poured some cold water on Michael's enthusiasm for Peter. Michael said, 'The reason that I chose him was because he is so good on radio and television.' I said I doubted this. I had heard him on radio and thought that he sounded too much like the rich, patriarchal businessman that he was. This exchange made me wonder about Michael's judgement but, other than that, I found myself being swept up in some of the euphoric enthusiasm that emanated from him. He was supremely confident not only about his ability to win a general election, compared with the ability of the rest of our candidates, but also to unite the party 'within twenty-four hours'.

'There is a lust for loyalty in this party,' he said. 'Of course I will be very careful in my appointments. They will be well balanced and you will find that everyone is united behind me within a day or two.'

Even I found it hard to resist his charisma and self-belief.

I decided to ask for advice from the most notable of the 'men in the grey suits'. Conrad Black, then owner of the *Daily Telegraph*, had called me 'one of the grey suits' when he visited me in my Commons office earlier in the year, and the turn of phrase stuck. So, the following morning, Wednesday 21 November, I left our mews house punctually at 8.20 a.m. for breakfast with Willie Whitelaw at another mews house a few blocks away. I was doorstepped as I walked out to the car. I mouthed some banalities about my job being to preserve unity in the party, and so on. The same thing happened when I got to Willie's street, Clabon Mews. There it was rather worse because I was unable to find No. 32, which appeared to be totally out of the right mathematical sequence, and I assumed the press records would have lots of pictures of me diving about trying to get into the wrong houses.

Willie and I talked over eggs and bacon and we agreed that I would say to the Prime Minister on his behalf, first, that there was a danger of her being humiliated in the second ballot. This he would bitterly regret. Secondly, that he thought that if she won by a very low margin, she would not be able to unite the party as the sniping would continue. Times had moved on and she simply would not be able to change that fact. Thirdly, Willie himself did not feel close enough to the parliamentary situation to say more, and he did not see himself as a man in a grey suit. Therefore, he did not propose to come and pay a call on her, but he would, of course, come to see her if she asked him to do so as a personal friend.

Willie was obviously relieved that I did not insist that he went round and saw Margaret himself, and he cheered up noticeably after I agreed to carry this message on his behalf. For the sake of the press we agreed that our meeting should have been at his request, and not mine. We thought this seemed a little less histrionic.

At 9.45 a.m. I went to the regular management meeting at Conservative Central Office to discuss next week's business. After that was done, Kenneth Baker asked me into his private room. He was very shaken by the prospect of a second ballot, and clearly and openly concerned that Michael Heseltine might win, which would put Kenneth himself out of the leadership race for ever – his age being too close to that of Michael. He insisted that the Prime Minister must go on as the only person who was likely to beat Heseltine. In

Kenneth's defence, it must be said that he had faithfully supported Margaret throughout the previous weeks.

At 10.20 a.m. I saw Geoffrey Howe in the room at the Commons next door to the one shared by his secretary and mine. This gave us a convenient and, I hoped, secret meeting place. Geoffrey confirmed to me that he was not intending to stand in the leadership election himself, and I agreed with this. I thought he would only attract criticism in the press and he would, at the end of the day, be humiliated. But we assumed then that it would be a straight contest between the Prime Minister and Heseltine. He himself was going to support Heseltine and he spent a minute or two telling me how good a minister Heseltine had been in various departments in which Geoffrey had worked closely with him, the Defence Ministry in particular.

At 10.45 a.m., back at No. 12, I rang John MacGregor, who had been asked by John Wakeham to ring round Cabinet ministers during the morning to find out their attitudes and those of their junior ministers. I had already advised MacGregor that, at midnight the previous night, just as I was preparing to leave for home, five Cabinet ministers, very relaxed after a late drink with Tristan Garel-Jones, came to see me and told me that they all felt that the Prime Minister could not win on the second ballot. They were Norman Lamont, Malcolm Rifkind, Chris Patten, William Waldegrave and Tony Newton. Rifkind acted as their spokesman. There was a good deal of embarrassment before he started to speak and I was pretty tired and not ready to receive their approaches too sympathetically. I suggested to them that they really would have to go and talk to the Prime Minister themselves or else, I asked, would they agree to my mentioning their names to her the following day? At that there was some hesitation particularly from Tony Newton. I suggested that he should think about it overnight.

John MacGregor told me that he was still in the process of ringing round various ministers and we agreed to meet at 12.15 p.m. in his office. Many colleagues rang me to tell me which way they were thinking of moving. Tony Newton rang to say that he was now prepared for me to mention his name to the Prime Minister, and Michael Howard also rang to say that he was convinced she could not win on the second ballot.

Eventually, I went into the regular Wednesday whips' meeting which had started an hour before. Between us, we did a further trawl of our parliamentary colleagues. We examined our lists of names with extreme care and decided that, instead of the figure of twelve of the night before, there were now twenty-six who might move over from the Thatcher to the Heseltine camp with one gain to her side, that is, a net loss of twenty-five. This would effectively wipe out her majority of fifty-two.

We made every possible attempt to identify those whom we thought to be telling us lies. For example, we felt sure that some of those who were now saying 'I voted for Margaret yesterday but I am certainly not going to be able to do that in a second ballot' had in fact voted for Michael Heseltine. It was a very difficult exercise in the judgement of the character and ambitions and personalities of our parliamentary colleagues. But it was what the whips' office was for. Collectively, we knew our parliamentary colleagues, and their strengths and foibles, better than anyone else and we took nearly two hours over this exercise. The net loss of twenty-five was our collective judgement.

At 12.30 p.m. I went along to John MacGregor's office and found Kenneth Baker there. As I went in I heard the end of a sentence of John's: '...a majority would probably not support her.' I confirmed that six of the Cabinet had told me that they could not encourage her to stand in the second ballot. John did not say much more about the Cabinet but said that around 15 per cent of the junior ministers he had talked to would not support her but the rest were all firm. Kenneth and he both seemed alarmed and they talked of calling a special Cabinet meeting in the evening for Cabinet ministers to make their position clear to the Prime Minister.

Cranley Onslow then joined me at No. 12. We had a glass of champagne together, offered to us by Nicholas Baker, the whip who had won our office sweep on the results of the first ballot. Cranley had come back from his meeting of the 1922 Executive whose conclusions were divided but not different from ours: Margaret would have a hard fight to win the second ballot but we could not be certain that she would lose. Therefore, there was no cut-and-dried case for either of us to tell her that she certainly should not go forward, a judgement which was Willie Whitelaw's as well.

At 1.15 p.m. Cranley, Kenneth, John MacGregor and I met the Prime Minister at No. 10 together with John Moore, Norman Tebbit and John Wakeham from her campaign team.

It was a strange meeting. It was lunchtime. We sat on different sides of a large table and, in between doing humdrum things such as passing plates of sandwiches and opening a can of beer or pouring a glass of water, we said our few words in turn, words that were helping to add up to a historic decision on an extraordinary day. Our pieces were not very different. Apart from delivering Willie's message, I emphasised that a number of colleagues, both ministerial and backbench, had told me that they did not think she would win on the second ballot. I gave her the figures, showing that our estimate of loss of support had changed from twelve last night to twenty-five today. I stressed that the view of the whips' office was that the result was now far too close to call. But there were five days ahead. A competent campaign, I said, would make a difference and there was no clear indication that, if she stood down, any other candidate would do better against Heseltine. Heseltine was, for Margaret, the bogeyman who had to be defeated.

Margaret listened very carefully, did not contradict and then moved on from me to ask Cranley for his views.

After we had all had our say there was a discussion about the nature of the election campaign ahead and how it would be improved; I did not join in this as it was not my business. I was just surprised that John MacGregor did not make more clearly and forcefully the point about the number of Cabinet ministers who were very doubtful about the Prime Minister going on to a second ballot. Perhaps this was shyness on his part. Eventually, Kenneth Baker came back to the point, emphasising that a large number of Cabinet ministers were thinking in this way and he wondered whether there should be a special Cabinet for them to make their views known. Peter Morrison suggested that she should instead see them in her office in the Commons individually or in twos or threes, and I supported this as the better alternative, thinking that a special Cabinet meeting would not only leak but also would be pretty chaotic. It was left that this would be organised for the evening. I still felt strongly that it would have been better if the talk with individual Cabinet ministers could have happened leisurely at No. 10 during the afternoon on a one-to-one basis, but Margaret was now committed to the debate in the Commons and there was no going back on that.

My clear impression as I left No. 10 at around 2.30 p.m. was that she intended to stand as not one of the seven of us had told her unequivocally that we did not think she had a chance of winning herself, nor had we stressed that any other candidate, Major or Hurd, would do better than her against Heseltine.

At 3.30 p.m. I went to the House of Commons and I listened to her bravely making her statement on the OSCE and the treaties that had just been signed in Paris. She was much applauded by our members for the contribution she had made to the cause of disarmament in the context of balanced troop reductions, and she got some tributes from the other side as well. I then listened to Tony Newton's opening speech on disability payments, which was a step-change from the immensely turbulent to the immensely quiet.

When I left the Chamber I was met by an agitated Murdo Maclean. He showed me the front page of the *Evening Standard* which had a headline to the effect that the Prime Minister's support was running away fast and that I was reported to have told her that she could not possibly win and must withdraw. This was incorrect and I said so to Charles Reiss, to the political editor of the *Evening Standard* and a few other journalists, at the same time avoiding to say what precisely I had told the Prime Minister.

In the light of that *Evening Standard* headline, George Gardiner, the head of the right-wing 92 Group (and one of those with whom Michael Heseltine surprisingly told me he had been in friendly communication), came into my office and virtually accused the whips' office and me of misleading the Prime Minister. Again I refused to tell him what I had told the Prime Minister but assured him that we were doing our job faithfully. He was angry that he had not been personally 'trawled' by the whips and asked for his opinion. Nor were many others of the 92 Group to which he belonged. I pointed out that we only had two hours in which to collect opinions the night before. It was selective but as accurate as our collective judgement could make it. He left my office with his feathers still ruffled.

At 6.15 p.m., while Alastair Goodlad was with me, a message arrived asking him to go along to see John Wakeham. Alastair came back to tell me that the scenario I had anticipated the previous day was taking place: a number of Cabinet colleagues were milling about on the Cabinet corridors (where all the Cabinet ministers have their House of Commons offices), being called in to see the Prime Minister in turn and firing each other up with determination between their conversations. One or two were said to have been quite abusive to her and she was reported to be visibly shaken. I thought again how foolish it had been not to leave the whole afternoon free to consult with her colleagues. If she had had them over to No. 10 one by one and separately for a quiet talk and a cup of tea, they would have found it much more difficult to stoke up each other's courage.

Later in the evening, I went along to talk to Douglas Hurd in his room in the Commons. Ken Clarke had put forward the suggestion that five 'wise men' should sit down during the night in the House and decide between them who was the best Cabinet colleague to stand and fight against Heseltine. His idea was that the group might consist of Alastair Goodlad and myself, together with three 'independents' who would be chosen by Hurd and Major.

Alastair joined me in Douglas Hurd's room and the three of us quickly agreed that the idea was a non-starter. There was no possibility of agreeing on one candidate, selected by a small cabal, and imposing him on the parliamentary party as the only alternative to Heseltine. If we chose Hurd, this would infuriate the Thatcherite coterie in the No Turning Back Group and the 92 Group. If we chose Major, this was likely to anger a number of those in the liberally minded groups such as the One Nation Club, Nick's Diner and the Lollards, a group founded by William van Straubenzee in the 1980s and curiously named after a fourteenth-century heretical sect. They, too, had been against the Poll Tax and regularly critical of Margaret's leadership.

If both Major and Hurd wanted to stand in the next round of the leadership election, the only solution was for them both to do so. Douglas agreed to this but wanted to put out a 'friendship and cooperation statement' when the nomination papers went in. This would be signed by Major and himself, pledging them to work together after the campaign was over. In a very Foreign Secretary manner, Douglas suggested to Alastair Goodlad that he should write a draft of this plan. I said I would ring and put this idea over to John Major who was still at his home in Huntingdon, recovering from a small operation to remove a dental abscess.

At around 10.30 p.m. I rang John, went through these plans with him and he agreed. He had some problems about the joint statement but said that he would think about it overnight and talk to Douglas. A further problem now arose in that the paper nominating the Prime Minister for the second round of the election campaign had already been prepared by Peter Morrison. As with the first round, Peter had planned that Margaret's two proposers should be John Major and Douglas Hurd, and Douglas had already signed. The paper had then been sent down to John's Huntingdon home for his signature. I was surprised to learn that 'the only car and driver available' for this mission had been Jeffrey Archer's even though he was no longer a deputy chairman of the party. No wonder he thought he deserved a peerage.

The sort of conspiratorial worry that happens late at night when ministers have been talking for too many hours now disturbed us. If John Major signed the nomination paper and sent it back to No. 10, where Peter Morrison was waiting for it, and it then fell into Bernard Ingham's hands, would he not immediately leak the news of this signed nomination paper to an impatient press? And could Peter Morrison then lodge it with Cranley Onslow, the chairman of the 1922 Committee, tomorrow morning and thus formally start the process of the second round, even if some Cabinet colleagues were saying they would resign from the Cabinet if the Prime Minister went ahead with taking part in the second ballot?

The thought of such double-dealing suited the mood and the time of the night. Already, Charles Powell had been evasive by saying specifically down the telephone to me from Paris that Douglas Hurd and John Major had agreed to propose and second the Prime Minister for the second ballot, whereas, in fact, Douglas had evidently chosen his words carefully and had simply said that the Prime Minister continued to have 'his full support'. I did not discover this until an hour or two after Charles had spoken to me and I had not yet had the opportunity to confront him with the apparent distortion, but on this turbulent evening it seemed perfectly possible that Hurd and Major might be bounced into formally nominating the Prime Minister for the second round at the very moment when they were wondering whether they should be putting pressure on her not to stand.

At 11.00 p.m. Peter Morrison rang from No. 10 and said he would like to come round and talk to Alastair and me. He arrived and we dealt with the problem of the nomination paper by getting Peter to agree in our presence that he would keep it, signed, in his pocket. He would not table it until after

Cabinet and, if there were threats of resignation at Cabinet, would not table it without consulting John Major and myself. This news was telephoned to John who was very relieved and, on that basis, put his signature on the nomination paper. Jeffrey Archer's car and driver had been waiting for over an hour while we sorted this problem out, and they were now released to drive back to London with a complete nomination paper.

Nonetheless, Peter Morrison's own opinion had changed. He talked about the Prime Minister's mood. She was still being lobbied by members of the No Turning Back Group. Michael Portillo was said to have just arrived at No. 10. Others were likely to turn up, telling her not to stand down. But she had turned pessimistic and gloomy since the evening meeting with Cabinet ministers in the Commons. Peter, Alastair and I all agreed that unless the Cabinet was wholly united, and publicly so, behind her, she could not go on. Peter said that this was Denis Thatcher's opinion too. I left the House at around midnight with a firm impression that she would stand down in the morning. Nonetheless, we had a last short, sharp, little discussion in the whips' office in which Neil Hamilton made it clear that he thought support for her was growing again. There had been a meeting of around fifty backbench MPs chaired by John Wakeham who were all ready to go out and fight to bring in the waverers, and Neil considered a bandwagon was rolling back in her direction. The wish was father to the thought.

On Thursday 22 November the first news that I heard on the radio as I awoke was that the newspapers had the full story of the five Cabinet ministers coming to see me after their drink at Tristan Garel-Jones' house. Clearly this has been leaked by one of them in order to put pressure on the Prime Minister or by Tristan himself who was, by nature, an inspired and clever conspirator. I was doorstepped again on my way to No. 12 but refused to make any comment.

Twenty minutes before Cabinet, Alastair Goodlad came into my room at No. 12 and said that John Wakeham and Peter Morrison had told him that the Prime Minister would be announcing in Cabinet that she was standing down.

At 9.00 a.m., the double doors of the Cabinet room were opened, we trooped in and sat in our usual seats, myself at the far end with Norman

Lamont as Chief Secretary on my right. The Prime Minister came into the room very soon after us. She sat in her usual place in the centre of the table, facing the windows that look over Horse Guards Parade. She was pale and looked very tired, with evident rings round her eyes, and the room, normally eager and active, was muffled in embarrassment.

After a short pause, and before we started on the regular business, the Prime Minister said quietly that she had consulted with a number of colleagues. Everyone had been very supportive, she continued, but many had said that she could not win on the second ballot. 'There is a danger of the policies that I believe in not being continued, and so I have concluded that I...' At this point she broke down and wept. Cecil Parkinson, sitting near her, compassionately and thoughtfully suggested that James Mackay, the Lord Chancellor, who was sitting on her left, read the statement for her. But she was determined to go on. After thirty seconds or so she recovered and finished her sentence. 'I have concluded that I should not let my name go forward for the second ballot.' I looked around the Cabinet table and noticed David Waddington sitting opposite her openly in tears.

Typically, after a further minute or two, she recovered her spirit and started talking about the campaign. 'It is vital that we stand together. It is vital that we win.' For her, winning meant stopping Michael Heseltine in his tracks. She had come to regard him as representing a reversal of all the policies for which she had fought for the past fifteen years. In fact, this was untrue save for the issue of 'ever closer union' in Europe where clearly she was on the one side and Michael on the other. But this issue represented the fault line to which other possibly imaginary splits, on the economy or the handling of the unions, could be traced. Although her face was looking thin and she was pale and weepy, the fighting talk started to come back. But there were moments when it was all quiet and uncomfortable; she commented that with three more supporters in the ballot she would have won and she would not now be withdrawing.

Talking about the Paris conference from which she had just come and the friendship shown to her by Gorbachev, Mitterrand, even, over lunch, by Chancellor Kohl, she said, 'The idea that one is not liked in Europe is absurd.' A touchingly naïve comment.

After Cabinet was over, she asked us all to stay on for a cup of coffee and we did. Some were already anxious to be unleashed and to start running their campaigns. Norman Lamont, sitting by my side, was particularly anxious to be off organising the campaign for John Major. But we talked on in a desultory manner. At one stage, Kenneth Baker said, 'The story will be that the Cabinet split and forced you out.'

Margaret immediately and instinctively replied, 'But this is true. That is why the advice changed between lunchtime and 6.00 p.m.'

I made a note of who might not be in the Cabinet in two weeks' time if Heseltine won. Howard, Wakeham, Parkinson, MacGregor were on my question mark list. And, of course, I wondered about myself.

The news of her resignation was out by the time we left Cabinet and walked along the narrow hallway to Downing Street. The world had changed and we had watched it do so in a painfully domestic scene of unhappiness.

The Commons was quite different from the day before. I had often admired Margaret at tense moments, but never as much as that afternoon when she was quick and witty at Question Time. In the morning she had feared that she might get damp-eyed at the despatch box, saying that she found it easier to deal with criticism than with sympathy, but she followed Milton's Samson Agonistes: 'Nothing is here for tears, nothing to wail or knock the breast; no weakness, no contempt, dispraise or blame.'

By the time Margaret started her reply to the No Confidence motion she was in top form. While Neil Kinnock had waffled in his opening attack, she was crisp. Where he had been made to look a fool when SNP members interrupted him with questions about Labour's policy on the Community Charge or on the single currency, she never let herself get into a corner. In the middle of a great tirade about the European single currency when she was asking the House: 'Do you believe in the European single currency, do you believe in the ECU taking over from the pound, do you believe in a single European Central Bank?' Skinner slipped in the words, 'But you will be the governor.' The whole House laughed. And she paused and thought and smiled and said, gaiety in her voice, 'I had not thought of that.' She paused again and added, 'I am enjoying this.'

She was relaxed in a way I had hardly ever seen her at the despatch box. Laying about her, she defended the principles on which she had fought to change the face of Britain over the last eleven years. When she sat down and the cheers and the waving of Order Papers had finished, she smiled across at Dennis Skinner, the persecutor of Tory MPs, the merciless interrupter. He was looking intensely at her with a half-smile on his face, and she said quite audibly, 'Thank you.' It was a tremendous performance, and I was told the following day by Andrew Turnbull that she was feeling much happier, having read the Friday morning papers and seen how complimentary they were about the last curtain call.

I was criticised by my old enemy Nicholas Winterton during the day on radio when he said that I had given the wrong advice to the Prime Minister and had misled her on purpose. He added, as in implied indictment, that I was a long-time friend of Geoffrey Howe. I assured the whips' office at our 2.30 p.m. meeting on Thursday that every word I had said at No. 10 the day before had been a firm reflection of their collective views. There was nothing that, a day later, I would wish to change. They all listened intensely and, I think and hope, wholly believed me. George Young said quietly from the far end of the room, 'Thank you, Tim.' Various people came up to me in the House and said that the whips' office had exercised its duty of impartiality fairly and correctly. I was glad of this. I could not, of course, expect the same reaction from either Winterton or Tebbit. Winterton glowered at me from the Bar of the Chamber and mouthed 'traitor' before Prime Minister's Questions started. I thought this was his revenge for my accusing him of disloyalty and of failing to support the government in July.

Tebbit refused to acknowledge a greeting from me later in the afternoon. Word reached me that he, too, was going round saying that the change of mood yesterday evening was largely my fault and due to the wrong advice I had given, saying that her vote was in danger of collapsing. I knew very well, though, that whatever my own views about the advisability of her giving up the leadership, nothing I had said had reflected that feeling. I had been as objective as I could and had reflected honestly the views of our office. If anything, I thought after the lunchtime meeting on Wednesday that I should have been more emphatic about the number of ministers saying that they did not think she could go on to the second ballot rather than leave John MacGregor to say so.

The next few days were a strangely quiet interim period. Heseltine, Hurd and Major put in their nomination papers and their campaign teams mounted their efforts but no one got in touch with me to ask for my vote. This was hardly surprising. On Monday afternoon I found on my desk in the House of Commons an envelope addressed to me. Inside was a list of allegations against Michael Heseltine that, the anonymous informant told me, the *Daily Mirror* were planning to publish during election time if Michael became Prime Minister. They would hold them until the time of the general election in order to cause us maximum embarrassment. There were many extraordinary and unpleasant charges. I made a personal guess as to who had left the envelope on my desk and thought it might be an outspoken right-winger. But, as there was a possibility that, within a day, the Queen might be asking Michael to form a government, I showed the paper to Robin Butler. He knew nothing of these allegations but said he would check them out as best he could. We both agreed that we were hardly in the business of advising the Queen not to send for Michael to ask him to form a government because of the so-called accusations.

I asked Michael to come and see me. He turned up after the 10 p.m. vote and I showed him the piece of paper. He was light-heartedly dismissive. I said that I was not interested in the truth of the charges but I wanted to be sure that he knew of them so that, if they appear in the press, he would be ready to answer them. I heard nothing more of these accusations.

Election day was Tuesday 27 November. After much thinking, I voted for Douglas Hurd. However likeable and intelligent he was, I did not consider John Major ready for the job yet. He needed another five years as Chancellor of the Exchequer. From my knowledge of him over many years I thought Douglas had a sensible pair of hands and would be able to unite the parliamentary party. He was not an exciting candidate but we did not need excitement at that moment. At around 6.15 p.m., Alastair Goodlad and I were talking in my room in the House when David Lightbown, the whip in charge, appeared with the figures of the vote which he had then to telephone directly to the Palace: 131 for Heseltine, 56 for Hurd, 185 for Major. John was two short of the critical 187, the absolute majority. Almost simultaneously, I watched Michael Heseltine on television walk out of his house in Chapel Street and address the newspaper reporters, saying that he would concede and would not let his name go forward to a third ballot. A few minutes later Cranley Onslow arrived in my room. By then, Douglas Hurd had also appeared on television conceding.

Cranley said that he thought the right thing to do was to cancel the third ballot, although there was no provision for this in the rules. I said I was certain this was what he should do. At that moment, Norman Lamont came through on telephone. Norman, who was in No. 11 Downing Street with John, asked about the third ballot. I said that Cranley had just decided that there was no point in holding one. Norman said, very excitedly, 'You mean that he is definitely cancelling it?'

'Yes,' said I, and I repeated the wording that Cranley had just been drafting for the statement to the press.

Norman realised of course that that meant that John was going to be the next Prime Minister. The tension in his voice relaxed.

Cranley, Alastair and I went round in my car to No. 11. There we joined a victory party with all sorts of people ranging from the newspaper reporter, Bruce Anderson, to Jeffrey Sterling, chairman of P&O, milling about, glasses of wine in their hands. It was all like the aftermath of a wedding. I eventually found John in his bedroom looking at a draft of what he was about to say to the press. I congratulated him and we talked warmly and in a friendly manner.

At one point I found myself on one side of a window peering out through the net curtain at the press in Downing Street below with Margaret Thatcher doing the same on the other side of the same window, cooing with evident delight at the success of her favourite candidate. The bulbs of the news cameras were flashing and John, with his arm round Norma, was talking to the press. I, in my heart, wished him all possible good luck ahead and all the strength that he could muster. I thought of the times in the past year when we in the whips' office discussed the fact that he got excessively worried and irritated about minor disasters – some backbencher had been rude to him for his not attending a committee meeting or whatever – and obviously I wondered whether he would have the strength for the enormous task ahead. I could only hope for him.

At the 10 p.m. vote I heard that Michael Heseltine had been in the whips' office in a near hysterical mood saying that four and a half hours had passed since the announcement of the ballot and no one had been in touch with him to offer him a job, yet he had got 131 votes and he could not be passed over. The whips were worried and suggested that I should talk to Michael. I saw him in the lobby as we were voting. I said that John must be given some time to make up his mind about how he was going to form his administration, but Michael was unstoppable.

'I hear they are going to offer me the Home Office. I know that is a plot. I was told about it twenty-four hours ago. But, as Iain Macleod told me years ago, that's a killer of a job and it's not in the mainstream. My talents are all in the business field. I want to be doing something that will help me to generate new interest among the businessmen and in the economy. I will not be able to do that in the Home Office.' Michael poured this out to me in the lobby while colleagues flocked past to vote.

I decided I had better see John Major once the 10 p.m. vote was finished and talk to him. I saw him on the front bench and asked for a few minutes immediately after the vote. We went back to the Chancellor's office, and typically he waved me into an armchair while he sat in an upright one. I offered him my congratulations on his victory and, at the same time, my resignation as Chief Whip, saying that I fully understood that any new leader of the party would want to appoint someone close to him as his Chief Whip. He thanked me and then I told him about my conversation in the lobby with Michael Heseltine, adding that I thought Michael was aiming to be appointed Chancellor of the Exchequer but I had told him, off my own bat, that there was no possibility of this happening.

'What do you think I should do with him?' said John.

'Well, I think I would give him the DTI and add Energy to that. You could take away some of the consumer protection side of the DTI so that Michael would concentrate on promoting British industry or the energy side of the North Sea.'

'But that is really a non-department now,' said John. 'There is really nothing in it.'

'Well,' I said, 'the alternative is to offer him the Department of the Environment if he will take it. But if you do that, you must be prepared for him to come forward with a scheme to reform the Community Charge which will involve relating the charge to ability to pay.'

'I am prepared to accept that,' said John quietly.

'So am I,' I said. We talked a bit more.

As I left, I noticed John Gummer and John Major's parliamentary private secretary, Graham Bright, hovering, their faces peering around the next door. Already, I thought, the camp followers want to be in on the act. They want to see who is gaining access to their king-in-waiting.

A few minutes after I had arrived at No. 12 the following morning, Andrew Turnbull rang to book me to see the new Prime Minister at 11.20 a.m. I went off to see Kenneth Baker at Conservative Central Office for our regular meeting at 9.45 a.m. to discuss next week's business with the management team. As I drove over to Central Office, I heard from Joe Bergin, my driver, that Cecil Parkinson had resigned and was not going to go on as Secretary of State for Transport. As usual, the drivers had the news first. After the management meeting Kenneth asked me to go along to his room and said that he had not yet had any message from John Major. He struck me as feeling quite lost and searching around for a mooring on the rock on to which he could cling. I told him a little of my discussion with John the night before about Michael Heseltine, and his eyes lit up at the mention of Home Secretary. It struck me that this was a post that he would enjoy and at which he would do very well, and I was glad a few hours later when I heard that this is what had been offered to him.

Meanwhile, back at the whips' meeting, we went through a list of those who might be promoted if there were any gaps. Names like Tim Yeo and Nigel Forman came up – people who had been passed over in Margaret's days but who, I felt, might now have a chance of getting the promotion they deserved. David Lightbown, one of our senior whips, said that, if Heseltine got the Department of the Environment and his job was to reform the Community Charge, the best possible person to help him would be George Young, only recently appointed a whip and an ex-minister who had fallen out with Margaret. Knowing that David's political persuasions were not at all the same as those of George, I felt this a very decent gesture on David's part and, sure enough, George Young was Minister of State at the Department of the Environment by the end of the day.

At 11.15 a.m. I left the large whips' room where we were meeting and walked through the back passages to No. 10. When I arrived, I was greeted by Charles Powell who told me that John was upstairs in the first floor study and that someone else had just gone in to talk to him. We wandered up and down the main reception room. I looked at the bowls of flowers that were on every table and thought that they had a strangely funeral parlour appearance about them. We talked desultorily, and I could not but think that this is what had happened to many others waiting to be seen by the Prime Minister during all the reshuffles that we had had in my year in the whips' office. I asked Charles what he was going to do and said that I presumed that he would be going to join the private sector. 'Oh yes,' he said. 'I see from today's paper that I'm going to join a bank whose name I've never even heard of'. He, and the whole place, had a surprisingly melancholic air about them.

After some minutes, I saw David Waddington leave the study looking distinctly bowed and grey. I learned later that he had been moved from Home Secretary to be Leader in the House of Lords. John Major asked me into his office and, as always, he was courteous and enquiring. If I had had a cough, I am sure he would have asked me if it was getting better.

We talked about some of the elements in John Major's proposed Cabinet reshuffle – Norman Lamont to become Chancellor of the Exchequer, David Mellor to come into the Cabinet as Chief Secretary. I cavilled at that and said that it did not really seem David's form. John replied that Leon Brittan, who was also a lawyer, had been one of the best chief secretaries and David had to prove himself in a really tough job. I asked about Michael Heseltine and he said that he was proposing to offer him the job of Environment Secretary.

'Will he take it?' I asked.

'I don't know,' said John 'but I hope so.' Then, with all the politeness that was his trademark, he accepted my offer to resign as Chief Whip but said that he would very much like me to stay in government and asked me to take on the job of Minister for the Arts.

I was surprised. Alice had shown prescience earlier that morning in saying that she thought I might be offered the Arts and adding that I had always said I would love to be the arts minister. True enough. I agonised for an hour or two, consulted Alice again over a sandwich lunch and then returned to No. 10 to accept the offer. Back in his office, I told John Major that I would stay on board and he, formally enough, expressed his pleasure and added, 'Well, remember you have to be tough. They are a very difficult lobby.'

I had already informed the whips that I was not going to go on as Chief Whip. Richard Ryder would step into my shoes and I knew he would do the job extremely well. He had been a whip before and was intelligent, popular and six years younger than the Prime Minister. It would be an important step up the ladder for him.

Thus ended thirteen months at No. 12. They were a unique period of history and I was lucky to have played my part in it. The trouble throughout was that Margaret Thatcher had ceased having an open mind. She only wanted to have her own friends around her and she had come to identify No. 10 and the job of being Prime Minister with herself. Anyone who stood in her way – from Nigel Lawson and Geoffrey Howe onwards – was to be dispensed with. They were not of the right faith. I tried very hard to get close to her and at times, most particularly on the day of Ian Gow's murder, I knew that I was. Yet underneath there was a deep suspicion of me which came to the fore again after Geoffrey's speech on the fringe of the 1990 Bournemouth Conference. It was inevitable, after Margaret's demise, that the right wing should look for a villain and fasten on me as an obvious candidate for the role.

The other villain was Geoffrey Howe himself. Arabella Warburton, his long-serving House of Commons secretary, told Alice and my constituency secretary, Mrs Harvey, of the abusive mail that he had received, including letters enclosing thirty pieces of silver. For someone as wholly committed to the success of the Tory Party, and who had agonised so much – too much – about his loyalty and faithfulness to Margaret, this was intensely painful.

At the end of the year, Geoffrey asked me whether Margaret was now in a mood of reconciliation. He seemed surprised when I told him of her continuing coldness towards me. An article in *The Economist* had quoted her as telling the Russian ambassador in London that she had been the victim of a plot which had been engineered by her Chief Whip.

'But you knew nothing of the contents of my speech in the House of Commons,' Geoffrey said, 'nor did I tell you that I was going to resign until just a few minutes before I went in to see Margaret.'

This showed the innocence of the man, but also my innocence in not realising the extent to which my friendship with Geoffrey was bound, when the fatal leadership election drew near, to be interpreted by Margaret's coterie as collusion with those who wished to get her out of No. 10.

Like other Government Chief Whips, I had become torn between loyalty to the Prime Minister who had appointed me and loyalty to the party of which I had been an active member for twenty years. I had come to the conclusion that, although I thought Margaret was likely to go on as Prime Minister until the next general election, this was not in the interests of either the Conservative Party or of the country and would certainly lead to our defeat at that election.

The details that pushed me on the way to this conclusion were not important in themselves. Among others, they were her incredible support for Michael Forsyth when he had been of such little help to Malcolm Rifkind, followed by her attempt to get Norman Tebbit back into government as Secretary of State for Education when he had caused so much division over the Hong Kong Citizenship Bill.

I remembered, also, the Prime Minister's comment to me when I had proposed political knighthoods for Tim Raison, Richard Luce and Tony Durrant, all well deserved for long and loyal public service. 'But you've not done anything for my friends,' she said.

These aggravating incidents were set alongside a growing admiration in my thirteen months of close working with Margaret for her personal courage, her determination and her extraordinary and thoughtful kindness to those around her. And also I felt an increasing sympathy for her for the loss of friends, her loneliness and the sense of isolation within her own Cabinet. It was impossible to be near her and not admire her, however irritating she was being.

By tacit agreement, we virtually never talked about her attitude to the European Community with which I profoundly disagreed. Late one evening, after one summit, I asked her whether she did not agree with the much-talked-about concept of subsidiarity: decisions should be taken at the lowest practical level involving a delegation of decision-making back from the European Commission to national parliaments. 'Not at all,' she said dismissively, and that was the end of that conversation.

I had for years felt that our future lay wholeheartedly within the Community and that we could not afford to be on the sidelines always complaining about the new rules. We had to be in the middle, arguing vociferously if we wished, accepting that the rules would change as the vision of the Community changed and doing our utmost to play an active and constructive part, looking forward all the time to a Community where the ties were bound to be deeper than they are at present. The Prime Minister's attitude was essentially one of looking backwards to past history, whatever her personal successes in bringing some sense into the European Community budget. We could never have been in agreement on this.

Arguably, I should never have become her Chief Whip at all as there was too great a philosophical divide between us. If someone else had been Chief Whip from the day of Nigel Lawson's resignation onwards, another David Waddington or John Wakeham, then the whips' office could well have behaved differently during the Meyer election. The whips could have been obviously partial in favour of Margaret on that occasion, and that would have paved the way for them supporting her in October and November 1990. Under those circumstances, she would have won on the first ballot but, as Willie Whitelaw had said to me at breakfast and as I said to her over lunchtime sandwiches on the famous Wednesday, her majority would have remained very small and the divisions in our parliamentary party would certainly have continued. I had no doubt that my insistence on impartiality had been wholly correct. The fact that after John Major's election only one of us lost his job in the whips' office – and that was me – meant all the rest of the whips' office, with its received wisdom about our colleagues, was there and ready to serve Margaret's successor. George Young moved to the Department of the Environment – a suggestion that I had made to John Major at my meeting with him the morning after his election – but that was as Minister of State and a clear promotion.

There is little doubt that Michael Heseltine made a miscalculation in not immediately conceding to Margaret after the first round when she won fifty-two more votes than he did and was just four short of the margin of victory required in the rules. This would have been seen as a magnanimous gesture and would have won him new and influential friends.

By 1991 Margaret, if she had still been Prime Minister, would have been losing by-elections and been way down in the national opinions polls. The certainty of losing a general election in the following spring could well have tempted a majority of Conservative MPs to change horses even at this late stage in the life of a Parliament. Michael Heseltine could then have success-fully challenged without any other candidates coming forward, and it would have been up to him to pull off the general election coup that fell to John Major's lot in 1992. 'The bastards', John Major's description of his detrac-tors on the right, would never have found a place in Michael Heseltine's Cabinet, and the history of the last decade of the twentieth century would certainly have been different. But hindsight is 100 per cent vision.

PART
TWO

SIX

The need for discipline

'Every hunt has a whipper-in whose job it is to ensure the hounds do not stray.' Sir John Sainty, Clerk of the Parliaments from 1983 to 1990, quoted these traditional words about the need for parliamentary whips to me when we first met. It remains as good a description as any.

On 25 November 1621, Sir George Calvert, Member of Parliament and one of James I's secretaries of state, wrote to Sir Julius Caesar, a remarkable man who combined a top legal job, Master of the Rolls, with being under-treasurer and Chancellor of the Exchequer. Calvert's letter required Caesar's attendance in Parliament on the following day and 'every day as long as the Howse sitts'.[1] This is the first recorded whip, summoning one of the King's men to Parliament to support his cause. Calvert's duty as secretary was 'to lay the King's necessities before Parliament'; he was an intermediary, regularly pleading for money and supplies for the King.

The Parliament of 1621 did not prove a happy experience for James, King of Scotland from 1567 as James VI and of England from 1603 as James I. He had published two books in which he expounded the theory of the divine right of kings to govern. But Parliament, after granting two monetary subsidies in February as a 'present of love' to the King, became increasingly concerned that James's son, Charles, should find a good Protestant wife rather than marry the Catholic daughter of Philip III of Spain. Before the Parliament to which Caesar was summoned opened, James left London to hunt at Newmarket and did not return until the final days of 1621. Then, furious that the Commons had presumed to discuss the Prince's marriage and claiming that was an act of high treason, he rejected a protestation from the Commons about their ancient rites and privileges. 'His Majesty erased it from the journal book with his own hand and ordered an act of council to be entered thereoff.' James dissolved Parliament by proclamation and went back to hunting at Newmarket. The tension between monarch and Parliament continued.

The 1600s were the turbulent century in British history. The execution of James's successor Charles I in 1649, the Puritan Commonwealth and the bloodless revolution of 1688, which got rid of the Stuart kings and placed the firmly Protestant William of Orange on the throne, destroyed the medieval view that there was a natural harmony between the head – the Crown – and the limbs of the body politic, the peers and the elected Commons.

Constitutional change became a slow-moving and erratic theme of the next century and with it the step-by-step increase in the influence of Parliament, sometimes in alliance, sometimes in conflict with the Crown. The rough and tumble, the occasional chaos at Westminster is well described by Horace Walpole, son of the great Prime Minister, Sir Robert Walpole, himself a Member of Parliament from 1741 to 1768 and reputed to be the best letter-writer in the English language. He commented on political struggles, fashionable scandals and social events throughout the reigns of George I, George II and George III. Many of his letters are addressed to an old friend, Sir Horace Mann, who was appointed in 1740 Minister from England in Florence, a post he occupied for forty-six years until his death in November 1786. Mann was thus out of the country for long periods of time and Walpole kept him up to date with 'everything that takes place both in the court and in society'.[2]

In 1741 the long premiership of Robert Walpole that had started twenty years earlier was broken. The Tory minority, known as the Patriots because of their support for the Jacobites, had seceded from Parliament for eight months in 1739. When they returned, they campaigned vigorously and Walpole's popularity was waning. The 1741 elections saw the Whigs with numbers reduced to nearly the same as the Tories; party discipline was scarcely existent. Horace Walpole described the scenario to Horace Mann from Downing Street on 3 December 1741:

The Parliament met the day before yesterday and there were 487 members present. They did no business, only proceeded to choose a Speaker, which was unanimously Mr Onslow, moved for by Mr Pelham [brother of the Duke of Newcastle] and seconded by Mr Clutterbuck. But the Opposition, to flatter his pretence to popularity and impartiality, call him their own Speaker. They intend to oppose Mr Earle's[3] being chairman of the committee and to set up a Dr Lee, a civilian. Tomorrow the King makes his speech. Well, I won't keep you any longer in suspense. The court will have a majority of 40 – a vast number for the outset: a good majority, like a good sum of money, soon makes itself bigger.

Walpole's prediction of a majority for the Court or Whig party was quickly proven wrong. On 16 December he wrote again to Mann.

Wednesday night, 11 o'clock, 16 December 1741. Remember this day. Nous voilà de la Minorité! Entens-tu çela? Hé? My dear child, since you will have these ugly words explained, they just mean that we are metamorphosed into the minority. This was the night of choosing a chairman of the Committee of Elections. Gyles Earle was named by the Court; Dr Lee, a civilian, by the Opposition, a man of fair character. Earle was formerly a dependent on the Duke of Argyll, is of remarkable covetousness and wit which he has dealt out largely against the Scotch and Patriots. It was a day of much expectation and both sides had raked together all probabilities; I except near twenty, who are in town, but to stay to vote on a second question when the majority may be decided to either party. Have you not read of such in story? Men, who would not care to find themselves on the weaker side, contrary to their intent. In short, the deter-mined sick were dragged out of their beds: zeal came in a great coat. There were two vast dinners at two taverns, for either party; at six we met in the House. Sir William Yonge, seconded by my uncle Horace, moved for Mr Earle: Sir Paul Methuen and Sir Watkin Williams Wynne proposed Dr Lee and carried him, by a majority of four: 242 against 238 – the greatest number, I believe, that ever *lost* a question. You have no idea of their huzza! unless you can conceive how people must triumph after defeats for twenty years together. We had one vote shut out, by coming a moment too late; one that quitted us, for having been ill used by the Duke of Newcastle but yesterday – for which, in all probability, he will use him well tomorrow – I mean, for quitting us. Sir Thomas Lowther was fetched down by him and voted against us. Young Ross, son to a Commissioner of the Customs and saved from the dishonour of not liking to go to the West Indies when it was his turn by Sir Robert's giving him a Lieutenancy, voted against us; and Tom Hervey [second son of the first Earl of Bristol and surveyor of the royal gardens] who is always with us but is quite mad; and being asked why he left us, replied, 'Jesus knows my thoughts; one day I blaspheme, and pray the next.'

So, you see what accidents were against us, or we had carried our point. They cry Sir R. miscalculated: how should he calculate when there are men like Ross, and 50 others he could name!

Walpole ends the letter with the words 'Tomorrow and Friday we go upon the Westminster election – you will not wonder, shall you, if you hear next post that we have lost that too?'

The prophesy proved all too correct. On Christmas Eve a week later Horace Walpole wrote again to Mann:

Last Thursday I wrote you word of our losing the Chairman of the Committee. This winter is to be all ups and downs. The next day [Friday] we had a most complete victory. Mr Pulteney [leader of the Tories] moved for all papers and letters etc. between the King and the Queen of Hungary and their ministers. Sir Robert agreed to give them all the papers relative to those transactions, only desiring to except the letters written by the two sovereigns themselves. They divided, and we carried it 237 against 227. They moved to have those relating to France, Prussia and Holland. Sir Robert begged they would defer asking for those of Prussia till the end of January, at which time a negotiation would be at an end with that King, which now he might break off, if he knew it was to be made public. Mr Pulteney persisted; but his obstinacy, which might be so prejudicial to the public, revolted even his own partisans, and seven of them spoke against him. We carried that question by 24; and another by 21, against sitting on the next day [Saturday]. Monday and Tuesday we went on the Westminster election... we went on the merits of the cause, and at ten at night divided, and lost it. They had 220, we 216; so the election was declared void. You see *four* is a fortunate number to them.

The difficulty of getting colleagues to come and vote on the night and on the right side despite attractive promises from the opposition was already a parliamentary hazard. Horace Walpole continued his account:

We had 41 more members in town who would not, or could not come down. The time is a touchstone for wavering consciences. All the arts, money, promises, threats, all the arts of the former year, '41, are applied; and self-interest, in the shape of Scotch members – nay, and of English ones, operates to the aid of their party, and to the defeat of ours.

The opposition promised a young Irishman, Lord Doneraile, 'brought in by the Court', that they would not petition against his election if he voted with them. Doneraile declared it was against his conscience but he still voted as they wanted and, wrote Walpole, he 'lost us the next question which they put (censoring the High Bailiff) by his single vote, for in that the numbers were 217 against 215, the alteration of his vote would have made it even; and then the Speaker, I suppose, would have chosen the merciful side and decided for us'. This is an interesting analogy with 28 March 1979 when Frank McGuire, an Ulster MP who would normally have supported Labour, was coaxed away by his wife before the vote, and a 77-year-old Labour MP was too ill to be brought to Westminster. Jim Callaghan, having expected to win, lost a vote of confidence by one vote, 310 to 311, thus ushering in Margaret Thatcher's first government.

A defeat in 1741 only meant a change of government if the King wanted it. Robert Walpole still retained the confidence of George II. After Christmas, the House of Commons met again and by the end of the first week of the new term was in a state of huge dispute. The question at issue was whether the Commons should set up a secret committee of twenty-one to sit and examine whatever persons and papers they should please and to meet when and where they pleased. This was proposed by Mr Pulteney and one of the opposition, Lord Perceval, said that he would vote for it as a committee of accusation against Robert Walpole's administration. There were, said Horace Walpole in his letter to Horace Mann,

> several glorious speeches on both sides… my friend Coke, for the first time, spoke vastly well, and mentioned how great Sir Robert's character is abroad. Sir Frances Dashwood replied, that he had found quite the reverse from Mr Coke, and that foreigners always spoke with contempt of the Chevalier de Walpole. This was going too far and he was called to order, but got off well

enough, by saying, that he knew it was contrary to rule to name any member, but that he had only mentioned it spoken by an impertinent Frenchman...

At eleven at night we divided, and threw out this famous committee by 253 to 250, the greatest number that was ever in the House, and the greatest number that ever *lost* a question.

In his book *Breaking the Code*, Gyles Brandreth describes in agonising detail the practice of bringing the moribund in ambulances into the precincts of Westminster in order to obtain their vote on crucial occasions. If he thinks it necessary, a whip from the opposing party will actually check that the invalid MP from the other side is still breathing. The eighteenth century was no different. Horace Walpole continued his account:

It was a most shocking sight to see the sick and dead brought in on both sides! Men on crutches, and Sir William Gordon from his bed, with a blister on his head, and flannel hanging out from under his wig. I could scarce pity him for his ingratitude. The day before the Westminster petition, Sir Charles Wager [Admiral Sir Charles Wager, at the time first Lord of the Admiralty, and aged 76] gave his son a ship, and the next day the father came down and voted against him. The son has since been cast away; but they concealed it from the father, that he might not absent himself. However, as we have our good-natured men too on our side, one of his own countrymen went and told him of it in the House. The old man, who looked like Lazarus at his resuscitation, bore it with great resolution, and said, he *knew* why he was told of it, but when he thought his country in danger, he would not go away.

There are no arts, no menaces which the Opposition do not practice. They have threatened one gentleman to have a reversion (a potential inheritance) cut off from his son, unless he will vote with them.

On the same evening my brother Walpole had got two or three invalids at his house, designing to carry them into the House through his door, as they were too ill to go round by Westminster Hall [the elder brother was Robert Walpole. He was Auditor of the Exchequer, and his house joined to the House of Commons, to which he had a door]. The Patriots [the Tories or Jacobites], who have rather more contrivances than their predecessors of Grecian and Roman memory, had taken the precaution of stopping the keyhole with sand.

Today's Members of Parliament, with their whips in constant contact via pagers, mobile phones and e-mails, might envy the blunt but simple tactics of their eighteenth-century predecessors.

Horace Walpole wrote as Alan Clark did, full of fun and gossip and little worried about the principle of what or who was being voted for. But clearly the chaos at Westminster that Walpole lovingly described could not continue for ever. George III succeeded to the throne in 1760 and took a far greater interest in domestic politics than either his grandfather or great-grandfather. Those who were regarded as the King's supporters were regularly summoned to Parliament at the opening of the new session by 'circular letters'. These requested the attendance of 'friends' and were a rudimentary form of the party whip.[4] In October 1763 George Grenville, Secretary to the Treasury, drafted a letter to go out from Downing Street. The letter treated its recipients with extreme politeness and courteous formality. It read :

Sir,

As business of great importance is expected to come on at the opening of the ensuing Session of Parliament, which is now fixed by Proclamation for the 15th of the next month, I persuade myself that your zeal for the public service at this critical juncture will induce you to give your attendance as early as possible: I flatter myself therefore that I shall have the pleasure of seeing you in Town before that time and am with great truth and regard,

Sir,

Your most obedient, humble servant

The Secretary to the Treasury was in a key position. It was very likely that, when the House divided, the Secretaries (the ministers of the day), would be named as tellers and in that position they could easily count the friends and foes of government.

As the Secretary to the Treasury had at his disposal information in regard to all the members who had received favours from the Government [such as pensions, places, contracts, or assistance in election, either for themselves or friends], he was advantageously situated to whip in those members, when an important vote was to be taken. In other words, the Secretary to the Treasury had unusual opportunities for managing the House of Commons.[5]

George III personally selected Lord North as Prime Minister in 1770. The Stamp Act, passed by Parliament in 1765, and intended to raise revenue from the American colonies that would help pay the cost of the regular troops stationed there, was strongly supported by the King, as were the Townshend Acts that attempted to put a tax on tea traded on the wharves of Boston. He believed in the right of a Westminster Parliament to raise an imperial revenue from the colonies for the purposes of defence, and he saw in this an extension of his own power. It was this belief that pushed the American colonies over the brink into their battle for independence.

By 1779, England was at war with France and Spain and, at the same time, fighting the American colonies. Out of this turbulence, much of it thought by the likes of Edmund Burke, the Whig Member of Parliament and the leading political thinker of his time, to be the result of incompetence, came a revival of political alliances against both George III and his Prime Minister.

From 1780 on, Parliament focused on two pivotal events: the American War of Independence and the French Revolution. By now the label 'Whig' and 'Tory' had come to be attached to most individual Members, the Whigs being primarily members of the great landed families and the Tories the patriotic supporters of the Crown. But they meant attachment to sets of principles rather than to formal parties. June 1781 saw the Whig Charles James Fox and the Tory Pitt the Younger in alliance, both speaking against the Prime Minister, North, and the continuation of the American War of Independence.

The friendship between Fox and Pitt did not last. First, after North's resignation in March 1782, Fox joined a government led by Lord Rockingham which survived for only three months until Rockingham's death. Then the younger Pitt, aged twenty-three, joined a government led by Lord Shelburne as Chancellor of the Exchequer. He wrote to his mother on 16 July 1782,

Our new Board of Treasury has just begun to enter on business; and though I do not know that it is of the most entertaining sort, it does not seem likely to

128

be very fatiguing... Lord North will, I hope, in a very little while make room for me in Downing Street, which is the best summer town house possible.

Shelburne, however, lacked a majority at Westminster to approve the treaties that ended the American War of Independence. Pitt went to see Fox in February 1783 to find out whether he would rejoin the Cabinet but Fox refused as long as Shelburne remained Prime Minister. Instead, three days after his meeting with Pitt, Fox met North and they combined, on 18 February, to defeat the government by sixteen votes. Resolutions pledging the House to preserve the terms of the American peace but declaring that the concessions to the French and Spanish were excessive were debated on 21 February. Pitt spoke for two hours and three quarters and was particularly rude to North:

> In short, Sir, whatever appears dishonourable or inadequate in this peace is strictly chargeable to the Noble Lord in the blue riband, whose profusion of the public money, whose notorious temerity and obstinacy in prosecuting the war which originated in his pernicious and oppressive policy, and whose utter incapacity to fill the station he occupied, rendered a peace of any description indispensable to the preservation of the State.

North, insulted as he had been, began his reply by a tribute to the 'amazing eloquence' of Pitt. His defence of the peace terms was successful and the opposition's majority, in a vote at 3.00 a.m., increased from sixteen to seventeen. Shelburne resigned two days later but then suggested to George III that Pitt should become Prime Minister. George III 'eager to escape the yoke already fitted to his neck – the yoke of the great Whig houses – grasped at the suggestion. He sent at once to Pitt, offering him the headship of the Treasury, with full authority to nominate his colleagues... It is perhaps the most glorious tribute to early promise that any history records.'[6]

Pitt, however, turned down the offer, much to his friends' consternation. It was repeated a month later after the Duke of Portland and North had failed to form an administration. The intervention of the King was direct and made no mention of the fact that Pitt was Chancellor of the Exchequer in a government that had just been twice defeated in the Commons. The King wrote to Pitt from Windsor; the letter is punctiliously timed and dated 24 March 1783, 5.12 p.m.

After the manner I have been personally treated by both the Duke of Portland and Lord North, it is impossible I can ever admit either of them into my service: I therefore trust that Mr Pitt will exert himself tomorrow to plan his mode of filling up the offices that will be vacant, so as to be able on Wednesday morning to accept the situation his character and talents fit him to hold, when I shall be in town before twelve ready to receive him. G.R.' Pitt replied the following morning, 25 March 1783, 'Mr Pitt received, this morning, the honour of your Majesty's gracious commands. With infinite pain he feels himself under the necessity of humbly expressing to your Majesty, that with every sentiment of dutiful attachment to your Majesty and zealous desire to contribute to the public service, it is utterly impossible for him, after the fullest consideration of the situation in which things stand, and of what passed yesterday in the House of Commons, to think of undertaking, under such circumstances, the situation which your Majesty has had the condescension and goodness to propose to him.

The King was, in turn, brief in his reply from Windsor, March 25, at 4.35 p.m.

Mr Pitt, I am much hurt to find you are determined to decline at an hour when those who have any regard for the Constitution as established by law ought to stand forth against the most daring and unprincipled faction that the annals of this kingdom ever produced. G.R.[7]

There is no thought in George III's mind that the Prime Minister should necessarily be able to command a majority in the Commons.

A week later Pitt resigned the office of Chancellor of the Exchequer and explained his future course: 'I desire,' he said, 'to declare that I am unconnected with any party whatever. I shall keep myself reserved, and act with whichever side I think is acting right.'[8]

The King had to wait another nine months before he got the Prime Minister he wanted. The 'infamous coalition' of Fox and North as joint secretaries of state was formed with the Duke of Portland as the nominal Prime Minister. Pitt was pressed to resume the office of Chancellor of the Exchequer but refused and spent some time in the coming months visiting Stowe, Brighton, partridge shooting (and narrowly missing being shot by his great friend, Wilberforce) and then on travelling to France. He returned in time for the opening of Parliament in November and the debate on the India Bill, drafted by Burke and backed by Fox. This was a remarkable Bill in that it gave to a board of seven people 'the absolute power to appoint or displace the holders of office in India, and to conduct as they deemed best the entire administration of that country'.[9] When the names of the directors were announced by Fox, the chairman of the board was to be Earl Fitzwilliam 'whom the Cavendishes are nursing up as a young Octavius, to succeed his Uncle Rockingham'.[10] George, the eldest son of North, came next and all the others were good friends of the new administration. 'There was not the smallest doubt that the new Board thus composed would be wholly at the bidding of Fox, whether in or out of office.'[11] The patronage involved was reckoned to be not less than £300,000 a year (about £30 million in today's money). Others calculated that it was worth more than £2 million.

The Commons passed the India Bill by a majority of 208 against 102 but the King quickly made known his intense dislike of so much patronage being in the hands of his enemies, the Whigs. Ten days later the Bill was thrown out by ninety-five votes to seventy-six in the House of Lords after the King sent a Tory ally a handwritten card stating that

His Majesty allowed Earl Temple to say that whoever voted for the India Bill was not only not his friend, but would be considered by him as an enemy; and if these words were not strong enough Earl Temple might use whatever words he might deem stronger and more to the purpose.[12]

The clash between Commons and the King was dangerously clear. On the same day as the Lords debated and threw out the India Bill, the Commons debated a resolution that

it is now necessary to declare that to report any opinion or pretended opinion of His Majesty upon any Bill or other proceeding depending in either House of Parliament, with a view to influence the votes of the Members, is a high crime and misdemeanour, derogatory to the honour of the Crown, a breach of the fundamental privileges of Parliament, and subversive of the Constitution of this country.

Pitt denounced the resolution; Fox, in turn, denounced Pitt in terms that would delight today's press: 'Boys without judgement, without experience of the sentiments suggested by the knowledge of the world, or the amiable decencies of a sound mind, may follow the headlong course of ambition thus precipitately, and vault into the seat while the reins of government are placed in other hands.'[13] The Commons passed the motion by 150 votes to 80 and the following day George III demanded that Fox and North, as secretaries of state, should deliver up their seals of office and send them by the under-secretaries 'since a personal interview on the occasion would be disagreeable to His Majesty.' This was stretching the royal prerogative to breaking point, but Fox and North duly surrendered their seals.

The next day, 19 December, the House of Commons was full and excited. Fox and North took their seats on the front opposition benches when a young Member, Richard Pepper Arden, rose from the government benches and moved a new writ for the Borough of Appleby 'in the room of the Right Honourable William Pitt who, since his election, has accepted the office of First Lord of the Treasury and Chancellor of the Exchequer.' It was the standard custom that Members, on being appointed ministers, had to stand down and be re-elected at a by-election since they were accepting offices of profit under the Crown.

One of the rare occasions when the Government Chief Whip speaks in the House of Commons is to propose in formal language the writs for by-elections. It may be fanciful to see in Richard Arden's action the first clear sign of a Government Chief Whip, but the somersaults of 1782 and 1783 showed the great need for firm party consolidation if a wilful and experienced King was not simply to ignore parliamentary votes and, at critical moments when he saw his power and patronage threatened, to appoint Prime Ministers of his own choice no matter whether they commanded a majority or not. The delicate constitutional balance of a non-executive Crown on the one hand and an essentially supreme Parliament on the other could well have been destroyed if George III's symptoms of madness had not appeared in 1788 or, three generations later, if Prince Albert had not died at the height of his powers in 1861.

One reason for the slow development of party organisation was that the likes of Edmund Burke were deeply concerned as to whether voting with a political party was compatible with the independence of thought and action that Members of Parliament increasingly promised to their electors. The philosophical idea developed that political parties were acceptable only if they were seen as good in themselves or, to use a more difficult word, 'virtuous'. For example, if the Crown was exercising its prerogative in a despotic manner or if the ministry was hopelessly corrupt, it was acceptable for politicians to band together as a temporary expedient in order to inaugurate a party-less reign of virtue.

> The question of *how* a party was to prove itself virtuous was given most celebrated consideration by Burke... A party might seek to legitimise its activity in the same way as an individual politician, particularly one engaged in opposition, by representing that activity as purely a matter of conscience and, more specifically, as arising from the upholding of principle.[14]

Burke is an interesting supporter of the principle of political party, given his own determined early independence from the wishes of the electors of Bristol. He told them when he first arrived in Bristol, 'Your representative owes you not his industry only but his judgement; and he betrays, instead of serving, you if he sacrifices it to your opinion.' But his political life was dominated by a fear of the power and aims of George III and he was insistent on building up the powers of the Whigs as the party dedicated to transferring influence and patronage away the Crown to the ministerial party. Ministers, however, still changed sides regularly. Fox, leader of the Whigs in the Commons, was opposed to the war which Pitt declared against the French Republic but his most important political friends first wavered and then went over to the side of the government.

> In July 1794 the Duke of Portland, Lord Fitzwilliam, Wyndham and Grenville took office under Pitt. Fox was left with a minority which was satirically said

not to have been more than enough to fill a hackney coach. 'That is a calumny,' said one of the party, 'we could have filled two.'[15]

Burke, who was passionately opposed to the excesses of the French Revolution, had, three years earlier, had such a tempestuous row in the Commons with his fellow Whig, Fox, over the merits of the Revolution that all informal relations between them ceased. Fox had charged Burke with inconsistency. Burke replied that he would never cease from advising the English to flee from the French Constitution.

> 'But there is no loss of friends,' said Fox in an eager undertone. 'Yes,' said Burke, '*there is a loss of friends*. I know the penalty of my conduct. I have done my duty at the price of my friend – our friendship is at an end.' Fox rose but was so overcome that for some moments he could not speak. At length, his eyes streaming with tears, and in a broken voice, he deplored the breach of a twenty years' friendship on a political question. Burke was inexorable. To him the political question was so vivid, so real, so intense, as to make all personal sentiment no more than dust in the balance.[16]

This profound disagreement between men as intelligent as Fox, Pitt, Grey, Sheridan and Burke on the issue of whether or not to welcome the French Revolution reveals the flaw in Burke's own philosophy that political parties were acceptable because, nine times out of ten, men sharing 'great, leading general principles'[17] would naturally tend to agree on matters of importance. When it came to the crunch, statesmen did not agree but changed political sides.

Nonetheless, the Burkean view came gradually to be accepted in that it was thought to be high-minded and based on principled beliefs. A claim to independence was compatible with this because those making the claim asserted that they were free from low or ulterior motives. This assertion was certainly based on wealth and social standing but also on an innate assumption of high principles. On the other side of the coin, independence did not mean a refusal to participate in altruistic joint action where issues of importance and principle were at stake.

This in turn led to the satisfactory conclusion that personal independence could be argued to be compatible with an increasing degree of party organisation and discipline. Thus political parties came to be accepted by individualistic and intelligent men who were paradoxically also ready to defend their personal judgement to the last.

I stress this point because the question I have had to answer most frequently is how our system of political parties, with the consequential and often heavy-handed whipping, is compatible with independence of individual judgement. Burke and his contemporaries started trying to find an answer to this in the reign of George III. Seriously divisive issues, such as support for the French Revolution, produced from the mid-1790s the beginnings of a progressive–conservative dichotomy in political opinion. During the reign of George IV and for a large part of Victoria's reign, after Prince Albert's death, the Crown essentially withdrew from politics. This meant that those naturally inclined towards conservatism (the Tories) ceased to regard themselves as necessarily attached to the Crown against a factious and difficult opposition (the Whigs). Instead, both sides saw the merits of an increasingly organised party as being the best hope for the survival and success of their ideals and ambitions. Thus by 1831 a Member of Parliament called Crocker was writing to Sir Robert Peel, 'Two parties are now generated which will never die', and the following year another Member, T. Raikes, was writing in his journal for 12 June 1832, 'such a season..., so little gaiety, so few dinners, balls and fetes. The political dissensions have undermined society and produced coolnesses between many of the highest families... The Tory Party think that a complete revolution is near at hand.'

Burke's insistence of the role of principle in politics may be said to have succeeded but only on the basis that 'truth is two-eyed.' In his *Essay on the English Constitution* Lord John Russell wrote in 1865, 'public affairs are so constituted that the truth scarcely ever lies entirely on one side.' By mid-Victorian times, partisans of both Whigs and Tories accepted that the other stood for genuine principles and were not taking a different view simply to be troublesome. The *Saturday Review* wrote in its issue of 28 February 1857, 'the opposite principles for which Pitt and Fox respectively contended had their source in an antagonism which is as perpetual as the laws of the human mind.' Thus it became possible to be a fervent party supporter, yet still principled and even, in a measure, to convince oneself that one was independent.

Until the 1830s there was little government legislation in the House. Treaties were approved or disapproved and there were a few Private Member's Bills – a Private Bill was needed until 1850 to get a divorce – but the King primarily used his Chancellor of the Exchequer and his Secretary at the Treasury as a means of raising money (supply) for his needs. In 1801 the post of secretary was split in two – the Parliamentary Secretary to the Treasury and the Financial Secretary. The Parliamentary Secretary to the Treasury became the official title of the Government Chief Whip. He was responsible for the circular letters requesting the presence of Members in the House, and these in turn came to be underlined with one, two or three lines, even at rare times, six lines, in order to emphasise the importance of the business that was to be discussed. This practice has continued to this day. Typically, a one-line whip will simply state the business for the day and add 'there may be divisions and your attendance is requested.' A two-line whip is much firmer: 'Your attendance is most particularly requested.' An example of a two-line whip, that for Edward VIII's Abdication Bill and signed by David Margesson, the Government Chief Whip of the day, is reproduced in the plate section of this book. Under normal circumstances, a one-line whip will be ignored by Members of Parliament unless they wish to take part in the day's debate. For a two-line whip, depending upon the majority of the government, a pair would in the past have been acceptable under which an opposition Member agrees with a government Member that neither of them will vote even if they are in the Chamber of the Commons listening to the debate. The present Labour government has, however, stopped this practice. A three-line whip, by contrast, requires attendance with no excuses being accepted. Typical wording will be 'Important divisions will take place and your attendance by 9.30 p.m. until government business is completed is particularly requested.'

John Hiley Addington, the Member of Parliament for Wendover, was the first appointment to the office of Parliamentary Secretary to the Treasury in 1801. It was not an immediate road to the top. It took him eleven years to rise to be under-secretary at the Home Office and, in the meantime, there were another six parliamentary secretaries to the Treasury, two of them for seven months only and none of them with distinguished ministerial careers.

This changed in 1832, the year of the first parliamentary Reform Bill. Charles Wood became Parliamentary Secretary to the Treasury having previously been private secretary to the Prime Minister, Grey. It is here that the story of the Parliamentary Secretary to the Treasury as Government Chief Whip effectively starts although the earliest contemporary reference to a parliamentary secretary as whip or whipper-in does not occur until 1839.[18] After two and a half years as Parliamentary Secretary to the Treasury Charles Wood went on to be Secretary to the Admiralty in 1835, Chancellor of the Exchequer in 1846, President of the Board of Trade in 1852, First Lord of the Admiralty in 1855 and Secretary of State for India from 1859 to 1866 when he was created Viscount Halifax. His last post was as Lord Privy Seal from 1870 to 1874 and he died in 1885. Thus his career spans the greater part of Victorian politics and, as Lord Halifax, he created a family dynasty that was to be very important in the 1930s and 1940s.

With the 1832 Reform Bill, and with the large additions to the electorate that it started, the concept of 'government' emerges – one which essentially relies on party support for survival and is relatively independent of the Crown. This inevitably leads to the increasing use of whips and of patronage to persuade Members of Parliament to come to Westminster and to do what the party wants them to do.

During the course of the years that followed, the Parliamentary Secretary to the Treasury became identical with the older, unofficial title of Patronage Secretary. This title was never officially recognised but it was frequently used, not least by John Biffen, (MP – and Secretary of State for Trade), with a mixture of irony and jest, when referring to me in the House of Commons during the year that I was Margaret Thatcher's last Chief Whip. For it was in the increasing spread of patronage – the ability to place friends in prestigious and well-paid jobs such as governor of remote cities in India and of states and provinces in Australia and Canada, to ease promotion in the army and navy and the church, to recommend for peerages and knighthoods and in gifts of money to help election expenses – that the growing importance of the Parliamentary Secretary to the Treasury lay.

As early as 1834 Robert Peel, the new leader of the Tory Party, referred to the position of whipper-in as 'the situation of all others the most confidential and important to me'. One symptom of this was that Peel issued dinner invitations on the advice of, indeed through, his whip. But Members of Parliament themselves were in two minds about whether the whipping function was or was not something that 'we should be better off without'. Whips were usually well liked personally but 'honourable members generally are very fond of snubbing whips'. Robert Peel in 1852 was quoted as saying that the post of the whip was 'a place which requires a gentleman to fill it and which no gentlemen would take'. One MP who was also a whip wrote in his diary for 9 August 1860 of 'men who are apt to treat the "whips" as if they were an inferior order of beings... worse still to believe that they are ready to perpetrate any trick or "dodge" for the benefit of their party'.[19]

The power and the accompanying notoriety of the whip increased throughout the mid-nineteenth century. Anthony Trollope, the master of clerical and political intrigue and himself an unsuccessful Liberal parliamentary candidate, wrote in 1873 of Phineas Finn, hero of two of his novels, developing conscientious scruples about supporting a measure to which his party is committed. The vote is approaching, and Finn meets in his club a young whip who insists that he should vote. Finn rambles on about his principles and receives a reply, 'Damn your principles, vote for your party.' The notorious reputation of the parliamentary whip had become part of the Westminster scenery.

Through the greater part of the nineteenth century there were only two secretaries at the Treasury, the parliamentary and the financial. A version of the 'Blue Notes', prepared by the Treasury to explain the Civil Service estimates and dated 1880–81, says this about the Treasury secretaries and their functions at that period.

The Secretaries ranked as first and second, the first being Parliamentary or Patronage Secretary, in direct subordination to the First Lord (the Prime Minister), and the second Financial Secretary, in direct subordination to the Chancellor of the Exchequer, as at present, only in early days the Parliamentary Secretary took a large share in the general correspondence of the office, which he does not now.

The 'Blue Notes' continued:

The Patronage Secretary

He is the Chief Government Whip, who administers the Secret Service Fund of 10,000 l. a year, under 1 Vict. c. 2, and in former days, distributed the patronage of the Treasury in the Revenue Departments and other subordinate offices amongst the nominees of supporters of the Government.

Patronage apart, the Patronage Secretary has nothing to do with ordinary Treasury business.

Financial Secretary

He is one of the hardest worked members of the Government. He has to attend the House more closely, and take charge of more Bills and Estimates that anyone else. He is very commonly the first lieutenant to the Leader of the House, answerable under him, and in conjunction with the Patronage Secretary, for the arrangement and due progress of the whole public business of the House.[20]

The words 'Secret Service Fund' produce a thrill of suspicion. This money was technically the King's private money. It was different from the Secret Service money paid to the secretaries of state and others. It was spent at the King's discretion and was not subject to any limit or to any form of audit. From the end of the seventeenth century, however, the custom grew that it was spent on the advice of the Lord Treasurer or the First Lord of the Treasury, and this convention inevitably added to the political strength of those who held these offices.

In 1782, the amount was limited by Burke's Civil Establishment Act, to £10,000 per annum, equivalent to around £1 million today.

Until 1837 it was paid out of the civil list and remained the King's money for which he gave his own receipt but on the accession of Queen Victoria this association was broken. The sum was removed from the civil list and made a charge on the consolidated fund, for administration directly by the Treasury. It was not abolished until 1886 and payments were always made exclusively to the senior secretary in the Treasury, that is to say the Parliamentary Secretary who doubled up as the Patronage Secretary. John Sainty writing in the *English Historical Review* for July 1976 produced a table, compiled from the Public Records Office, that showed that Charles

Wood, during his two and a half years as Patronage Secretary, received £22,500 of Secret Service money and Brand, who is the subject of the next chapter, received £72,500 between 1859 and 1866.

There is no specific description of how the Secret Service money was to be used except that the 'Blue Notes' for 1880–81 state that the annual sum of £10,000 was 'administered by the Patronage Secretary of the Treasury, and it was intended primarily to defray the expenses of the Treasury Whip.'[21]

There is no doubt that the cost of duplicating and circulating letters to government supporters, informing them what the business of the Commons was to be, cost money. A Treasury Clerk administered the business and the 'letter of notice to members of the House of Commons who support the administration'[22] was distributed by four carriers. However, Professor Hanham's researches have shown that the unexpended balance of the money received by a Patronage Secretary was kept by him and used to meet the expenses of his party when it went into opposition. The fact that the allowance of £10,000 a year did not all go on paying for circular letters to be issued to government supporters meant that once the Tory Party were out of office after the fall of the Wellington government they suffered financially from their relative exclusion from power during the next fifty years. Of the £529,500 disbursed as Secret Service money between 1830 and 1886, £380,000 (72 per cent) was received by Whip patronage secretaries and only £149,000 (28 per cent) by their Tory counterparts.[23] Of course, this will have had an effect in terms of party organisation but, even more important, the Patronage Secretary, as the distributor of this money, knew who had received it and what favours he could demand in return.

In this lay the core of the power of Government Chief Whips in both the nineteenth and twentieth centuries. They had patronage to dispose of, they knew who wanted what in terms of promotion, honours or money and, in addition to loyalties and ideology, this provided the cement with which to bind together political parties. One of the most surprising effects of the independent commission that Tony Blair has set up to recommend the names of cross-bench peers is that the Prime Minister is removing from his own grasp and from that of his Chief Whip one of the remaining fountains of patronage. An important question is whether the Prime Minister will be able to recover this heady influence in the case of either nominated or elected members of the Upper House. I discuss this in the last chapter.

The Secret Service money was the precursor of the large donations to political parties of the late nineteenth and twentieth centuries. It is surprising that this money lasted for so long and with little parliamentary criticism. This can only have been because opposition parties anticipated that, when they found favour with the ever-enlarging electorate and formed a government, then it would be their turn to receive the money. Too much criticism was therefore out of place.

SEVEN

Whipping with elegance –
Henry Brand 1859–66

In between resigning as Chancellor of the Exchequer in June 1783 aged twenty-four and being appointed Prime Minister by George III in December aged twenty-five, Pitt the Younger enjoyed 'the charms of advancing summer' at the Wimbledon villa of William Wilberforce. 'One morning,' Wilberforce wrote, 'we found the fruits of Pitt's earlier rising in the careful sowing of the garden beds with the fragments of a dress-hat with which Ryder (another friend) had overnight come down from the opera.' But, out of office and in addition to behaving like any well-connected young man of the day, Pitt found time to introduce a detailed plan for parliamentary reform.

It contained three resolutions. By the first the Commons would pledge themselves to take measures for the better prevention of bribery and excessive expenses at elections. The second provided that in any borough where the majority of voters were convicted of gross corruption the borough itself should be disenfranchised and the innocent minority would be entitled to vote for the county. By the third one hundred new members were to be created including an increase of representatives from London. The two joint secretaries of state took opposite sides. Fox warmly supported Pitt's plan and Lord North denounced it. When it came to a vote Pitt's resolutions were rejected by a large majority, 293 to 149. The Commons did not yet have any appetite to reform itself, although a year later they were willing to indulge in a vicious prosecution of Warren Hastings for charges of corruption in India.

Matters changed once the Napoleonic Wars had ended in 1815. The battle for parliamentary reform in Britain grew hotter. Lewes, the county town of Sussex and home of Thomas Paine, the author of *The Rights of Man*, was an example of this. Nestling in the Downs, it was host to a number of outspoken Whigs determined to oust the two local Tory MPs, Sir John Shelley and George Shiffner. The electorate was around 900, with the clerics, the lawyers, the doctors and bankers and their followers making up the Tory numbers and the tradesmen, the dissenters and the backstreet households making up the Whigs.

The local Whigs were strong supporters of Princess Caroline, the wife from whom the Prince Regent, the future George IV, had separated. When his Divorce Bill failed in the House of Lords, the people of Lewes rejoiced, church bells rang and the town band paraded. In the election of June 1826 Shiffner retired, having previously moaned at the cost of victory: 'Had I been aware of this, I certainly should have kept out of the business altogether.' Shelley succeeded in keeping his seat but it was the Whig, Thomas Reed-Kemp, who topped the poll with 569 votes to Shelley's 306. When Kemp's daughter married in 1829, the taverns were opened and free coal dealt out.

At the next election, in June 1830, after George IV's death Shelley and Kemp were again returned for Lewes but Wellington's government had lost popularity through resistance to parliamentary reform and making it possible for Roman Catholics to hold public office. A Whig resurgence brought Earl Grey to government. He, in turn, introduced the first Reform Bill of 1832 which started the process of increasing the numbers of those who had the right to vote. The forty-shilling freehold vote – a vote to every man who owned land that produced an income of forty shillings a year – was retained in the counties, but in the boroughs, the new centres of population, the vote was offered to the £10 householder, the man who occupied – either as owner or tenant of one landlord – buildings that had an annual value of £10. This was calculated by Lord John Russell, who introduced the Reform Bill in the House of Commons, to add 455,000 voters, more than doubling the previous number of voters.

In fact the actual increase in the number of voters was less than Russell expected;[1] in London, for example, the increase amounted only to 44,000

143

rather than the expected 95,000. In 1836, it was calculated that the total number of electors was now 813,000; but this was still a very considerable increase. As a result of the July revolution in France the qualification for the franchise was lowered from an annual income of 300 to 200 francs. In consequence, out of a population of 31 million, there were 160,000 who possessed the vote, one voter for every 200 citizens. In England, with a population of 24 million, by contrast there were now 800,000 voters, one voter for every thirty citizens.

It is hard for us, comfortable in the knowledge that every adult has a vote even if they do not bother to use it, to understand what excitement the extension of the suffrage aroused. Cobbett, the radical Tony Benn of his day, wrote thus in his popular *Political Register* about Russell's Bill:

> This measure is one the adoption of which will form a really NEW ERA in the affairs of England, aye, and of the *world* too: it will produce *greater effects* than any that has been adopted since the 'PROTESTANT REFORMA-TION': it will be called… 'THE REFORM', as the change made in the time of Henry VIII is called 'THE REFORMATION', and as that made in 1688 is called 'THE REVOLUTION'.

Jeremy Bentham, who for years had been committed to the reform of Parliament, died on the morrow of the 1832 Reform Act, having spent the last twelve years of his life working on a constitutional code 'whose object was the bettering of this wicked world, by covering it over with Republics'.

The Tories changed the official name of their party to Conservative but still only had 150 Members in the new House. In January 1833, Robert Peel, the defeated Prime Minister, was given the following estimate of the composition of the new House: Conservatives 150; Ministerialists 320; Radicals, Repealers etc. 190. Among them were thirty-three merchants and tradesmen and thirty-six bankers. Most were still country gentlemen and 'members of the aristocracy'. But nonetheless the overwhelming majority were committed to parliamentary reform and among these were a number of outspoken Radicals.

The reformed Parliament met for the first time in January 1833. The scene was described in a letter by one Conservative opponent of reform on 25 January: '…for two nights and a half the vehemence and disorder were so great that people began to think that the national convention was begun. Peel told me that it was "frightful – appalling".' Two years later it had not changed. Greville wrote in his memoirs for 4 April 1835:

> ...in better, or at least more gentleman-like, times, no noises were permissible, but the cheer and the cough... Now all the musical skills of this instrument is lost and drowned in shouts, hootings, groans, noises, the most discordant that the human throat can emit, sticks and feet beating against the floor. Sir Heworth Williamson, a violent Whig, told me that there were a set of fellows on his side of the House whose regular practice it was to make this uproar.

Four years later another Member of Parliament, Charles Thomson, wrote in his diary for 21 September 1839: 'I will give up the Cabinet and Parliament... The interruption and noise which prevails so much in the House *cows* me.'

Against this changing background of a Parliament moving from a general support of the status quo to one that was increasingly committed to parliamentary reform, and with representatives from the growing industrial boroughs – Birmingham, Leeds and Manchester – being constantly pushed for further extensions of the suffrage, the rapid development of party whipping was inevitable. Many of the old loyalties, based on blood relationships and the ownership of land, were strained by petitions from constituents, political unions and campaigns by the Radicals who wanted to move quickly towards universal suffrage and the secret ballot.

The Government Chief Whip emerged as the behind-the-scenes figure whose job it was to pull together the discordant elements in an increasingly rowdy House.

Sir Thomas Fremantle was a Conservative whip from 1837 and became the parliamentary secretary and Chief Whip when Peel won the 1841 election. In opposition he was expected to help those Conservative members who could not get to the House of Commons to vote. A letter to him from Eliot Yorke from Saint Germans, Cornwall and dated 1 May 1840 read:

> My dear Sir Thomas, I am very much obliged to you for your letter and my only reply is, that *I cannot make any arrangement to be up on the 6th May*. You

must therefore be good enough to pair me – even with a bad man – I sincerely hope that this is the last time I may have to trouble you – for I do not like being altogether absent from the House of Commons.

Eliot Yorke could not resist a bit of gossip about corruption in his area. His letter continued:

Totness will strengthen you with one vote. The bribery there has been, I am told, beyond precedent. There are two men little above the rank of common labourers who will swear that they were offered respectively the sums of £100 and £130 and three years' labour at a certain price per week if they would give their votes for Gisborne – and the intimidation was equal. One voter was carried out through a hole at the back of his house – made in the brickwork – to ensure his voting – the front door being besieged by the opposite party and the voter being in fear of his life. There is some thought of bringing this before the public... Pray let me know who is my pair. Very faithfully yours, Eliot Yorke.

The pressure increased when Peel was in office. A letter to Fremantle from James W. Lyon in the summer of 1844 read in part:

In East Gloucestershire, we are peculiarly circumstanced. Both our Conservative members are and have been absent... Lord Fitz Hardinge and all the Whigs are for fixed duty – in short, for any measure to embarrass the government.

It became necessary for someone to move the farmers – and, *faute de mieux*, I have been actively engaged for the last month in doing so thro' the medium of Peter Matthews, an influential Cotswold farmer who looks after my farms and property there and himself holds a farm at £1,000 a year.

We are to have a public meeting. They have written to me to prepare resolutions – these can easily be done but it is wished to go a step further – to present petitions from every Parish against any further alteration of the corn laws. Upon this latter point, I wish to have solicited your *personal* advice and, for that purpose, have called the Treasury, on Thursday, and yesterday –

I will wait again upon you this afternoon between 2.00 and 3.00 o'c in the hopes that you may grant me one minute's audience... I need hardly add that your counsel will be received in entire confidence – tho' it will guide me.

The Government Chief Whip's role came to be seen as one of the ways of catching the Prime Minister's ear. Lord Glengall wrote in September 1842 to Fremantle giving details about the patronage in Ireland. He not only complained about the amount of money and the number of people involved but also hoped that, if the matter were sorted out, the government might be able to get their hands on some of the proceeds.

My dear Sir Thomas, the following observations I have made to you several times in our hurried conversations. I now write them to you in order that if you think fit you may communicate them with Sir Robert Peel, for you may rely upon it that however the subject may be turned or twisted, there is perfect truth in what I remark.

I know 'the interior' of every department in Ireland and how its patronage is worked.

Almost all the patronage in the country is virtually in the hands of the various Boards – viz;

the Poor Law Commissioners – their patronage is enormous – Clerks have excellent salaries – Surveyors, Engineers etc., etc.

the Board of Works – the same as regard Engineers, Surveyors and Contractors. The great works carrying on, on the Shannon, give them very great patronage indeed – the Solicitors of these Boards receive sums, of which you can have no idea. Barrington received £18,000 for his legal experiences on the Shannon vide the parliamentary returns...

Glengall listed a number more of shocking examples and then ended his letter with the words:

of course I am aware that the Government has patronage to a certain intent in some of these Boards – and that the Acts of Parliament give the Boards the patronage in a variety of instances. Still I am certain that the Government by looking into the matter would be able to appropriate to themselves much more than they at present have, and that fairly.

I could say much more on this subject but I am sure you understand the case in all its bearings.

When Peel took office as Prime Minister in 1841 he found the deficit in the public finances for that year was estimated at well over £2 million. The solution that he proposed involved two changes to both of which he had previously been opposed: the restoration of income tax and the general reduction of protective duties. The first was intended to help achieve the second and from 1842 until 1845 the argument raged about the repeal of the Corn Laws of 1815. They prohibited the entry of foreign corn into Britain until the price at home reached 80 shillings for 4 hundredweight, with 67 shillings as the corresponding figure for wheat from the colonies. This was the measure that, a generation earlier, the landed interest in Parliament had fought for two years to achieve, but it was never a success. In spite of the Corn Laws the price of wheat fell from 71 shillings and 6 pence per quarter in March 1815 to 52 shillings and 10 pence in January 1816. There was no steady price for the home farmer as the quantity of imports and the quality of harvests varied widely.

In the Budget of 1842, a Budget as bold as Geoffrey Howe's in 1981 which abolished exchange control, Peel set about the reduction of import tariffs. Out of the 1,200 articles that were then subject to tariff 750 were reduced and, to make up the lost revenue, an income tax of 7 pence in the pound was introduced. Two years later Peel removed another 430 articles from the tariff list and many Conservatives with broad acres correctly feared that Peel might abolish the import duty on foreign corn. The spirit of this is captured in Peel's letter to his Chief Whip, on 25 November 1842 replying to a letter that Fremantle had sent him from another Conservative, Sir Charles Burrell:

My dear Fremantle, I came to Town last night and shall *remain* here for some days.

Sir Charles Burrell's letter surprises me. This is the *first* intimation I have had that the thanksgiving for a good harvest was deemed *inappropriate*. The wheat crop of Sir C. Burrell and three or four of his neighbours − who attend his parish church − failed, probably from want of draining and bad farming, and therefore we are not to thank God for a harvest which, considering the appearances and prophecies in May and June, was providentially good...

If Sir Charles had such cases before him, as I have before me, of thousands and tens of thousands in want of food and employment at Greenock, Paisley, Edinburgh and a dozen large towns in the manufacturing districts, he would instruct me to rend my garments in despair 'if some excellent jerkes of beef from South America' should get into the English market, and bring down beef from 7 ½ pence or 8 pence a pound... R. Peel.

The debates which followed on the question of whether to repeal the laws restricting the import of foreign corn and thus on the core question of protectionism against free trade, split the Conservative Party for two generations in the same manner as the issue of being part of closer European union divides the Conservative Party now.

When the final vote took place in May 1846, Peel had 231 Conservative backbenchers voting against him and only 112 with him. He commented that posterity would justify him but the young Disraeli, the brilliant, sarcastic rebel in Peel's own camp, remarked that posterity was a limited assembly 'not much more numerous than the planets'. 'Maintain the line of demarcation between parties,' Disraeli protested and that is what Peel signally failed to do.[2]

Six years later, the most respected Government Chief Whip of mid-Victorian times entered Parliament. He came from a charmed and influential background. His mother-in-law was Eliza, the natural daughter of Georgiana, Duchess of Devonshire, and of her great love, Earl Grey, the father of the 1832 Reform Bill.

Henry Brand became a Liberal Member of Parliament for Lewes in 1852. A generation earlier, his father, General Brand, had inherited Glynde Place, a handsome collection of buildings two miles outside Lewes, of Elizabethan origins with Georgian additions, a fine courtyard and a magnificent pair of gates. Brand then became the Liberal government's Chief Whip in June 1859 when Lord Palmerston was returned as Prime Minister. Gladstone was

Chancellor of the Exchequer, Russell Foreign Secretary and Sir George Grey Home Secretary. On 14 June 1859 he wrote to his wife Eliza:[3]

Dearest Izy

Matters are going on well and I have heard nothing about myself from Head Quarters, so that I am still not without hope that I may be spared to you & to my children.

I believe that Sir George Grey will be included in the Cabinet...

I suppose that no man ever was so indifferent about an office – value £2000 a year [£102,000 in today's money] – as I am – not that I am the least indifferent about the money of which I greatly stand in need.

Yrs HB

By the following day the news was different.

Dearest Izy

I am to be Secy to the Treasury – and my heart sinks into my shoes – while you are no doubt in a high state of exultation.

I have really no time for more at present. Gladstone is of the Cabinet at one end & Cobden [MP for Stockport and a chief advocate of free trade] is to have an offer at the other – but don't mention this till you see it in the Papers.

I do not much admire either of these appointments, but I think they are called for.

Everybody very civil about me & my office, but I confess that I feel very nervous.

Yr HB

Eliza and Henry Brand had eight children and even in the excitement of becoming Government Chief Whip he did not forget his family. On June 16 he wrote again to his wife:

Dearest Izy

I have very formidable work to begin with: attending meetings of the Cabinet & so forth. I write early lest in the hustle of the day I should not find a corner of time for you.

At 12 I am to meet the Cabinet at Cambridge House, at 3 Hayter upon various matters, at 4 to discuss the knotty point of Election Petitions.

I have ordered fish for 8 from Saturday till Tuesday both inclusive.

I will find Gerty [one of their daughters, aged 15] a present, if you will tell me what. Is it time for a watch? I may perhaps write again today.

Yr HB

Two days later Brand confides to his wife, 'I had a very satisfactory talk with Palmerston this morning, when we vowed mutual confidence and all that sort of thing.'

Brand remained Chief Whip and Parliamentary Secretary to the Treasury until July 1866 when, Palmerston having died two years earlier, Russell was defeated by a combination of Lord Derby in the Lords and Disraeli in the Commons. Ironically, Disraeli's second Reform Bill of 1867, many of the principles of which Brand had regularly supported, reduced the numbers of Members of Parliament for Lewes from two to one. Brand lost his seat, and gave up being Liberal Chief Whip, but was soon chosen instead as Member of Parliament for Cambridgeshire which he represented from 1868 to 1884.

Brand had the gift of inspiring confidence. He was never a member of Cabinet and only attended at the suggestion of the Prime Minister but his opinion was sought by Palmerston and then Russell on a wide variety of issues, and Gladstone, closer to him in age, consulted him continuously, ranging from the details of his Budget to the question of how to handle religious teaching in schools.

The *Northern Star* wrote of Brand on 2 April 1868:

any visitor to the lobby of the House of Commons, in the last 10 years, could not fail to remark amongst the gossiping crowds of members, who occupied the sacrosanct portion of this privileged hall, a gentlemanly little man, of rather urbane appearance and decidedly cool and collected manner.

Dressed to the very nicety of neatness, with an air of precision that in no way savoured of primness, but was rather the expression of what, for want of a better word, may be called correctness, he seemed one of those men who you might confidently approach if you had any business with him, but whom you would not for worlds approach through mere vanity or curiosity.

His well-cut features, well set off by a fresh ruddy complexion, which gave him a juvenile look not to be confounded with a jaunty air, irresistibly attracted attention and it was as impossible to avoid inquiring who he was, as it was to avoid stretching head and neck for a peep beyond the door which the elected alone could pass.

This was Mr Brand, the Secretary of Treasury, or as he was better known the whip of the Liberal Party. He lately resigned this responsible and laborious office, and on Saturday last leading members of his party, with Mr Gladstone at their head, assembled to pay him a tribute of respect, not unworthy of those who tended it or him who received it.

No one saw the late whip flushed or agitated or nervous. Always presenting the same tranquil aspect, he might be taken for the one indifferent member of the House for whom the fate of principles and the fortune of party had no concern... To Mr Brand's exertions must be attributed the union, such as it was, which availed in the Liberal ranks during the last five or six years. None but he could have kept the party together after the death of Lord Palmerston. His personal influence, his sound judgement, his amiable manners, won over many an intractable character, actuated by the least controllable of all motives – selfish ones... To appear calm and imperturbable is an essential quality for Chief Whips. Whatever may be going on in the Chamber in terms of noise, misunderstanding or protest, he, or she must sit on the front bench in the Commons looking like a contemplative Buddha.

The Tories in Sussex would not have agreed with all the comments in the *Northern Star*. The Christies lived, as they still do, a mile away from Glynde at Glyndebourne, and the Christie of the day was the leading Tory candidate for the parliamentary seat of Lewes.

At a local meeting of the Conservative Association at the White Hart Hotel, Mr Christie announced his intention of standing against Mr Brand. A Mr Baxter moved the resolution supporting Mr Christie and waxed eloquent about the Tory in comparison with the Liberal.

He is associated with us by every tie that we can value and esteem in an independent borough like Lewes. I must say I look on Lewes, my native town, as disgraced by Mr Brand; for this reason, we have lost our independence and we shall never regain it so long as he is our Member and holds the whipper-in-ship of the Whig party. He has no voice in the House of Commons, he cannot give an independent vote and he never has done so. Therefore if we would be an independent borough, if we would hold up our heads among our neighbours we would have an independent representative and not one who, as whipper-in, is necessarily bound and tied down to his party.

These charges came to no avail and Brand continued to hold the Lewes seat.

In government, Brand took his job as Patronage Secretary seriously. He was a principal source of honours and of paid employment in the public service. Some of the letters Brand received from his parliamentary colleagues asking for favours have survived as have some copies of his replies.[4] These are annotated carefully with the name of the letter writer, the date of receipt and the subject written in Brand's neat hand.

Lord Granard was a persistent applicant for favours. On 28 January 1863 he wrote from Castle Forbes:

Do you think there would be any chance of Lord Palmerston being induced to give the Governorship of the Isle of Man, which I perceive is vacant, for my brother, the reason I am anxious that he should get some appointment is that, from the course I took at the recent Longford election, his chances to success at any future election are much diminished.

I may mention that my brother served for 7 years in the army, and I consider that from the continued support I have always given to the present Government and their candidates that it *would* be no great stretch of favour to give him the appointment.

Two months later he was at it again with another letter to Brand.

I see, by the papers, that the Governorship of the Mauritius is vacant, and as I should be glad to serve in that capacity for a few years, I should feel greatly obliged if you would let me know if anyone is as yet designated for the vacancy, as, if not, I should apply to the Duke of Newcastle for it.

He got his come-uppance very quickly. Two weeks later, on 8 April 1863 Newcastle wrote to Brand:

> My Dear Brand, you had better tell this bumptious young Irishman that one who has been accustomed to Colonial Government for 30 years has been appointed to Mauritius – one of the most important and *therefore* best paid of the Governorships.
>
> His reason for not writing to me direct is no doubt that he took it upon himself to write about a year ago a very impertinent letter pointing out to me his opinion of my conduct in not appointing J Marshall to Antigua – a letter which of course I put behind the fire without answer.
>
> Yours sincerely, Newcastle.

Sir George Grey and his wife Caroline were friends of the Brands as well as political allies. Caroline Grey wrote one September around 1860:

> Dear Mr Brand, I have been wishing for some time passed to bring my cousin Edward Hamilton's name before you, lest you should forget in the midst of your many occupations how anxious he is to come into Parliament. Vacancies may occur unexpectedly, and you may be glad to remember a very clever man, whose great ambition is to have something to do, who will support the Government, and who does not mind spending money.
>
> Mr Edward Hamilton is brother to the present Bishop of Salisbury. He distinguished himself at Cambridge, studied and practised the Law and then went out to Australia where, with a brother of the Speaker's, he interested himself in managing a large Estate. He has now returned to England, and being of a very active nature tires with doing nothing.
>
> I think his name was brought before Mr Hayter sometime ago and probably Mr Gladstone may have mentioned him to you. Will you forgive my troubling you on the same subject also. He would, indeed, do honour to the cause, I feel sure, if he were fortunate enough to get a Seat as he is remarkably clever, well read, and extremely quick and ready in conversation on all topics of interest.
>
> This requires no answer, but oblige me by making a Mark on your tablets of the purpose of my request, please.

With love to Eliza and your belongings, I remain dear Mr Brand, yours truly, Caroline Grey.

One good turn deserves another. Lord Grosvenor wrote to Brand on 3 January 1863:

Mr Faulkner Lloyd, one of our Flintshire Squires or rather the eldest son of one, and one of the most active politicians on the right side in the county is very anxious to obtain some employment under government, suited to his age etc. Would there be the remotest chance of his being able to obtain a Commissionership of Tythes (and something else) which he understands is now vacant. He is a man about 45 years of age.

Would it be possible to do anything in the matter? He is well known to everyone in that quarter, Gladstone, my father etc., and I should be glad to help him. He seconded my brother at his nomination.

Peerages and church appointments were always at the heart of applications to the Chief Whip. A pathetic letter came to Brand from Cosmo Reid Gordon of Christ Church, Manchester:

I have now been in holy orders for seven years. I was senior curate to Canon Stowell, and for the past four years have had all but the sole charge of one of the most influential churches in this city. When I entered upon the duties, it was only half let, whereas now people are waiting for pews. About a month ago I was in the metropolis and saw about 40 Members of both Houses of Parliament, who are now using their influences on my behalf with the Duke of Newcastle and the Lord Chancellor. I did not meet with a single refusal but was told by many that had they known my wishes earlier, an independent sphere would have been obtained for me long ere this time. I believe you will also assist me in my efforts with these two Members of the present administration.

It may be some proof of acceptance that I am paid a salary unequalled by any other assistant clergyman in the church. I have declined chairs in Scotch and Irish Colleges, preparing clerical work... Most of my friends seem desirous that I should go out to the colonies, as they state difficulty has sometimes been experienced in finding bishops of sufficient literary standing and parochial influence for the different posts as they become vacant.

Brand, presumably, wrote back regretting that he could not help, for, four days later, Gordon writes again:

> I regret that my former note was not sufficiently explicit on the matter about which I troubled you last Friday. I quite understood that you had no clerical patronage to dispose of but the fact of your knowing me and your being kind enough to write to the Duke of Newcastle or the Lord Chancellor as a private Member of the House and not as the Patronage Secretary of the Treasury was all that I desired. If I am not too troublesome, I will feel greatly obliged for this favour, as your recommendation would have great weight.

Irish peers were not unlike suppliant clergymen. They wanted to move up the ladder to full-blown United Kingdom peerages, which would automatically enable them to sit in the House of Lords. The letter that follows from Lord Gort contains a pleasant little hint of blackmail. If he were only elected as one of the Irish representative peers, he might well have to support Derby, the Tory leader, but if he were chosen to be a United Kingdom peer then matters would be different. He wrote to Brand from 12 Merrion Square North in Dublin in March 1866:

> I understand it is intended forthwith to confirm peerages of the United Kingdom upon several Irish noblemen. In the present anomalous position of the Irish peerage, such a decision appears probable and judicious – and in case I am rightly informed, I wish to say a few words about myself.
>
> My opinions have always been moderate and I took little part in politics during my father's life – but since Sir Robert Peel's death I have invariably given my humble support, in Limerick and elsewhere, to the Liberal Party – my father only held the representative peerage for four months, and from this circumstance my claims upon it appear strong to some of my friends. But from the existing system, if elected, I would be bound in honour to support Lord Derby, which I will not do. At the same time I do not think I am self-sufficient if I believe that my presence in the House of Lords would

be useful − the unusual difficulties with which I had to contend for many years, though now happily succeeded by present independence and bright future prospects, have given me a detailed knowledge of railway matters, commercial finance and cognate subjects, which is much wanted in dealing with the vast map of private business that comes yearly before Parliament but with which, though familiar to many in the House of Commons, a wealthy hereditary body like the Peers can hardly ever acquire more than a very superficial acquaintance.

You know me I think well enough to understand my motive in writing, and to feel that I do not seek a seat in the House out of vanity, but with the intention and hope of using it with some benefit to the public, and some advantage to my political friends.

The requests for permission to be away from the House of Commons have not changed from the nineteenth century to the present day. Thus Mr Gilpin writing to Brand from the Bedford Hotel in Brighton on 23 January 1860:

I am *slowly* making my way out of a long and severe illness, and my medical men positively prohibit my being in my place in Parliament.

They speak, however, with great confidence of my being able in a few months to go through my duties as usual.

Now will you kindly ask for leave of absence for me for a short time (say six weeks) and would it be possible to get me a good 'Pair' for that time? I hope to keep you furnished with my address, and in case of need would do my best to come from any part of the kingdom for a critical division.

I am reminded of the backbencher who recently wrote to the Chief Whip asking to be excused for missing a vital three-line whip with the words, 'I got so carried away by the discounts at the Army and Navy sales that I forgot about the vote.'

The letters from Gladstone, as Chancellor of Exchequer, flowed regularly. On 26 March 1864 he wrote to Brand:

In dealing the figures of my budget which I expect will make a pretty tight fit, I shall, bearing in mind what has passed between us, assume that income tax is a better horse to ride than fire insurance duty: and at the same shall anxiously enquire whether any mitigation of the latter subject, at a moderate cost, can be desired, which will enable those who have a disposition generally friendly to make a stand against the agitation in future, until greater and more urgent matters should be disposed of.

If you have more to say on this, please let me see or hear from you.

On 4 January two years later, a few months before the Liberal defeat on electoral reform, Gladstone writes to Brand about 'treasury arrangements on which we have conferred at great length'. He then adds: 'the conflict between the Principles of Good and Evil (I forget which *you* represent) about the Treasurer of County Court is now in the hand of Russell. Happy New Year to you and Mrs Brand.'

More serious was the possible rebellion in 1861 by fifty-one Liberal Members of Parliament on the question of defence expenditure. Led by Morley and Cobden, they signed and sent Palmerston on 15 January a letter requesting that government expenditure should be reduced in the following session. They pointed out, in particular, that 'the country was not engaged in an European war' and thus 'a great responsibility will rest on the Government and the House of Commons if it [expenditure] should not be materially reduced at the earliest opportunity.' The letter concentrated on the peace that existed between Britain and the rest of the world.

The foreign relations of the country at the close of the year are such as to encourage a reasonable confidence in the maintenance of peace. The war with China is at an end. The Italian revolutions appear to be issuing in the establishment of the constitutional rule of Victor Emmanuel over the Peninsula, whilst the neutrality which has been observed by England is acknowledged both at home and abroad to have been the policy of wisdom.

Above all our relations with France have become decidedly amicable having obtained the guarantee of a commercial treaty favourable to the interests of both countries, and being made still more friendly by the abolition on the part of the Emperor of the passport system in France specially on behalf of the subjects of Her Majesty.

Under these circumstances the country will naturally expect a considerable reduction of our warlike establishments from the extraordinary scale of the present year.

Palmerston reacted with style. He wrote immediately to Brand on the very same day:

as to the Morley memorial which was written by Cobden and sent over to Morley it can only be looked upon as a declaration by those who sign it as a want of confidence in the Government.

It is a leap in the dark at the bidding of that political fanatic Cobden who proposed once in the House of Commons that England and France should send their fleets into the middle of the Channel and there burn them so that the French might be able to invade us whenever they chose without our having any armed ships to resist them. But the true meaning of the memorial is that we should have no more rifled muskets, rifled cannon, iron ships or defensive work, that we should have no sufficient army or navy, that we should cease to be an influential power in the world, that Spain should have Morocco; France, Egypt, Syria and the Rhine; Russia, Constantinople and European Turkey; that our commerce should be shut out from the Mediterranean. That we should hold our existence as a nation at the goodwill of France and Russia, and that we should sink down to the object of contempt and derision to the nations of the world.

Whatever the foolish people who sign the memorial should fancy or ask, I will never be responsible for such a state of Things, and I am quite sure that a nation that has turned out 150,000 volunteers will back up a Government resolve to maintain it in a state of sufficient defence.

I can hear Margaret Thatcher expressing similar sentiments in a defence debate in the Commons to anyone who advocated that we should not try to recapture the Falklands from the Argentinians.

Brand replied five days later with a typical whip's caution. First he dealt with recommendations for a Lord Lieutenancy, then he got onto the serious business.

With regard to the retrenchment address, it was no doubt conceived in mischief by Cobden and Bright but it has been signed by many of our friends... with no desire to embarrass your Government or to mark want of confidence. They ought to have known better.

He enclosed a list of those who had signed and then continued:

I have marked with a capital X those who may have signed from *mischief*. The others have, as I think, signed from foolish motives but may be roughly depended upon. I understand that Crawford and Baines have been deputed to present the address to you...

I entirely agree with you as to the feeling of the country about defences. But I should not be disposed to treat this address to you as an expression as a want of confidence. I should rather regard it as an abstract declaration in favour of economy, but not intended to fetter the discretion of the Government in providing against dangers abroad and at home.

It may indeed be so intended by Bright, Cobden and Co but not, I am persuaded, by a majority of the men who have signed and to these I should like to give a lesser intention.

Later in the same year Brand obviously felt that he has gone too far on a matter of patronage and, in combining the roles of Patronage Secretary and junior Treasury minister, he might have offended the Prime Minister. On 6 December he wrote a private letter from Glynde:

Dear Lord Palmerston, I signed yesterday at the Treasury a memorandum for transmission to you, through Ashley, on the case of Mrs Deans, whom Lady Dunmore and others recommended for a situation in Edinburgh.

I am much annoyed that through inadvertence in my department your wishes in favour of Mrs Deans have been overlooked.

I submit for your consideration that it would not now be desirable to appoint her to the situation – firstly because the Commissioners of the Inland Revenue have, with the sanction of the Treasury, placed another person in the situation; and, secondly, because it appears from the report of the Comptroller General of the Inland Revenue, at Edinburgh, made in October last, that Mrs Deans is not well qualified for the situation.

It seems to me that it would be very awkward, to say the least, to dismiss a person who is in charge of a situation, nominated by the Commissioners of the Inland Revenue, with the sanction of the Treasury, and to put in her place a person who has been reported upon as unfit by the officers of the Inland Revenue department.

I think you would be better to reserve the first vacant appointment of the Board for Mrs Deans.

However, I must leave this entirely to your better judgement, and must confess to being ashamed at having to trouble you about such a trifle at a time when so many weighty matters are before you.

Brand did not get away with this. The very next day Palmerston replied in a hand that is far more shaky than his letter at the beginning of the year but with a spirit that is still formidable.

I cannot allow myself to be tricked and foiled by a combination of underlings – I was repeatedly told upon enquiry through my private secretary that Mrs Deans would be appointed the moment the office became vacant and in consequence of such information I repeatedly told Lady Dunmore that Mrs Deans had been put into the office; in consequence of that report I wrote to that effect to Lady Dunmore.

I will *not* stand being made a fool of by a lot of intriguing subordinates, and I must positively insist upon my promise being kept. Pray see that this be done forthwith.

After his signature, Palmerston added a postscript: 'as to Mrs Deans not being fit, that is all nonsense, the whole thing is a Scotch job in favour of some friend or relation of the local people.'

A year later, in an even shakier hand, Palmerston wrote to Brand about a candidate for a Kent parliamentary seat:

...as to Doring he seems to be a most inveterate jobber, and he wants Kent to turn up trumps on both sides of the card. Some time ago he wanted to get a peerage on condition that he should not stand for Kent, and now he wants to extort a peerage as a condition on which he should be willing to stand. Pray tell him he must do what he likes about standing but that I cannot hold out to him any expectation of a peerage whether he stands or not. There are plenty of better and sounder men for the House of Lords when recruits may be wanted for that branch of the legislature.

In October 1863 Gladstone wrote from Hawarden to Brand about the budget for 1865–6 and the possibility of the total repeal of income tax. When Peel reintroduced this tax in 1842, it was at a rate of only 3 per cent and Peel stressed it was intended as a temporary tax only. Gladstone filled five pages with detailed handwritten calculations but concluded that the expected deficit of £1¼ million in 1865–6 was too great. He then wrote:

> I do not think this difficulty, or this deficit, would exist if the country were possessed with a really strong spirit of economy; but at present we still seem not much less remote from such a state than from one of great enthusiasm for the enlargement of the elective franchise... I am very glad that these calculations, rude and of necessity questionable as they are, should be in your hands, for the Parliamentary Secretary has more power to give the effect of them than the man who fills my office.

The issue that dominated Brand's time as Chief Whip was, in Gladstone's words, the enlargement of the elective franchise. Brand had always been a reformer but one who recognised that increasing the number of those who had the vote, by reducing the amount of annual income or of property-value that they had to show in order to get on to the electoral roll, was much easier to get through the Commons than changes in the distribution of seats. The first was a matter of general principle and followed on from the first Reform Bill of 1832. The second directly affected the interests of individual members of Parliament, their patrons and their lives. When some Members looked at a Reform Bill that both increased the number of voters and disenfranchised a number of small boroughs, they saw that they would lose their seats and they threatened to vote against the measure.

As early as December 1859, six months after Palmerston's victory over Derby, Brand as Chief Whip was writing to Sir George Grey.

I am uneasy at the disposition which seems to me to be gaining ground to make your Reform Bill too strong.

The House don't want a strong bill, and in this respect it certainly represents public opinion. It would certainly reject a strong bill, and you could not venture to appeal to the country on such a cry. If you did, it is my belief that you would set up the Tories for the rest of our lives.

But, you will say, what constitutes a 'strong' bill?

Well, the debate on the bill of '59 pretty clearly showed how much or how little that House was prepared to stomach. The present House is still more squeamish. That House demanded a larger enfranchisement of persons – a £6 franchise in boroughs being clearly pointed out, but there was no cry for a larger disfranchisement of places.

In fact the limited disfranchisement of places very nearly floated the bill of '59 through the House, not withstanding its gross defects, while the large disfranchisement of places of the bill of '54 wrecked that measure. Take care you don't get wrecked upon the same rock.

You may indulge with impunity in a further extension of the franchise beyond £6 rating provided you can show by your returns that the standard which you take will not in the aggregate swamp the existing constituencies.

But a larger disfranchisement of places is a dangerous experiment.[5]

Palmerston died in October 1865. His life, a member of the Reform League Executive remarked, was a security against the introduction of a measure of franchise reform. He was succeeded by the elderly Russell while Gladstone took over leadership of the House of Commons. By contrast, Russell was reputed to have been carrying a Reform Bill in his pocket for the last ten years. Brand clearly thought that he would have even more influence over Russell than over Palmerston. Within days he was in touch with him about possible changes in the Cabinet.

On 28 October 1865 he wrote:

Dear Lord Russell, the more I think of the proposal that DeGrey and Cardwell should change places, the less I like it.

The objections to it are: (1) both men are doing their work well in their respective places, Cardwell having a special and important work in hand – the

Confederation Project; (2) both would be unwilling to change; (3) we should suppress Hartington who among the young men ought to be brought forward; (4) we should gain no actual strength on the Treasury bench in the House of Commons.

It is true that the Government boats do require trimming there being too much weight among the Lords; but the true remedy for this state of things lies in throwing a Peer overboard – a most unpleasant remedy no doubt.

I don't think that it is absolutely necessary that this remedy should be applied at present – perhaps not at all – but you ought to be prepared to apply it in the event of public opinion settling strongly against the present distribution of offices in the House of Commons. On the whole I should recommend suspension of action in this matter for the present.

By early 1866 there was strong opposition within the parliamentary Liberal Party to any further franchise extension. A group of thirty Liberal MPs, led by the anti-reformer Lowe, promised to support the Conservative opposition in defeating the government if it brought forward any measure on the subject.

'What sort of a measure do you mean?' Sir Charles Adderley, a Conservative, asked of Lowe before Gladstone introduced a mild Reform Bill on 12 March.

'Any bill that lowers the borough franchise by one sixpence,' replied Lowe. He soon gathered around him more than thirty disgruntled Liberals whom John Bright, the Quaker industrialist of Rochdale, a great orator and moraliser, christened the 'Adullamites' – 'a sullen cabal cowering in the darkness of a small cave'.[6]

Gladstone's Bill extended the county franchise to include tenants paying an annual rent of £14 or more and the borough franchise was to be lowered from £10 to £7 annual rent. The right of voting was also given to men who had had a deposit of at least £50 in a savings bank for two years. Gladstone's relative moderation did not satisfy the anti-reform Liberal group. They kept the government majority down to a mere five votes on the second reading of the Bill.

Gladstone and Russell then introduced a separate Redistribution Bill in May that was again purposely moderate in tone. Small boroughs were not to be abolished altogether but 'grouped' together in larger units: Woodstock, Wokingham and Abingdon, for instance, were to become one constituency with two Members. But the Liberal government was now tottering over the question of the extension of the franchise. Brand was at the heart of the discussions. He wrote to Russell, the Prime Minister, on 3 June 1866:

> I hear that a movement is afoot among your supporters to wait upon you on Tuesday with a request that the Reform Bill be postponed. I have no doubt that they will give expression to what are believed to be a general wish both inside the House and out of it that, while the Bill is postponed, the Government should not resign.
>
> It seems to me that the Government would suffer much discredit, and the character of public [opinion] may be lowered if you were to acquiesce in the withdrawal of the Bill unless you were sustained by a distinct vote of confidence.
>
> I think that such a vote might be just carried, although I have not ventured to consult anybody upon the subject, and my object in writing to you now is to suggest that the movement above named should be directed to that end, if you approve of the idea of a vote of confidence.

Brand then went on to mention the views of Gladstone whom he had seen that morning. 'He is in favour of pressing the franchise clauses, and is not clear that we can properly retain office, even with a vote of confidence until those clauses have been passed.'

Russell replied on the same day from Pembroke Lodge in Richmond Park. 'I am convinced that there is no use in pressing the franchise clauses. The alternative is between a vote of confidence and postponement or resignation. I prefer the last, but will not insist if my colleagues think otherwise.' The Chief Whip clearly thought otherwise. He wrote again to Russell on 20 June.

> I have gone over the constituencies of E and I [England and Ireland] name by name and I have made an estimate of the several places where we might gain or lose by dissolution. The list is enclosed. You will see that I estimate 24 losses and 16 gains. We should thus be, if my estimate is correct, 8 seats worse off than we are now.

I put our present strength in round numbers at 320, resting upon the division of Monday last; we should thus be reduced to 312... I feel bound, however, to add my strong opinion that a dissolution at the present crisis would be a fatal mistake. I believe that it would go far to destroy the popularity which justly attaches to the Government, and that it would be the making of the Conservatives for many years.

Brand's argument had two strands to it. First, as Chief Whip, he calculated that the Liberal Party would lose seats at a general election. Second, as a politician, he believed in an extension of the franchise and wanted a Second Reform Bill to be the hallmark of a Liberal government rather than a Conservative one.

The debate came to its height on 23 June 1866. Brand sent Russell a draft parliamentary resolution which Sir George Grey had approved but about which Gladstone still had doubts. The terms were precisely those which a Chief Whip, anxious for his government to stay in office, might have drafted at any time:

That in the present state of public affairs both at home and abroad, this House would see with regret any change in the Councils of Her Majesty.

That this House has pronounced no opinion adverse to the principles of the extension of the franchise and the increase of the representation of populous counties and towns on which the Bills for the amendment of the representation of the people introduced by Her Majesty's Government are based; but is of (the) opinion that it is not advisable to proceed further with these Bills in the present session of Parliament.

That this House, however, is anxious for an early settlement of this important question, and with this view will be ready to take into consideration any measure which Her Majesty's Government may introduce in a future session founded on the principles and leading provisions of the measures introduced by H.M. Government during the present session.

Brand added, with a tone of desperation coming into his letter:

having failed to find you in C. G. [Carlton Gardens] I have consulted G. [Gladstone] about the resolution. He adheres, as you will see by his memorandum, within, to the precise terms agreed upon at the Cabinet yesterday.

Sir G. Grey has seen the resolution and approves.

I am thus placed in a most embarrassing position, for I expect to see several friends today upon this subject of a vote of confidence, and I am without instructions how to deal with them. I cannot in the face of G's opinion tell them to go forward. In the meantime, the hours are slipping away fast, and it will soon be too late to organise a resolution. Our supporters should be summoned tonight for a meeting on Monday, if the movement is to be made at all.

As to a dissolution at the present juncture, my opinion grows stronger every day. It would be fatal not only to the Government but would break up the Liberal Party and throw back reform many years.

I trust that you will not advise it and that, if you do, you will release me from taking any part in it; for I could not be a party to an act which I firmly believe is opposed to the true and lasting interests of the country. I am fully alive to the great responsibility which I take in making this statement, but there are times when men must speak out, and I am bound to do so now.

Geoffrey Howe, when he made his resignation speech in the Commons in October 1990, echoed the theme that 'there are times when men must speak out, and I am bound to do so now.'

Brand did not convince Russell who wrote back on the same day:

with respect to dissolution, I shall state to the Cabinet my opinion that it is the right course to take, but I shall not propose it to the Queen unless they all agree – which they will not.

Indeed, I am resolved no longer to lead unless the Whig and Radical wings of the party agree to support me. By the Whigs, I mean the Whig portions of the 306 – the other 44 I give up.

But then unless some 10 of the 44 return to us we can have no majority and must resign.

I think you must ask some prominent men whether they will vote for such a resolution as I now return to you. If not, I will not accept their resolution as justifying our remaining in office with the present Parliament. Yours truly, Russell.

Russell added a footnote with a different pen. 'You are quite right, with your opinion, to resign in case of a dissolution – but we shall all linger together.'

Brand immediately acknowledged Russell's letter, doubting that the Liberals would have a sufficient majority on a vote on a resolution 'to float us through the crisis'. In the same letter he did not forget his patronage duties. He proposed that Sir James Matheson was a very proper man for the Lord Lieutenant of Ross-shire and added, 'I enclose a few names for baronetcies.'

Gladstone disagreed with Brand's tactics. He wrote to him the following day.

I say it without the least doubt that in my opinion the resolution is inadmissible. It certainly specifies reduction in lieu of extension of suffrage; but it in no degree alters or advances the position of the House of Commons as compared with that which it held in February, in other words it throws the session's work away.

Brand's health cracked under the strain. A day later Gladstone wrote to him, 'I am extremely sorry to hear of your illness,' and continues, 'the Cabinet will not accept, I believe, anything which merely recognises reform as apart from (not all but any of) the votes and proposals of this session.'

But time had run out and two days later the arguments were finished. An Adullamite, Lord Dunkellin, introduced a motion to substitute a narrower town suffrage than that the government proposed. Russell was defeated by eleven votes (315 to 304) and resigned. He wrote from 37 Chesham Place, Belgrave Square, to Brand. His priorities, and the order of precedence that he gives to subjects, are interesting.

Dear Brand, I submitted the names you mention to the Queen yesterday together with some other. The Queen told me today that she would write to me upon the subject, so that I cannot give you any information till the Queen has decided. The Queen has asked Lord Derby to undertake to form a government, and to report in person to Her when he has anything to tell.

Thus the Liberal reign ended and Derby and Disraeli with an overall minority of seventy took office. The Chief Whip had failed to keep the parliamentary Liberal Party together: the division over franchise reform was too great. The challenge and the prize of getting a Second Reform Bill through the Commons became Disraeli's.

On 5 July 1866 Russell wrote to Brand:

I am glad to tell you that as a last act of power I advised the Queen to make you a Privy Councillor. Her Majesty at once assented and I trust you will be able to go down with us [to Windsor] tomorrow at 12.15 from Paddington Station. Had we carried the Reform Bill and you had retired, it was fully my intention to have proposed that the Privy Council should open its doors to you.

Brand duly went to Windsor and was sworn of Her Majesty's Most Honourable Privy Council, an honour that meant more in Victorian times than, sadly, it does today.

Two weeks later Brand spoke in his constituency at the inauguration of the Lewes Liberal Registration Society and he was quoted in the local paper, the *Sussex Advertiser*:

I feel very strongly that it is in consequence of the disunion of the Liberal Party that the Liberal Party does not at this moment guide the administration of public affairs. I am not disposed to say of that body of men who recently severed themselves from the Liberal Party that they are all opposed by conviction to Liberal principles but I am disposed to look upon some of them, not all, as stray sheep who may come back to the fold [renewed cheers].

But all was not gloom. The local Liberals organised festivities and a massive tea party on the Mount Field in Lewes, next to the railway station. The newspaper reporter enjoyed himself:

To supply hot water for a picnic on an ordinary scale is sometimes found a troublesome task, but where 'a small tea party' of 1,200–1,500 is concerned, it becomes a rather arduous undertaking. To improvise a tea-kettle of sufficient capacity was one main point and this was accomplished... a locomotive and boiler were pressed into the service – forming, it must be admitted, a tea-kettle as novel as that was admirably suited for the object. [Fireworks followed] The final piece, displaying the words Brand and Pelham in white diamond and crimson fire, was very beautiful.

Lord Pelham was Lewes's second MP.

The Chief Whip's problems with the rebel Adullamites, like those of John Major's whips with the Maastricht Treaty rebels and the No Turning Back Group, refused to go away. Russell asked him on 22 July: 'What sort of Reform Bill would not cancel their capacity for digestion?'

Brand replied to Russell from Glynde:

> I will sound the Adullamites as far as I can; but the truth is most of them look upon reform as naughty children do on physic. They will not believe that they will be the better for what they don't like and would throw it out of the window if they were not afraid of their constituents. I expect that Disraeli will present us with a bill nearly if not quite as large as ours.
>
> I agree with you as to our cause. If he brings in a bill, we will shape it as best we can in committee. If you don't, we should raise the question by resolution.

He added as a footnote: 'I am going to Aix La Chapelle on Thursday, having been advised to go there to wash out the effects of the Crisis, from which I still suffer a good deal.'

Brand's prophecy quickly proved correct. Soon after the new government took over, Lowe, the Liberal rebel who had helped them into power, wrote to his brother, 'I hold Bright and his mob in such sovereign contempt that I require no external support to fortify me against their abuse. What I am afraid of is your friends *the Tories*, and above all, Dizzy, who I verily believe is concocting a very sweeping bill.'

Within six months, Disraeli, previously all for delay, had come to the conclusion that the right procedure for his party to follow was to introduce some general resolutions on reform and then quickly to proceed to a Reform Bill. It was, of course, at this moment that the Liberals realised that the Tories were stealing their clothes. Equally, a number of them were suspicious of Gladstone's leadership in opposition. Forty or fifty Liberal Members of Parliament, meeting in the tea room of the House of Commons (the typical place for such plots to be started) decided to oppose Gladstone. They included a sprinkling of Adullamites, a radical group led by Henry Fawcett, and several Russell Whigs 'who cannot bear Gladstone as their leader'.[7] The Adullamites were afraid of 'a coming democracy and trades union tyranny'; the Radicals wished 'to get the largest measure of reform whether it should come from the hands of the Government or from the Opposition'. Disagreed though they were in their principles, the members of the 'Tea Room' group were successful in checking Gladstone at this early stage in the story of the Bill. 'This was the first real breach in the defences of an opposition which had to remain united if it had any chance of success'.[8] On paper the Liberal opposition still had a large majority but they failed to make use of it.

The pleasant surprise of finding themselves in government brought the Conservatives together.

> Derby made a powerful plea for unity, calling a meeting of Conservative peers at his London house where he told them not only that the bill was the most Conservative measure that could be adopted and had the almost unanimous support of the House of Commons, but that his objects for the whole of session had been 'to act so as to place the Tory Party permanently in power and not to place them in a position to be beaten as soon as they have served the purpose of the Opposition'.[9]

He wanted to break the deadlock of the previous twenty years and he succeeded. The Second Reform Bill passed through the Commons being strengthened as it went, and then passed the Lords with few important changes.

Brand's career as Government Chief Whip ended with the defeat over the 1866 Reform Bill. George Grenfell Glyn was marked out by Gladstone as Brand's potential successor as Liberal Chief Whip but in a letter to Brand of 13 August 1866 Gladstone wrote:

> I am fearful about Glyn. His father begged us we would not press for an answer, to which request for time I answered as he willed. But rumours of his [illness] at a moment's interview that I had with him were not very encouraging. In the *present* state of the party, these duties are far greater *even* than their ordinary importance and I am anxious about the result. I suppose that it is best to say nothing to F. Cavendish until we know who the chief is to be.

Cavendish was private secretary to Gladstone. He rose to become Chief Secretary and was murdered in 1882 in Phoenix Park.

Brand was watched closely by the press to see which way the Liberal Party in opposition would turn on the issue of a Tory Reform Bill. One newspaper reported, 'the principal whips [of the Liberal opposition] have opportunely lashed the life out of a whole flight of canards in reference to the internal condition of his party.' 'Mr Brand has been closely watched throughout the recess by those who attach unlimited importance to the doings of the highly placed…' The Liberals 'were not going to be again led into a tight place by Mr Gladstone'; the regular supporters of the government 'had had enough of it'. The alliance of Russell and his principal colleagues with the Radicals had 'disgusted everybody'.

In February 1867 Brand made another speech to his Lewes constituents in which he obliquely criticised the rebels in his own party.

> The Cave of Adullam sent out some gloomy and discontented spirits, and they, in an unholy alliance with the Tory Party, made an end of the measure. If I had to write the epitaph of the Reform Bill of 1866, I should say that it was a bill which even its enemies admitted to be honest and it was lost owing to the defections of those who ought to have been its friends.

Thus Brand himself, despite being a hardened Chief Whip, was willing to support a Bill that dealt with the enlargement of the franchise no matter whether it was introduced by the Liberal Prime Minister Russell or the Tory Prime Minister Derby. It was this broadness of spirit that put him in line to become Speaker of the Commons after Gladstone returned to power as Liberal Prime Minister at the end of 1868.

The possibility was first raised with him by Glyn, now Government Chief Whip. Brand wrote to Glyn on 31 May 1870.

> I have been detained here [Glynde] today which I am sorry for as I should have liked to see you to correct what I said to you too lightly yesterday. On reflection, I ought not to be so idle as I painted myself. I should never seek office and be quite content (probably more content) without it. If I can be of service I should be a coward to shirk work. Having so far retracted what I said

yesterday, I wish to add that if you ever think of me, it must be on public ground, for I don't wish for office upon any other grounds.

You mentioned the Speakership. I question whether I should be big enough either in body or mind for so higher a place. Be that as it may, I adhere to what I said yesterday – on public grounds I should if I were your place give the preference to Bruce above all others. In a matter of this moment, we must not consider persons. Bruce will never succeed as Home Secretary; but I think he will make a good Speaker.

Eighteen months later the matter moved on and Gladstone, as Prime Minister, decided to nominate Brand to be Speaker. Brand wrote to Gladstone at 10 Downing Street on 10 November 1871:

Dear Mr Gladstone, I am your willing servant and will do all in my power to justify your choice. I had hoped to have seen you tomorrow to tell you this face to face but I am unexpectedly to see tomorrow a solicitor in the neighbourhood who is very ill; so I take leave to write.

If you wish to see me after tomorrow, I will attend your summoning when and where you please. In the meantime, I will mention the matter to no one nor have I mentioned it except to my wife who, although a woman, can keep a secret.

Brand and his wife, Eliza, had by now been married for thirty-two years.

Gladstone replied the following day: 'My Dear Brand, I have received your letter with great pleasure. We propose to keep the whole matter secret as long as we can.' At Christmastime Brand told his friends. One of them, J.P. Bouverie, wrote back:

My Dear Brand, I got your letter this morning and it was just like yourself, which is the highest praise I can give, to write to me as you have done. You deserve any post or employment or like and so I am heartedly glad… I will not say that I have not had aspirations for the chair myself – but I can honestly say that that does not make me for a moment grouch seeing *you* there – which I should have done as to anyone else – and *I quite approve* of your saying yes. I think I may possibly be able to help you occasionally – especially till you get well into your saddle – and I think you know that all I can do, be it little or much, to make your duties less troublesome or trying, will be done by me *with a will*. My best congrats to the Mrs and a Merry Xmas to you all.

John Bright, the reforming scourge of Palmerston, was asked by Brand to propose him for the Speakership. Bright replied from Rochdale on 26 January 1872.

Dear Mr Brand, you pay me a high compliment where you ask me to propose you, and I value it as it deserves to be valued. I would undertake the office if I were well enough to do so but, unfortunately, I dare not attempt to speak at present, and it is uncertain if I shall be able to be in the House at its meeting. My nerves have not yet recovered their tone, and I look upon going down to the House as upon something which I scarcely know how to meet.

I need not tell you how much I approve of the choice which has been made. You will have the wholehearted support of all the parties in the house, and no one will be better pleased to see you in the honourable office as Speaker than I shall. I thank you for your most friendly proposition, and regret that I am not able to take the duty you would assign to me.

Brand's name went forward to the House of Commons and was accepted in February 1872. From the start he was very conscious of the duties of his office.

A few Tory 'croakers', as *The Times* put it, said it was a mistake to suppose that a gentleman who had been, for many years, 'whipper-in' to the Liberal Party could by any possibility be an impartial Speaker but, the paper continued, on 20 July 1872, 'the result shows that their fears were utterly unfounded. Mr Brand is a model Speaker, impartial to a fault, dignified in manner, and in every respect worthy to rank as "first commoner of the realm".'

In February 1874 while a general election was in process *The Times* wrote again:

although it was thought a hazardous step when a late Patronage Secretary was promoted to preside over the House of Commons, it must be admitted that the result was justified and more than justified at the choice. Mr Brand has proved to be a Speaker of the first order of merit. He is at once firm and impartial, clear, prompt and dignified, in the exercise of his authority.

In the event the re-election of Brand as Speaker was proposed on 5 March 1874 by a Conservative Member and seconded by a Liberal Member. No Conservative candidate was put forward.

Later in 1874 Speaker Brand had the embarrassment of standing up in the House of Commons and announcing that his son Harry had been unseated after winning a by-election for the seat of Stroud in Gloucestershire, 'a notoriously corrupt borough where the Tory landowners and the Liberal woollen merchants were locked in battle'. Harry had won by 2,695 votes to 2,613 but the Conservatives claimed that a secret fund had been started by Liberal supporters and a sum of £1,200 had been raised. This was described as a 'decoration fund' for paying for flags and bunting. It was too large a sum for bunting; some, without Harry's knowledge, must have gone on bribes and the judge decided that Harry must lose his seat. His father remarked in his diary : 'few men have laboured more earnestly than I have and with practical effect for a long and active career to achieve greater purity in elections. Yet it has come to this.' But all was not lost. Harry was returned for Stroud in 1880 and two years later his father noted in his diary:

> Gladstone came to see me in the Chair to say how sorry he was not to be able to secure Harry's service in his ministerial promotions. He spoke very highly of his position in the House. He had nothing at his disposal but a Lordship of the Treasury (a whip) and certainly he could not offer him that, that he might be placed higher.

Brand's most famous moment as Speaker came on Wednesday 2 February 1881 when there was what the newspapers referred to as 'an organised obstruction' which lasted for forty-one hours. The subject under discussion was the Protection of Person and Property (Ireland) Bill. Brand retired at about eleven o'clock in the evening and took his seat again at about ten the next morning. Thus the *Standard* of 16 March 1892 two days after Brand's death:

Having slept upon his difficulties he came down prepared for prompt action. When he entered the House Mr Biggar was speaking and he necessarily paused until the Speaker had taken his place. But without calling on him to go on Sir Henry Brand declared the debate closed. 'The present sitting,' he observed, 'having commenced on Monday last has continued to Wednesday morning... a necessity has thus arisen for the intervention of the chair. The usual rule has proved powerless, the credit and authority of this House are seriously threatened and it is necessary they should be vindicated. A new and exceptional course is imperatively demanded, and I am satisfied I shall best carry out the wish of the House if I decline to call upon any more members to speak and at once proceed to put the question to the House.'

'The Speaker's coup d'état' as it was called gave entire satisfaction to the country generally and it was felt that Sir Henry Brand by his patience and forbearance at the earlier stages of a sitting and the firmness and courage which he had exhibited at the close of it had shown himself possessed of that combination of qualities which Sir Roundell Palmer had described [when proposing Brand for the chair]. The culminating point of disorder was reached two days afterwards when the whole body of Irish members, defying the authority of the chair, had to be removed by force. The Speaker never flinched; but the new urgency rule by itself was not sufficient to meet the difficulty and Sir Henry Brand himself framed the new rules of procedure, 17 in number, which were very soon brought into operation.

It was for his manner of dealing with the Irish obstructionists that Speaker Brand was best remembered and in this his experience of dealing with rebels in his own party served him well. On 4 September 1881 he wrote to his old friend, Sir George Grey, from Glynde again:

Many thanks for your letter, your approval is particularly grateful. Certainly, Parliament had a heavy job last session – (1) to keep order in Ireland (2) to keep in check rebels within the House (3) in such straits to frame and to pass remedial measures for Ireland.

Gladstone did his share of the work admirably. He was slow, however, to find out that, of which I had long since been assured – i.e. that Parnell and Co. were rebels and would stop at nothing within the law to degrade and destroy

Parliament and government. His eyes are now open and he knows with whom we have to deal.

This question of non-stop opposition continued to bother Gladstone and Brand. The possibility of standing committees to which matters could be referred from a House where there was too much filibustering had to be examined. Brand wrote to Gladstone on 15 October 1882:

> I fear that the House will continue at the mercy of a dominant minority unless it assumes the power in some form to close a debate; the tactics of obstruction are by now by bitter experience thoroughly understood, and the wilful obstruction of all time will know too well how to thwart the will of the House by choking it with debate. In saying this, I have not only the Irish party on my mind but many other parties in this and future parliaments which may be formed but bent upon opposing the deliberate wish of the House.
>
> I should advise that whatever rules you pass be made 'standing orders', otherwise you will have to do your work over again, for which the House will not thank you.

Brand's view was prophetic. Standing orders – agreed rules of procedure by which the Commons are run – became a vital feature of regulation of the manner in which the House conducted its business. They remain so today.

Henry Brand died on 14 March 1892 and was buried at Glynde. The local paper commented that it was remarkable how many 'persons of the working class' attended the funeral. 'It seemed as if all the poor of the district, men, women and children, had left their homes to pay a last tribute of respect to the memory of the deceased nobleman and his family.' Another obituarist wrote that in his opinion Henry Brand was the only man who in an emergency could exercise an authoritative influence over Mr Gladstone. 'He did not attempt to confute the great statesman in argument. On the contrary he would say, "Well, Mr Gladstone I can't argue with you, but it won't do".' This is a facility that other Chief Whips have wished they possessed.

EIGHT

Whipping with force –
Aretas Akers-Douglas 1885–92

The warning note sounded by Brand to Gladstone that the tactics for the obstruction of parliamentary business were now all too well known proved frustratingly accurate. Parnell, the great Irish politician, and his followers had learnt that it was all too easy to bring the business of the House of Commons to a standstill. This, together with the increasing obsession of Gladstone for Irish Home Rule, were to be a continuing theme for the next twenty years.

Aretas Akers-Douglas entered Parliament as the MP for East Kent in 1880 while Brand was still Speaker. He was a landowner, a staunch Conservative like Lord Salisbury, the leader of his party, but, unlike Salisbury, easy to talk to. He was thought of as one of the few Conservative successes in the 1880 general election which had been won by Gladstone and the Liberals. Disraeli is reputed to have conferred his personal blessing on Douglas while visiting Lord Abergavenny at Eridge Castle in Kent. He was regarded as a young man of ability, integrity and discretion 'who was unhappily married and willing to spend any amount of time away from home'.[1] His contemporaries considered him a born whip, and, after three years in Parliament, he was invited to become a junior Conservative whip, becoming the second whip in 1884 and the Chief Whip the following year.

In the same year the Representation of the People Bill was brought forward by the Liberals. Northcote, leading the Tories in the Commons, and Salisbury, the leader in the Lords, were in a quandary about their tactics regarding the Bill. Salisbury had long assumed that Gladstone's government would expand the county electorate by bringing the counties into line with the borough occupier franchise of 1867. There was much discussion as to whether a Tory majority in the Lords should throw out a Franchise Bill passed by a Liberal majority in the Commons. Randolph Churchill, by now the commanding young figure in the Tory Party, handled the matter badly by announcing, at the opening of the parliamentary debate in 1884, that adding 'two million or so yokel voters' to the existing total of three million was not worth Parliament's trouble. It would be better for Parliament to attend to serious matters such as the country's finances and the recession in trade. In addition, he and many other Conservatives were opposed to Ireland being put on exactly the same basis as the rest of the United Kingdom for parliamentary representation purposes.

The first draft of the Bill was thrown out by the Conservative peers on 8 July 1884 with a majority of fifty-nine. They wished to be certain that the redistribution of seats was resolved at the same time as the increase in the franchise. They were afraid, otherwise, of the Conservative Party being put in the wilderness for years as a result of a combined broadening of the right to vote with a Liberal manipulation of seats in favour of the new towns and against the Tory counties. Salisbury said that Gladstone was deliberately provoking a battle and Gladstone, in return, announced an unusual autumn session of Parliament. Winn, the Conservative whip, was all for continuing the fight as he saw the electoral tide turning in favour of the Conservatives and he wished to force a dissolution. But the majority of Conservative chiefs were against Winn, and Salisbury finally settled with Gladstone that the Lords would let through the Franchise Bill as long as an agreed Bill on the redistribution of seats had been published beforehand.

October and November 1884 saw intricate negotiations between teams led by Salisbury for the Conservatives and Gladstone for the Liberals. Single-Member constituencies became the rule for everywhere except the City of London which was reduced from four to two Members. Eighty-nine single-seat boroughs with a population of under 15,000 lost an individual Member and were absorbed into bigger constituencies. Thirty-nine two-Member boroughs were deprived of one Member. Altogether, 182 seats were available for redistribution. Of these, ninety-seven were to form new county divisions and the metropolitan area was boosted with thirty-nine new single-Member seats. Very few existing constituencies were left undisturbed.

The Irish remained over-represented because Salisbury did not wish to disturb Parnell and his followers. As Salisbury said to Northcote, Parnellite MPs were preferable to Radicals determined to bring in universal suffrage in Britain. Parnell, Leader of the Irish Home Rule party, had now been in Parliament for nine years and the Conservative attitude to him was ambivalent. They were ready to do deals with him over legislation that affected Ireland in order to win votes from the Liberals.

On this basis an agreed Redistribution Bill was presented to the House of Commons on 1 December and passed its second reading without a vote on 4 December. The third reading of the Franchise Bill passed the Lords on 5 December and received the royal assent the following day.

In effect, these reforms in 1884 carried Disraeli's measures of 1867 to their logical conclusion by extending household suffrage to the counties and franchising the agricultural labourers. What was new was that the growth of the towns such as Manchester was recognised and the counties lost members to the new industrial areas. Winn, the Conservative whip, was unhappy with all of this. He was observed once by Northcote, as looking 'very Cassandra-like, and thinks of us as in an evil case'. In the circumstances it was not surprising that the mantle of Chief Whip was transferred from his shoulders to those of Akers-Douglas. At the same time George Bartley was dismissed as the principal organising agent of the Conservative Party outside Westminster. He was succeeded by Captain Richard Middleton, nicknamed 'the Skipper'.

Middleton and Akers-Douglas developed total confidence in each other's efficiency and methods of working. With Middleton at Central Office and Akers-Douglas at No. 12 Downing Street, the National Union of Conservative Associations was reformed and full-time professional party agents began to be recruited. There followed ten years of almost mythic cooperation and growth in the Conservative Party. Salisbury once commented, 'Douglas and Middleton have never put me wrong,' and in her biography of her father his daughter wrote, 'that was the classic period in Conservative electioneering. Under Mr Akers-Douglas' whip and Captain

Middleton as Chief Agent, the organisation attained a completeness that could hardly have been improved upon.'[2]

At the time of his dismissal as principal agent, George Bartley wrote in the *Fortnightly Review* of May 1885, 'the aristocratic leaders live in a lofty sphere but in a limited one. The upper ten thousand is a very important body, but now that there are to be five million voters it is very small numerically, and will carry less and less party weight.' The 'upper ten thousand' was Bartley's slightly mocking description of what he might privately have called the ruling class. The decade that followed showed that fundamental reorganisation of the party could prove his argument wrong. Every constituency was required to form an association and every association affiliated with the National Union, with England divided into eight provincial unions and Wales divided into north and south. Distinctions between county and borough were done away with and Conservative Clubs were set up throughout the country. This new professionalism outreached the Liberal Party and led, surprisingly soon, to the Conservatives starting to win the new town constituencies that they had feared would always be prizes for the Liberals. Speaking at the end of this period of change, at the National Union conference in 1900, Salisbury said, 'but what strikes me as most extraordinary is that the great strength of Conservative feeling lies among the owners of villas of every kind which surround London. In my time they were a certain "find" for every Radical candidate but a notable change has taken place there.'[3]

Akers-Douglas soon won his spurs as a whip. He specialised in knowing the idiosyncrasies of Members on the backbenches. The day after the defeat of Gladstone's five-year-old second government on 8 June 1885, he wrote to Salisbury:

Sir Richard Cross [the future Home Secretary] tells me you are anxious to know the names of the Liberals who walked out to avoid voting last night. I am sorry I cannot ascertain their names as none were seen to go out within a quarter of an hour of division. No member was seen in Central Lobby during division – sixteen Liberals who did not vote were in the House earlier in the evening.[4]

The implication was clear. There were at least sixteen Liberal Members of Parliament who had been in the House some time before the vote but had then purposefully abstained with the result of bringing their government down. These were potential recruits for an anti-Gladstone government. Akers-Douglas was getting his intelligence service into place.

A short-lived Salisbury government followed. Akers-Douglas at the age of thirty-three was appointed Chief Whip with the office of Parliamentary Secretary to the Treasury. This gave him the rank of a junior minister and the official title of Patronage Secretary. It was the start of the long and trusting association between Salisbury and Akers-Douglas that was a landmark of stability in the changing domestic scenario of the twenty years ahead. Salisbury was seen as detached, highly intelligent and innocent. He was once described as a 'Grand Lama' on the 'distant red benches of another place'.[5] Akers-Douglas filled the gaps for him. He made it his business to know the likes and dislikes of every one of his backbenchers and quickly became the ideal chain of communication between the Chief, as Salisbury was always known, and party rank and file.

The unique circumstances of the break-up of the Liberal Party due to Gladstone's determination to bring his plan for Home Rule for Ireland to fruition gave the new Conservative Chief Whip every opportunity. On 26 January 1886, after six months of Salisbury's government, the Conservatives were defeated on an unlikely cause, an amendment to the address on the Queen's Speech which urged the provision of allotments for labourers. Salisbury resigned at once but eighteen Liberals had voted with the Conservative government and seventy-six stayed away. The months that followed were full of intrigue in which Salisbury and Akers-Douglas sought to persuade the anti-Home Rule members of the Liberal Party to form some alliance with the Conservatives. Two leading Liberals, Hartington and Goschen, had voted with the Conservatives on 26 January, and now the feelers were put out to them. The Marquess of Hartington had been in the Commons for nearly thirty years and was regarded as straightforward and conscientious, someone around whom 'respectable and moderate old Whigs would rally'. Goschen was, by contrast, clever, obstinate and meticulous. Both had held office under Gladstone.

On 9 February, Salisbury reported to Akers-Douglas:

My dear Douglas... Goschen came to see me today – among other things to talk of the possibility of some treaty between us to secure his friends from

Aretas Akers-Douglas (seated), Conservative Chief Whip 1885–92, with his fellow whips (left to right) Arthur Hill, W. H. Walrond and Sidney Herbert.

'The Unionist Whips, 1904': left to right, Marquess of Hamilton, Sir Alexander Acland Hood, Ailwyn Fellowes, S. Crossley, H. W. Forster, Lord Balcarres, Viscount Valentia.

POLITICAL NOTES.

THE CREATION OF PEERS.

THE WHIP'S LIST.

It has for some time been understood in Ministerial circles that the Master of Elibank, as Chief Whip, has had the preparation of the list of names of supporters of the Liberal Party which the Ministry will submit to the King if the Constitutional crisis ends in a creation of peers. The number 500, with which the public have been familiarized, there is reason to believe was taken as the number that might be required in extreme eventualities, and it is stated that there are more than 500 names now on the list. Some, it is understood, are members of the House of Commons, and a large number are supporters of the Liberal Party outside the House. If the crisis ends with a creation of peers there would thus be a number of by-elections to the House of Commons. It is evident that the members of the House of Commons on the list for the most part would vacate seats in districts in the country which are favourable to Liberalism, for in such districts the Liberals have for some time past shown great activity, and it is these preparations which have been thought on the Unionist side to be preparations for a General Election.

The list is no thing of yesterday. There is reason for saying that a good deal of the work in connexion with it was done in the month of May. During that month the Master of Elibank was sometimes absent from the House of Commons, and his absences led to a rumour that he was again taking an active interest in the work of a Government Department and would enter the Cabinet when the Government was reconstructed. It is now apparent, however, that at this time the activities of the Master of Elibank were required outside the House in connexion with the Government's list.

"The Times"
July 12th 1911.

Cutting from *The Times*, 12 July 1911, with inscription written by the Master of Elibank's Private Secretary R. H. Davis: 'These are the Master's notes given to Nicholson [of *The Times*] in the Chief Whip's Room, House of Commons, on the evening of July 11th 1911 to bluff the Tories.' (See pages 230–1.)

On Friday,11th December,1936,the House will meet at 11 A.M.

        Motion to take Private Members' time this day, and
to suspend the 4 o'clock rule.

                    ————————————————

        His Majesty's Abdication Bill; all stages.

        Your attendance by 11 A.M. and throughout the Sitting

is most particularly requested.

                                DAVID MARGESSON.

The two-line whip issued by David Margesson for Friday 11 December 1936 to cover the passing of King Edward VIII's Abdication Bill. (See page 260.)

'Usual stuff I suppose – national interest, stand on own two feet, not our fault, shop around and what the devil do they think they're playing at!'

Above: Cartoon by Nicholas Garland in the *Daily Telegraph*, 4 May 1971.
Below: Cartoon by Stanley Franklin in the *Sun*, 20 April 1988.

'Arrggh! Maggie's brought in a tougher chief whip.'

THE SHEEP-DIP

"Give me a chance, Herbert. Don't send them through so fast."

Cartoon by Leslie Illingworth entitled 'The Sheep-Dip', published in *Punch*, 10 July 1946 and featuring Herbert Morrison, then Leader of the House of Commons. This copy was given to the author by Bernard Weatherill, Speaker of the Commons, on his appointment as Government Chief Whip in October 1989, and inscribed: 'I hope that as Chief Whip you will ensure an orderly passage of Bills for the remainder of this Parliament!'

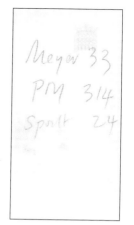

(i)

(ii)

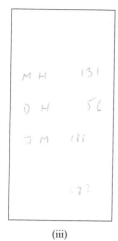

(iii)

Notes brought by the whip on duty to the author as Chief Whip immediately after the count of votes in the Conservative leadership elections, 1989 and 1990, with a cartoon by Bill Caldwell in the *Daily Star* signed 'To the Chief Whip. Margaret Thatcher, 5 December 1989'.

The notes concern (i) Sir Anthony Meyer and the Prime Minister, 5 December 1989, (ii) Michael Heseltine and the Prime Minister, 20 November 1990, and (iii) Michael Heseltine, Douglas Hurd and John Major, 27 November 1990.

Prime Minister Margaret Thatcher with the Government whips in July 1990. The author is on Mrs Thatcher's right, with Deputy Chief Whip Tristan Garel-Jones on her left. Behind them are, left to right, Alastair Goodlad, Tim Wood, Tom Sackville, Nicholas Baker, Kenneth Carlisle, Greg Knight, David Lightbown, Sydney Chapman, John Taylor, Michael Fallon, Irvine Patnick and Tony Durant.

being opposed by us at an election if they joined us in opposing the government. I acknowledged the importance of coming to an understanding on the point and said I would consult you. I said it would not be worth our while unless they would break definitely with Gladstone. He admitted this, and further limited his proposal to those places, where, without a split, our chances were hopeless. Without pledging himself I gave him general hopes of an understanding. Yours very truly, Salisbury.[6]

Gladstone, back in government again, brought forward his Irish Home Rule Bill on 8 April, and Randolph Churchill, now deeply committed to the cause of the Protestants in Ireland, invented the term 'Unionist' to cover the varied political elements who were opposed to Home Rule. This was seen by some as a break-up of the Empire of which they were so proud. To others it was a surrender to Roman Catholics who were still described in terms of 'rebels and traitors'. Randolph Churchill, father of Winston and ever an opportunist, saw his political chance. He wrote to his friend, the Irish Lord Justice Fitz-Gibbon, 'I decided some time ago that if the GOM [Grand Old Man, a euphemistic description of Gladstone now seventy-eight years old] went for Home Rule, the orange card would be the one to play.'[7] On 19 April, eleven days after the first reading of the Home Rule Bill, 'Skipper' Middleton sent a letter 'to every county and borough in England and Wales' suggesting non-party meetings to defend the safety of the Union, and Liberals and Conservatives started to appear on the same platform.

Lord Brabourne, a former Liberal whip and a neighbour of Akers-Douglas in Kent, wrote to him from Italy on 15 April:

...If you are organising any demonstrations against Gladstone's separation policy, I should be happy to go anywhere and do anything... Considering that I left Gladstone's party in 1880–81, when he took to my mind a new departure in Irish policy which I thought *must* lead him to where he is now, it would be eminently satisfactory to me to see so many of my old weak friends practically confessing now that I was right... I have been reviled, abused and ostracised for five years past simply because I saw a little further ahead than they did, and could not stop them to support and strengthen Gladstone or his march to separation. However, the thing *now* is to overthrow him, and this can only be done by vigorous and united action...

Events moved quickly. On 14 April, the Conservative leader, Salisbury, and the leading Liberals Hartington and Goschen shared the same public platform at Her Majesty's Theatre in London. Cowper, a former Lord-Lieutenant appointed by Gladstone, chaired the meeting and Salisbury and Hartington were on either side. It was as momentous a cross-party occasion as the pro-Europeans' launch of Britain in Europe in October 1999, with Tony Blair sitting in the middle, Charles Kennedy on one side of him and Michael Heseltine and Ken Clarke on the other. Randolph Churchill, although not present, described the event as a concurrence unparalleled in the annals of English history, the terms of a coalition based on one great principle, the safety and integrity of our empire.

But in 1886, as in 1999, caution took over quickly. Ten days later the *Western Weekly News* wrote:

> there is something of a pause in London politics... Meanwhile, a separate organisation on the Liberal side against the concession of Home Rule has been set on foot. It became a necessity after the meeting at Her Majesty's. That was much too Conservative an affair to be pleasant to the Liberals who spoke at it. They seemed like captives of the bow and spear of Mr Akers-Douglas. To avoid that dangerous appearance in future Lord Hartington and his friends have started a Liberal Unionists Society, which will manage the great movement.[8]

The next month was full of activity. Gladstone was reported to have accepted the amendment of another leading Liberal rebel, Joe Chamberlain, which said that Irish members should not be excluded from the Westminster Parliament. On hearing this news, Akers-Douglas took all the members of the recent Conservative Cabinet down by special train to Hatfield for an urgent consultation with Salisbury. But his fears never materialised. Instead, Gladstone said that, as representation must go hand in hand with taxation, Irish MPs would be admitted to Westminster when questions of Excise or Customs were being discussed. This compromise proved inadequate. On 8

June the Government of Ireland Bill was defeated by 250 Conservatives voting with 93 Unionist Liberals against 228 Liberals and 85 supporters of Parnell who believed in total separation for Ireland. Brookfield, a Conservative Member for the Rye division of Sussex, wrote in his *Annals of a Chequered Life*:

> when the Bill was at last defeated, what I recall better than anything is the deep sincerity of our satisfaction; how Members who perhaps hardly knew each other shook hands and shouted, and how the crowd outside – I forget what hour of night or morning it was – sang 'God Save the Queen' in a way that showed they meant it.

The immediate challenge to Akers-Douglas and Middleton was to make sure that they honoured the pledge that had been made through Hartington to Liberal Unionists that Conservative candidates would not fight against them for their parliamentary seats. A special May conference of the National Union was held at which the chairman suggested that it might be better to avoid the names Tory or Conservative and drop, instead, into Loyalist, Unionist or, preferably National. This would help 'many of our patriotic Liberal friends' who would be happy to collaborate with the 'great national party'. In the July election which followed there were some individual problems in constituencies such as Bath but in the end only four seats were fought by both a Liberal Unionist and a Conservative. The result was an overwhelming defeat for Gladstone. The Gladstonian Liberals dropped from 334 to 191, the supporters of Parnell remained at eighty-five, the Conservatives increased from 250 to 316 and Liberal Unionists won seventy-eight seats in the new House.

Akers-Douglas advised Salisbury that the Liberal Unionists broke down into 'six men pledged either to follow Salisbury or Hartington whichever is in power – forty-three followers of Hartington – twenty-one followers of Chamberlain and eight who mean to rejoin Gladstone at once. If Hartington remains outside he can with Chamberlain hold the whole of his seventy-five votes'.[9]

Frantic negotiations followed. The position of the Liberal Unionists was crucial. If they split and a large number of them went back to Gladstone, he would be able to form another government. If they stayed, as Unionists, in alliance with the Conservatives, then the Queen would have to summon Salisbury. In fact, Salisbury, acting with typical detachment, was quite content to suggest that Hartington form the next government. He met Hartington on 24 July and told him that he wished to advise the Queen accordingly. On Chamberlain's advice, Hartington declined. They both concluded that, if Hartington accepted, the Liberal Unionists would be swallowed up into a great nationalist party that would effectively be dominated by the Conservatives. If they refused, Conservatives would be in power for a few years but then, with Gladstone out of the way, the Liberal Party could 'probably pick itself together again, and I hope may be strong enough to turn them out'.[10]

Akers–Douglas was greatly relieved. He wrote to Salisbury on 17 July 1886:

> I have seen Brand [son of the former Speaker and a leading Liberal Unionist] and several other Whigs and from what I can gather from them Hartington shows no desire to or intention of coalescing. In the first place they do not desire a split with Chamberlain and secondly they persist in their view that a Tory govt. would be stronger with their united support outside the govt... but I am bound to say that the majority would decidedly welcome a pure Conservative government.[11]

Typical Chief Whip's advice: stay with your own party, don't try and meddle with others.

Akers–Douglas was returned unopposed in the July election and went back to the post of Government Chief Whip, which he held for the next six years. These were years of great volatility. The Conservatives were the largest party in the Commons but their life as a government depended on Liberals who were dissatisfied with Gladstone and Home Rule, and their adherence to the government was made in turn even more variable by the occasional conflict in the views of Hartington and Joe Chamberlain.

One of Akers–Douglas's first actions upon becoming Patronage Secretary for the second time was to abolish the annual £10,000 (now worth £540,000 in today's terms) of Secret Service money for which he was not obliged to give any account.

Although it had become the custom to spend a large part of the money on the routine expenses of the Chief Whip's office, the newspapers of the day started to point out that means might be found of diverting the money to pay the election expenses of impecunious members of the ruling party. In July 1886 the *Whitehall Review* made a clear accusation:

> it is an open secret at electioneering headquarters that the general election was delayed until after Quarter Day purely in order that Mr Arnold Morley, the Liberal Chief Whip, might draw a second Quarter's instalment for distribution among impecunious Gladstonian candidates. Mr Akers-Douglas drew the money down to Lady Day [25 March]; and then Mr Morley drew it down to mid-summer. He has now drawn it down to Michaelmas, and the whole of the money (£5,000) has been spent on the elections.

The Sheffield *Daily Telegraph* added on 28 August: 'I understand that at the end of Mr Gladstone's administration last year something like £30,000 of the Secret Service money had accumulated. This presumably was spent to promote the interests of Liberal and Home Rule candidates at the election.'

Akers-Douglas drew attention to the Secret Service money when, at the end of his first period in the office of patronage secretary, he handed back a surplus to the Treasury. Again in office in July 1886, he persuaded Randolph Churchill, now Chancellor of the Exchequer in Salisbury's government, to sponsor a Bill to amend the old Acts.

The Liberals were thought to have benefited so much in the recent past from the Secret Service money that they could not oppose the Bill abolishing it. This was passed at the beginning of September. Randolph Churchill, announcing the Bill for the repeal, gave full credit to Akers-Douglas:

> ...the main credit of it will be due to my Hon. friend the Parliamentary Secretary to the Treasury who, from the day he came into office last June, took a great interest in this question, and, by measures which he induced the Treasury to adopt, anticipated the Minute of the Public Accounts Committee which had been set up to make recommendations on the subject.

This was a wise public move from a Chief Whip who was also the Patronage Secretary and under constant pressure to recommend peerages or baronetcies for his parliamentary colleagues. Akers-Douglas showed a certain fastidiousness on this subject. As Richard Shannon wrote in *The Age of Salisbury*, 'the exchange of honours for money was of course scandalous and not to be officially countenanced. But there were many gradations both of time and circumstance.' Akers-Douglas, in an illustrative case in 1891, refused an application for a baronetcy and an offer of financial assistance in return with the reply that no hope could be held out 'until those who had long laboured for the party and bled for it had been considered'. The applicant had to wait fourteen years.

The difficulty for many parliamentary candidates was that the extension of the franchise meant more voters, and this in turn led to the running and organising of an election becoming much more expensive when there were thousands to be wooed rather than hundreds. The need for money became a constant theme. Mr Fred Milner, a former MP for York, wrote from 138 Piccadilly to Akers-Douglas on 2 July 1887:

> I do not think you are behaving well to me. I know that my name has been brought more than once before you in connection with some of the vacant seats, and that you have thrown cold water on the idea. You seem to require but one qualification for a candidate, and that is wealth. I have heard this very strongly commented on by more than one MP – I have never sought a constituency, and never shall, but I think it is very hard that when my name is brought forward no encouragement should be given. I have worked very hard and at great sacrifice for the party, and have always been content to contest hopeless seats, and think it is rather hard to see preference continually given to those who have nothing but wealth to recommend them.

The association of money with parliamentary seats and honours grew. Salisbury was sufficiently uninterested that more and more of a burden fell on Akers-Douglas. Abergavenny, head of a family that had long dominated Kent, told Douglas of two candidates for Mid Kent: 'I am convinced Beresford Hope would not go down even if he had money... the other I have never heard of but Ralph [Abergavenny's brother] says he can speak and has money.' Sometimes the Patronage Secretary gratified the desires of his colleagues and was rewarded with thanks and compliments; sometimes the whole process was carefully wrapped in conscious obscurity. As one recipient declared:

> An interview with you is likely to be under difficulties from other ears in the lobby, or in your own room. Therefore I write to thank you very sincerely and very heartily for your efforts in getting my father a peerage. Not only am I grateful to you for the trouble that you have taken, but also for the tact which you have shown in managing, under circumstances which both of us know, a touchy and delicate matter. You will not take it a fulsome compliment when I say that it is 'tact' that makes you the good head whip that you are – I will not write more – but I am not the sort of chap to forget a good turn, and in fair weather or foul hope you will count on me as a good pal in the future...[12]

Even after he ceased being Chief Whip and was promoted first to Minister for Works and then to Home Secretary Akers-Douglas's involvement with patronage continued. Schomberg McDonnell, Salisbury's private secretary, wrote to him in September 1898: '...the Queen has played the mischief with the list, reducing the Knights and CBs by 1/3 each! So there will be many sore backs... the Peers, Baronets and PCs are all right.'[13]

Following the election of 1886, Randolph Churchill rapidly became the Heseltine of the Conservative Party of the day. He combined being the glittering star, the possible future Prime Minister, with a capacity for self-destruction that had a potential for destroying the party as well. Lord Carnarvon wrote in his diary, 'Randolph is already a rival that can compel, or thwart, or drive, or hold back. At any moment he can force Salisbury's hand in the House of Commons, and in Cabinet-making he is taking a very strong part.'

Salisbury offered Churchill the twin posts of Chancellor of the Exchequer and Leader of the Commons. Herbert Maxwell, one of his contemporaries, then wrote in his book, *Evening Memories*, 'Men went back to the younger Pitt for a parallel to this heaven-born leader. For the first time since 1832 it was possible to look hopefully on the prospects of the Conservative Party.' But Churchill was not able to control the make-up of the 1886 Conservative Cabinet, and it was here that the seeds of his failure was sown. W. H. Smith, the 'book-stall man', who had been in Disraeli's Cabinet of 1874, was appointed Secretary for War and Lord George Hamilton continued as the senior Lord of the Admiralty. Within five months Churchill had quarrelled with them both over the army and navy estimates and had resigned.

At the beginning of October, Churchill made a speech at Dartford in which he paid a handsome tribute to his friend, Akers-Douglas: 'There is a cause to which success is due... it is due to the indefatigable energy, to the tact, to the good humour, to the zeal, and to the knowledge of one of your members of the county of Kent – Mr Akers-Douglas.'[14] But he then outlined a wide-ranging agenda that included a number of generous proposals for Ireland, a scheme to reduce national expenditure and the reorganisation of local government. This was published under the title of 'The new Conservative programme' and Churchill was said in contemporary newspapers to be speaking 'as in England only the head of a government speaks'. Churchill had strayed way beyond his own areas of responsibility and many read this as throwing down an obvious challenge to Salisbury's leadership.

The route that Churchill then followed seems to us, a century later, a strange one. He picked a quarrel with W. H. Smith, the War Minister, on the grounds of the increase in the War Office's financial requirements. An additional demand for £560,000 prompted the following explosion from Churchill: 'I can't go on at this rate. Whether on foreign policy or home policy or expenditure I have no influence at all. Nothing which I say is listened to. The Govt. are proceeding headlong to a smash and I won't be connected with it; the worst feature of all is this frantic departmental extravagance.'[15] This was followed up by a reference to 'your frightful extravagance at the War Office'.

Smith, who had had Cabinet status for twelve years, was regarded as a quiet, thorough, almost plodding individual. But there was a limit to his tolerance of Churchill. He sent Salisbury a note saying, 'It comes to this – is he to be *the* Government? If you are willing that he should be, I shall be delighted, but I could not go on on such conditions.' On 20 December Churchill met with Smith who later reported to Douglas:

He dined with Joe [Chamberlain] on Friday and that I think settled it, for after trying for two hours on Monday to beat me down, he told me, quite in a friendly way, that he should resign, and he let out frankly that his 'rapprochement' was towards Joe rather than to any other politician of the present day: and unless they quarrel we shall see the two working together.[16]

The bond between Churchill and Joe Chamberlain was intended as a threat that would curdle the blood of Smith and through him Akers-Douglas and Salisbury.

On the same night of 20 December Churchill, accompanied by Hamilton, dined with Queen Victoria at Windsor Castle and from there he sent his letter of resignation to Salisbury. He followed this up with a letter of explanation to Akers-Douglas in which he fulminated that 'the character of the domestic legislation which the Government contemplate in my opinion falls sadly short of what the Parliament and the country expect and require.' The conduct of foreign policy was 'at once dangerous and methodless'. He maintained his stand on expenditure and finance on the grounds that these 'involve and determine all other matters'. The letter to Akers-Douglas read like a manifesto stating where Churchill would stand publicly in opposition to Salisbury and the Conservative Party. He assumed that the party could not survive without him. He was wrong.

'A more patient man would have waited' was Winston Churchill's verdict on his father. Joe Chamberlain, the leading tariff reformer who managed to be a Radical while falling out with the Liberals, was amazed. 'Whew!... the cat is among the pigeons with a vengeance.' But nonetheless he reassured Randolph: 'the Government is doomed, and I suspect we may have to reform parties on a new basis. You and I are equally adrift from the old organisations.'

They both whistled in the wind. Churchill gave Buckle, the new editor of *The Times*, advance information of his resignation but all *The Times* wrote was that despite 'inconveniences' that would follow, Salisbury was right to back Smith and Hamilton. He was 'wise and patriotic'. Only one minister, the colonial under-secretary, followed Churchill and, on Christmas Eve, Akers-Douglas was able to reassure Salisbury, writing to him:

I have refrained from bothering you with any letter before as to the condition of the party but take this opportunity of mentioning that I have had a large number of letters and telegrams from your supporters in the House of Commons assuring you of their loyalty and continued support. Middleton [the Chief Agent] has also received many to the same effect. I am quite sure the party is sound – even those of R.C's own section and several of his personal friends who I have seen have expressed their regret at the step he has taken and say they cannot defend him...[17]

Salisbury, however, continued to play with the idea that Hartington, as the head of the Liberal Unionists, should become Prime Minister in his place. With Queen Victoria's support an offer went to Hartington, en route to Rome, inviting him either to form a coalition government or to take the leadership of the Commons. Akers-Douglas took a different view. Although he had been Government Chief Whip for only six months he wrote on New Year's Eve to Salisbury emphasising that

the policy of a coalition Cabinet with Hartington at its head... would be highly undesirable in the interests of the party. As I told you yesterday the party are loyal to you to a man... What I most fear would be the effect of your resigning first and then the Queen sending for Lord H. to form a Govt. Your resignation would be taken by large members of our party as an acknowledgement that you were afraid to go on though you had 320 followers and would magnify the position of Churchill. Such a coalition as this with Hartington at its head would be a Liberal coalition in the eyes of many and it would offend many who now say freely that by giving you the majority at the last election they expressed their confidence in you which confidence you wd. seem hardly to appreciate.[18]

Akers-Douglas considered this letter important enough for him to keep a copy in a special leather-bound book.

His advice won the day. By the time Hartington was back in London, the idea of a coalition led by a Liberal Unionist had gone the same way as bright paper on a Christmas parcel.

There followed some days of anxious discussion as to who should succeed Randolph Churchill as leader of the party in the Commons and Chancellor of the Exchequer. Salisbury wanted to try out George Goschen to see whether he would join the Cabinet as a Liberal Unionist but also as Chancellor of the

Exchequer. Goschen was a close friend of Hartington and highly regarded for his financial knowledge. He had been 'detached' from Gladstone and official Liberalism[19] for six years but he had no seat in the Commons. A by-election opportunity in Liverpool was quickly found for him but he lost by seven votes. Akers-Douglas did not appreciate the delays. On 13 January he wrote to Salisbury '…I hope you will complete the Govt. as soon as possible as delay gives cause for various rumours and creates jealousies.'

Salisbury's choice fell on W. H. Smith, 'Old Morality' as fellow MPs called him. Winston Churchill wrote of him in his biography of his father, Randolph: 'of all the characters with which the story deals scarcely one of them improves so much upon acquaintance as this valiant and honest man. He was a true type of what Disraeli calls "an English worthy".'

W. H. Smith was not without his own worries. He was concerned that Hicks Beach, leader of the Commons before Randolph Churchill in the last Salisbury ministry, might feel put out, but Beach reassured him that Ireland was his first consideration and he would continue as Chief Secretary for Ireland. Smith also had more trivial concerns. He wrote to Akers-Douglas from the War Office.

> There are two or three matters on which we ought to meet if my nomination goes on…[20]
>
> Are the mover and the seconder of the Address fixed upon?
>
> When will you and Salisbury both be in town again?
>
> Have you any idea when we shall have to go to Osborne? [Queen Victoria's home on the Isle of Wight]
>
> What is the form of invitation to the dinner given the night before the House meets?
>
> Is it the First Lord of the Treasury requests the honour etc. or simply Mr W. H. Smith?
>
> I should prefer the simpler and plainer – but the cards will have to be printed – *if I go on.*

Smith did go on as leader of the Commons and, unusually as First Lord of the Treasury as well. Parliament met on 27 January 1887 and Akers-Douglas, within a month, on 23 February, anonymously and perhaps unintentionally, wrote the epitaph to Randolph Churchill's career in a letter to *The Times*:

Sir, The recent differences in the Cabinet have evoked so much discussion, even in the ranks of the Conservative Party... that I ask leave to refer in your columns to some remarks made by Lord Salisbury at the Foreign Office meeting yesterday... Lord Salisbury, in alluding to the resignation of Lord Randolph Churchill, expressed his regret at the loss which the party had sustained by that resignation and his high sense of the noble Lord's great ability. He went on to say that he hoped with confidence that the separation would only be transitory, and that ere long they would again have the advantage of Lord Randolph's services...[21]

Akers-Douglas, as a professional politician, knew well that, whatever the pious hopes, resignation from the highest rank, when the prospect of being Prime Minister has been deliciously close, makes the barriers to return almost insurmountable. Randolph Churchill, although he continued to write friendly letters from Rome to Akers-Douglas and didactic ones to Smith, never held Cabinet office again.

Akers-Douglas's powers grew. Although his party did not have a majority in the Commons, he managed to get through a reform of procedure which, providing there were at least 200 members voting, allowed the Speaker, at his discretion, to move the closure of the debate on a bare majority of one.

Obviously this led to very strict whipping by the government whips in order to ensure that the quorum in the House did not drop below 200. The whips, as a contemporary press correspondent said, were being kept to their posts for four nights a week from four o'clock in the afternoon to nearly three on the following morning. Another paper wrote:

Hon. gentlemen strolling in at 1 a.m. in dinner dress were held prisoners for the Navy vote, and when it was found that an all-night struggle had become imminent official messengers were sent to scour the party clubs, and even bring hon. gentlemen out of their beds... The wife of a well-known hon. and learned gentleman [J. Addison QC] received a telegram at eight o'clock for her husband signed 'Akers-Douglas', calling for his immediate attendance at the House. The Senator had not been home. His wife rushed to the House and found her spouse in evening dress. He vowed he had been at his post despite the incriminating telegram which was shaken ominously in his face.[22]

I remember well one of my junior whips telephoning for the same purpose: to persuade a colleague who had gone home to return to the House for a late vote. His wife answered the phone, put her hand over the earpiece and muttered to her husband in his pyjamas, 'It's the whips' office; they want you to come back for a vote.'

'Tell them I am not here.'

This message was duly passed on to the whip who replied, 'Well, please tell whoever it is next to you in bed to come back here immediately.'

The pressure continued. The session of 1887 lasted from January to September and was regarded as one of the most exhausting ever. Divisions took place endlessly. On 8 May W. H. Smith wrote to Akers-Douglas:

> I think it very likely we may want to put on the closure at half past six or seven tomorrow, and again after dinner at ten or half past. We have been talking a good deal about obstruction and it will be necessary therefore to use all the powers we have got even at some risk at being defeated.
>
> Perhaps you would pass the word to men to be down at the House by six.

A week later he wrote to his wife on 13 May:

> The obstruction of the two oppositions [Gladstonians and Parnellites] now united in one is beyond anything that has been seen in this House, and unless it gives way under the pressure of public opinion very drastic measures will have to be taken. Here I am again droning on, while the Irish and their allies spit and splutter and obstruct. It is desperate work, unmitigated obstruction, utterly regardless of all consequences to Parliament or the country. We have now been eight days over one clause, and we have not finished it yet... I got to bed at four this morning...[23]

Smith survived in office as Leader of the Commons for four more years. He and Akers-Douglas had become firm friends. In July 1891 he had a severe attack of gout and collapsed. A few days later his daughter wrote to Akers-Douglas asking him 'to look in and see him on your way to the Treasury this morning, if you do not mind paying him a visit in his bedroom'. In August he was still writing to Akers-Douglas about sending telegrams to Conservative electors at a Lewisham by-election in order to remind them to return from holiday for the day and vote. He died on 6 October, the same day as Parnell. The following day Sydney Herbert, Akers-Douglas's closest lieutenant, wrote to him from Ireland, regretting Smith's tragic death, worried that Parnell's death would make life more difficult by uniting the Irish and then moving on to discuss the future. 'The Irish papers say that Goschen is to lead the House. Why not send Ritchie [president of the Local Government Board] to Ireland, make Arthur [Balfour] First Lord and Leader, with leisure to help Ritchie with his bills etc.! I fear that our boys will kick at Goschen.'

The Leader was dead and the task of the Government Chief Whip to find the right successor began again.

The spotlight immediately fell on Arthur Balfour. The fact that he was the nephew of the Prime Minister, Salisbury, would have made him an impossible choice even a generation later. Such considerations did not apply in 1891. Despite his reputation for dilettante indolence and the fact that he seemed to enjoy playing tennis and shooting grouse more than sitting on the front bench in the Commons, Balfour had enormously added to his reputation in the four years that he had been Chief Secretary at the Irish office. Contrary to expectation, he had proved hard working and unapologetically tough in his dealing with the Parnellites. His success, along with Randolph Churchill's increasing ill-health, finally put an end to the possibility of Churchill's return to the Cabinet.

The Liberal Unionist Alliance with the Conservatives stayed in place and six days after Smith's death, Lord Wolmer, the Liberal Unionist Whip, wrote to Akers-Douglas:

…As to the question of future leadership I have no hesitation in giving you my *private* and personal view – A.J.B. [Balfour] is the right man. But can he remain Chief Sec. and lead the House? I don't see why not. I don't think Arthur should chuck the Chief Sec. before the dissolution; so if it is decided that he can't remain Chief Sec. and lead, you must make some temporary arrangement, and for that you have got Beach all ready to your hand.

The next day Jackson, the Financial Secretary to the Treasury, and a possible candidate for the office of Chief Secretary for Ireland, wrote to Akers-Douglas:

There is no doubt that *you* ought to be put in a position to know who should be put forward as Leader in the House without delay. The first question is are you to have a man put in temporarily or one who is to be tried permanently. From the party point of view, in view of a general election, the advantages of a permanent leader being now selected are I think very great and I incline to think you had better make up your mind to select your permanent man. The choice, I think, lies between Beach [Hicks Beach, the President of the Board of Trade] and Balfour, the former would do very well for the House but the latter would carry the country better. Goschen is very valuable in his present position but I doubt his success as a Leader of the House, his defect of sight places him at a disadvantage and he would not at present be looked on as the leader of the Conservative Party. On the whole my view is that you had better jump the fence and select Balfour. Details must be settled after and they must be made to fit.[24]

George Goschen, who was now in the Cabinet as Chancellor of the Exchequer and who had acted as Leader of the Commons during Smith's illness, was, as Jackson had said, the most likely alternative but he was still a Liberal Unionist. Hicks Beach was a third possibility but Akers-Douglas was in no doubt that Balfour was the right man. On 16 October he wrote to Salisbury:

...I saw Goschen yesterday and urged him to follow Beach's lead in publicly stating what he told me privately, viz: that no jealousy existed between himself and Balfour and that he would serve under the latter if desired.

He demurred to this at the time but I see by the papers today that he practically did so after all. Has it occurred to you that Goschen's disappointment might be lessened by being appointed to the Cinque Ports?

The office of the Lord Wardens of the five ports on the south coast of England has a ceremonial importance long after the end of any practical function. Recent Lord Wardens have included Winston Churchill and the Queen Mother.

Salisbury had already decided. He wrote to his wife on 14 October, 'Arthur must take it. Beach was possible: Goschen is not. But I think it is bad for Arthur, and I do not feel certain how the experiment will end.'[25]

Within a few days Salisbury had obtained the agreement of Hartington, the leader of the Liberal Unionist wing, and A.J.B.'s appointment as First Lord of the Treasury was announced. Akers-Douglas immediately turned his attention to considering who should succeed Balfour in the key position in Ireland. He wrote to Schomberg McDonnell:

> ...there is an objection to both Ritchie [the president of the Local Government Board] and Jackson [the Financial Secretary of the Treasury] which you will no doubt have thought of viz: the social position of their ladies in respect of entertainments at the Chief Secretary's lodge – but this is a minor consideration.
>
> Would the Chief put Jackson in Cabinet? I conclude not at first. So that Arthur can have a greater hold on policy.

Akers-Douglas' strength in recommending senior ministers to Salisbury lay not only in his own experience and knowledge of his colleagues but, on the other side of the coin, in Salisbury's innocence and ignorance. Salisbury had strong views about whom he met. Sir James Fergusson, baronet, Member of Parliament, and Under-Secretary of State for Foreign Affairs when Salisbury was Foreign Secretary, wrote to him on 5 August 1890 saying that the 'Queen of Sedang', a French lady who was daughter of the Marchise de Nerine (sic) desired an interview regarding the position of the country over which her husband is king. Fergusson then questioned Lord Salisbury, 'Is it desirable to enter into such a conversation as is proposed? If this lady is to be received, by whom should it be done? I have had no charge of Burma frontier affairs. The lady is said to be very attractive.'

Salisbury replied in pencil on the same day: 'I make it a rule never to see ladies officially – they are so interminable. I would not recommend anyone to undertake this lady. She will give trouble. S.'[26]

Salisbury maintained the same attitude of aloofness to his parliamentary colleagues. Aretas Akers-Douglas had to fill the gaps. On 15 August 1892, Sir Algernon Borthwick, MP for South Kensington and proprietor of the *Morning Post*, complained to Akers-Douglas: 'Lord S. does not understand the value of the H. of C. nor the feeling of the constituencies' and, fifteen months later, the *Pall Mall Gazette* wrote:

...There is a well-known story, which, if not true, is *ben trovato* that Lord Salisbury was walking across the Horse Guards Parade with Mr Akers-Douglas when a gentleman passed and just raised his hat. 'Douglas,' said the Chief, blandly, 'pray who is that fresh-looking young man?' 'That, Lord Salisbury,' answered the whip, 'is a member of your Government — Walter Long, the Parliamentary Secretary to the Local Government Board.' Again, Lord Salisbury has been begged to show himself at the Carlton, but he has always answered that if he did he would only get into a corner between Sir William Blank and Sir Henry Asterisk, and never escape.[27]

The government reshuffle after the death of W. H. Smith and the placing of Arthur Balfour as the new leader of the Conservatives in the Commons, a leader who was to be in the forefront of politics for the next generation, marked the zenith of Akers-Douglas's career as Government Chief Whip. An election followed in June 1892. Salisbury had been in power for seven years and it was time for the tide to turn. Early in the year Akers-Douglas forecast that the Conservatives and Unionists would be in a minority of twenty-eight to thirty. He was not far out. The Gladstone-cum-Irish Nationalist majority was forty, though Akers-Douglas himself, as in 1886, was returned unopposed. Three years passed in opposition and then, in June 1895, the Liberals, now headed by Rosebery, were beaten in an unexpected division on the army estimates. The *Daily Telegraph* reported on 22 June 1895 that the crucial paper with the division figures 'was banded backwards and forwards between the ministerial and the Opposition tellers, the latter of whom were slow to realise the victory which their party had won. It was not till the record of the division had been twice placed in the hands of Mr Akers-Douglas that he announced its result to the House...' Salisbury became Prime Minister for the third time.

It was necessary for Members of Parliament accepting offices as ministers under the Crown to vacate their parliamentary seats and to submit themselves for re-election. While this was taking place, Akers-Douglas temporarily acted as Leader of the House and then he was appointed First Commissioner of Works with a seat in the Cabinet. A few weeks later the *Morning Post* wrote:

It would be a great mistake to suppose that Mr Akers-Douglas has ceased to manage the party organisation because he has become First Commissioner of Works. Although Sir William Walrond is now Chief Whip... Mr Akers-Douglas is still the party 'boss', just as Lord Tweedmouth continued to manage the Radical Party after he became Lord Privy Seal. The truth is that Mr Akers-Douglas has a knowledge of *le dessous des cartes* which makes him indispensable, at all events for a time, until Sir William Walrond is educated in the mysteries of the post.[28]

In 1902 after the final resignation of Salisbury, Akers-Douglas became Home Secretary. There he introduced a controversial Aliens Act, the first occasion in which government attempted to control the landing of immigrants in Britain. In February 1904 it fell to Akers-Douglas as Home Secretary to wind up the six-day debate on the Loyal Address in answer to the Royal Speech spelling out the government's programme. Arthur Balfour, now Prime Minister, was absent due to flu, Austin Chamberlain, the Chancellor of the Exchequer, was away because of the death of a friend. Gerald Balfour, Arthur Balfour's brother, had, as President of the Board of Trade, taken a somewhat different view in the debate about the impracticability of duty preferences for the colonies to that of brother Arthur. The Colonial Secretary, Alfred Lyttleton, had also taken a different view. This aroused deep suspicions among the free traders who formed the bulk of the Conservative Party, and Akers-Douglas, in winding up, concentrated on an appeal to party loyalty to paper over the cracks. This did not work. Balfour's niece, Blanche Dugdale, wrote in her biography of her uncle: 'Finally, the Home Secretary, Mr Akers-Douglas, failed lamentably in an appeal to party loyalty. He struck the wrong note with a quavering finger, and the upshot was that some twenty-seven Unionists went into the Opposition Lobby, and seven others abstained from voting.'[29]

Such a revolt must have been distressing to an ex-Chief Whip. If Akers-Douglas had a fault, it was that he rated party loyalty above everything else and failed to realise that moods, views, and even convictions change. This is particularly difficult for a Home Secretary where the minister's brief arouses passions that cross party lines as in asylum, police and prison matters today.

Akers-Douglas's task as Home Secretary was made no easier by the fact that both the new King, Edward VII, and Queen Alexandra took an interest in murder cases and prison sentences and, writing through their private secretaries, did not hesitate to let Akers-Douglas know of their feeling:

> HM... desires me to let you know that he feels very strongly that Miss Doughty's sentence should be substantially reduced, and that he thinks it merciful she should be informed of the reduction as soon as you are able to do so. (9 August 1905)
>
> The Queen is distressed at seeing that two women are to be hung tomorrow – and she has had an appeal also for their lives – could you send me [the private secretary, Sydney Smith] a line to show the Queen that it is not possible to do anything as she seemed interested in their case. (3 February 1903)

In each case Akers-Douglas wrote letters which dealt with the kind and humane thoughts of Their Majesties.

Even more difficult was King Edward's interest in the Royal Prerogative of Mercy and this caused Akers-Douglas to send the following note to the King on 26 September 1903:

> Mr Secretary Akers-Douglas with his humble duty begs leave to enclose a Memorandum which he has prepared at Your Majesty's desire on the Royal Prerogative of Mercy – or rather on the constitutional practice as to the exercise of the prerogative.
>
> Mr Douglas thinks it is most important that the practice of the last eighty years at any rate, should not be departed from. He would particularly emphasise the three following points.
>
> (1) There are from 5,000 to 6,000 petitions every year against convictions and sentences. If Your Majesty is to deal personally with any of them, you ought to deal personally with all. It would be invidious to pick and choose.
>
> If Your Majesty is to deal with death sentences your attention must be available at all times from sentence to final decision. The practice of the Secretary of State is to deal not only on the evidence at the trial: but on evidence which accumulates until the last moment.

The power of reprieve involves the power, and duty to refuse to reprieve. This latter power is sometimes bitterly attacked, and public opinion is lashed up by an unscrupulous partisan press… It is, in Mr Douglas's opinion, the Home Secretary's duty to bear the brunt of such attacks, and to defend himself if necessary in Parliament.[30]

But it was not the problems of capital punishment that caused Akers-Douglas to alienate Tory MPs when he wound up the debate on the Address of February 1904. It was the old bugbear of free trade against protectionism, the issue that had split the Tory Party and divided Peel from Disraeli sixty years earlier.

As with John Major on Europe, A.J.B. tried to keep both sides of the party happy, the free traders on the one hand and, on the other, those who thought that a degree of higher tariffs was necessary to protect industries at home and in the colonies. Balfour's means of doing this was over elaborate. He would make a number of obscure statements of policy and then declare that there would be no tariff change during the currency of the existing Parliament; that if the Conservatives won the next election the colonies would be invited to a conference on taxes and tariffs; and if an agreement were then reached, it would be submitted to the country at another general election. No loyal Unionist quite understood where Balfour was going to and even the exceptionally loyal Akers-Douglas was confused. As he wrote to an old friend, Arthur Wollaston, on 7 June 1905:

Though I am not a protectionist and am opposed to any permanent duties which will in the aggregate raise the price of food of the working classes I was then [the election of 1885] and am now in favour of Tariff Reform.

Tariff Reform was a policy of the government in the sense laid down [in] Mr Balfour's declarations at Sheffield and Edinburgh.

The Prime Minister has over and over again explained his position with regard to it…[31]

The last sentence sounds like a despairing summary put out by No. 10 Downing Street's Press Office on the issue of joining the Euro or of the war against Iraq. In January 1906 at least, uncertainty and confusion on a key subject led to an overwhelming defeat for a Conservative government at a general election

Akers-Douglas was one of the few ministers who survived. Balfour was defeated at Manchester and out of 369 Unionist members only 157 kept their seats. The Liberals increased their representation from 186 to 377 and, for the first time, the new Labour Party had material strength. They won fifty-one seats. A long period of twenty years that had been dominated by Conservative government ended and it was not until 1921, fifteen years on, that a government was once more led by a Conservative.

Akers-Douglas again temporarily led the Conservatives in the Commons until Balfour got another seat. The battle between the 'whole hoggers' who wanted the Conservatives to adopt a strong programme of social and tariff reform and the older and more cautious veterans of Balfour's government continued. Akers-Douglas received letters from all sides, but no clear policy was decided on. In 1906, the Conservative Chief Whip, Acland Hood, formed an 'Advisory Committee' to consider 'democratising' the National Union and 'bringing the Central Office under more effective popular control'. Akers-Douglas's expert knowledge made him an obvious member of the committee and of other party councils.

In October 1910, a year after the threat to British naval supremacy from the increasing size of the German navy had woken Asquith and the Liberal government up to the dangers of war, the Chancellor of the Exchequer, Lloyd George, submitted a memorandum to Asquith and other government colleagues, including Winston Churchill, in which he suggested that war was sufficiently close for there to be a truce to party conflict. All outstanding domestic questions should be speedily settled in as friendly a manner as possible. With Asquith's agreement, Lloyd George submitted this proposal to Balfour and a number of leading Conservatives were then reported to be in favour. However, Balfour later said that the bulk of Conservative Members of Parliament were hostile and the main problem was the personality of Lloyd George himself.

This story appears in the memoirs of Lloyd George, published in 1938, under the page heading 'Akers-Douglas kills it':

He [Balfour] then told me that there was one other man he felt he would have to consult. He said: 'You will be surprised when I give you his name!' When I heard it I think I was rather surprised that this individual should still hold such an important and influential position in the councils of the party, for he had retired from active political life for a good many years: it was Mr Akers-Douglas, who had formerly been Chief Whip of the Conservative Party, and was then Lord Chilston. I remember one of the last things Mr Balfour said to me on that occasion. Putting his hand on his forehead, looking down and more or less soliloquising, he said: 'I cannot become another Robert Peel in my party!' After a short interval he added: 'Although I cannot see where the Disraeli is to come from, unless it be my cousin Hugh [Hugh Cecil, fifth son of the 3rd Marquess of Salisbury], and I cannot quite see him fulfilling that role!' Mr Akers-Douglas, however, turned down the project for cooperation in settling these momentous national issues, and there was an end to it. It very nearly came off. It was not rejected by the real leaders of the party, but by men who, for some obscure reason best known to political organisations, have great influence inside the councils of a party without possessing any of the capabilities that excite general admiration and confidence outside.

This assessment in Lloyd George's memoirs both exaggerates and minimises Akers-Douglas's importance. He was never a Potemkin to Salisbury's Catherine the Great. He was not a designer of major party policies or much interested in party philosophy. His natural strength lay in assessing where party feeling lay among Conservative members of Parliament and in trying to bring that feeling into agreement with the policy wishes of the leader of the party.

When Balfour finally decided to retire in October 1911, after the Parliament Bill had passed the Lords two months earlier, the first persons he informed were Lord Lansdowne, the leader of the party in the Lords, and Akers-Douglas, though the latter had stopped being a minister five years earlier.

Akers-Douglas lived on for a further quiet fifteen years. His obituary, written by Sanders, Balfour's private secretary, contained the friendly summary:

He wanted nothing for himself; it was with reluctance that he yielded to the persuasion that at the Coronation he should accept the peerage. He would gladly have stood aside for another's claims. His contempt for the appetite for party honours was deep, and he scorned at the man who voted in the government lobby in the hope of being turned into a nobleman.

It was about this last aspect of a patronage secretary's life and powers that Akers-Douglas's successors as Chief Whip were to be particularly concerned.

NINE

Honours without honour –
Whiteley and Pease 1905–10

The 1867 Reform Act, passed by a Conservative government led by Derby in the House of Lords and by Disraeli in the Commons, virtually doubled the electorate from around 1,430,000 to 2,470,000, about a third of the adult male population.[1] The result of extending the household suffrage to the boroughs was that the votes of the artisan class, that is, the semi-skilled workers in the new manufacturing industries, was increased by nearly 140 per cent. The next Reform Act, that of 1884, was the work of a Liberal government led by Gladstone. It extended the borough franchise of 1867 to the counties. This, in turn, doubled the county electorate and increased the total electorate to about five million. Nearly 60 per cent of the adult male population could now vote. The long overdue Redistribution Act of 1885 gave the big cities and the new centres of the manufacturing industries their proper electoral weight for the first time. 'Vast rings of suburban constituencies sprawled over the major conurbations. London spilled over the home counties. The modern pattern of politics was established.'[2]

This led to a sea change in Westminster politics. New seats from the manufacturing towns meant a new breed of Members of Parliament and a quick strengthening of the national party associations. Although the Corrupt and Illegal Practices Act restricting electoral expenditure had been passed in 1883, many new parliamentary candidates sought help with their expenses from the party headquarters, and this in turn led them to the party Chief Whip and the new national offices.

In introducing secret voting, the Ballot Act of 1872 had made payments to individual voters less effective since the means of checking how individuals voted disappeared. Nonetheless, in the days before radio and television, election costs remained extremely high by our standards. The cost of a Conservative vote at current prices in the 1880 election was 158 pence. At 1980 constant prices this is equal to 3,780 pence, or nearly £38 per head. By contrast, when I was elected to the Commons in February 1974, the Conservative vote at current prices cost 6.7 pence, equal to 16.4 pence at constant 1980 prices.[3] Although declared election expenses fell further after the 1883 Corrupt and Illegal Practices Act of 1883, they remained a substantial political hurdle which became harder and harder for the official Liberal Party, led by Gladstone, to surmount.

Joe Chamberlain, a highly successful businessman, mayor of Birmingham at the age of thirty-seven and MP for Birmingham at the age of forty, pioneered the National Liberal Federation which, from a Birmingham base, oversaw Liberal constituency organisations throughout the country. Yet he was driven from the official Liberal Party by Gladstone's support for Irish Home Rule. He considered Gladstone's Home Rule Bill of April 1886 too far-reaching and correctly judged that it would be fatal for the Liberal Party. He led a strange coalition of Radicals and Whigs into the lobby against Gladstone and Parnell, the leader of the Irish Nationalists. Along with the Conservatives, they threw out Gladstone's Bill by thirty votes in July 1886. Although the National Liberal Federation stayed officially with Gladstone, Chamberlain took with him much of the Liberal Party's powers to raise money from successful and newly rich industrialists. In the election of 1886, 'Liberal financial disadvantage is shown by the fact that the party allowed 117 Conservative and Liberal Unionist candidates to enter the House of Commons unopposed whereas only 37 Liberals were unopposed.'[4] Of the eight general elections that had been held between 1847 and 1885, the Liberals won seven. Of the four elections to be held over the next fifteen years, they won only one, in 1892, and that by an inconclusive margin.

Shortage of finance for the party is the background to the indulgence in the sale of Honours which cast a dark shadow over the administrations of Asquith and Lloyd George. The Conservatives had captured, as Lord Salisbury hoped they would, the votes of the suburbanites, newly enfran-

chised, enjoying higher living standards and 'keen to take part in local associations since this gave them a chance to mix with prominent social
personalities and receive occasional invitations to gatherings in their homes'.
By contrast the local Liberal organisations 'became pale, middle-class imita-
tions of their Conservative counterparts'.[5]

Subsidies from Headquarters became the life support system for Liberal
associations and many Liberal candidates declined to accept nominations
until money was available from the Chief Whip, first Herbert Gladstone,
son of the former Prime Minister, and then George Whiteley. The involvement of a Prime Minister was a little more delicate. Before the 1892 election,
Middleton, the Conservative Chief Agent, was confident that he could raise
£80,000 to give as aid for English and Irish seats. 'With a little management
this could easily be done.' However, his sense of what was proper meant that
he did not require Salisbury, the Prime Minister, to write letters asking for
money. 'All finance of this kind is of so delicate a nature' that Middleton did
not wish Salisbury's name 'connected with it, in any way whatever'. Not so
with Chief Whips. The years of Conservative government saw a steady
decline in the approach to Honours. Permissible shaded off into the corrupt.
Under Arthur Balfour, Salisbury's nephew who succeeded him as Prime
Minister, the Government Chief Whip Acland Hood, helped by Akers-
Douglas and Balfour's confidential private secretary, Jack Sandars, inherited
a fund of £150,000 but felt he needed to be able to invest £200,000 of which
£100,000 would be spent on financing the election in January 1906. Five
years later, after the 1910 election, won by Asquith and the Liberals, the new
Conservative chairman of the party wrote to Bonar Law, who had just
succeeded Balfour as the Unionist leader, saying that a 'nest egg' of over
£300,000 had been built up by the Conservative Chief Whip partly because
'a year's peerages are hypothecated'.[6] This was shorthand for saying that
Conservative supporters had already paid for peerages which they would
have to wait for a Conservative victory to receive.

In 1905 the political pendulum was ready to swing back from
Conservative Unionists to Liberals. Since 1903 Joe Chamberlain had led the
Liberal Unionists in a tariff reform campaign against free trade.
Chamberlain's belief in imperial preference (preferential tariffs for the
colonies and Dominions), and in retaliation against foreign tariffs and cheap

imports, was well received by Unionists in the Commons but not by senior colleagues in the Cabinet nor by Balfour. In November Chamberlain won over the support of the National Union of Conservative Associations. A month later Balfour, hard-pressed in his own party by Chamberlain, resigned as Prime Minister but did not ask King Edward VII to dissolve Parliament. He hoped the dissension in the Liberal Party over Home Rule would remove their new popularity before an election was called. He was wrong. Campbell-Bannerman, whose reputation for shrewdness and common sense had grown since he became Liberal leader in the Commons in 1898, called an election within weeks. In the landslide that followed the Liberals won 377 seats, the Unionists only 157 but these were classified 'more realistically as 109 Chamberlainites, 32 Balfourians, 11 Unionist Free Fooders, and a few uncertain'.[7]

Herbert Gladstone had raised much of the cash the Liberals needed for the 1906 general election from just seven rich men, all of them successful entrepreneurs. All became either a peer or a baronet. He was rewarded with the Home Secretaryship.

The Liberal Government Chief Whip, George Whiteley, already an MP for twelve years, continued down the steps already trodden by the Conservatives. A wealthy cotton manufacturer and former Conservative, Whiteley's appointment was not appreciated by his deputy whip, Jack Pease, himself a member of a powerful Quaker dynasty from north-east England that contributed eleven members to the House of Commons in the nineteenth century. Whiteley put Pease in charge of disciplining the large numbers on the Liberal backbenches of whom 181 were newcomers. Pease compiled a voting record for the session and some of these backbenchers reacted in the traditional manner when they were listed as not being present when they should have been or as having voted the wrong way. One elderly member advised Pease to drop his inquisitional return 'as an ungentlemanly and possibly libellous proceeding and which I feel sure is not countenanced by the Prime Minister.'[8]

Whiteley himself quickly earned even stronger criticisms. A backbencher, Rudolf Lehmann, voted with fifty-seven others for a reduction of 10,000 men in the army in an attempt to persuade the government to commit itself to a reduction in the army budget for the following year. He was invited to come to the Chief Whip's room and there he was scolded 'as if I had been a schoolboy and he a headmaster'. According to his diary for 19 March 1906, Lehmann told Whiteley that if he continued to bully backbenchers he would 'make a ghastly failure of his whipship, and that he hadn't been a Liberal long enough to warrant him in taking this line.'[9] In fairness to Whiteley, at this time he had only been Patronage Secretary for four months but the complaints were echoed in the Prime Minister's office by his private secretaries, including the comment that Whiteley 'enjoyed the money-squeezing part of the degrading occupation' of compiling the Honours list.[10]

These hostile noises were not forgotten when Campbell-Bannerman resigned as Prime Minister on 3 April 1908 and Asquith went to the spa town of Biarritz to be appointed his successor by Edward VII. Within five days Pease wrote to Asquith suggesting that the eleven years he had spent in the Liberal whips' office entitled him to some promotion and that he would prefer to be in what he referred to as an administrative job rather than continuing as a whip. Asquith replied on his return from Biarritz that he would like Pease to succeed Whiteley; 'there is no one in the party who possesses the same qualifications as yourself to succeed him and I need not say that the office is one of the most responsible and important in the government.'[11]

Whatever Whiteley's failings in the treatment of difficult backbenchers, his success in raising money in his thirty months as Chief Whip was evident: 'We then discussed Whiteley's characteristics and his methods, the way in which money had been collected from those given Honours was obviously most distasteful, but the chest was fuller than it had been since the days of Pitt, and the sooner the securities (and) consols were taken out of Whiteley's name and put into Trustees the better, half a million nearly in hand'. Thus, according to Pease's diary, ran part of his discussion with Asquith. A month later Whiteley confirmed to Asquith that he had 'handed over £519,000 (actual and collectable, all good money)… less than under £5,000 overdrawn at the bank' and £400,000 in consols.[12] (Consols was the colloquial way of saying Consolidated Fund, guaranteed by the Bank of England and equivalent to today's government bonds.)

The time in government had not been wasted. Whiteley, despite the insomnia which was the official reason for his retirement, had refilled the

Liberal pouches and this, along with a vast majority in the Commons, gave the confidence to Asquith that he had previously lacked. This confidence was shown in the battle with the Tory majority in the House of Lords that started a year later with Lloyd George's Budget and Finance Bill of 1909 and that put government and opposition Chief Whips in direct conflict.

The Pease family fortunes had come from the staples of the industrial revolution in north-east England – coal, iron, railways, engineering, banking. Unfortunately Jack Pease's father, Joseph Pease, himself an MP for nearly forty years, had managed the businesses disastrously and was nearly declared bankrupt in 1902. A consortium of friends got together to support Jack Pease's career in politics but the issue of money is ever present in the diary that he kept of his nineteen months as Government Chief Whip. His attitude to the sale of Honours in return for financial support for the Liberal Party was either naïve or bordering upon the dishonest but this must be seen against the glittering Edwardian background of dinners, balls and huge bags of birds at shoots. Money that had been quickly made was lavishly spent and the newly rich longed for titles and respectability. It was the age of the plutocracy. Those who had made millions from textiles, railways and banking – and often from clever inventions like bleaching powder and durable hard soap – wished to catch up quickly with the landed families who had been hand in glove with the Crown in ruling Britain for centuries. Knighthoods, baronetcies or, preferably, a peer's title were seen as the appropriate way of blazoning successful wealth. No one could challenge the right of the baron and his wife to sit above the salt at dinner.

Pease's naïvety is shown by an entry in his diary for 5 June 1908, a few days after he had been officially appointed Chief Whip: 'At 11.20 found Asquith with Margot and Violet trying a motor in Downing Street.'[13] Asquith did not drive himself but was fascinated by cars and had owned one since 1900. His chauffeur had two speeding convictions, the most recent on 16 March 1908 for driving his 'very busy' master at more than 10 mph in St James's Park.[14]

After the examination of so important an asset in relation to a Prime Minister's movements, retired into the Cabinet room, where H.H.A. does all

211

his work... I suggested the Cabinet must decide before Monday 15th whether the Old Age Pension Bill should be treated as a Money Bill...

He [H.H.A.] told me the King had not demurred to the Honours List except for grumble there had been too many knights. Crewe [Liberal leader in the Lords] had sent in several names and he thought his list must be cut down.

He said Whiteley had been skating on too thin ice in selling Honours and asked me to pursue a different course. I said I had no intention of associating money and titles, but was anxious to interest those I could in helping my scheme for devolving work on [Liberal] Local Federations which I should have to subsidise if constituencies were to be effectively organised.

I saw Herbert Roberts [Liberal MP and timber merchant], congratulated him on prospective baronetcy and he said he recognised the necessities of party and asked me to suggest what help I would like. I said £5,000, he offered £4,000 with further £1,000 if I needed it.[15]

Six days later Pease wrote, 'I placed to credit of my a/c £30,000 at London and Westminster Bank. The clerk said this is the biggest cash payment ever received in bank notes he had experience of, Holden's son gave it me night before, I trusted it in a Govmt dispatch box – as I never knew them tampered with.'[16] The Holden who provided this cash bounty was Sir Angus Holden, a woollen manufacturer in Bradford and France. He had been a Liberal MP for fifteen years until 1900 and his peerage was announced a fortnight later. The following day, 12 June, the diary entry reads: 'Saw Lord Blyth – who asked to pay two sums of £2,500 to us, 1/2 yearly in place of annual sums of £5,000 in June, I agreed... Asquith gave garden party to Liberal Party and LRC [Labour Representative Committee] Liberal members and their wives – a great success fine afternoon.' Sir James Blyth, a philanthropist who lived in Pease's constituency, had been ennobled a year earlier.

On his first official day as Government Chief Whip Pease recorded that six Liberal MPs had been to see him asking him for Honours – one wanted to be a Baron, one a Privy Councillor, one a Baronet and three Knights. By 1910 all had received the Honours they sought except for one who had to wait until 1928 but then he had only been an MP since 1906 and he lost his seat in 1910. As to Pease himself his 3 June diary notes read, 'Asquith... told me I would get a PC on King's birthday, but not now as I had hardly been promoted and it would look as if I was in too great a hurry.' The luckiest person appears to have been J. W. Philipps, ship owner and Liberal MP for Pembrokeshire, who had married an orphaned heiress, Leonora Gerstenberg, in 1888. Pease's diary for 11 June records 'I asked Asquith about Honours; he showed me the list – put his pen through several. He asked me whether Philipps' incident of trying to seduce a girl barred him from peerage, I said, "No".'

It is against this background of incessant pursuit of Honours, with the aspirants pledging large sums of money with their next breath, that the dispute about the rejection of Lloyd George's Budget of 1909 by the Tory majority in the House of Lords and the consequent threat by the Liberals over the next two years to create any number from 150 to 600 of new Liberal peers must be seen. The danger to the Tories was real. They were terrified that such a flood would lose them for ever their historic ability to amend or reject in the Upper House Bills of which they disapproved. With the advent of Labour members in the Commons and with Lloyd George, a Welsh Nonconformist MP, as Liberal Chancellor of the Exchequer, legislation that heaped new taxes on land ownership and thus attacked the basic income of heirs to great estates was a real possibility.

Some had already diversified into industry and commerce. By the 1890s, one in four of the partners in London's leading merchant banking houses were married to daughters of peers. But the threat of radical legislation came after twenty years of agricultural depression in which overall agricultural land values halved.[17] A clash between the Tory majority in the House of Lords and the Liberal majority in the Commons was inevitable.

The dispute began in the summer of 1908 with the Old Age Pension Bill. The Budget of that year, drafted by Asquith before he became Prime Minister and introduced by him in person, forecast a modest surplus. Part of this, £1.2 million, was dedicated to providing non-contributory pensions for the first time. A pension of five shillings a week for 'necessitous and worthy' persons of seventy years or over was promised. Pease suggested that a guillotine was the quickest and best method of getting the Bill through the Commons and Asquith took the unusual step of designating it as a Money Bill to stop spoiling amendments in the Lords. By unwritten tradition the Lords did not intervene in Money Bills. They attempted to tamper with the

Old Age Pensions Bill but the Commons asserted 'privilege' and they desisted.[18]

At the same time the Lords rejected at second reading a large-scale Licensing Bill, the aim of which was to reduce 'the then monstrous evil of intemperance – how monstrous it is perhaps difficult for the present generation to realise'.[19] King Edward VII summoned Lord Lansdowne, leader of the Tories in the Upper House, and urged him not to reject the Bill but a party meeting decided otherwise. Influential brewing interests felt the Bill would be very bad for their business.

By the end of 1908 it was clear that that year's budget surplus was going quickly to turn into a major budget deficit. Old Age Pensions had been provided for for only three months of the financial year; in 1909 they were going to cost four times as much. Adding in the extra battleships that were to be built in order to keep ahead of German warship building meant that a total of over £15 million would have to be found by new taxation. By the standards of those days this was a vast sum, one without precedent. The Budget of 1900, with a South African war to pay for and in a period of trade boom, had increased taxes by only £12.1 million.

Lloyd George, the Chancellor of the Exchequer, saw his opportunity. The Lords' destruction of Liberal Bills appeared to him and to Asquith to be a golden opportunity to change the balance of power in Parliament. The defeat of the 1908 Licensing Bill by 'the trade' in the Lords and by a huge majority (272 votes to ninety-six) acquired a transcendent importance.

Lucy Masterman, wife of the Parliamentary Secretary to the Local Government Board, found herself sitting next to Winston Churchill, now President of the Board of Trade and soon to become Home Secretary, at dinner in the Commons on 26 November 1908. 'He was perfectly furious at the rejection of the Licensing Bill by the Lords, stabbed at this bread, would hardly speak,' she recorded in her diary. 'We shall send them up such a Budget in June that should terrify them,' he thundered; 'they have started the class war, they had better be careful.'[20] Churchill had put well behind him the fact that he was born in Blenheim Palace, a grandson of the Duke of Marlborough.

A few days later Sir John Branner, who regarded himself as a radical MP and who led the campaign against an increase in the building of battleships, counselled Asquith after a meeting on naval policy 'that if he and his colleagues would now enter upon the fight with the Lords, his followers would back him with enthusiasm and that the stronger he showed himself the greater would be that enthusiasm'. Asquith's only comment in reply was 'The House of Commons has never received a greater blow in its existence than it did last week.' Nine days later, at a dinner of the National Liberal Club, Asquith made it clear that he intended to bring to an end the ability of the House of Lords to determine 'what shall and what shall not be the legislation of the country… I invite the Liberal Party tonight to treat the veto of the House of Lords as the dominating issue in politics – the dominating issue, because in the long run it overshadows and absorbs every other'.[21]

Asquith's speech was rapturously received and he added that 'the Budget of next year will stand as the very centre of our work, by which we will stand or fall, by which certainly we shall be judged in the estimation both of the present and posterity.' The Budget was Lloyd George's People's Budget of 1909 and the legal vehicle for this Bill, the Finance Bill, was to be at the heart of acute controversy for the next two years.

Measures in the Bill to which the Lords most objected were the increase in death duties on estates between £5,000 and £1 million, the creation of a supertax for the first time, albeit fixed at a low rate, on incomes of over £3,000 and above all Land Value duties, a duty of 20 per cent on the 'unearned increment' of land value, to be paid whenever land changed hands, and also a duty of a half-penny in the pound on the capital value of undeveloped land and minerals.[22] It had been a tradition since the seventeenth century that the Lords did not challenge the supreme authority of the Commons over 'supply', the provisions for annual expenditure. The peers might be expected to make angry noises from the red benches but in the end they would submit. In 1909 the Tory majority chose not to do so.

It was Pease's job to get the Finance Bill through the Commons. The committee stage began on 21 June. Clause Two was still being considered on 7 July when Pease was authorised by Cabinet to negotiate with Acland Hood, the Conservative Chief Whip since 1902, on what are technically called Closure Resolutions – arrangements to guillotine sets of clauses after a determined period of time for debate. Lloyd George accused the Tories of filibustering and refused to withdraw the new Land Tax. Pease used the large Liberal majority to establish a rota for Liberal members under which batches were allowed off for a week or two of rest. The Clerk of the House of Commons suggested that the Speaker be given a new power to select amendments and Churchill made a speech saying that, if the Lords insisted on amendments to the Budget, a dissolution and a general election were inevitable. For this he was criticised by his Prime Minister but unsurprisingly remained unrepentant.

It was a heated political summer. On 29 July the Clerk of the Commons recorded: 'Lloyd George has a fantastic notion, probably suggested to him by Winston Churchill, that, for the purpose of putting a stronger screw on the Lords, the passing of the Appropriation Bill ought to be postponed until after that of the Finance Bill.'[23] The purpose of an Appropriation Bill would have been to provide some temporary finance to keep the public services and the armed forces going while the Finance Bill continued to be argued out. Without either an Appropriation Bill or a Finance Bill the public services would, in theory at least, have ground to a halt.

On 12 August, the all-important day when grouse shooting started and many members would have expected to be on the moors, Pease wrote in his diary:

> Called into Cabinet to state what dates I proposed to give to budget the following week and to explain how I proposed we could secure clause fourteen this week. I said by threat of Saturday's sitting and to take it on Friday after third reading of Appropriation Bill. I was entrusted to do this – and got arrangements through later with Hood.

On the same day Asquith wrote to his Chief Whip, 'Dear Jack, I do not propose to return to the House after dinner tonight, as I am rather done up with the heat and have to prepare for Bletchley tomorrow. Ever Yours H.H.A.'[24]

There was no let-up. Pease came back from six days of shooting in Scotland and immediately started talking with Asquith about the possibility of a general election in January. It was his job to deal with parliamentary candidates and to make sure that there were no three-cornered fights between Liberal, Labour and Tory candidates as a result of which the Tories would win seats on minority votes. He could not himself believe that the Lords would reject the Finance Bill as he, rightly, saw that this was bound to lead to restriction or abolition of the Lords' right to veto Bills that had passed the Commons. But the two issues of Lloyd George's radical Budget and the Lords' veto had become inextricably mixed. The Irish Nationalists were especially keen on reducing the Lords' veto. They knew that, if they were to obtain their objective of Home Rule, they had to cripple the powers of the Tory majority in the Lords first.

Pease himself got caught up in the argument. Speaking at a meeting of his Essex constituents, he was reported in the press as saying that, although the Commons recognised that the Budget had to go to the Lords and have the King's sanction, 'the Commons did not recognise the right of either King or Lords to reject these proposals from the representatives of the people.'[25] His knuckles were rapped by Lord Knollys, the King's private secretary, for what was regarded as the unnecessary introduction of the King's name and he wrote a rambling apology: 'My remarks had reference only to the method by which the veto powers of the Upper House might be limited, and that if the necessity arose advice might be given by ministers to secure the creation of peers to enable the mandate of the country to be carried through, if ordinary means failed.'[26]

And so the story of the creation of more peers in order to limit the power of the Lords spread around. On 4 November 1909, the Finance Bill passed its third reading in the Commons by 379 votes to 149. It passed on to the Lords where Lansdowne proposed that 'this House is not justified in giving its assent to the Bill until it has been submitted to the judgement of the country.' On 30 November the Lords threw out the budget by 350 votes to 75. The clash between Commons and Lords could not have been more evident. Asquith announced the dissolution of the Commons and elections in January 1910. He also, following the example of 1832, when William IV was asked, but refused, to create additional peers, asked Edward VII how he would answer if he was requested to make sufficient Liberal peers to ensure the passage of the Finance Bill through the Upper House. The King's answer was conditional. He would only agree to do this if a Liberal majority was again returned in a further general election after that of January 1910.

Although Liberal ministers knew that this had been the King's answer, most of the Liberal Party did not. They, and much of the country, thought that Asquith had obtained a firm royal promise that the Lords would be coerced by a mass creation of peers.

The election destroyed the overall Liberal majority. The Conservative Unionists gained over 100 seats and the Liberals could only remain in government with the support of the Irish Nationalists and the Labour Members. The hope that reform of the House of Lords, and taxation of privileged land owners – about whom Lloyd George and Churchill had been making bitter public comments – would arouse a radical spirit in the electorate proved quite wrong. Pease, who had forecast that the Liberals would keep 315 seats as against the actual result of 275, lost his own Essex seat at Saffron Walden by 4,283 votes to 4,011. As soon as he heard the result Asquith wired Pease saying, 'This is the worst incident of the election and grieves me more than I can say.' Two weeks later he offered Pease a seat in the Cabinet as First Commissioner of Works, and Pease, hard pressed by his wife to have a Cabinet seat with £4,000 a year, accepted gratefully. Asquith then changed his mind and Pease joined the Cabinet in the largely honorific role of Chancellor of the Duchy of Lancaster but later became President of the Board of Education. The safe seat of Rotherham was handed over to him by Sir William Holland, who was indignant that he had already paid £10,000 for a baronetcy but was now, in recompense, given a peerage.

In his nineteen months as Government Chief Whip Pease had steered Asquith through gale-force winds in Parliament. Although Lloyd George and other members of Asquith's Cabinet thought little of Pease's brain, Asquith was determined to keep him and use him as a faithful friend, one to be regularly consulted on difficult issues. He was succeeded by the Master of Elibank who had been with him in the whips' office and had something of a reputation as a slick operator. Pease himself was not totally happy with him and J.A. Spender, the editor of the *Westminster Gazette*, wrote later, 'beside Elibank I felt myself a mere beginner in the art of smoothing.'[27]

Pease, like all Chief Whips at this time, only attended Cabinet by invitation but almost invariably he spoke to Asquith after Cabinet and was told all that had happened. Asquith constantly went over the problems of managing government business in the Commons with him. Edwin Montagu, the

Prime Minister's parliamentary private secretary, is said to have reported to Walter Runciman (President of the Board of Education) on 12 May 1909 that he had nothing to do and he never saw Asquith. 'Pease gains in influence and reputation for infallibility every day.' In his diary for 20 October 1908 Pease wrote, 'It is more obvious to me than ever that the Chief Whip should be in the Cabinet, if he is to look after the time of the House and keep ministers with departments in touch with Private Members' views.' The next two years were to underline the importance of Chief Whips.

TEN

A game of bluff –
Elibank and Balcarres, 1910–12

The Liberal Prime Minister, Asquith, appointed Alick Murray, the Master of Elibank, as his Government Chief Whip at an extraordinarily difficult time. The election of January 1910, far from producing the small Liberal majority over the Conservative Unionists which Pease had forecast and which Asquith desperately needed, returned 275 Liberals to 273 Unionists with the Irish Nationalists and the Labour Party holding the balance. The parliamentary Labour Party were to prove a reliable ally for the Liberals but the votes of the Irish Nationalists could only be assured if they saw progress towards Home Rule. This meant either a radical change in the membership of the Lords or the abolition of its veto. Lloyd George's 'People's Budget' of 1909 had still not passed the Lords.

Elibank, always referred to by his staff as The Master, came from an old Scottish family. He had been in the whips' office since 1905. Although Asquith had briefly removed him to make him under-secretary of India in 1909, he now returned as an experienced hand for an extraordinary parliamentary battle. For some weeks after the election it was not clear how Asquith intended to play his cards. David Balcarres, who had been in the Conservative whips' office since 1903, wrote in his diary for 24 February 1910:

Oh, the temperament of the new House of Commons! For the last four years we have worked under disadvantages of unique extent – and our fight was courageous in the extreme, for we were throughout disheartened by the terrible paucity of numbers, by the overweening bearing of our opponents, and by the galling sense of our own defeat. Now all is changed. We attack a glum and dejected government. Cheers now greet our speakers from the furthermost benches on the Speaker's left [the opposition side of the Chamber]. Even a bad argument now receives greater applause than would have been granted twelve months ago to a brilliant repartee. And the more I survey our new men the more confident do I become that among our recruits there are many who are not only keen and zealous, but active and competent allies.[1]

The reverse was true on the government side of the House. The Liberals had lost ninety-eight seats. They found this hard to believe and the new Chief Whip wrote a despairing memo for his own records:

The general situation was much complicated by the misinterpretation of the Prime Minister's statement at the Albert Hall in December to the effect that he would neither hold Office nor assume Office without obtaining Guarantees from the Sovereign. When it was found that there was no doubt that this speech had been completely misinterpreted in the Country, and that the Government were retaining Office without any attempt, so far as the public were aware, to come to grips with the House of Lords, a flatness fell on the Liberal Party... Mr Asquith's speech on the Address – the very worst I have ever heard him make – reflected this feeling, and he himself for the time being lost his accustomed nerve, strained as he was to the utmost by continual Cabinet meetings and the growing discontent of his Party, culminating in disagreeable speeches from our own benches and open attacks from the Tories on his alleged breach of faith. In a week, the Prime Minister's prestige fell to so low an ebb that at one moment I despaired of his ever recovering it... On the Saturday afternoon following the meeting of Parliament, I had a long talk with Edward Grey at the Foreign Office on the situation. Grey was on the point of resignation, but I pointed out to him how much the Prime Minister had lost ground in the House of Commons and in the Country, and that at this juncture his, Grey's, resignation would deal a blow at the Prime Minister from which he would never recover...

My main object at this time was to prevent the Party getting completely out of hand. There is no doubt that the Cabinet in these early days was absolutely discredited. It was well known that they were wrangling amongst themselves, because some of them were indiscreet enough to give hints to their friends as to what was occurring round the table. The Prime Minister, as I said before, had lost his nerve, he had no grip of the situation, and at any moment the secession of important Ministers would have brought down the whole fabric. I pressed on Ministers, separately and individually, that a disappointed Party in the Country looked at the Cabinet to cease their internecine quarrels and to pull the Country through its difficulties. In the House of Commons, the position was intolerable. Groups of Liberals were meeting constantly, rebellion was in the air, the Irish, suspicious of the Whig element in the Cabinet, were, through that astute Parliamentarian, T.P. O'Connor, unceasingly stirring up our militants to action. No sooner had I headed off one group than another was on me!...[2]

Elibank used this quiet, uneasy period to give a private lunch for the Prince of Wales, the future George V, who was generally considered to be a Tory supporter. However, Elibank, as a senior whip, had had the title of Comptroller of the Royal Household after the Liberal victory in 1906. The daily duty of keeping the King informed of what was happening in Parliament had passed on to him, but this also brought him in touch with the Prince of Wales who fell into the habit of visiting the House of Commons. A note from his private secretary, Bigge, on 27 February showed a commonplace worry about the detail of a visit:

The Prince of Wales would like to come to the House of Commons to-morrow afternoon if you could kindly arrange that he and his Equerry could have a seat. He will arrive at 3.30, and says he really does not wish to trouble anyone to meet him, so long as he can leave his coat in the Whip's room, but *I* think if you *can* do as before and ask John Fuller or any one of your colleagues to be there, it would be better. Please send me word by telephone to say 'all right'.[3]

Elibank's aim was to soften up the Prince of Wales about the coming parliamentary crisis and to persuade him of the moderation of the Liberal government despite their connection with the Irish Nationalists and the commitment to House of Lords reform. The Elibank papers contain an agenda for the lunch in the handwriting of R.H. Davis, the Master's private secretary at 12 Downing Street. It was dictated to him by Elibank and it starts:

Objective:

1. To initiate opinion and conduce the more favourable view of our policy.

2. To suggest to mind some possible acts of mediation to avert crisis.

3. To bring about arbitration between the 2.

There follow sixteen pages of handwritten notes concerning what was said to the Prince of Wales. It ends with the words:

Ground of approach.

Dangers: deadlock

Majority – all P would press for C support.

If assured, general election would succeed and strengthen Position.

If refused – inevitable general election with C introduced on party platform.

(Balfour could not carry on. Could not get supply and so must call Parliament together – defeated by combination)

This would mean great and grave crisis – which might *endanger* C's position.

The one force which is irresistible in country is electorate. If it returned same number of members of all parties, government could not carry on. Liberals must refuse unless guarantees and (are) to be put in force without more delay.

U. could not govern – with Irish against them.

Alliance with Irish would break up U party – none too solid now.

Always preserve in discussion preliminary essential that veto must be *abolished* in finance and *curtailed* otherwise.

Room for negotiation and compromise in second – none in first.

That is key of situation

Bear in mind also   Socialists and

Labour and

Irish and

Extreme Radicals if joining in one party would make liberalism impossible and must give Tariff Reformers better opportunity than they would ever have expected.[4]

Despite his friendship with Elibank, the Prince of Wales remained suspicious of the Liberal government. For two months it was not clear whether Asquith and the Liberal government would press ahead with Lloyd George's People's Budget. Then, on 14 April, the die was cast. Asquith made his concordat with Redmond, the head of the Irish Nationalists, and announced resolutions in the Commons to limit the veto of the Lords. He added that, if the Lords did not accept this policy, 'we shall feel it our duty immediately to tender advice to the Crown as to steps which would have to be taken if that policy is to receive statutory effect in this Parliament.'[5] Elibank recorded that Asquith had scored a great parliamentary triumph that evening and that all his lost prestige had been recovered. Balcarres, the Conservative Deputy Chief Whip, saw matters from a different, opposition point of view:

> The House was excited and petulant when he [Asquith] began. Balfour roused some animosities, and when Lowther [the Speaker] adjourned the House tempers were roused, cries echoed, and members did not leave the Chamber. For two or three minutes one expected a fiendish explosion... I caught sight of Walter Erskine [Assistant Sergeant at Arms] and he promptly acted on my suggestion of lowering the lights. This cooled ardour and the Chamber rapidly emptied itself – but the lobby continued a scene of splutter for any minutes.[6]

Three weeks later King Edward VII died. A sense of gentlemanly propriety required that the new King should be given time before the crucial request to use his Royal Prerogative and create many more Liberal peers was revived. A private constitutional conference between the leaders of the two main parties took place to see whether they could reach agreement on reform of the House of Lords. The conference met twenty-one times between June and November. 'Exactly like a Cabinet,' said Balfour, 'but much more united.' But, despite the friendly atmosphere, the search for a solution inevitably failed. Given the mood of the times, no compromise was possible. The conference broke up without agreement and without any disclosure of its proceedings.

Churchill himself took a typically bellicose line, assuming that there would be another election in the autumn and that the Liberals would only win this if the constituencies were 'properly manned'. For action on this he turned to Elibank, and Elibank, in turn, was praised by Balcarres for what he was doing to keep up the Liberal associations. 'His work in the constituencies has been admirable. He has spent his holiday travelling about, rousing enthusiasm among local magnates, forcing them to adopt candidates, distributing cash with judgement, and generally rehabilitating an organisation which was going to bits under the clumsy handling of Jack Pease.'[7] Balcarres knew an equal when he saw one. He added, 'Whatever be the outcome of the fight, Elibank stands out as one who has done much for his party; and he starts with the advantage of being a gentleman.'

The election took place in December but did nothing to resolve the stalemate. The Liberals now held just one more seat than the Conservative Unionists, 272 to 271, and Asquith again was only kept in power by the votes of Irish Nationalists and the Labour Party.

As early as the 17 December, four days before the last of the election results was announced, Lloyd George, the Chancellor of the Exchequer, wrote to Asquith:

Is it not vital that you should see the King at the earliest possible moment? Everything depends on the next few days. The Tory papers which he reads, and whose opinions in the main he accepts and assimilates, are busily engaged in persuading him that our majority is inadequate.

Many if not most of those who came in contact with him are hostile to the Liberal Government and imperceptibly influence his judgement.

If he adopts the Tory view of the election now, and each aspect of it sinks into his brain, the difficulties later on will be enormously increased and may well become insuperable.

An interview with him now would see him right and as he means well he would then remain right.

Moreover, is he not entitled to see his Chief Minister and talk matters over with him as soon as the election is finally ended?

It is a very grave position for him and it can hardly be treated as if it were a matter of trivial consequence that could stand over until a more convenient season.

Elibank wrote back to Lloyd George from 12 Downing Street on 21 December:

> My dear Chancellor, the PM has seen the King: the interview was cordial and satisfactory. Asquith pointed out that the majority was cohesive and formidable and had been 'returned' after what in effect had been a referendum. HM complained that he had not been 'trusted' to do the right thing but the PM made short work of the 'secret agreement' grievance remarking that he had sacred obligations to Colleagues and that he would have acted precisely in the same manner to the late King.
>
> The King trotted out the Bigge [the King's private secretary] arguments re Irish [that the government only had a majority with the help of the Irish members] which were at once demolished – the British majority being evidently a new idea to him!
>
> He is anxious that the Parliament Bill should be passed before the coronation. We must try and do it, but the *necessary* business to be taken will make it difficult. The King also wished to send Knollys [also a private secretary] to sound A.J.B. [Balfour] as to his intentions, but the PM has dissuaded him from this course – much to the relief of Knollys!
>
> Bigge comes to see me tonight and I hope to keep him friendlily inclined to us; at any rate much patience is necessary in dealing with him. I have received a fairly reasonable letter from him since my two conversations with him.[8]

'The Secret Agreement Grievance'[9] which Elibank mentions obscurely refers to the point as to whether Asquith had earlier obtained a firm but secret agreement from either Edward VII or George V that, if the Liberals won the second 1910 election, the Crown would definitely agree to the creation of enough new peers to get a Bill reforming and reducing the powers of the House of Lords through Parliament. It is also questionable whether the Liberals had, in statistical terms at least, a majority after the December 1910 election, given that they only had 272 seats out of a total of 670. Nor had any specific figure for the number of new peers ever been agreed between King and Prime Minister. This was the point that was at the heart of the game of bluff to be played between Liberal and Conservative Chief Whips in 1911.

On 21 February Asquith introduced the Parliament Bill in the Commons, removing the right of the Lords to veto any Money Bill and restricting its veto rights on other Bills to a delay of two parliamentary sessions. It was a short Bill but its consequences were huge. Elibank's brother, Arthur Murray, wrote proudly of him: 'since Alick had taken over the Office of Chief Liberal Whip the first hand of the "Commons v. Lords" rubber had been played. It had not been an easy hand – the next was to prove no easier.'[10]

A month earlier Balcarres had been approached with a view to his taking over as Conservative Chief Whip but with the responsibilities being divided. He would be responsible for patronage and parliamentary business but organisation of the constituencies, selection of candidates and office work would move to a new chairman of the Unionist Party. Balcarres was Balfour's obvious choice but he wrote in his diary:

> I hate it. One gets no thanks, and much blame, and one is treated as a hewer of wood, a drawer of water, by men who haven't a tenth of our experience but who think the Whip has always to be in attendance, that he is a kind of fag to all and sundry, and that if anything goes wrong the unpaid and overworked slave must bear the blame.
>
> Seven years of this is enough to ruin any man, for all parliamentary skill is atrophied by this restless incessant work. One has no time to attend to the debates, no leisure to practise speaking. All one's work is done in the lobbies. Two or three more years of it and I shall have to abandon all hope of successful office.

A few days later, he is more cheerful. 'We are going to strengthen the Whips' room by two new men, Wilfrid Ashley and a Somersetshire foxhunting squire with maroon countenance, and incredible astuteness, one Sanders, a pleasant fellow: loyal, keen, witty and a worker. This will relieve me a good deal.'[11]

Three days later he added a complaint in his diary that every Chief Whip has repeated: 'Ex Ministers must attend better: Whips must be better informed, conferences more frequent – discussion invited rather than deprecated.' But he also wished to see a closer connection between the political parties in the two Houses and he expected to become responsible for reforming the Whips and 'the speaking departments' in the Lords.

The Parliament Bill, limiting the Lords' power of veto but not attempting to change the composition of the Upper House, passed its Commons third reading on 15 May and a week later reached the House of Lords. There it was amended out of recognition, most significantly by effectively removing Irish Home Rule from the veto-limits on the Upper House, an amendment that could not possibly be acceptable to the Irish Nationalists.

The tension between the political parties became worse. A letter appeared in *The Times* towards the end of May denouncing those Liberals who had attended a fancy dress ball given by two Conservatives, one of them a good friend of Churchill, now First Lord of the Admiralty. The Churchills' presence at the ball did not please Balcarres: 'Mrs Churchill by the way created no little stir by going to the fancy dress ball the other night disguised as a nun, and obviously about to enrich the world with offspring. Increase duly arrived within 48 hours. Her profile caused disagreeable comments. Churchill also, as a cardinal, did not inspire much respect.'[12]

The question of how many peers the Liberal government might have to create in order to get the Parliament Bill through the Lords dominated conversation. Balcarres reported sarcastically that a rich man, whose money bags the Liberals were anxious to squeeze, was virtually promised a peerage in return for £120,000 or more which would pay for an extension of the Science Museum at South Kensington but he then withdrew the gift as he did not wish to be one of several hundred new peers. He had however 'received a definite assurance that for the time being there was no intention of asking H.M. to create peers in any abnormal numbers'.[13]

Almost the only day when reference to the new peerages vanished from the pages of Balcarres's diary was on 22 June when he commented on George V's coronation.

One of the great successes of the Coronation was a stand-up fight between the two kilted princes after the service in Westminster Abbey. By some imprudence the Prince of Wales and his sister were sent in a state coach with the younger brothers, but without a controlling prelate or pedagogue. When fairly started from the Abbey a free fight began to the huge delight of the spectators in Whitehall. The efforts of Princess Mary to mollify the combatants were sincere but ineffectual, and during the strife she nearly had her sweet little coronet knocked off! Peace was ultimately restored after about fifty yards of hullabaloo.

Balcarres officially became the new Conservative Chief Whip on 1 July. Thus two new Chief Whips faced each other, both from old Scottish families and both very close to their political masters, Elibank to Asquith, Balcarres to Balfour. In the days that immediately followed Balcarres's appointment, Elibank stepped up the bluffing as the Conservative majority in the Lords passed more amendments to the Parliament Bill. Balcarres argued to Balfour that he found it incredible that backwoodsmen in the Lords, by their amendments to the Parliament Bill, would force the creation of more peers, 'thus prostituting their order and at the same time making a potential majority for Home Rule'.[14]

Elibank was not going to take anything for granted. He was an early master of political spin, and newspaper owners and journalists, much more naïve than today, were eager to swallow the morsels he threw at them.

On 11 July Elibank had lunch with Kennedy Jones of the *Daily Mail* and saw Nicholson of *The Times* on the evening of the same day. To both he made it clear that he had a list of potential peers ready. To *The Times* he implied that there were more than 500 names on the list. The following day he wrote two mildly boastful letters from 12 Downing Street. The first was to Bigge who had been created Lord Stamfordham in the Coronation honours:

Please look at today's "*Daily Mail*" where you will find an article headed: 'Indiscretion of a Whip' – which will do much good! I think it is quite unnecessary to say more than that various newspapers on both sides have been publishing lists of possible peers for sometime back, as it must be a very obvious deduction for anyone to draw that, when a constitutional crisis of this magnitude is taking place, any Chief Whip would be a fool who did not prepare for eventualities. I, of course, have a list, as I told you some time ago, but the suggestion contained in the "*Daily Mail*" article that it has been handed about is obviously untrue. No one has seen it outside the Whips' room. I may, perhaps add for your information that the writer of the article lunched with me today. When we meet in Wales, I will tell you what passed between us.

The second letter is to the Prime Minister:

> Please see accompanying article in today's "*Daily Mail*" – also copy of a letter that I have written to Bigge on the subject. The writer of the article is – Kennedy Jones. He lunched with me today!
>
> I do not despair of getting the "*Daily Mail*" to help us, but the curvature may take a little time. Harold Harmsworth [younger brother of Alfred Harmsworth. Together they founded the *Daily Mail* in 1896 and the *Daily Mirror* in 1903] was with me this morning and returns to see me this afternoon.
>
> Kennedy Jones tells me that Arthur Balfour on the 25th of this month in the City is going to call upon you to create the Peers, but he [KJ] adds that, if you will agree to accept the amendments dealing with the Crown, the Protestant succession and the Speaker's Committee (which he said was advocated by Peel and is very popular in the country) and moreover would allow our intention to do so to reach the "*Daily Mail*" before Balfour speaks, it will spike Balfour's guns, and "*Daily Mail*" will urge the opposition and its readers to let the Bill pass. He says that these concessions will save the Opposition leader's "amour-propre".
>
> Kennedy Jones spoke pretty freely about the Tory Party, saying that it was completely broken and leaderless. I chaffed KJ about the accompanying article which I said he would not have taken the trouble to write had he not attached very great importance to the possibilities of the creation of peers. I hope to see you tomorrow.

On the same day, 12 July 1911, a note appeared in *The Times* headed 'Political Notes – the Creation of Peers – the Whip's List'. This read:

> It has for some time been understood in ministerial circles that the Master of Elibank, as Chief Whip, has had the preparation of the list of names of supporters of the Liberal party which the ministry will submit to the King if the constitutional crisis ends in a creation of Peers. The number 500, with which the public has been familiarised, there is reason to believe was taken as the number that might be required in extreme eventualities, and it is stated that there are more than 500 hundred names now on the list... The list is no

thing of yesterday. There is a good reason for saying that a good deal of the work in connection with it was done in the month of May. During that month the Master of Elibank was sometimes absent from the House of Commons, and his absences led to a rumour that he was again taking an active interest in the work of a Government Department and would enter the Cabinet when the Government was reconstructed. It is now apparent, however, that at this time the activities of the Master of Elibank were required outside the House in connection with the Government's list.

On his copy of Political Notes R. H. Davis, Elibank's private secretary, wrote, 'these are the Master's notes given to Nicholson in the Chief Whip's room, House of Commons, on the evening of 11 July 1911 to bluff the Tories.' The fourteen typewritten pages, on 10 Downing Street paper, that followed have in fact just 249 names on them, some just as a plain name: Muspratt; Duncan; Caird Esq.; Dundee; F. Harrison Esq. or R.H. Harrison Esq.

The actual number that Asquith and Elibank thought they would have to create was around 125 but the number of 500 was thrown around in order to alarm Tory peers. On 18 July Lloyd George met Balfour and confirmed that George V had agreed in the last resort to create peers to pass the Parliament Bill. Balcarres's diary reads:

Lord Knollys saw the Chief today and repeated the story, but as emanating from the King... Lord Knollys nervous and distressed. He is a regular jackal of the government and has throughout acted as a politician rather than as a courtier. He deserves to be sacked...

I urged most strongly that our party could not be invited to settle its attitude on the strength of verbal statements from a maundering old courtier and an unscrupulous minister. I urged that the Prime Minister who is responsible for the advice to the Throne must himself be the official agency of communications to ourselves. This is a matter where form is as important as substance. Knollys could be thrown over, (Lloyd) George might lie.

My view was accepted.[15]

And Balcarres had only been Conservative Chief Whip for seventeen days.

The Tories were caught in an awful dilemma. Throw out the Parliament Bill altogether, and they would lose, perhaps for ever, their majority in the Lords. All the peers created would be Liberal and hereditary. Vote for the Bill, and they were voting not only for a huge reduction in the power of the Lords but also, given the current make-up of the Commons, for Irish Home Rule which most of them, as befitted the Unionist Party, abhorred. As with most such dilemmas, the end results were attacks on the leadership for sitting on the fence and the cry 'Balfour must go'.

The Shadow Cabinet met two days later, again at Balfour's house in Carlton Gardens. Balcarres made a list dividing those present into three classifications: for acquiescence without forcing creation of peers, ten led by A.J.B.; for driving government to create peers, eight including a fairly reluctant Chief Whip; and uncommitted either way, five. Lansdowne, the Tory leader in the Lords, appears twice, in both the first and the last category. This seems appropriate as it was hard to discover Lansdowne's precise views. Those in the second category were the ditchers, ready to die in the last ditch; the remainder were hedgers, their views liable to trimming.

Balcarres summarised the conflict in one word: quantum. He wrote:

A.J.B. would not mind 150 peers but he is desperately afraid of 400. 150 would equalise conditions in the Lords: would show that the peers do not insist upon preserving their social status, and we should none the less retain the sole asset of the Parliament Bill, namely the two years' delay.

On the other hand, Asquith may say that 150 will not suffice. By appointing 400, he would secure immediate passage of all his bills, and we should lose our one advantage in the measure as it now stands.

Balcarres, as Chief Whip, found himself part of the dilemma. His nature was to be a ditcher, and, above all, he hated the thought of any Conservative peer voting for the radical Parliament Bill. The pragmatist in him realised that the end result of defeating the Bill, though, could be the worst of all possible worlds, the appointment not of 150 Liberal peers but of several hundred. The loyalist in him required him to support his leader's judgement. And, in the end, that is what he did.

The Commons met on 24 July to deal with the Lords' amendments to the Parliament Bill. MPs were in an emotional mood and they behaved accordingly. The opposition taunted the Government by shouting 'Who killed the King?', echoing the gossip that Edward VII's death had been brought on by worry about the determination of the Liberal government to create peers in order to push through their Parliament Bill. Balcarres failed to control the thirty who, as he put it in his diary, kept up an organised outcry.

Shortly before meeting of the House, I learned that F.E. Smith and Hugh Cecil [later respectively the Earl of Birkenhead and Lord Quickswood, Provost of Eton] had determined to howl Asquith down. I had hurried interviews with the ringleaders, but without avail. A scene followed which did our party no credit notwithstanding the recollection that they did it to us in the old days.

Moreover, as I warned the malcontents, our rowdyism was unsuccessful, for although Asquith could only utter disjointed sentences, the noise issued not from a party but from a small fraction, and Elibank turned the tables on us by letting Balfour have a quiet hearing.

The House adjourned in great disorder, A.J.B., as he told me, furious at having been accorded a hearing from Radicals after Tories had refused it to Asquith...

Our behaviour was inexcusable. It was stupid, will create reaction against us, and will further split our party.

That diary comment proved horribly true. Sandars, A.J.B.'s man for all seasons, had written to Balcarres the previous Friday: 'A.J.B. begged me to tell you that it would be quite an error to suppose that he – or for that matter Lansdowne – is opposed to peer creation, say of 100 or 150.' That point of view never got across. The ditchers came to regard both A.J.B. and Lansdowne as unable to take a firm stand and as excessively frightened of the Liberal threat. A.J.B. was strangely unwilling to counter this impression and Balcarres found this difficult to deal with. On 25 July he made the following emotional note of a conversation that evening with his Chief:

A.J.B.: You know my view that the end of the world will not come if x number of peers are created: that also, though perhaps in a modified sense, is Lansdowne's view also [x is the figure quoted in Balcarres' note].

Balcarres: Then can I tell our men? Their position is substantially your own.

A.J.B.: You must not tell our men that I can compromise. There can be no collusion between ourselves and the govt, no manipulation of the division lobby. That would mean complicity and I will have none of it.

Balcarres: At the same time our men are entitled to know the innermost facts, and they, as I repeat, do not really conflict with your views.

A.J.B.: …You can tell them what you think fit, but I dislike whispering in the lobby.

Balcarres: But if you say nothing in public, whisperings are inevitable. I have to safeguard your position. It may prove untenable. Why cannot I do my utmost in this direction?

A.J.B.: I quite understand that both Lansdowne and I may have to resign in consequence of this. I am not certain if such a solution would not be a happy issue. I don't know who for the moment could replace us, but I am ready to contemplate this as a distinct possibility.

Balcarres was turning to resignation of the leadership as the easy way out of a historic problem.

The following days were occupied by a crisis with Germany over the status of Morocco. In between dire warnings about the worsening international scene, Balcarres had time to calculate that it would take 3,000 minutes or 50 hours to swear in 300 new peers and that would destroy the vocal chords of the reading clerk in the Lords. But he was even more alarmed by the growing evidence of the number of Tory peers who, for a wide variety of usually selfish reasons, would support the government. He still thought this the ultimate disloyalty and the worst possible outcome to the crisis.

On Saturday 29 July he noted in his diary:

In Carlton [Club] found that the rot has spread more than I conceived possible. Here is my provisional list of our men who are actually prepared to vote for the Revolution.

Camperdown, sensible and robust; Shaftesbury, always thought him so too; Harris; Sturt, snob; Beaulieu, snob; Ridley, brother-in-law of R; Galway, weak; St Aldwyn, always a funk; Desborough, incredible, but courtier, I suppose; Cromer, a Radical; Donoughmore, inexplicable; Suffolk (USA); Richmond, can't understand; Roxburghe (USA); Ilchester, can't understand; Barrington, gaga; Dunmore (USA behind); Farquhar, toady; ? Rutland – inconceivable; Revelstoke, courtier; Winchelsea, never heard of him; ? Bishop of St David's; ? Curzon (USA).

One of the delightful features of this typically monosyllabic and frank whips' list is that the insertion of USA shows that Balcarres thought the American wives of these peers were pressurising their husbands to ensure that there was no devaluation of their titles. What was special about being a Viscountess or Baroness if suddenly the market was flooded with another three or four hundred of the same description?

The most revealing entry in Balcarres's diary for these extraordinary few weeks was that for the following day, a quiet Sunday, when he suddenly realised the power he had. By changing the way in which he put over his views, or the emphasis that he gave to the different possibilities, he could direct the course of events:

Tomorrow I have to see Elibank. Is it not rather hard that A.J.B. who has my views and knows I am to talk over the matter should leave me without guidance? Lord Lansdowne I have not seen and I suppose I must go into the conference without a word of direction.

I confess a great temptation comes over me. Were I to assume a particular tone in our conversation tomorrow Elibank would report accordingly to his cabinet and in twelve hours orders would be issued for the creation of peers. How far am I for instance entitled to assume that Lord Lansdowne will stop the rot among our own men who propose to support the administration? If I am correct in thinking he must do so, and I make that point clear to Elibank, then again the government loses the support on which it was confidently counting, and must secure its own position by its own agents.

Of course, I can temporise, say I am unprepared and so forth, but Elibank and Asquith want our lead, and are bringing the King up from Cowes on Wednesday (or possibly earlier) to conclude this sordid transaction.

Balcarres was far too honest, too much of a gentleman, to alter the way he presented the possibilities in order to achieve the result that he personally wanted. Other Opposition Chief Whips might have done differently. The argument went on, sometimes furious, sometimes absurd for the next ten days. It was the height of summer, and offices in the Commons were small and hot. Balcarres kept his sense of humour. He noted on 2 August: 'Elibank says that the only compliment he can pay us is to offer to the opposition whips an electric fan to cool our heated brows. We accept the offer.'[16]

In the meantime, Liberal MPs did not hesitate to jump on the bandwagon and suggest suitable names to Elibank. Herbert Lewis MP wrote to him on 2 August:

In the event of a creation of Peers being necessary, may I submit to you the following names :

E.D. Jones of London and Fishguard – a great contractor, member of the firm of Topham, Jones & Railton of George Street, Westminster. Carried out the great harbour works at Gibraltar.

Alderman W.H. Williams, ex-Lord Mayor of Liverpool. Exactly the kind of man who would be elected to a reformed second chamber as the representative of a great municipality. Has a wife who would adorn the Peeresses' gallery. No son.

Thomas Rowland Hughes, Treasurer of Bangor College, formerly General Manager of the North & South Wales Bank, Liverpool. Has a son.

The letter ends with two other names : 'Peter Roberts of Bromfield Hall, Mold and Mr Aralli of Mia Hall, Dysurth, Flintshire are two very wealthy Liberals.'

As the days passed and he realised how many Tory peers would either abstain or vote with the government, Balcarres personally became more of a ditcher and even less ready to compromise. He tried to push both Balfour and Lansdowne in that direction.

Balfour's frivolous sense never left him. Balcarres records him as saying after a disputatious meeting with Lansdowne and Alfred Lyttelton (MP and former Colonial Secretary), 'What funny people I have to deal with: I wonder why people are quarrelsome and so jealous of each other – I love them all but at times they vex me with their naughtiness.'

Balcarres also found time to jest. He had often commented on the amount Asquith drank, especially champagne. A diary note for 2 August, the same day as the offer of the electric fan, says, 'Asquith's troubles are only just beginning. Action has to replace bluff, and the prospect of making 200 or 300 peers is not alluring. To add to his difficulties he yesterday committed the folly of changing his diet. He substituted Amontillado for Marsala – with the result that he is now absolutely speechless.'

But Balcarres found Balfour's failure to give a strong personal lead increasingly irritating. On 4 August he commented sourly that the post of a Chief Whip was always difficult,

> but still more so when his Chief spends so much time in the country. This afternoon, Thursday Balfour and Lord Lansdowne depart from London till next week. Their absence from the 3rd to the 7th is most embarrassing. These are the days preceding the crisis during which their presence here is more than ever imperative. Though not a valetudinarian Balfour thinks much about his health... The Chief fancies that his internal organisation differs from that of everybody else, and he likes going from doctor to doctor discussing symptoms. His bedroom is like a chemist's dispensary. He is longing for Gastein, with its peaceful detachment together with the healing baths which have already done him much good. All this is a source of trouble during these stirring times!

Although the number of ditchers was increasing in the Commons all the time, Lansdowne, badgered by Lord Curzon, had made up his own mind that he might speak against the Liberal government and the Parliament Bill but he was not going to vote against it, and Balfour, with his dislike of organised discipline, was not going to try and dragoon him.

The fatal vote in the Lords came on 10 August, and 131 voted not to insist upon amendments to the Commons amendments and therefore supported the government and the Parliament Bill, 114 voted against. Eight dukes voted against the government, none for the government. Both archbishops and twenty-five Tory peers voted with the Liberal government. None of those listed by Balcarres voted against.

Balfour left for the healing baths of Gastein without waiting for the final verdict. In contrast to his copious notes of previous days, Balcarres's entry for 10 August was of two lines only: 'Bade farewell to A.J.B. at Victoria, on his road to Gastein. At night the Parliament Bill carried by Conservative votes.'

Six days later, as an afterthought, he expanded a little:

The departure of A.J.B. for Gastein before the division on the Parliament Bill is seized upon as a sign of apathy – and makes the hostile critic allege complicity in its most naked form. J.S. Sandars [A.J.B.'s private secretary for nineteen years] is blamed for having allowed it though he was powerless in the matter: it is no good pointing out that A.J.B. booked his tickets for Thursday last (after repeated postponement) in the belief that the division would have taken place the previous night.

Meanwhile, he has written to say that no letters are to be forwarded to him as he can't be bothered to read them.

Balfour's excuse was a feeble one. He could of course have stayed, cancelled the rail tickets and set off on his curative holiday a day or two later. There is a strong sense of unspoken disappointment in Balcarres's notes about the comments that A.J.B. made to him. As loyalty to the Conservative Party was so all-important for Balcarres, it was inevitable that he would have liked Balfour to have come down on the side of the ditchers.

But Elibank had played a very successful game of poker. By giving the impression to both the *Daily Mail* and *The Times* that he was expecting to have to appoint up to 500 peers, by letting it known that he had a list of around that number although, in fact, the list in his papers was half that size, he made the leading hesitant Tories – A.J.B. and Lansdowne and Curzon – fearful of being swamped and thus losing for ever their control of the Upper

House. Conversely, if it had been clear that only around 125 peers would be created, Lansdowne would have voted against the Parliament Bill.

Elibank was a more successful tactician than Balcarres. He got the Parliament Bill through the Lords on a low vote, when he had no outright majority in either House and he had to create no new peers – but he knew the facts. The King, whatever guarantees had been given, was loath to create hundreds of peers and Stamfordham was writing to Elibank from the Royal Yacht saying how much he hoped that the government would win in the Lords, if only with a small majority. Thus Elibank enjoyed the typical advantage of a Government Chief Whip as opposed to an Opposition Chief Whip. He knew far more of the inside story than Balcarres did. But he recorded no jubilation or Te Deum in his diary. By contrast his younger brother, Arthur, could not resist the superlatives. His diary entry reads:

> A day memorable in Britain's history. The great Veto fight is over and democracy has won. In the House of Lords tonight, the crucial division took place on Lord Morley [the Lord President]'s motion that the destructive Lansdowne's amendment excluding Home Rule and including the Referendum and joint Committee, should not be insisted on.
>
> The final scene was played out in a crowded House. It was a strange spectacle. Arrayed against each other were Lord Halsbury's obstinate 'No surrender' party and the little band of Liberals. The scene and the occasion will linger in the memory. Various small bands could be observed watching each other jealously; if one showed symptoms of voting then the other was determined to go into the opposition lobby. Finally the result of the division was announced. The defeat of the 'die-hards' was greeted with loud Liberals cheers and 'Ditcher' hisses...

Arthur Murray's gift for bathos did not leave him; even at historic moments. His next paragraph reads: 'The Royal Observatory at Greenwich reported today, for the first time in its history, a temperature of 100 degrees in the shade.'[17]

Once the Parliament Bill was settled the question of votes for women came back to prominence and occupied much of Elibank's last year as Chief Whip. Asquith was strongly opposed to giving votes to women. Although both Churchill and Lloyd George voted against a so-called Conciliation Bill in 1910 that would have given votes to women but only on a very limited basis, by 1911 a clear majority of the Liberal Cabinet was in favour of helping a Bill on its way. It was agreed that the women's claim should be included in a major Reform Bill which would abolish plural voting and extend the male franchise from eight to ten million voters. Lloyd George and Churchill were worried in different ways.

Lloyd George wrote to Elibank on 5 September 1911:

> I think the Liberal Party ought to make up its mind as a whole that it will either have an extended franchise which would put the working men's wives on to the register as well as spinsters and widows, or that it will have no female franchise at all. The only basis upon which women's suffrage has been conceded in any other country, as you know, is the former. Now, it looks to me that, through sheer drifting, vacillation and something which looks like cowardice, we are likely to find ourselves in the position of putting this wretched Conciliation Bill through the House of Commons, sending it to the Lords and eventually getting it through. Say what you will, that spells disaster to Liberalism; and, unless you take it in hand and take it at once, this catastrophe is inevitable... You alone can save us from a prospect which fills me with despair. I have given a good deal of thought to it; and, when you get this report, I shall be in a position to make one or two suggestions to you as to the best way out.

Churchill, not surprisingly, took a different view. Writing to Elibank on 20 December from the Admiralty, he let off steam in a typical manner:

> We are getting into very great peril over Female Suffrage. Be sure of this: – the Franchise Bill will not get through without a Dissolution if it contains a clause adding 8,000,000 women to the electorate. Nor ought it to get through.
>
> How can the PM honourably use the Parliament Act to force it upon the King, when he has himself declared it to be a 'disastrous mistake'? In the second year of passage of this and the Home Rule Bill the Tories will demand a Dissolution. Votes for women is so unpopular that by-elections will be unfavourable. The King will be entitled obviously to say to his Prime Minister,

'You cannot conscientiously advise me to assent to this vast change. The constituencies have never been consulted. No responsible government is behind it. You do not believe in it yourself.'

The King will dismiss the Ministry and Parliament will be dissolved on the old Plural Voting Register. We shall be in confusion ourselves. With us will go down the Irish cause. The situation that is developing is very like the free trade split in the Tory Party in 1903. I do not understand L.G. [Lloyd George] at all. Our one hope was the referendum which alone gave a reasonable and honourable outlet. He knew my view. And yet he has gone out of his way to rule it out at the very beginning.

He is exactly like Joe [Chamberlain] in 1903: it is with most profound regret that I watch these developments. I have been through it before.

Do not, I beseech you my friend, underrate the danger.

What a ridiculous tragedy it would be if this strong government and party which has made its mark in history was to go down on Petticoat politics! and the last chance of Ireland – our loyal friend – squandered too! It is damnable.

No doubt you have made some deep calculations as to voting in the H of C. Please let me know what they are. But I do not think there is any safety there. If L.G. and Grey go on working themselves up, they will have to go, if Female Suffrage is knocked out. And the PM's position will become impossible if it is put in.

The only safe and honest course is to have a referendum – first to the women to know if they want it: and then to the men to know if they will give it. I am quite willing to abide by the result.

What I cannot stand is making this prodigious change in the teeth of public opinion and out of pure weakness.

Alexander the Great (your forerunner) said the peoples of Asia were slaves because they were not able to pronounce the word 'No'. May you and we avoid this pusillanimity and this fate. Your sincere friend, W.

The Prime Minister's wife, Margot Asquith, added her piece. She wrote to Elibank from the Hotel des Alpes in Murren:

When Henry gets back do see him at once he should be with you first or second. *Don't* recommend the referendum for suffrage which is Winston's idea and the Westminsters. Every female would very properly say he had betrayed them. Let him stick to what he said and try and stop any more stupping (sic). Henry's present position is hopeless and even ridiculous, he alas! never saw the importance of enduring silence on Grey[18] and L. George and this fearful mistake will break us to a certainty – what a subject to smash over!! Get L.G. and all of them to hold their tongues if possible – no PM could be placed in a worse position by colleagues and his own want of anxiety as he is at this moment. Do all get together with sagacity and elasticity to get him out of it if you can. You are my one hope.[19]

Asquith and Elibank, however, were let off the hook by the failure of Bills promoting votes for women to make any progress though the House of Commons. In the most important case Speaker Lowther ruled that a women's suffrage amendment would so change a Bill primarily designed to increase the male suffrage that the Bill would have to be withdrawn and reintroduced. Irish Home Rule, the threat from Germany and the increasing sums of money to be spent on building war ships came back to front stage, and votes for women were postponed until after the First World War was over.

In March 1912 Elibank fell ill and Asquith sent him away for a fortnight. Walter Runciman[20] wrote to him the day before his return:

I am sure that we are all hoping to see you back again tomorrow – cheerfully well – and this is only a line of welcome. It is always pleasant to know that one is missed, and I am saying only the bare truth when I say that your absence left a big gap in our world. John Gulland and Percy [Liberal whips] were excellent, they could not make up for your personality.

You did well to have a complete holiday while you were about it, and I would say one thing alone about your return – don't overwork yourself again – for your health is something of great importance to us as well as of *all* importance to you.

Elibank decided to retire at the end of the 1912 summer session. He was immediately made a peer and he accepted a job in the plutocratic Lord Cowdray's firm, Pearsons. But the news of his retirement came as a surprise to colleagues and friends, not least to Margot Asquith. She wrote from 10 Downing Street on 6 August:

> Dearest Master, I want to ask you a great favour. Of course it will never be the same for me talking to Illingworth [Elibank's successor as Chief Whip] but I wish you would just say to him that I am absolutely trustworthy and helpful with Henry... It is not from personal vanity. I want to know so much that it saves Henry having to tell me and at the rare times when we *are* alone we can close in quickly – you see I see very little of him and if we didn't keep in close and constant political touch our lives would really be apart. He is never surprised with whatever I know and I often *don't* tell him even that I know.

There is no evidence that Elibank passed on this touching message to his successor.

Both as Government Chief Whip and as Patronage Secretary, Elibank made one substantial error of judgement. In April 1912 he along with Lloyd George, the Chancellor of the Exchequer, and Rufus Isaacs, recently appointed Attorney General, bought shares in the American Marconi Company. Rufus Isaacs' brother was Godfrey Isaacs who, in turn, was managing director of the English Marconi Company. They bought shares at £2 and, on the first day that the shares were available to the public, they closed at £4. The lack of judgement lay in the fact that a month earlier, in March, the English Marconi company had signed a contract with the Post Office to build the first six of what was to be an Imperial Chain of wireless stations linking the British Empire together from Australia and Africa to Canada. The system would be owned by the state but Marconi were to be the prime contractor and were generally supposed to be making a very large profit out of the deal. It was easy to assume that the American Marconi would in some degree benefit from the English Marconi's success.

The Tories, smarting from their defeat over the Parliament Bill the year before, fell with relish on the fact that the managing director of Marconi was the brother of the Attorney General. The sinking of the *Titanic* on its maiden voyage a month after the tender added a tragic boost. The few passengers who had been saved owed their lives to the new wireless apparatus on board the *Titanic* and the messages that were sent over it, urging the nearest ships in the North Atlantic to come to the rescue of the lifeboats. Shares in the English Marconi Company which had been £3. 6s. 3d. at the end of December 1911 were £9 by March 1912.

Throughout the summer of 1912 Members of Parliament pressed the postmaster general, Herbert Samuel, to publish the contract with Marconi and to have an opportunity to debate it. Motions were inevitably put down for a select committee to consider the whole matter.

On 19 July Samuel tabled the contract in the House and, the following day, an article appeared in a weekly journal, the *Outlook*, which beat the drum of speculation about insider dealing as hard as possible: 'The Marconi Company has from its birth been a child of darkness. Its finance has been a most chequered and erratic sort. Its relations with certain Ministers have not always been purely official or political.' The Isaacs brothers and Herbert Samuel were Jews, and anti-Jewish bias was rampant in the article:

> It is also a matter of common knowledge that the postmaster general for the time being bears the honoured name of Samuel. Here we have two financiers of the same nationality bidding against each other, with a third in the background acting perhaps as mutual friend... The Marconi Company have published their version of the contract more than once, and on the strength of it their shares went up from the 6/3d of 1908 to about £9, yet the postmaster general is still busy dotting its i's and crossing its t's.

Another journal, *Eyewitness*, founded by Hilaire Belloc and edited by Cecil Chesterton, a brother of G.K. Chesterton, was even ruder.

> What progress is the Marconi scandal making? We ask the question merely from curiosity and under no illusion as to the inevitable end of the affair. Everybody knows the record of Isaacs and his father, and his uncle, and in general of the whole family. Isaacs' brother is chairman of the Marconi Company, it has therefore been secretly arranged between Isaacs and Samuel that the British people shall give the Marconi Company a very large sum of money through the agency of the said Samuel, and for the benefit of the said Isaacs. Incidentally, the monopoly that is to be granted to Isaacs No. 2,

through the ardent charity of Isaacs No. 1 and his colleague the postmaster general, is a monopoly involving antiquated methods, the refusal of competing tenders far cheaper and far more efficient, and the saddling of the country with corruptly purchased goods...

Another reason why the swindle, or rather theft, impudent and barefaced as it is, will go through is that we have in this country no method of punishing men who are guilty of this kind of thing...[21]

A select committee was set up in the autumn of 1912 and, after many months, the contract with Marconi was approved. A libel action was brought a year later by Godfrey Isaacs against Cecil Chesterton, and Chesterton was found guilty and ordered to pay a fine of £100 and Isaacs' legal costs. Asquith stood by Lloyd George, who continued as Chancellor of the Exchequer, and by Rufus Isaacs who became Lord Chief Justice and Marquis of Reading and, then, Viceroy of India. The claim that there had been insider knowledge in the purchase of the American Marconi shares did not, after months of accusation and debate, stand up to rigorous analysis. But Elibank resigned on 7 August, the day Parliament broke up for the summer recess but also the day before the first inflammatory article in *Eyewitness*. As Patronage Secretary, Elibank was in a particularly difficult position and used ill health as the excuse for giving up his very sensitive job. His brother simply recorded in his diary for the day: 'The House rose today for the summer recess. A.O.M. [Alick Murray] resigns his seat in Parliament and the Chief Whipship. Everyone is tired and exhausted physically and mentally.'

Balcarres, by contrast, prospered after his and Balfour's defeat over the Parliament Bill. Balfour, recuperating in Bad Gastein, wrote with magnificent detachment to Lady Elcho, his constant friend and fellow letter writer for thirty years, on 15 August, five days after the Liberals' victory in the Lords and three days before the Parliament Act became law:

I have for the moment forgotten politics. I gather from my correspondence that every one in England is furious with someone else – especially is every Unionist furious with some other Unionist. I also should be furious if I thought about it; but I do not; and all party clamours, strikes and rumours of strikes come to my ears dim and deadened by sheer distance.

Balfour had by now taken the decision to resign at leader of the Conservative Party. He returned from Bad Gastein on 2 September and went almost directly to Whittingehame, the large Balfour family house in East Lothian. Balcarres rented a house nearby and visited Whittingehame three times over the next few weeks, first trying to persuade Balfour not to retire and then, realising that that was a lost cause, persuading him to delay his departure until Parliament met again and he had had the opportunity to make a number of reputation-rebuilding speeches in Scotland and in Parliament at the end of the recess. He wrote a charming memo for himself on 2 October after an hour alone with Balfour: 'I reverted to the objection I advanced yesterday – told him that the first duty of life was to part with it handsomely – that to retire 48 hours before the House met would involve us in confusion, and would shroud his position with ambiguity, besides laying him open to the charge of cowardice.' This from a 42-year-old to a past prime minister old enough to be his father.

Parliament met again on 24 October. Balfour spoke on both the first and second days and Balcarres recorded a conversation with Harry Chaplin, owner of the Derby winner in 1867 and an MP since 1868: 'Says that Balfour's speeches in Scotland, together with those delivered here yesterday and today, show him to be not only the best living parliamentarian, but also the only conceivable leader of our party.' Balcarres added in his diary that he felt proud that he had persuaded Balfour to make these speeches. But it would not make the task of his successor any easier.

Austen Chamberlain[22] was the preferred choice of Balfour and Lansdowne to succeed. Although he had opposed Balfour over the Parliament Bill, Chamberlaine was regarded as loyal to Balfour and by Balcarres who wrote in his diary for 25 October:

For my part I can only look to Austen Chamberlain. Walter Long[23] is hopeless, impossible. He is stale and turgid: his temper is peppery and twelve months hence will be uncontrollable. Bonar Law[24] won't do. He seems almost to be retiring from politics so sporadic is his attendance, and so reluctant is he to take an active part in our work. Moreover he is more reserved and unapproachable every day.

He added, two days later:

> Bonar Law is interested in subjects, not in politics. Whole branches of public
> life are a closed book to him, whereas Austen, approachable, interestable, and
> wedded to the whole field of political thought, has the further advantage of
> varied experience: whip, treasury, postmaster general, admiralty, exchequer –
> quite a large range.

As so often with elections, it did not work out as the Chief Whip intended.
Three weeks later, on Monday 13 November, Bonar Law was Balcarres's
new chief.

After a few more protestations and resolutions from dubious allies
expressing total confidence, Balfour announced his resignation on the
afternoon of Wednesday 8 November at a meeting in the City, 'twenty or thirty
people present in a grubby little city office at the end of a squalid passage – no
convenience for the reporters, a telephone bell which refused to be silenced –
a good deal of emotion in the Chief's speech with those occasional hesitations
which mar the effect of his public speeches.'[25] The secret, although gossip had
been on many tongues, had been well kept, and no newspaper achieved a scoop.

Later that evening, at 6 p.m., Balcarres sent telegrams to all members of
the parliamentary party to attend a meeting at the Carlton Club at midday
the following Monday. He had for some days been stressing that, if there was
a meeting, he was the only one who could summon it. The intention was to
have a ballot, for the first time in Unionist history, and even a second ballot
which would enable the Irish Unionists to vote for their leader, Carson, on
the first ballot but, reckoning that he had no real chance, to transfer their
votes to Walter Long on the second ballot.

On Thursday 9 November, at lunchtime at the Carlton Club, Balcarres
recorded the betting as 6 to 4 in Walter Long's favour, but also a growing
feeling that somehow a ballot was not right for the party. Both Chamberlain
and Long started to tell Balcarres that they might withdraw in favour of a
neutral candidate, assuming the other did the same. Henry Chaplin told
Balcarres in the evening that he concurred 'in ballot if desired by our men, but
says he hates it for parliamentary purposes, a fortiori for use at a private club
gathering'. Meanwhile, Bonar Law made it clear that he intended to stand.

By the next day the decision had been taken. After further separate talks with Balcarres, Austen Chamberlain and Walter Long both agreed that they would withdraw and, instead, support Bonar Law, Long proposing him, Chamberlaine seconding him. The unity of the party was the only reason advanced by either men; the rancour of the Parliament Bill remained; Long had been a hedger, Austen a ditcher, whereas Bonar Law was listed by Balcarres as one of the uncommitted. Sitting on the fence between hedge and ditch may not have been a notable triumph of principle but was certainly rewarded in this case.

More fundamentally, the parliamentary party was not yet ready for a straight vote among themselves for a new leader. Although some complained that one of the many objections to what Balcarres told them on the Friday afternoon was that it was 'arranged' and undemocratic, the majority were quite unaccustomed to full-blooded democracy in any aspect of life. They expected to be consulted and, then, the decision to be arranged by those in charge, notably by the Chief Whip.

In the long comments in his diary note for Sunday 12 November, Balcarres showed no regret at the withdrawal of Chamberlain; he had moved on. He was now concerned about the influences on Bonar Law, particularly the influence of Max Aitken, an MP since 1910 and newly knighted:

Harry Forster [a Tory whip since 1905] says he would prefer W. Long with all his absurdities to any whisperer. Bonar Law does whisper, and whispers into the ear of Sir Max Aitken whose judgement must not weigh unduly with a House of Commons leader – if such he prove to be.

I make no forecast of tomorrow's meeting; but there is always a danger that an important person will change his mind.

No important person changed their mind.

Two hundred and thirty one members were present at the Carlton Club on the Monday morning. Chaplin opened the meeting, Long and Chamberlain both spoke in Bonar Law's favour. Carson fetched Bonar Law and introduced him to the meeting, and Balcarres records that by now 'all doubts and hesitations had vanished. On entering Bonar Law had an ovation – all stood and cheered, with one exception, namely Banbury [a Tory MP since 1892] who remained seated in the front row. This caused comment afterwards.'[26] The meeting lasted only fifty-five minutes. There is a parallel with the ease with which Michael Howard became leader of the Conservative Party following Iain Duncan Smith's dismissal. Conflict was expected, but avoided

The Chief Whip felt a justifiable sense of relief but no great sense of personal pleasure or sorrow, merely satisfaction at a job done well. He ends his diary note for the Monday on an unusually reflective note:

> Up till the last moment there was a real risk that one indiscreet comment, or one pointed question might have given rise to debate which, once started, could not readily have been controlled. The result of any discussion whatever would have been wounding.
>
> Too many compliments were paid to me. This in a sense was tactless as it depreciated the personal responsibility of the two protagonists. I have learnt much during this week of stress. Never once have I lost my temper or displayed annoyance. I put every man on his honour, whatever may have been his motives or desires. I have used oblique flattery in the process: I have throughout kept my nerve. On the other hand many people now probably look upon me as an intriguer and wirepuller – not justly – but that is the penalty of a whip who carries instructions to their conclusions.

Instructions? A strange word for Balcarres to use. Nowhere in his lengthy diary entries for the three weeks in question does he ever mention receiving instructions from anyone. Rather, he gives the strong impression of being in charge, of being the conductor of a large orchestra where the violins did not always agree with the winds which, in turn, were out of harmony with the brass. Perhaps, when he wrote of carrying instructions to their conclusion, he was unconsciously justifying the fact that the end result was precisely what he had not wanted when his great friend, Balfour, announced his determination to resign.

He got on well, however, with Bonar Law and became increasingly impressed by the latter's growing confidence and command of language. His team of whips worked increasingly well. At the end of what he described as 'a dramatic, scandalous and paradoxical week about Irish Home Rule', he wrote on 16 November 1912:

The opposition whips have shown how strong is their control over Unionist members – not in driving them into one lobby or the other which is the only thing the government whips think about – but strong in a far more essential matter. We can now convey information to every member of the party in incredibly short spaces of time – and our men recognise so fully that whatever we suggest is based upon careful thought, that they accept our advice like lambs... Then again as regards ourselves we preserve anonymity – we don't figure in the press... Our influence is all the stronger from the fact that we move in the shadows; and our men know that whatever credit is earned is ascribed directly to themselves.

Any Chief Whip would be proud to have enough confidence to write that in their diary.

After his father's death on 31 January 1913 Balcarres went to the Lords as the Earl of Crawford and his party career ended. His remaining duty was to advise Bonar Law on the choice of a successor as Chief Whip. He wrote to his leader with unusual vacillation on 2 February:

...I fear this is a problem on which I am obsessed with hesitation and doubt.

This very fact brings home to me the necessity of having a man who can make up his mind – right or wrong. I have been through a hundred affairs of infinite greater moment but never can I recall a parliamentary difficulty about which I was unable to offer any opinion whatever.

Let me however lay certain alternatives before you: it is of course essential that the Chief Whip should lead a life of abnegation since all his ideas must be freely placed at the disposal of others, and his aim must be to watch other harvests fructify – hence the man with individual not collective ambition will not succeed. This eliminates various people, for a whip must not desire to get on.

Balcarres himself had moved forward since his hesitation two years earlier at taking on the Chief Whip's job. He had lost some of his prejudices. He had been tested in the fire of extreme controversy and found that he could survive without changing his own innate honesty. In a sense it is not surprising that, in the First World War, he served as a volunteer in the ranks, and then as a Royal Army Medical Corps orderly in a Flanders front-line dressing station. He had learned to live with himself and his heredity.

ELEVEN

The total whip –
David Margesson, 1931–40

The Representation of the People Act of 1918 finally gave women the vote, but not all of them. The prime purpose of this Act was to ensure that every male soldier who had survived the war had a vote. A woman was enfranchised only if she was thirty or over and either she or her husband qualified on their local franchise by owning or occupying a property with a value of more than £5 per annum. There was much debate about the appropriate age at which women should be allowed to vote and it required a Speaker's conference to agree on the age of thirty, partly in order to keep women in a minority at a general election. Universal suffrage became the right of all men aged twenty-one and over on the basis of residence, and the total number of electors more than doubled from eight million in 1915 to twenty-one million in 1918. Permitted campaign expenses were reduced at the same time to less than half the amount permitted by the 1883 Corrupt Practices Act, and provision was made for a free postal delivery to each elector and the free use of schools for meetings. Ten years later, in 1928, the franchise for men and women was at last put on totally equal terms. 'Elections became calmer; petitions became much rarer; registration procedure became much more efficient; party machines became stronger; and the administrative machinery worked more smoothly.' By the time David Margesson became Government Chief Whip in 1931, the boisterous electioneering settings of the previous centuries had disappeared. The scene became more sober, with a high percentage of the population voting.

If one politician of the twentieth century deserves to be remembered for his work as Chief Whip, it is Margesson. He was constantly described by the newspapers as a martinet, a strict disciplinarian, a man whose most important objective was the survival of the Conservative Party and of its majority in the Commons, and this was a view of him shared by many Members of Parliament. Others who knew him well outside Westminster saw a different side to him. He was talkative, handsome, plain-speaking. Jock Colville, Winston Churchill's long-term private secretary, spoke of him as a man who was exceptionally endowed with charm, and Chips Channon, writing in his diaries of a holiday in Austria in September 1937, repeated the compliment: 'In the evening late, David Margesson arrived from London and my cup of happiness was full, with the Chief Whip here. He is so charming and so powerful, and I only hope that he will enjoy himself...'

With his daughter, Gay Charteris, he preferred to go to the theatre than to talk politics. On holiday, she told me, his first words in the morning were 'What is the programme for today?' To ride in the morning, play tennis in the afternoon and croquet in the evening, that was the perfect programme. 'He made fun with it all. That was where his energy lay,' she wrote to J.E.B. Hill, author of his entry in the *Dictionary of National Biography*.

Margesson's father, himself son of a village rector, was for many years private secretary to the Earl of Plymouth and brought up his family in Worcester.

Early in his life, when he was twelve years old, Margesson wrote a touching document: 'I promise my father and mother that I will not smoke or drink alcohol in any form (except by a doctor's orders) nor lend or borrow money until I am twenty-one years of age. So help me God. Father and mother promise, on their side, to give me £100 on my 21st birthday if I keep the above promise inviolate.' This note was signed by Margesson himself and by both his parents.[1]

Margesson's father was able to send him to Harrow and then on to Magdalene College, Cambridge, but he left the university early without a degree and went to the USA to seek, unsuccessfully, his fortune. The First World War broke out. Margesson returned and, knowing nothing about soldiering except how to ride, he volunteered as a trooper in the Worcestershire Yeomanry. Commissioned in November 1914, he served with the 11th Hussars for four full years in France. He won the Military Cross and in 1916 married Frances Leggett, the only child and heiress of a rich New York wholesale grocer. Although the cavalry did not suffer as much as the infantry, he was sufficiently influenced by the horror of the trenches never to want to see war in Western Europe again. Thus he joined the large group of thirty- and forty-year-olds who dreaded the thought that another world war was ahead of them and who were natural allies for the appeasement policies of Neville Chamberlain and natural opponents of the determination of Churchill to re-arm and not to trust Hitler or Mussolini.

According to family notes, after the 1914–18 war ended he was seriously tempted to become Master of the Bicester hounds. Thanks to his wife, there was no shortage of money but the war had widened his horizon. At a meeting of young ex-officers he met Arthur Lee and it was he who persuaded Margesson to stand as a Conservative candidate in the general election of 1922. Lee was First Lord of the Admiralty in Lloyd George's National Government and owner of Chequers until he gave it to the nation in 1921. His wife, Ruth Lee, wrote in her diary for 15 July 1923:

We spent the weekend at Hinchingbrooke with the Sandwiches. The young David Margesson was there and he unconsciously amused A. [Arthur] very much by the way in which he laid down the law about politics and the 'iniquities' of the late Government. It was only a year ago that A. first suggested to him that he should go into politics and that he, who was then First Lord and had some influence, would try to find him a seat. At that time Margesson was so frightened at the prospect of entering Parliament that he literally ran away to Devonshire to hide, but A. had relentlessly dragged him back to London and almost forced him to stand at the General Election. Now, in less than twelve months, Margesson seems to have forgotten all this, and lays down the law to A. as if he were a seasoned statesman of long standing and experience. It made us all laugh very much.

Times change and men with them. Sixteen years later Ruth's husband, now Lord Lee of Fareham, wrote in his diary for 1939:

Early in May we spent a weekend at Chequers with the Chamberlains; only the second time we had stayed there since we left in 1921. Amongst other guests were the American Ambassador [Joseph Kennedy] and his wife, both only remarkable for her juvenile appearance and their much advertised surplusage of children; Oliver Stanley, a typical 'Derby', with his wife a typical 'Londonderry' of the 'I'm not rude, I'm rich' variety; and my one time protégé David Margesson, who had developed from the timid neophyte of 1922 into the totalitarian tyrant of 1939, which only shows how far masculine pulchritude, unencumbered by brains, can carry one in the Tory Party.

Margesson entered the House of Commons in 1922, lost his West Ham seat in 1923, stood successfully for Rugby the following year and then represented Rugby until 1942 when he left the Commons. He was blessed by an offer of patronage from the start. On 7 January 1924, although he was only thirty-three years old with one year of experience in Parliament behind him, Eyres Monsell, the Conservative Government Chief Whip wrote to him from 12 Downing Street:

> My dear David, it has occurred to me that a knighthood might do you some good in Rugby – you know I wanted to get you a job – a K. will be looked upon only as a retainer… Best of luck and *wire* me 'yes' or 'no' if you want to be put forward… As always, Bobbie.

Margesson did not accept this tempting offer and remained plain Captain Margesson until he was made a peer in 1942. He became a whip in 1926 and Government Chief Whip in 1931. He then had the unique experience of serving, for nine years, as Chief Whip to four successive Prime Ministers, one Labour, three Conservative – Ramsay MacDonald, Stanley Baldwin, Neville Chamberlain and finally Winston Churchill. These were extraordinary political times, dominated first by the fear of acute economic crises that led to Ramsay MacDonald forming a National Government in 1931 and then of growing dismay at the rise of Nazism and the fear of German expansion and rearmament.

Between 1924 and 1929 Churchill had held the office of Chancellor of the Exchequer and was widely regarded as the natural successor to Stanley Baldwin, the Prime Minister. However, after the Conservatives' narrow defeat in the election of May 1929, Baldwin and his Cabinet resigned to be replaced by a Labour government that was supported by some factions in the Liberal Party. The Liberals were splitting up and being led in different directions by Lloyd George, Sir Herbert Samuel and Sir John Simon, all of whom held varying views about whether to join a coalition led by Ramsay MacDonald.

The moment he was out of office, Churchill took up a strongly independent line and his subsequent isolation from the official Conservative Party in the 1930s and his personal ostracism by many old friends is one of the distinctive features of that decade. The issues of free trade, which he favoured, and Dominion status for India, to which he was violently opposed but which was strongly supported by Stanley Baldwin, were his first battlegrounds.

In the summer of 1931, the rise in unemployment in Britain and the stock market crash in New York caused such concern about the economic situation that King George V asked the Labour leader, Ramsay MacDonald, to form the first of the all-party National Governments. Churchill was already so out of favour that he was not invited to be a member of the new Cabinet which consisted of four Conservative, three Labour and two Liberal ministers. Six weeks later Parliament was dissolved, Labour were reduced to fifty-two seats from 288 and the Conservatives, with 473 seats, had a huge majority. Ramsay MacDonald remained Prime Minister but in the new National Government Cabinet the Conservatives now held eleven posts as opposed to the three held by Labour. Churchill was not one of the eleven and, at the age of fifty-six, after four years out of office, he could not reasonably expect ever to be a Cabinet minister again. The natural consequence was for him to turn increasingly to opposition to the policies of the two Conservative successors to Ramsay MacDonald, first Stanley Baldwin and then Chamberlain. This rift caused continuing problems for Margesson as Chief Whip, despite the large Conservative majority in Parliament. The schism in the 1930s over whether to trust Hitler in his rebuilding of German economic and military strength became as profound as the disagreement in the 1990s over Britain's place in an ever closer European Union. In the 1930s, though, political enemies still stayed in the same large houses, played golf and shot grouse together. In the 1990s they found it difficult to speak to each other in that home of Toryism, the Carlton Club.

Within six months of becoming Chief Whip, the splintering of the Liberal Party into three groups – National Liberals headed by Lloyd

George, the official Liberal Party led by Sir Herbert Samuel and the Liberal Nationals led by Sir John Simon – caused Margesson serious problems in the make-up of the National Government Cabinet. He wrote on 17 June 1932 to Neville Chamberlain who, as Chancellor of the Exchequer, was attending the Conférence de Lausanne with Ramsay MacDonald:

> I had a talk this morning with S.B. [Stanley Baldwin] about the vacancy which has occurred in the Cabinet due to Donald Maclean's death. He suggested that I should write confidentially to you to let you know the feeling in the party in case you should be asked your views by the PM and Samuel while you are in Lausanne.
>
> I am afraid of a real row in our party if the vacancy is filled by a Samuel Liberal. In the first place the Samuel Liberals always had one more place in the Cabinet than they were entitled to. They had three members, the Simon Liberals only two. This has always been a sore point with the Simon Liberals since they are actually numerically stronger than Samuel's lot [thirty-five as opposed to thirty-three]. I see no reason why this outweighing of the Simonites by the Samuelites should continue now that an opportunity has come to alter it.
>
> Secondly there is no Liberal of either denomination worthy of promotion into the Cabinet. I am sure it would be resented in the country and indeed it would not be right to put a man into the Cabinet whose only qualification was that his inclusion would maintain the balance of the parties in the Cabinet. I am confident that the country demands at this juncture the help of its very best men regardless of party.
>
> Thirdly our supporters would never understand why another member of the group that agrees to differ should join the Cabinet to augment the dissenters.

This is reminiscent of the comments about the 'bastards' in John Major's day, but the difference in this case was one of shades rather than primary colours, the Simonites being more obviously in favour of the National Government than the Samuelites.

Margesson concluded:

Finally, the last Honours list in which the Liberals got away with the lion's share went very badly with our party and was criticised severely. I fear that if the Samuelites get away with it again we really might have trouble and a weakening of support for the National Government. Probably you are perfectly alive to all these considerations but I felt I must make sure of bringing them to your notice. It will be time enough to discuss persons when we are asked to give names to fill the vacancy but Kingsley Wood to Education and Douglas Hacking to the Post Office, on the understanding that he stays there for the duration of this parliament, seems to me a good selection ...

The moment for a general reshuffle does not appear to me to have arrived yet.

Neville Chamberlain replied from Lausanne two days later: 'My dear David, thanks for your note. Neither the PM nor Samuel had said a word to me on the subject of filling Maclean's place. If they did I should say the same as you do, viz: that party labels ought not to enter into consideration but the best man should be chosen and if I were further asked who was the best man I should say Kingsley.' Neville Chamberlain finishes his short letter on a personal note reminiscent of present-day Councils of Ministers of the European Union: 'I am hoping still that we may not be detained here too long, but there seems to be a wide difference on that, as on other points, between the French and ourselves.'

From the start of his career as Chief Whip Margesson got on particularly well with Stanley Baldwin, now Lord President of the Council. A month after the exchange with Neville Chamberlain, Baldwin wrote to Margesson from 11 Downing Street (13 July 1932):

My dear David, you have done excellently and I am proud of you. Let that be recorded of the session that is passing.

And selfishly – you have been of the greatest help to me, and being lazy by nature, you know what that means to me !

Get a good holiday and the best of luck to you.

Yours ever. S.B.

I am just going to have breakfast.

Thus, within seven months of becoming Chief Whip, Margesson had settled in easily and carried through one of the most difficult of his jobs, putting the pieces together in a Cabinet reshuffle, and asserting his authority in the process.

A newspaper report of Margesson commented that he would address the new Members privately when they got to Westminster. Said one: 'He put such a Prussian terror into me that it took me months to find out that, like Pagliacci, his heart beats with human passion.' A celebrated political lady once asked him how he mastered those turbulent men, supporters of the government. 'You must remember,' replied Margesson, 'I was once adjutant of a cavalry regiment.'

But this is a one-sided view. Sidney Herbert, wounded in the war and an ex-cavalry officer like Margesson, wrote to him on 18 October 1935:

My dear David, this is a line to thank you from my heart for your sympathy and understanding last Tuesday – it was not the first time since my life, affections, ambitions, hopes and health started to go to hell, that you have given me a fresh lease of new hope and energy.

I remember so well the time when you and I, rather disillusioned war veterans, had become in 1922 young parliamentary candidates and were used, with great seriousness and hope, to discuss the future. What strange and bloody things have happened to us since !

Don't think me sentimental when I say that not only have I been delighted by the success of your career and the skill and wisdom with which you have guided our intellectual but often asinine leaders but that I have got real help from the example of your amazing guts and courage in adversity.

Two weeks later, Baldwin, who had become Prime Minister for the third time in June 1935, wrote in surprisingly emotional terms to his Chief Whip:

My dear David, your letter touched me very much. There is no relationship between men so close as that of a Prime Minister and his Chief Whip. For my part, it has been a joy to work with you: you have never failed me and few can realise what difficult times we have been through...

Englishmen may appear to take these mutual loyalties for granted: we don't talk about them. But it is good once and again to break the silence of our instinctive reserve, and say to each other what we might regret never having said if death came to one of us unexpectedly.

Margesson's relationship with Baldwin was cemented by the problems caused by the young King Edward VIII's infatuation with Mrs Simpson and the King's eventual abdication in December 1936. Margesson always agreed with the Baldwin line that any arrangement was unacceptable that permitted the King to marry the twice-divorced Mrs Simpson and have her as his queen with the cover-up title of Princess or Duchess. Margesson knew the young King well and had played and beaten him at squash. He himself had been separated for some years from his American wife but nonetheless he did not fall in with the ideas being put forward particularly by Winston Churchill, supported by Lord Beaverbrook, that a solution could be found which would fudge the issue and would give time for the King to get over his infatuation.

Tommy Dugdale, the MP for Richmond in Yorkshire, was Stanley Baldwin's parliamentary private secretary throughout the crisis period of November–December 1936. He had married Nancy Tennant, a half-sister of Margot Asquith, and thus brought up in intensely political surroundings, only a month earlier. In the diary she kept of the crisis,[2] she was deeply critical of the entourage around the King. She pithily described three of its main members:

Lord Beaverbrook of the *Daily Express* and the *Evening Standard*; Mr Esmond Harmsworth (son of Lord Rothermere) of the *Daily Mail* and the *Evening News*; and Mr Winston Churchill of nothing in particular, but whose name carries a certain publicity. None of these men is English in the sense that Mr Baldwin is English. If compared to a wireless, Mr Baldwin has his earth in the British soil, and his aerial listening in to the British public. They are three men in public life unashamedly out for themselves, all wanting to make personal capital out of a public tragedy. Thus differing wholly from S.B. [Stanley Baldwin].

A few pages later Nancy Dugdale described the meetings which took place on Tuesday 24 November.

Neville Chamberlain summoned Attlee the leader of the Opposition, Archibald Sinclair, leader of the Liberal Party 'and the possible snake in the grass, Mr Winston Churchill, whose very freedom from loyalties makes him a "dark horse is a loose box"'. All were asked whether they would come down on the Government's side against the marriage of the King and Mrs Simpson or would they form a government if summoned by the King. The first two pledged their absolute loyalty to Mr Baldwin, by saying they would not form an alternative government. Mr Churchill said, although his outlook was a little different, he would certainly support the Government.

A few days later Nancy adds the comment,

Walter Elliot[3] was full of fears as to what Winston Churchill would do in conjunction with Lord Beaverbrook as to forming a King's party. An essential factor in forming a party is a support of followers – Winston has none, and he has no power in the country, so I was in no way afraid of him.

Churchill himself thought that the King was being rushed by his ministers into a uniquely severe constitutional decision, an act of abdication, and that he should be given time to reconsider, time preferably until Mrs Simpson's divorce was made absolute the following April. He issued a statement that was published in the press on Sunday 6 December which started with the words 'I plead for time and patience'. But he was howled down when he pressed for delay in the Commons the following day. He was ruled out of order by the Speaker for trying to make a speech at Question Time and, walking out of the chamber, he shouted at the Prime Minister – according to Lord Beaverbrook's account – 'You won't be satisfied until you've broken him, will you?'

Neither the press, nor Baldwin, nor finally, the King himself agreed with Churchill. Within the previous few days the King had decided that he would marry Mrs Simpson at all costs and he wanted to do so immediately in order to stop rows with his ministers and speculation in the press. On Thursday 10 December the King signed a deed of abdication and Margesson issued a two-line whip for the following day in which attendance of Members of Parliament was, in the usual archaic language, most particularly requested for the passing of His Majesty's Abdication Bill. The Bill was three pages long and passed through all its stages in Commons and Lords in under three hours of debate.

A constitutional crisis of first importance was avoided. But Churchill had once again shown his ability to rouse passion and to be on the different side of a formidable cause to that taken by Stanley Baldwin. The feeling against Churchill ran high. Nancy Dugdale wrote in her diary for Wednesday 9 December:

> The telephone rang and a rather commanding, peremptory voice asked to speak to Captain Dugdale. This was from Mr Winston Churchill, who subsequently spoke to Tom at No. 10, only to ask, soaked in apprehensive egotism, what Mr Baldwin was going to say about him the next day!
>
> 'You are not even going to be mentioned tomorrow,' was the answer. It is astounding you cannot kill Winston with any known political axe. Throughout the crisis he and Beaverbrook worked together. This was subsequently admitted by Winston. Upon one of his visits to the King this out-of-date Roman mercenary is purported to have said to him, 'Fight, Sir, fight! And I shall be behind you with two thousand men!' Two thousand men, where from? Whom? Unemployed? Paid? Unpaid? What to do? This shows how his boundless imagination transports him into an unreal world of fairy-tale heroics. Winston was the magnified image of himself all through this crisis, as was Mr Baldwin. In what different guise those images appeared.

Winston Churchill later wrote in the *Yorkshire Post* that it was almost a universal view that his political life was at an end. 'There were several moments,' he wrote, 'when I seemed to be entirely alone against a wrathful House of Commons. I am not, when in action, unduly affected by hostile currents of feelings; but it was on more than one occasion almost physically impossible to make myself heard.'

When Stanley Baldwin was succeeded by Neville Chamberlain in 1937, Tommy Dugdale ceased to be his parliamentary private secretary and entered the whips' office under the command of David Margesson. A fellow MP, George Penny, wrote to him wishing him every possible good fortune and adding, 'You will find David and James Stuart wonderful fellows to work with and that is half the battle.' With him Dugdale brought the baggage of suspicion of Churchill that was at the heart of Margesson's problems for the next three years until Churchill became Prime Minister on 10 May 1940.

Appeasement did not then have the stigma that history has attached to it. Many sources recognised that the economic burden placed on Germany in 1919 by the Treaty of Versailles was too severe. They admired Hitler as a useful leader who was rebuilding his country after the crazy inflation of the Weimar Republic. E.W.D. Tennant, chairman of the Anglo-German Fellowship and a distant cousin of Nancy Dugdale, wrote an 'account' of him after a visit to Germany and Austria in 1938:

> Germany is governed by one comparatively young man risen from low beginnings with no personal experience of other countries and surrounded by advisers of similar type, all men of vital, dynamic energy who have gone through an incredibly hard school,... who are tough, ruthless but immensely able and who believe themselves to be governed by very high ideals. I still believe that it should not only be possible, but easy, to make friends with them...

Rab Butler[4] was sufficiently impressed by these comments that he sent them forward to Chamberlain and Halifax, appointed Foreign Secretary a month earlier, with the comment, 'I think you will find his [Tennant's] account remarkably true.'

Margesson never had the close relationship with Neville Chamberlain that he had had with Baldwin. The few personal letters that survive take the form of Chamberlain thanking Margesson for enquiries about his health: a 'slight' heart attack, a cold and sinusitis. The last of these is written from Angus on surprising mauve writing paper. After dealing with his illness Chamberlain writes:

> With regard to the Windsors, I was very interested to have your impressions and be able to compare them with those of W. Monckton whom I have now seen myself. He and I had a good talk with one another and then with the King and I have now drafted a reply to the Duke putting him off until next year and limiting his visit.

Chamberlain was a complex character. Brought up in a free-thinking family in Birmingham, a family that was more liberal than conservative, he believed when he became Prime Minister in 1937 that Hitler and Mussolini were both men with whom he personally could make a bargain that they would keep. His motives and methods were neither dishonourable nor unreasonable but, as an anonymous essayist put it in the autumn of 1939, 'His mistake was only that of the little boy who played with the wolf under the impression that it was a sheep – a pardonable zoological error, but apt to prove fatal to the player who makes it.'

Margesson had no difficulty in supporting Chamberlain's attempts to avert war. Although a military man, his own experience of the First World War made it natural for him to support all possible attempts to avoid another European struggle. His son recalled that he jokingly called the period of Neville Chamberlain's Prime Ministership his 'golden period'.

> He always remained sceptical of the wisdom of hindsight. Although he did not totally defend Munich, I have often heard him present the case for it, without the benefit of hindsight, by citing fact and the circumstances that existed at the time which subsequent events and the passing of time had led many people to forget. I also once heard him argue the case, from the same standpoint, for Pontius Pilate, pointing out that Jesus had 'put him in a very awkward position'!

By the spring of 1938, however, the stress between Chamberlain and Churchill had become constant and almost intolerable. Anthony Eden resigned his post of Foreign Secretary in February in protest against Chamberlain's intention to recognise the Italian conquest of Abyssinia and to start negotiations with Mussolini in order to foster Anglo–Italian friendship. Churchill supported Eden's views while Margesson was on the other side of the fence, putting pressure on the chairman of the Parliamentary Foreign Affairs Committee to water down a communiqué backing Eden's firm stand.

In March Germany invaded Austria. In the ensuing parliamentary debate Churchill was expected to repeat a recent Labour Party call for an inquiry into the weakness of British Air Defences but Margesson commented to

Cabinet that he 'did not think that Mr Churchill is getting or is likely to get much support for his request for an inquiry.' At the end of September Chamberlain met with Hitler, Mussolini and the French Prime Minister Daladier in Munich to agree the transfer of the Sudetenland and some three and a half million Germans from Czechoslovakia to Nazi Germany. The Czech government, led by Benes, accepted these terms on the understanding that the rest of their country would not be invaded and in the afternoon Chamberlain flew back to London with the famous piece of paper in his hand setting out the Munich terms. In 1878 the then Conservative leader, Disraeli, and Lord Salisbury had returned in a triumphant mood from the Congress of Berlin and Disraeli had announced, from a first floor window at No. 10 Downing Street, that he had brought back peace with honour. Sixty years later, at his wife's suggestion, Chamberlain used the same phrase about his agreement with Hitler. 'Tell them,' she said, 'that you have brought back peace, but not just peace – peace with honour,' and this is what Chamberlain did, speaking from the first-floor window that was Disraeli's bedroom.

The Foreign Office did not agree with either the Munich terms or Chamberlain's assessment of them. The deputy under-secretary, Sir Orme Sargent, surveyed the scene from a balcony in the Foreign Office building on the other side of Downing Street. 'You might think,' he said to John Colville, 'that we had won a major victory instead of betraying a minor country.'

The phrase 'Peace with Honour' has never been forgotten, nor has Chamberlain ever been forgiven for it by historians. Chamberlain, though, was suffering from a strange illusion that he was right in his recent approach to Mussolini and Hitler, and only he knew how right he was. 'The Führer' he described as 'being profoundly and favourably impressed by my personality... He would not deliberately deceive a man he respected, and with whom he had negotiated... He was extremely anxious to secure the friendship of Great Britain.'

But, even in the agonising years of 1938 and 1939, while an increasing number of Conservative Members of Parliament backed Churchill's calls for speedier and more extensive rearmament – and some hoped that a Ministry of Supply would be created with Churchill recalled to the Cabinet in order to head it – Margesson's faith in Chamberlain appears never to have wavered.

As one newspaper wrote about him:

As Chief Whip Margesson applied the principle: the government and the party right or wrong. He never deviated. Mistakes could always be remedied but once the party was split unity would be lost, and with it perhaps democracy in Britain. Churchill menaced a united front by his opposition to government policies. It did not matter whether he was right or wrong; he menaced unity; and so under the Margesson command the voting legions of the Conservative-dominated National Governments were paraded and marched and they rolled over Churchill.

Thus the National Government changed its commanders but never broke its team ranks. In its nine years there have been two parliaments, four premiers: MacDonald, Baldwin, Chamberlain and Churchill – but only one Chief Whip.

As late as April 1939, after the debate in the Commons on the Italian invasion of Albania, Churchill approached Margesson and, according to a letter Chamberlain wrote to his sister, told Margesson of his 'strong desire' to enter the Cabinet. There is no record of Margesson pressing Chamberlain to accept this suggestion. Chamberlain commented to his sister, 'I told D.M. that I would let this suggestion simmer a bit.' Five days later a Ministry of Supply was established but the head of it was not Churchill, as some of his friends had hoped, but the relatively unknown Leslie Burgin, the Liberal National MP for Luton who had been Minister of Transport for the previous two years. It was not until the evening of 3 September, after Hitler's invasion of Poland and Chamberlain's subsequent declaration of war between Britain and Germany, that Chamberlain offered Churchill the job of First Lord of the Admiralty with a place in the War Cabinet.

The eight months of the Phoney War followed in which neither side made great strategic moves, and then, in early April 1940, Hitler invaded Denmark and Norway. British troops were landed here and there without success. Norway fell amid a growing dissatisfaction with Chamberlain's ability to be a commanding war leader.

On 7 and 8 May, there was a confused and angry two-day debate in the Commons on the fall of Norway and the conduct of the war. Attlee, the leader of the Labour Party, had said at the beginning of the second day that the Labour Party would force a vote against the government at the end of the debate in order to show disapproval of the government's handling of the war.

Chips Channon describes the result most graphically in his diaries.

At last the Speaker called a division, which Winston nearly talked out. I went into the Aye Lobby, which seemed thin for a three-line whip, and we watched the insurgents file out of the Opposition Lobby (Teenie Cazalet could not make up his mind and abstained). 'Quislings,' we shouted at them, 'rats. 'Yes-men,' they replied. I saw all the expected ones, and many more – Hubert [Duggan] among them and my heart snapped against him for ever. Then I voted, as usual everyone wondered how many had dared to vote against us: so many threaten to do so, and funk it at the last moment. Anthony Eden and Jim Thomas in our lobby looked triumphant, and I saw Winston and his PPS Brendan Bracken there. I went back to the Chamber, and took my seat behind Neville. 'We are all right,' I heard someone say, and so it seemed as David Margesson came in and went to the right, the winning side of the table, followed by the other tellers. '281 to 200,' he read, and the Speaker repeated the figures. There were shouts of 'Resign – Resign'... and that old ape Josh Wedgwood began to wave his arms about and sing 'Rule Britannia'. Harold Macmillan, next to him, joined in, but they were howled down. Neville appeared bowled over by the ominous figures, and was the first to rise. He looked grave and thoughtful and sad.

The majority was not nearly large enough. Thirty-three Conservative MPs voted against the government and sixty-five were absent, unpaired or abstained. Neville Chamberlain was bound to resign.

In his diary two years earlier, on 12 September 1937, when he was on holiday in Yugoslavia with David Margesson, Channon wrote of Margesson's efforts to persuade Ramsay MacDonald to retire in November 1934 after a disastrous by-election result. Baldwin and Chamberlain were both seen as the natural successors to an aged MacDonald but it took until the following Whitsun for MacDonald to sign his letter of resignation. He was followed as Prime Minister by Baldwin who had 'much appeal and no enemies whatsoever, then, at least'. Channon added, 'I gleaned from long bedroom chats with David Margesson that the government, backed by the Baldwinites and the whips' room are pushing Inskip[5] forward for the premiership after Chamberlain, instead of Sam Hoare who would certainly give them more trouble.' At that time Margesson would never have supported Churchill. As the *Daily Mirror* subsequently wrote 'When he [Churchill] was opposing Mr Chamberlain's appeasement policy, Captain Margesson did his utmost to silence Mr Churchill. If Captain Margesson had had his way, Mr Churchill would have been driven out of public life.'

Had Margesson changed his mind by the time of the debate on the 8 May? He must have been shocked by the fact that the Conservative majority had fallen from a possible 213 to only eighty-one but Jack Profumo, elected only a month earlier as a pro-Chamberlain candidate in a by-election, was an unexpected voter against the government. His interview with Margesson the following morning remained in his memory fifty years later. 'And I can tell you this,' Margesson said, 'you utterly contemptible little shit. On every morning that you wake up for the rest of your life you will be ashamed of what you did last night.' Margesson's personal loyalty to Chamberlain had not wavered even though, six months earlier, he had accepted that Chamberlain's attempts to appease Hitler were finished and that war was inevitable. Chips Channon's diary for 2 September 1939, the day before war was formally declared, said, 'Broken-hearted, I begged David Margesson to do something; but he was already determined. "It must be war, Chips, old boy," he said. "There's no other way out."'

On 9 May Chamberlain asked the Labour Party leaders, Attlee and Greenwood, whether they would join a coalition government. On 10 May they refused to join, making Chamberlain's resignation inevitable. There were then two contenders for the premiership, Lord Halifax, the Foreign Secretary and the preferred choice of the King and Queen and a substantial number of Conservative MPs, and Churchill. Churchill had, of course, a number of followers who regarded him as the only person who could lead Britain to victory in a war that was becoming increasingly desperate. Others regarded him as a political turncoat, a dangerous adventurer, at best 'a delightful rogue who lacked political judgement', at worst 'unscrupulous, unreliable and unattractively ambitious'.

The Foreign Office team remained loyal to Halifax but he ruled himself out on the grounds that the country at this critical moment could not be led from the House of Lords. He then slipped away for a vital part of the afternoon of 10 May. Channon's diary described the afternoon graphically.

> Action had to be taken immediately. Neville hesitated for half an hour, and meanwhile Dunglass [later Alec Douglas-Home] rang me – could not Rab persuade Halifax to take it on? Rab was doubtful, as he had already this morning and yesterday had such conversations with 'the Pope' [Halifax's nickname] who was firm – he would not be Prime Minister ... Nevertheless, I persuaded Rab to go along to Halifax's room for one last final try; he found Halifax had slipped out to go to the dentist without Rab seeing him – and Valentine Lawford, the rather Second Empire secretary, who neglected to tell Halifax that Rab was waiting, may well have played a decisively negative role in history ... We rang Number 10, but Alec Dunglass said that already the die had been cast. A message was sent to the Palace and an audience arranged for 6 o'clock ... We were all sad, angry and felt cheated and outwitted. Alec who, more than any other, had been with the Prime Minister these past few weeks, and knows his words and actions by heart, let himself go.

Churchill was irrevocably on his way to the goal that had eluded him for so long, the office of Prime Minister.

Margesson was not someone naturally given to writing. Rather the opposite. He left no diaries and very few letters. His family have no record of whether, or when, over the crucial interval between the decisive vote on 8 May and the afternoon of 10 May, the Chief Whip felt it right to put his weight behind Churchill. But Bob Boothby had spent his time successfully organising opposition to Halifax among Conservative Members of Parliament and it was clear that both Labour and Liberal MPs supported Churchill. By the afternoon of 10 May, whatever their past disagreements over policy, Margesson accepted the inevitable. Colville writes in his diary for 10 May that, after Attlee's telephone call that Labour would agree to join a government provided Chamberlain was not Prime Minister, Margesson proposed that Chamberlain should lead the House, as Lord President, as Bonar Law had done in the First World War while Winston, as Prime Minister, would be the new Lloyd George. He added that, provided Chamberlain and Halifax remained in the War Cabinet, 'there will at least be some restraint on our new War Lord.'

By 7.00 p.m. that evening the new Prime Minister had come back from the Palace, ministers not in the Cabinet were being sent for and told they would have to resign and Alec Dunglass, Rab Butler, Chips Channon and Jock Colville met at the Foreign Office and drank in champagne to the health of Mr Chamberlain, 'the King over the water'.

Churchill saw the wisdom of keeping Margesson as Chief Whip in order to gain the support of those sections of Conservative Members of Parliament who were still deeply suspicious of him or who thought that Chamberlain had been unnecessarily rustled out of office. Churchill set up his office in Admiralty House and by 14 May Colville is describing how he went there after dinner. While waiting for Churchill to arrive, he read

> a large number of letters suggesting various appointments. A note by Brendan Bracken referred to a number of 'our friends' disliked by 'the parachutist' by whom he meant David Margesson (who, owing to the reconstruction, has landed in the enemy camp, I suppose). At about 10.30 Winston came down, and then by degrees a motley gathering appeared, David Margesson, Sinclair, Eden, Beaverbrook, the American Ambassador (who told me the most disquieting evidence of Italy's intention to enter the war) and Pug Ismay. Strange bed fellows indeed![6]

But Churchill was determined not to let bitterness and disagreements of the past prevent him from building up the support behind him. On 17 May Margesson formally re-accepted the position of Parliamentary Secretary to the Treasury, the official title of the Chief Whip.

There were those who were not happy with Margesson continuing in the job that he had now held for nine years. Tommy Dugdale had been in the whips' office since 1937. At the end of 1939 he joined his old regiment, the Yorkshire Hussars, and he went with them in early 1940 to the Middle East. In October 1940 his wife, Nancy, received a letter from John Crowder MP in which he suggested that Tommy came back from the Middle East and rejoined the whips' office as the office had 'gone from bad to worse since Winston became Prime Minister'. He told Nancy that he had made this suggestion at a private meeting of the backbench 1922 Committee and his remark had been received with loud applause from all parts of the room. A deputation went to see Churchill a few days later and were handled with skill. Crowder wrote again to Nancy on 27 October reporting that 'Winston said that there was no one he would like better than your husband in the Whips' Office but he is reported to have added, "Do you think he would be willing to come back just when developments may be taking place in the Middle East?"'

A fortnight later, on 12 November, another Conservative MP, Captain Vyvyan Adams, took up the theme in an unusual adjournment debate in the Commons. Adams, who was on active war service and therefore rarely in the Commons, attacked Margesson in bitter language, accusing him of muzzling parliamentary freedom and of driving huge majorities to support policies which had culminated in the catastrophe of the war. He added,

> Those of us who worked for years for a Churchill government he chose to treat as a bad smell. In May the façade which the Right Hon. and gallant Gentleman thought so safe suddenly collapsed, and some of us who were serving far from Westminster sighed with relief. At last, we felt, this evil, unhappy tyranny was over. No longer would the criterion of great decisions be the convenience of the Chief Whip and his little knot of friends… I did expect to hear by post, or perhaps on the wireless, that the Chief Whip, who had at last been exposed after nine long years as a huge political sham, had gone either to the Suez Canal or the House of Lords.

The language was too extreme and Margesson was defended, among others, by Quintin Hogg who described it as a very unjust and improper attack upon him. The Prime Minister wrote four days later to Vyvyan Adams saying that the appointment of Margesson as his Chief Whip had been his unfettered decision. He continued,

> It has been my deliberate policy to try to rally all the forces for the life and death struggle in which we are plunged, and to let bygones be bygones. I am

quite sure that Margesson will treat me with the loyalty he has given to my predecessor. The fault alleged against him which tells the most is that he has done his duty only too well. I do not think there is anyone who could advise me better about all those elements in the Tory Party which were so hostile to us in recent years. I have to think of unity, and I need all the strength I can get.

Moreover, I ought to tell you that even during the bitterest times I have always had very good personal relations with Margesson, and knowing what his duties were I never had any serious occasion to complain. Several times when I heard the whips were putting stories about which were not true I spoke to him plainly and he stopped them. The Liberal and Labour whips have the very highest opinion of his integrity and good faith in all House of Commons relations, and there is no doubt that he is the most efficient servant who could be found for these functions in a Three-Party Government.

Finally, I may tell you in confidence that I have long had a very high opinion of Margesson's administrative and executive abilities, and that when I formed the new Government I offered him a Secretaryship of State. He declined this but offered in the frankest manner to go out altogether. I can assure you he has been a great help to me on many occasions since I became Prime Minister, and I am absolutely sure he will go on to the bitter end.

But Margesson, in fact, only went on as Chief Whip for another six weeks. Perhaps Churchill paid some heed to the remarks made by John Crowder and Vyvyan Adams. Certainly he knew that the Conservative Party in the Commons was now entirely behind him. In wartime, with a coalition National Government and few votes at Westminster, an efficient, capable organiser, used to handling difficult colleagues, might better exercise his talents elsewhere than in the lobbies of the Commons. On 23 December 1940, a moment when the tide of war was running at its strongest against Britain, *The Times* had as its front page headlines: 'Lord Halifax goes to Washington. Consequential changes: Mr Eden returns to the Foreign Office. Capt. Margesson Secretary for War.' The *Daily Mail* of the same day wrote in its leading article:

The first two appointments caused no surprise. The third undoubtedly does. Capt. Margesson, who has never held high ministerial office before, now finds himself at the head of one of the greatest ministries. His ability for the task remains to be demonstrated.

Certainly no man who has brought on his head so much criticism for 'disciplining' Conservative MPs is lacking in character or personality.

The Times supported this view, writing, 'he has created a reputation for himself as probably the most efficient Government Chief Whip of all time.'

A week after his appointment, the *Sunday Times* said reasonably enough that it was too early to pass a judgement on David Margesson in his new job.

He has been condemned for doing his job as Chief Whip too well. That is a charge which needs to bring a flush to his cheek. A few months ago he was accidentally locked in a closet and nearly suffocated. The memory of that unpleasant episode may recur to him from time to time at the War Office. All his former slaves of the Lobbies wish him good luck and goodbye. Even the Russians lamented Ivan the Terrible after he had gone.

The War Office was known as a hideously difficult job. The minister had to marshal the supplies, the munitions, the troops, the tanks, and at the same time receive daily notes from Churchill, Prime Minister and Minister for Defence rolled into one, requiring action that day. On 4 March, barely six weeks after his appointment, he wrote in reply to a letter of congratulations from Stanley Baldwin saying that the last few months had been

very trying and painful, but then political upheaval is always like that. The House of Commons is a mighty queer place but its collective voice does represent the country's view, right or wrong. Last year the country took the view (rightly, I think) that you can't fight a war on a division of political opinion. Party politics take people's minds off the essential of going all out to win; so no matter how big a majority we had had in the fateful division, or if the House had not divided at all, the result would have been the same, the govt was doomed since a coalition was impossible under poor Neville. It was all very sad. He had done much magnificent work, he was such a fine administrator, he had such a clear brain and such courage, but he engendered personal dislike among his opponents to an extent almost unbelievable.

At the end of his six-page handwritten letter, sent from the War Office, Margesson writes attractively like a boy reporting to his parents on the new school.

> I am getting on all right here. Naturally I am finding it pretty difficult since I have never had any departmental experience before and to take on this job in wartime as one's first effort is nerve-racking. I was *so* happy in the Whips' Room. I hated to leave; it had become a second home to me. No one was more surprised than I was when Winston asked me to come here. I advanced every reason good and bad why he should not make the appointment and for a time I thought I was making some progress, but in the end he came back to his old vomit and naturally I could hold out no longer. In wartime one has to do as one is told. I got a good blooding my first day in the House as I had to answer 40 questions. Rather an ordeal! They went all right and that has given me confidence. Now on Thursday as ever is I have to introduce the army estimates. I don't mind saying I am apprehensive. I have done so little public speaking and speaking in the House is so much a matter of practice. However I have worked hard at the speech. I must hope for the best.

And the speech was very well received. *Punch* referred to it as a distinguished maiden speech and the *New Statesman* and *Nation* went even further:

> Margesson made a very good speech. He has surprised the House ever since he became Secretary of State for War by his conciliatory attitude towards critics and by the broad humanity of his approach to the difficulties of the private soldier and to the problem of the alien. Those very qualities which in the eyes of his critics made him too efficient as Chief Whip are likely to stand him in good stead as War Minister.

But Margesson only lasted another eleven months in the post, until 21 February 1942. He was working in his office on a Saturday when James Grigg, his permanent under-secretary and senior civil servant, appeared and had the embarrassing task of telling his boss that he was personally replacing him. To some extent Margesson was a sacrificial lamb. Singapore had fallen and the war was not going well. Although the attack on Pearl Harbour on 7 December had brought the Americans into the war, there were too many delays, too many frustrations in the build-up of tanks and ammunition, and the number of red boxes at night may have been somewhat too high. Margesson's number two, Grigg, had been Churchill's principal private secretary at the Exchequer from 1924 to 1929. As early as 30 September 1939, he had written to his father, 'I am told that Winston's stock is going up and that people are expecting him to be PM before long.' Grigg was to make the War Office the supremely efficient partner of the Ministry of Supply and Ministry of Defence.

It was not until a day later that Margesson got his official letter from Churchill at No. 10.

My dear David, I am very sorry to tell you that the reconstruction of the Government, which the pressure of events and opinion have rendered necessary, makes me wish to have the War Office at my disposal.

I have never regretted the efforts which I made to overcome your diffidence about accepting this Secretaryship of State. On the contrary, I think you have done extremely well, and I am very glad that your last speech on Thursday was so successful. I know that you realise what my trials are in these very difficult times, and I am very grateful to you for the way in which you responded to James Stuart's tentative opening of the subject.

I hope you will keep in touch with me, and let me have the benefit of your advice from time to time.

Margesson sent a dignified and decent reply two days later.

From long experience I well know the difficulties of reconstructing a Government under the pressure of events and public opinion. So I hope that my going will make things easier for you and to some extent lighten your almost unbearable burden.

I hate leaving the War Office; but what do personal feelings matter in days like these.

The unwritten sentence in either of these letters is that the surrender of Singapore had been a great blow to British pride, and setbacks in North

Africa and the eastern Mediterranean had aroused deep gloom. Not only a scapegoat but a more efficient team was needed.

Victor Cazalet wrote to Halifax, now British ambassador in Washington, on 26 February:

> David Margesson dined with me last night. He only heard about his dismissal on Saturday afternoon when he was working at the War Office... to add insult to his injury his permanent under-secretary [Sir James Grigg] came back from a visit to Chequers and had the unpleasant job of telling him that he was taking his place. David has not seen Winston yet. Perhaps he will get another job. [He didn't.] At the moment, poor fellow, he is out after eleven years of office without a penny, after having done the best job he has ever done in his life... Changes qua are not much good, and the general impression is one of confusion.

The socialite journalist Mollie Panter-Downes took a different view from Cazalet's. In the 'London War Notes' that she wrote regularly for the *New Yorker*, she had been deeply critical about the fall of Singapore, saying that this was due to 'the lack of prevision, the absence of dynamic planning, and the sahib mentality which made the supposedly impregnable fortress a push over for the first determined nation that came along'. A week later she warmly welcomed the reshuffling of senior ministers. 'Disasters sometimes accomplish quickly what the slow will of the people, bent on the same results, can't achieve in months. It took a Singapore to bring about the remodelling of the War Cabinet and the shifting of unpopular Ministers for which the Country had been hoping for so long.'

This marked the end of Margesson's ministerial career. He was quickly made a viscount but he is reputed never to have spoken in the Lords. Others heard him talk and much enjoyed it. James Lees-Milne wrote in his diary for Friday 11 May 1944:

> An enjoyable dinner at Emerald [Cunard]'s tonight. Lord Margesson is quick-witted and teases Emerald deliciously. He is a good talker when he gets onto beastly politics, as Emerald remarked, and has a beautiful timbre to his soft voice, which he never raises even when roused; on the contrary he lowers it. I

suppose the House of Commons teaches a man to control his emotions. Emerald was tonight quicker with her repartee than I ever remember. I was amazed by her brilliant, incisive mind. Conversation flitted from nonsense to seriousness. Lord Gage said, 'Once in Berlin a painted young creature said to me, "Darling don't be county now." Imagine such a thing to me, who literally am the County of Sussex.' Emerald said the Minister for Food invited her to sit on his knee. Lord Margesson spoke well about the Bolshevik situation. He said Churchill was terribly depressed by their sudden non cooperation, and the blackout they have lowered over their side of the German front. They will allow no one to penetrate it, and no one to enter Vienna. It is thought they are putting all Germans to the sword, with the exception of those thousands they are deporting as slaves to Russia. This is a most terrible and sickening thing. Clarissa [Churchill] said one must not mind.

Compton Mackenzie wrote of a lunch in November 1948:

I recall lunching with the Birkenheads in Chester Street and meeting for the first time David Margesson by whom I was much attracted. As Chief Whip during what I thought were the two disastrous 'national' governments and as Minister for War when war came I expected to find ourselves completely out of sympathy. The Birkenheads had to go off to some affair at Church House soon after lunch. But Margesson and I stayed talking until half past four. I wish I had made some notes of that talk but alas, what he told me about the Abdication, about Baldwin, and indeed about so much in that fatal decade of the thin-faced 30s was not recorded by me at the time... What I do know is that it was one of the most absorbing conversations I have ever enjoyed.

The 'thin-faced 30s' – this is an unusual description but it comes from one of the best observers of the time.

What the traditional view of Margesson missed was that, out of parliamentary school, he was not only amusing and witty but an insider with a unique knowledge of the turmoil that lay below the large Conservative majorities in the 1930s and in 1940. Lady Cunard accused him of being only fit for politics and love, and knowing nothing of anything else. But, of course, she went on inviting him to dinner and he was one of a circle of friends who regularly stayed at Leeds Castle with Lady Bailey. Lord Ampthill met him there and I asked him over lunch what David Margesson had been like. 'Very funny,' he said.

TWELVE

From Chief Whip to Prime Minister –
Ted Heath 1955–74

Ted Heath remains a paradox, a man of huge skills and great achievement with whom, for many people, it became almost impossible to communicate. Elected in 1950, he was then eight years in the whips' office. A junior Conservative whip after only one year in the Commons, Deputy Chief Whip a year later and Government Chief Whip under Anthony Eden before he was forty, he was regarded by Eden as having 'especial qualities of patience, adroitness and dependability'.[1] Eden wrote in his memoirs, *Full Circle*, 'though Mr Heath's service in Parliament had been short at that time, I have never known a better equipped Chief Whip. A ready smile concealed a firm mind.'[2]

Thirteen years later when I met Ted for the first time the grace had gone. It was 1969, Ted had been elected leader of the Party four years earlier and one of his shadow ministers, Ernest Marples, had formed a small Public Sector Research Unit for which two friends of mine, David Howell and Mark Schreiber, worked. I was prospective parliamentary candidate in a hopelessly Labour seat in Sheffield and was asked by Mark to write a paper on the machinery of government that Ted had requested. This meant looking at the various departments in Whitehall and seeing which of them might either be split up or merged together. I said that I knew nothing about the subject and I was told that that was the point. I had no axe to grind and no preconceived opinions. The paper had to be ready before Easter and I worked like an excited beaver to produce it. It was finished in time, I sent it round to Mark, I was told it had been passed to Ted and then I heard nothing more. After some weeks I asked what had happened to it and I then received a short note of thanks from Ted, inviting me to come round to his set of rooms in Albany to discuss it. I arrived around 9 a.m. in my best suit and very nervous. I waited some minutes in a handsome room, full of books, papers and a grand piano, and then Ted came in in sailing mufti – slacks, an open-necked shirt – and carrying a large, tantalising cup of coffee. We sat down, we talked in general terms about my paper (about which nothing was ever done), and I left. My main memory is that he did not do what would have been my first action: offer me a cup of coffee.

Music became the only subject on which it was possible for a relative stranger to talk to Ted. Patrick Wright[3] told me of the time Ted visited him when he was ambassador to Luxembourg at the end of the 1970s. Ted arrived in the evening, and was totally silent before going out to dinner with Christopher Tugendhat, then an EEC Commissioner. Virginia, Patrick's wife, insisted on going to bed when Ted returned as she had found him so difficult to talk to. Patrick offered him a glass of whisky and then, as he was about to suggest that it was time for bed, asked him first if he would like them to play some music together. Ted made a deprecatory noise but Patrick, a serious musician himself, insisted that he was not talking of school concert stuff. He took him into the next room where there were two grand pianos – a requisite in any embassy which Patrick graced. They sat down and played together until 3.00 a.m., with shouts of pleasure and demands for encores from Ted. Next morning at breakfast the musical interlude was not mentioned.

As a Conservative whip, Ted was a man of his time. He fitted the changing nature of the parliamentary party. His very arrival in the whips' office was symbolic. His predecessor was a substantial landowner in Cheshire, Lieutenant Colonel Sir Walter Bromley-Davenport, a scion of Eton and the Grenadier Guards, who had been put on duty one evening by the Chief to stop unpaired Conservative members slipping away from the House before an unexpected vote. He saw a grey suit slipping through an exit door, kicked hard and felled his victim. Story has long had it that the victim was either the French or the Belgian ambassador. Ted himself claims that it was another MP. An apology was not accepted, Bromley-Davenport retired to Capesthorne Hall where his family produced excellent amateur dramatics, and Ted, educated at Chatham House Grammar School and Balliol, that most serious of Oxford colleges, took his place. At Oxford, he had joined the Bach Choir and become the college organ scholar. He attended the Nuremberg Nazi Party rally as an observer in September 1937 and then spoke passionately a year later in the Oxford Union against the Munich Agreement, attacking Chamberlain for a 'policy which brought us to the brink of war, that pulled us out at such a terrible cost and that points at we know not what future tragedies'.[4] He accused Chamberlain of 'turning all four cheeks to Hitler at once', a comment that was judged at the time as being over the top.[5]

Paul Bryan[6] joined the whips' office a year after Ted became Chief. He commented in his autobiography[7] that the whips' office were a warlike squad. A brigadier, six lieutenant colonels, three majors, a naval commander and a fighter pilot. Of Ted he wrote that he felt lucky, in his first parliament, to serve under him.

> Considering he had only been in the House of Commons for five years he had a remarkable grip of the day-to-day parliamentary situation. He had complete confidence in ordering about the senior ministers. He was serious but with a sense of humour which anyone will know who has heard him give an after dinner speech. He used his whips relentlessly. He seldom gave his own view until he had squeezed us dry. We worked hard for him but great were the rewards in the Whips' Office. Most of us became ministers in due course.[8]

Reliability was the key characteristic assigned to him by Robert Carr[9] who entered the House at the same time as he did. 'If he promised you that he would do something, you knew that he would,' Robert remarked to me. Patrick Buchan-Hepburn,[10] Chief Whip from 1951 to 1955 during Churchill's final years as Prime Minister, went further. 'A Chief Whip has to take the responsibility and be jolly rude at times, then the Deputy has to pick up the pieces. He [Ted] became very good at that. He could be very nice to people.'[11]

Buchan-Hepburn himself was given to writing and receiving irreverent notes during Churchill's Cabinet meetings. One of them, unsigned, reads, 'It looks as if all must be well! You'll notice the cigar box has crossed the table.' Buchan-Hepburn scribbled his reply: 'He's taking much too much interest in things again!' Another note from his old friend, James Stuart, then Secretary of State for Scotland but a previous Chief Whip, was written in Cabinet on 28 October 1953 after a discussion on meat marketing. It simply said, 'Would you mind going out and buying me a revolver?' Yet another from James Stuart is dated 8 April 1955. It reads, 'The (sausage) mills of God grind slowly – but it is always nice to see, at the end of thirty years' grinding, the Perfect Foreign Secy emerge attired like Solomon in all his glory.' Two weeks later Churchill finally resigned and the Perfect Foreign Secretary, Anthony Eden, became Prime Minister.

As Chief Whip, James Stuart had played a part in the attempt eight years earlier to advise Churchill that in view of some of his Shadow Cabinet colleagues it would be in the better interests of the party if he sought peace in retirement. In his autobiography[12] he tells of his delivery of this message and Churchill's reaction.

> I was not surprised that it was agreed unanimously (if you don't count me) that the man for the job was the one who had no axe to grind and was, after all, the Party's Chief Whip! Winston received me alone in his room at the House ... I then told him of the unanimous view expressed by our colleagues at our meeting. He reacted violently, banging the floor with his stick and implying that I too had joined those who were plotting to displace him ... It did take a few days before he could treat me normally again ... No more was heard of his retirement for several years and none of the others present at our private meeting repeated to him the views which they had so kindly invited me to convey.

Eight months after Eden, now Prime Minister, won the May 1955 general election, Buchan-Hepburn moved to the Cabinet post of Minister of Works at the same time as Macmillan became Chancellor of the Exchequer, Rab Butler Leader of the House of Commons and Selwyn Lloyd Foreign Secretary. The promotion of Ted to Chief Whip was accepted as a natural progress, with Martin Redmayne as his deputy. Ted took a different view to Buchan-Hepburn about the role of Government Chief Whip. He told me that he thought Buchan-Hepburn had personally spent too much time concentrating on how many MPs went through the lobbies and how to get them there. He delegated that to Redmayne while he concentrated on seeing that ministers were better informed on what was happening and the mood of the moment in the parliamentary party.

With this in mind, the index card on each MP was improved. He wrote in his own autobiography:

> I wanted to transform communication between Whips and backbenchers by encouraging much closer, friendlier and more personal contacts between each Whip and the members for whom he was responsible. To help bring this about, I introduced a system of immediate reporting of all forms of intelligence on writing pads back in the office. One copy of each note would be placed at once on the responsible Whip's desk, a second would be kept by the Whip who had gained the information and the third was left for everyone in the office to read. It quickly became the established habit that the first thing for each Whip to do upon returning to the office was to look for these reports on the views of our members on the major topics of the day.[13]

The same system was in force when I became Chief Whip thirty-three years later. It can, of course, be said that this system may have encouraged 'friendlier contacts' but it could also be seen as the whips having the latest possible information on who was in a rebellious mood and what unacceptable amendment to a government Bill they were plotting to table.

Within seven months of Ted's appointment the débâcle began that was to lead to Eden's downfall. On 26 July 1956, the Egyptians' militant leader, President Nasser, nationalised the Suez Canal. At the time, the Canal still had great strategic importance in the transport of goods and people. Nasser's seizure of it was a hostile retaliation to the United States' refusal to finance his pet project, the building of the Aswan Dam. Ironically, in view of current events, Eden was entertaining the Iraqi Prime Minister, Nuri es-Said, to dinner on the evening of the nationalisation.

At first it seemed as if the Labour opposition, newly led by Hugh Gaitskell, would support Eden in considering how to regain the Canal, asking only that the problem should be handled through the United Nations. But Ted quickly advised Eden that Gaitskell's agreement was only paper-thin. 'Gaitskell was too new in office to deliver it, even if he wanted to. Moreover, he was no Attlee. When the opinion in his party changed, I was sure that he would go with it. This subsequently proved to be the case.'

Throughout the summer holiday months the unanimity of the parliamentary Conservative Party also begin to crack. The Suez group, led by Julian Amery, Fitzroy MacLean and Charles Waterhouse, wanted speedy action to regain the Canal; others, among them Nigel Nicholson and Bob Boothby, were against such a military adventure. It was the task of the Government Chief Whip to try to reassure both sides.

The opening sentence in Chapter 7 of Ted's autobiography which covers the Suez crisis says,

> The job of the Chief Whip is, above all, to hold the parliamentary party together. There are many different approaches to this... it is essential to have an immensely strong personal bond of trust with the Leader of the Party... but a particularly unhappy episode, perhaps the unhappiest of Britain's entire post-war history, tested my loyalty to breaking point, and I was forced to take the hardest decision of all. In doing so, I subjugated my own views and doubts to the overriding need to hold the Conservative Party together at a time of crisis – not for my benefit alone, not even for that of the party but, I profoundly believe, for the long-term benefit of the country.

This can be read as an apologia for the fact that Ted was a member of the inner circle who knew, in October 1956, that the Israelis had secretly agreed with France and Britain that they would invade Egypt. In the words of Eden, 'We shall then send in our own forces, backed up by the French, to separate the contestants and regain the Canal.'[14] This agreement, which was against all of Ted's instincts, came to be known as the Sevres Protocol. The Americans quickly destroyed it by refusing to support sterling when our currency collapsed and, jointly with the Soviets, putting down a resolution at the UN demanding a ceasefire and withdrawal of all forces. This was carried by sixty-four votes against five, the minority being made up of Israel, France, Britain, Australia and New Zealand. The role reversal between the United States and France in relation to Egypt in 1956 and its near neighbour Iraq in 2003 shows the degree to which the United States has taken over the duties of a world power and France has withdrawn from them.

Only Selwyn Lloyd, Harold Macmillan, Rab Butler and Ted Heath were told about the Sevres Protocol. At the Cabinet meeting the following day, other ministers were kept in the dark and Eden repeated what he had said at the Conservative Party Conference about the need to use force only if necessary. Walter Monckton, the Minister of Defence, was the only Cabinet minister to resign but he was followed by Anthony Nutting, Minister of State at the Foreign Office and Edward Boyle, the Economic Secretary of the Treasury.

The fact of the matter was that Anthony Eden lied to Cabinet and to the House of Commons. The excuse for using armed forces to invade Egypt and to regain the Canal was to stop the fighting between Israel and Egypt, but this was a pretext only. Britain and France had, by the Sevres Protocol, connived at Israel's invasion of Egypt and many quickly guessed this. Events moved with speed. On 30 October, ten days after the signing of the Sevres Protocol, Eden advised the House of Commons that Israel had attacked Egyptian territory and was moving towards the Canal. A day later he gave the order to bomb airfields in Northern Egypt alongside the French and, in the Security Council, Britain and France vetoed an American resolution calling for Israel's withdrawal. At the same time the Anglo–French task force set sail from Malta for Port Said. Four days later there was a massive protest meeting in Trafalgar Square and a march down Downing Street. And on the same evening, after a broadcast appealing for national unity by Eden – the first occasion on which a Prime Minister used television to address the British people at a time of war – Gaitskell as leader of the opposition quickly followed with a declaration, also on television, that only Eden's resignation could 'save the honour and reputation of our country'.

A day later the army was making good progress after landing at Port Said but, the very next day, 6 November, the Cabinet agreed that without American support for sterling which had been the subject of massive selling, Britain had no alternative but to accept a United Nations solution to the conflict. Later that evening, Eden announced in the Commons that agreement had been reached over the use of United Nations forces and that military operations were to cease at midnight. Two days later there was a Commons debate on a vote of No Confidence in the government. Ted described in his autobiography how, during the debate, he was having dinner at the Chief Whip's table in the corner of the dining room when Charles Waterhouse and Julian Amery asked to see him on behalf of the Suez Group. 'Waterhouse told me he could ensure that all members of the group would vote with the Government in the division that night, provided I would give an undertaking to bring about Eden's downfall as Leader of the Conservative Party. I told him to go to hell and, without further discussion, went back to finish my dinner.'

In the event none of the Conservative MPs voted against the government and there were only six abstentions.[15]

Ted then added that he received a number of letters thanking him for holding the party together during the crises '...and for doing so with courtesy... I was perfectly clear in my own mind that it was one thing to save the Conservative Party from the abyss, but it was quite another to convince the British people that we were still fit to govern.'

Two questions arise from this humiliating failure. The first is whether Harold Macmillan, one of those in the inner circle from 21 October, when he learned of the Sevres Protocol, was aware from his own extensive American contacts that sterling would crumble and that the Suez invasion would be a quick disaster, but he neither said so nor resigned as he saw this as a means of hastening Eden's departure and his own succession as Prime Minister. It is significant that, in writing about the Cabinet meeting on Tuesday 6 November, Ted described Macmillan taking him off into a corner and asking what was the party going to say. Ted then added, 'We had come full circle. Macmillan, who had supported the venture from the beginning and who had so strongly and consistently urged a full-blown military operation, was also the first to recognise that it could not be completed.'

The second question is why Ted, who was opposed to the operation from the moment he heard of the Sevres Protocol and did his utmost, in his own words, to change Eden's mind, did not himself resign. His reasons for this are a classic summary of the difficulty of a Chief Whip's position. When I asked him the question he briefly said, 'No. When you take on the job, you take on all of it. You cannot pick and choose.'

A longer apologia occurs in Ted's own autobiography:

The Chief Whip's relationship with the Prime Minister is a special and personal one. He owes his complete loyalty to the Prime Minister who is entitled to count upon it... To my mind it is no exaggeration to say that the resignation of a Government Chief Whip on a major issue of policy would be a mortal blow to confidence in the Government. Certainly a Prime Minister could hardly survive it. For a Chief Whip to resign, particularly during a national crisis such as Suez, would be an act not only of utter disloyalty, but of wilful destruction.

Forty-five years later, this may seem a slightly doubtful argument, confusing the duties of office with personal conviction. But no contemporaries blamed Ted for not resigning. He was known to be convinced more by those against the resort to military action than by the Suez Group and their demand for a speedy removal of the Suez Canal from Egyptian ownership. The Suez crisis was, in fact, fortunate for Ted's reputation. He was seen by all sides as the man who had held the party together in what could have been a disastrous crisis. Robert Carr told me of his respect, even fondness, for Ted and he thought this was the view of the majority of the party. It is not often that a Chief Whip attracts affection. Ken Clarke,[16] himself a government whip from 1972 to 1974, told me that Ted was very proud of his role in the Suez crisis. He regarded Ted as having been a whip by instinct. Chief Whip was a post that suited him and he was the last Government Chief Whip who, when there was a vote in which opposition from some of his own party was expected, acted as a teller in the opposition lobby, personally counting his rebels. When Ted did this, it was equivalent to a six-line whip.

Eden had been ill before and during the Suez crisis. Ten days after winning the confidence vote in the Commons he went to Jamaica for a month. In his absence the leadership battle between Harold Macmillan and Rab Butler grew intensely. At the last meeting of the backbenchers' 1922 Committee before the Christmas recess it was the natural prerogative for Rab Butler to address the committee as he had been left in charge of the government in Eden's absence. Ted, however, arranged for Macmillan to speak after him and it was Macmillan who, in Heath's own words, turned in a magnificent performance while Butler was uninspiring. Three weeks later Eden told Ted that, on doctor's advice, he had decided to resign. After informing his colleagues, he went to Sandringham later in the day to tell the Queen. There was no question of Tory MPs, let alone members of the party in the country, being balloted as to who they would like to see as Eden's successor. Lord Salisbury and Lord Kilmuir, respectively the Lord President of the Council and Lord Chancellor, interviewed members of the Cabinet separately about their position and Ted Heath himself and his whips' office quizzed their parliamentary colleagues. Kilmuir described the interviewing of the Cabinet ministers in the Privy Council offices in the following terms:

> There were two light reliefs. Practically each one began by saying, 'This is like coming to the headmaster's study.' To each Bobbety [Salisbury] said, 'Well, which is it, Wab or Hawold?' As well as seeing the remainder of the ex-Cabinet, we interviewed the Chief Whip and Oliver Poole, the chairman of the party. John Morrison, the chairman of the 1922 Committee, rang me up from Islay the next morning.[17]

The 1922 Committee was founded to help Conservative MPs elected that year 'to find their feet' in the Commons. It meets weekly on Wednesday evenings during the parliamentary session. Its influence depends heavily on the character of the chairman and John Morrison was a long-serving and particularly powerful chairman.

The following day Ted went to see Sir Michael Adeane, the Queen's private secretary, and told him that in his judgement a substantial majority would prefer Macmillan to Butler and that he personally was certain that Macmillan would be the right appointment. The next day Adeane telephoned Ted. He said that the Queen was sending for Macmillan but asked Ted to break the news to Butler personally. Ted found Rab waiting in the Privy Council Chamber, sitting at a table deep in thought. He described what followed in his autobiography:

> Unusually for him, for he was a prodigious worker, he had no papers or folders in front of him. He was just patiently waiting for the news. As I entered, his face lit up with its familiar charming smile. Every newspaper that morning, save one, had announced that he would be the new Prime Minister. All but one were wrong. I had a sad mission to carry out, but there was nothing I could do to soften the blow. 'I am sorry, Rab,' I said, 'it's Harold.' He looked utterly dumbfounded.[18]

Ted undoubtedly got on well with Eden. He got on even better with Macmillan whom he served for another two and a half years as his Chief Whip.

A few hours after Macmillan had accepted from the Queen his appointment as Prime Minister he took Ted Heath, who has been poring over the list of potential ministers with him, to the Turf Club for dinner. Macmillan originally suggested the Savoy Grill but Ted persuaded him that that could attract too much publicity. After a dinner of oysters, steak, coffee and brandy, Macmillan refused the club manager's suggestion that they left by the back door into Shepherd Market. 'How very kind,' he said, 'but I think it is perfectly all right for me to leave by the front door. I am not ashamed of being Prime Minister, you know.'[19] Unfortunately, the media had by then tracked Macmillan and Ted Heath down and the assumption in the press the following day was that Macmillan was paying off a debt for Ted's support. More realistically, Macmillan's staff had not yet moved into No. 10 and his wife, Lady Dorothy, had not stayed in London but had gone to Birch Grove, their home in Sussex, to continue her gardening. From the Turf Club Macmillan and Heath went back to Downing Street to complete the task of forming a government. The names were announced the following day.

Macmillan came to rely on Heath totally, moving from regarding him as an 'admirable assistant' to meriting the adjective 'superb'. This tribute was after one of the few upsets of these years when Thorneycroft, as Chancellor of the Exchequer, objected to departmental plans for an increase in government expenditure in the year ahead. He wanted a reduction of £153 million, was promised economies amounting to £100 million, but still resigned over a gap of about £50 million. Nigel Birch, the Economic Secretary at the Treasury, and Enoch Powell, the Financial Secretary, resigned with him. Macmillan was suitably cross that his three Treasury ministers should have resigned over such a narrow difference between them and the rest of the Cabinet, and he was particularly irritated as he was leaving for a Commonwealth trip lasting six weeks the following day. Ted drove down with him to Heathrow where Rab and most of the Cabinet were waiting. Ted records in his autobiography, 'As we said goodbye, Macmillan turned to me and said, "Now, look after the show. Rab will do all he can to help you."'[20]

In October 1959, after winning a majority of 100 in the general election, Macmillan appointed Ted to the cabinet as Minister for Labour and a year later made him Lord Privy Seal with responsibility for negotiating Britain's entry into the European Economic Community – a responsibility that culminated in de Gaulle's 'Non' in 1963. For the year in which Douglas Home was Prime Minister Ted moved further up the Cabinet ladder with his appointment as President of the Board of Trade and then, in 1965, he won the first leadership election in which Tory MPs were directly balloted, beating Reggie Maudling by 150 votes to 133. Five years later, winning the 1970 election with a small overall majority of thirty, Ted as Prime Minister resumed the pursuit of membership of the EEC that had eluded him in 1963. For this passage of arms Francis Pym was his Chief Whip from June 1970 to December 1973.

Shortly after winning the June 1970 election, Ted Heath as Prime Minister reopened negotiations to join the European Community. De Gaulle had now exercised his veto twice, once against Harold Macmillan's effort in 1963, then again against the tentative application by Harold Wilson, as Labour Prime Minister, in November 1967. Two years later de Gaulle resigned. He was succeeded by President Pompidou. Much more open-minded than de Gaulle, he got on well with Ted Heath and over twelve hours of talks he became convinced that he should encourage Britain's entry. By this time Harold Wilson had changed faith and had convinced himself that there was more political gain in opposing rather than supporting the terms that Heath and his chief negotiator, Geoffrey Rippon, battled to win. A White Paper outlining the terms was published in July 1971 along with a glossy brochure setting up the case for entry. The great argument began in which we are still engaged thirty years later.

After a preliminary debate at the end of July in which the Commons simply took note of the terms, the stage was set for a six-day debate at the end of October which invited the Commons to approve the principle of joining the European Community 'on the basis of the arrangements which have been negotiated'. The smallness of the Tory majority coupled with the knowledge that any number from thirty to fifty Tory MPs would either abstain or vote against the term put the Chief Whip into a position of extraordinary difficulty. Francis Pym came to the conclusion that the government had much more chance of winning the crucial vote by a reasonable majority on a free vote rather than on a three-line whip. He put it to me that

> I had been in the whips' office since 1962. I knew exactly the feelings of every Member of Parliament in our party and I knew that none of them would change on such a matter of principle. Our not having a three-line whip but having a free vote instead made it much more possible for Labour MPs to abstain or to vote with us even though the opposition officially had a three-line whip against the motion.

Three weeks before the debate, on 5 October, Pym sent a Personal and Private note to Heath detailing the number of rebels on either side and giving a masterly summary of the reasons why he would risk having a free vote on an issue of such huge importance. With Francis Pym's agreement, this is reproduced as an appendix on pages 352–6 below.

Ted Heath took a great deal of convincing. At the start he felt very strongly that he was 'entitled' to ask the government members to support him in the lobby and he expected that the governments of the six existing members of the Community would be surprised if he did not use his majority to endorse the terms that had been agreed.

As the annual Conservative Conference opened in Brighton on 11 October Ted was still insisting that a free vote was out of the question.[21] Francis Pym has described the battle to persuade Ted 'as the hardest he ever had', but Willie Whitelaw, his predecessor as Chief Whip, eventually supported him and a week later, three days before the debate opened, Heath was won over. On the Conservative side, the whips came off. On the opposition side, led by Tony Benn who wanted to commit Labour firmly against the European Community and who argued that the Tory government could be defeated if Labour polled its full strength, Labour MPs voted by 140 to 111 not to allow themselves a free vote. The result was a triumph for the European Community cause. The Ayes were 356, the Noes 244, giving a majority of 112 for entry on the terms that had been negotiated. The bookmakers had been giving odds of 25–1 against a majority of over one hundred. Eighty-nine Labour MPs had either voted for entry or abstained. Forty-one

Tories had voted against or abstained. In his memoirs Ted Heath acknowledges a little grudgingly that Francis Pym's minute to him of 5 October in which he had predicted thirty-eight defectors from the Tory Party had proved 'incredibly accurate'. In his biography of Ted Heath, John Campbell says bluntly, 'The three-figure majority for Europe which was triumphantly secured on 28 October was not Heath's achievement but Francis Pym's.'[22]

Pym agreed that it was totally different the following year when it came to the Bill that put into legislative force the Treaty of Accession.

> We had to have a whip to deal with all the detail in committee stage. Our majority got down to single figures on several occasions but Tony Royle, another long-time Conservative whip, and Ken Clarke acting as the official Government Whip for Europe, worked with pro-Euro Labour MPs and particularly with John Roper[23] who later joined the Social Democrat Party. When we needed their help, we told them and we got just enough support to make certain we were not defeated. But I had never to ask for more than I really needed. If I had, they would have lost confidence in me.

The majority fell to four on one occasion. Ted Heath became impatient and worried about the narrowness of their victories, and Pym replied to him, 'If you don't have confidence in me, you can get yourself another Chief Whip. But you can't ask me to change my ways.'

Effectively, the government only got the European Communities Bill through the Commons with the help of Labour rebels and the small Liberal Party. At the end of the second reading debate Bob Mellish, the Labour Chief Whip, had to restrain his angry left-wingers from 'lifting Jeremy Thorpe [the leader of the Liberals] across the chamber'. They were furious that, if five Liberal votes had gone the other way, the government would have lost by two votes.

By 27 April, the Bill had spent nearly ninety hours in committee without finishing Clause 2, so the Chief Whip decided that the government must resort to the guillotine which strictly limits the time available for discussion. The resolution to enforce this was carried by only eleven votes, with thirteen Conservatives voting against the government, but the third reading of the Bill, the final stage at the Commons, was agreed by a majority of seventeen votes, 301 to 284. Michael Jopling,[24] himself a junior whip under Francis Pym and due to become Chief Whip under Margaret Thatcher in 1979, told me that he had never known a more successful or more complex exercise of whipping than that organised by Francis Pym on our entry into the European Community.

John Roper supported this view saying that the free vote of 28 October 1971 'was a triumph – a masterly move by Francis Pym'. He pointed out that there were eight or nine stalwart pro-European Labour MPs who were about to retire from the Commons and who were always willing to absent themselves when Ken Clarke needed them to do so. But Roy Jenkins had to be careful. He was still in the Shadow Cabinet and in the six-day debate he and two other members of the Labour front bench, George Thomson and Harold Lever, were all condemned to silence. The Labour Chief Whip, Bob Mellish, was 'reasonably relaxed' about his rebels. He knew that there was still a strong pro-European element in his party and it was questionable whether he really wanted to defeat the Bill.

When the Accession Bill was finally won, a photograph was taken of Ted with the whips who had helped to get the Bill through the Commons. The influence of the Chief Whip and the whips' office on Ted remained strong, sometimes to good advantage, sometimes not. Ken Clarke told me that there was a moment when Ted was proposing to sack Margaret Thatcher, as Secretary of State for Education, from the Cabinet because she was considered to be ineffective and too unpopular in her determination to cut free school milk. He was dissuaded from doing this by Francis Pym on the grounds that Ted must have one woman in the Cabinet. In early 1974 Ted attended a whips' dinner at which, not unusually, a great deal of wine was drunk. He asked the whips whether he should go for an immediate election or delay. Because of the miners' strike, most voted for delay and one, Sir Walter Clegg, who represented a northern constituency, argued most passionately for the election to be put off for a few more weeks. Ted accepted the argument and the election date, which could have been in late January, was postponed until 28 February. This proved disastrous. At the start, the Tories were favourites to win at 2–1 on but events went against them. Bad retail price figures showing that prices had gone up by 20 per cent in the previous year were announced two weeks before the election, and a record monthly balance of payments deficit was published three days before. The impression gained ground that Labour's apparent reasonableness might be better than the Tories' toughness.

A row broke out during the election campaign between the Coal Board and the National Union of Mineworkers about the accuracy of the statistics contrasting their pay with that in other industries. The story was blown up by the press and the government was blamed for what appeared to be an unnecessary miners' strike. Enoch Powell gave up his seat as a Conservative MP without giving any notice to the offices of his association or his agent and, a week before the election day, after criticising Ted's policy of accession to Europe, let it be known that he had cast a postal vote for the Labour Party. Ted always felt that if he had followed his own gut feeling and held the election in January before the miners' strike broke out, he would have won it. As it was, Harold Wilson made hay with the claim that an arithmetical error had thrown the country into an unnecessary national pit strike, and the final score was Labour 301, Conservatives 297 and Liberals fourteen. After some days of unsuccessful negotiation to see whether he could form a coalition with the Liberals, Ted resigned from office and Francis Pym ceased to be Government Chief Whip.

I entered the Commons at that election and soon became a member of the One Nation Dining Club – a cheerful organisation of which Ted Heath himself had been one of the founders. I noticed that a number of its senior members like Maurice Macmillan and Charles Fletcher-Cooke could not forgive Ted for never having thanked them for supporting him in the long nights debating the Accession Bill. Pro-European or not, they felt that they had gone out of their way to see that Ted had his triumph and that Britain entered the European Community but Ted had never uttered a word of gratitude. And this was echoed to me by others such as Paul Bryan who said that Ted did not have a capacity for making or keeping up with his friends.

Willie [Whitelaw] left trails of friends behind him. When he retired, the twenty-four policemen who had looked after him at one time or another gave him a farewell dinner. They would never have done that for Ted. When I sat next to him at lunch at No. 10 he never mentioned the years that we had spent at the whips' office together.

This seems to be at the heart of what went wrong for Ted soon after he became Prime Minister. The year 1971 had been an extraordinary year for him. He had reversed de Gaulle's 'Non' and had won the approval of Parliament and Pompidou for Britain joining the European Community. He had reopened negotiations about Northern Ireland with Jack Lynch, the Taoiseach of the Irish Republic. He had conducted the London Symphony Orchestra at a gala concert and he had skippered the British Team, including his own yacht *Morning Cloud*, in winning back the Admiral's Cup. A unique polymath display of skills. He should have been on top of the world, yet the signs of remoteness and rudeness were increasing, even to those who had worked loyally for him in the years in opposition. David Howell, whose membership of the small Public Sector Research Unit brought him so close to Ted between 1965 and 1970 – 'I virtually lived in his rooms in Albany' – thought that the ease and that the jokes had disappeared very quickly when Ted became Prime Minister. 'He used to write me notes that laughed at people that he and I had met. Ted was both perceptive and funny but, even before 1970, critical and somewhat contemptuous of his parliamentary colleagues.' Once he became Prime Minister, the spontaneity disappeared. 'He became wooden,' said David. 'I would talk about a problem with him and he would not answer except with a grunt. The civil servants told him that our Public Sector Research Unit had no official standing. It was not headed by a senior civil servant and could not be taken too seriously.' David found himself quickly sidelined as a junior minister in the Civil Service Department.

It was this feeling of being slighted and ignored that caused so many Tory MPs not to support Ted in the leadership campaign of early 1975. Airey Neave, the MP for Abingdon since 1953 and a successful escaper from Colditz during the war, ran a clever campaign for Margaret Thatcher but there is no doubt that pent-up irritation with Ted rather than Margaret's virtues and skills caused her to win and Ted to lose.

There is another side to the story. Jim Prior, Minister of Agriculture and then Lord President and Leader of the House of Commons under Ted, told me that 'none of those who worked closely with Ted between 1970 and 1974 felt he was so difficult... He would thank people without them realising that they were being thanked.' He did not remember Ted ever thanking him 'but it did not matter.' He told me that at the end of the Cabinet in March 1974, when Ted and his colleagues decided that their attempts to woo the Liberals were not working and that they had to hand over office to Labour, it was Margaret Thatcher who had proposed the vote of thanks to Ted. John Peyton, Minister of Transport Industries in Ted's government, felt much the same as Jim Prior. 'I have always had a soft spot for Ted. He was a powerful Prime Minister. I was responsible for developing the idea of the Euro Tunnel between France and ourselves. When Ted decided that it was important, Willie Whitelaw and the others were much more attentive.' He remembered affectionately the evening concert which he and his wife had arranged to celebrate William Walton's seventieth birthday. Only a few friends were invited, including Ted Heath, who then asked them whether they would mind the party being transferred to 10 Downing Street. A marvellous evening followed. The guests included Georg Solti and his wife, Benjamin Britten, Peter Pears and Sir Arthur Bliss, the Master of the Queen's Music. The evening ended at midnight with a performance of Schubert's B Flat Trio. Ted had remembered that, ten years before, he had heard Walton being asked whether there was any piece of music he wished he had composed himself. This was the piece that he wished he had written.

I asked Nancy-Joan Seligman, married for fifty years to Madron Seligman, Ted's close friend since they were at Balliol College, Oxford, together, whether she saw changes in Ted over all the years of their friendship. She did not. She described him as 'a wonderful friend. He made our lives much richer. When Madron was in hospital, he sent flowers and rang every day to see how he was'. For four years running she and Madron and their four children spent Christmas with Ted at Chequers. 'He loves Christmas,' she said. 'He always has a big Christmas tree in his house. I used to fill a Christmas stocking for him and he came down to breakfast one morning on Christmas Day complaining that I had put some little brown balls in his stocking. He tried to eat one of them, only to find that it was made of brass.'

The Seligmans used regularly to take a house near the coast in Brittany where they kept a small boat. Ted had never sailed before but he found the sailing exciting, took sailing classes when he came back to Broadstairs and the answer in due course was *Morning Cloud*, the yacht of which he was justifiably extremely proud. To learn sailing to the degree of proficiency demanded by *Morning Cloud* was a remarkable feat for a man already in his late forties and not brought up in boats. But Nancy-Joan commented that, in sailing as in other matters, he was very competitive. Sailing with him was not a matter of a gentle passage and gin and tonic on the deck but very serious, with no time for small talk. But then Ted never had any small talk. Nancy-Joan remembered a dinner at No. 10 when the Queen was the Guest of Honour and was sitting on Ted's right. Nancy-Joan recalled winking at the Queen and trying to suggest that she nudged Ted in order to wake him up.

I asked whether she thought that Ted would have been an easier person if he had married. Would marriage have changed him for the better? She mentioned Moura Lympany, the famous pianist whose name was associated with Ted for a long time. 'I think she chased him,' she said. 'She was too obvious. It would have been another dimension if he had married.'

This was a theme picked up by Peter Rawlinson, the Attorney General in Ted Heath's government. 'A wife would have made all the difference. He needed someone to consult.' This remains true both for Prime Ministers and for Chief Whips.

In his biography of Ted Heath,[25] John Campbell explicitly blames the fact that Ted was Chief Whip for his failure with the Tory parliamentary party.

> It gave him an essentially disciplinary view of party management. It is on the face of it one of the central paradoxes of his career that a leader who had been Chief Whip should lose the leadership in 1975 precisely because he had lost the support of the party in Parliament. The explanation would seem to be that just because he had been Chief Whip – at a period when the party was chastened and relatively biddable – he took it for granted that backbenchers would always ultimately do what the whips told them, as they had in his day. He assumed that his own Chief Whips, Francis Pym and Humphrey Atkins, should be able to keep the troops loyal to him as he had done for Macmillan.

This may be partially true but the full answer is a little more complex. Ted is a uniquely ambitious and determined person who genuinely believed in one-nation Conservatism. When, as Prime Minister, he did not turn the nation round as he expected, he became, for most of us, reclusive and drawn into himself. He could never forgive Margaret Thatcher or the parliamentary Conservative Party for voting him out of leadership in 1975. He then clearly needed the support of a family both to distract him and to share his burden with him. That said, he remains the only Chief Whip to have become Prime Minister.

THIRTEEN

The man behind Alec Douglas-Home – Martin Redmayne, 1959–64

This chapter goes back a little in history to 1959, when Martin Redmayne succeeded Ted Heath as Government Chief Whip after the October election. He had already been in the whips' office for eight years and had been Deputy Chief under Ted. Paul Bryan, to whom I referred in the last chapter, told me that Ted and Martin were never close and that Ted treated Martin as his deputy very badly. He summoned Martin to London during the holidays and then kept him waiting for three days before he saw him.

Martin Redmayne himself wrote of Ted that he was 'supremely self-sufficient and at times could be very tough'. He recalled how Ted had once told a Tory rebel, 'You're nothing but a bloody Fascist.' He regarded him as incomparable in argument. 'He knew his facts and bludgeoned an opponent with dates, figures, logic. I certainly am no compulsive talker – perhaps rather a compulsive listener. It always seemed better to me to let the other chap do the talking.'[1] This is precisely what Ted said of himself – in his autobiography – that he did the listening and let others do the talking.

Redmayne served under Macmillan as Prime Minister for four years, until October 1963, and then under Douglas-Home for the single year of his premiership. Redmayne was shy and dour. He did not have the polymath qualities that Ted had but he wrote under the pseudonym of John Gilpin some bad poetry of which he was proud. Most of it was about the House of Commons and some of it appeared in newspapers and articles. I quote an example below that describes a week in an MP's life:

Whip

On Monday, Mountain brings forth Mouse
On the Adjournment of the House
A Full attendance is required

▬▬▬▬▬▬▬▬▬▬▬

(That mountain may be mouse inspired)
Thereafter: Mr Edwin Ratz,
'Impending shortages for cats'

Tuesday and Wednesday, per adventure,
We risk defeat by vote of censure.
Vital Divisions will take place

▬▬▬▬▬▬▬▬▬▬▬
▬▬▬▬▬▬▬▬▬▬▬

Attend by 9.15 or face

▬▬▬▬▬▬▬▬▬▬▬
▬▬▬▬▬▬▬▬▬▬▬

Our grave displeasure

▬▬▬▬▬▬▬▬▬▬▬
▬▬▬▬▬▬▬▬▬▬▬

        Charles de Vere
On the adjournment: 'Price of Beer'

The Negroes (Denigration) Bill
On Thursday, 2nd Reading, till
Your dinner time. And after dinner
Debate the boundaries of Pinner.

Your presence is expressly sought

▬▬▬▬▬▬▬▬▬▬▬

Unless you're paired.

▬▬▬▬▬▬▬▬▬▬▬

        And it is thought,
The Pneumo-Byssinosis Bill
On Friday (here's a bitter pill)
Demands that you should be on call

▬▬▬▬▬▬▬▬▬▬▬

At 4.15 pm.

▬▬▬▬▬
▬▬▬▬▬

    That's all.

Note
The balance of the week is free
Attend your fete, your surgery,
Your sale of work, your church bazaar
On Saturday.
    Your Sundays are
Reserved, of course, for private life
– On Sunday you may see your wife.

Redmayne's family owned a sports business in Nottingham and he worked in that before and after the Second World War. This was not the precise background of most of the Conservative whips at that time – they tended to be both military and landed – but Redmayne had had 'a good war', serving in the Sherwood Foresters, commanding the 14th battalion in the Italian campaign and then forming and commanding the 66th infantry brigade. He won a DSO in 1944 and was made an honorary brigadier in 1945.

He ran the whips' office like a military headquarters with strong emphasis on knowing the exact position and number of his troops at any one time. He sent copious typewritten notes to Macmillan and then to Alec Douglas-Home about a very wide range of subjects. On 12 June 1961 he compiled a list of suggested and consequential ministerial changes. It included the words, 'Home Secretary would like to promote Renton to be Minister of State in place of Vosper.' This refers to David Renton, an old friend but no relation.[2] A sense of humour occasionally slipped into the formalities. For a new UK Commissioner to Malta he suggested, 'I could try [Alan] Noble but his wife is now busy breeding race horses and I suspect that she would not want to live out of the country.' On 11 July 1963 he sent a minute to Macmillan about the date, before the holidays, on which he should attend a meeting of the backbench 1922 Committee: 'The later date is preferable because the opportunity for mischief thereafter is less.'

In October 1962 he wrote in some anger to Macmillan complaining, as Government Chief Whips have so often done, that ministers did not spend enough time in the Commons. They should 'reserve an hour or two for the House of Commons on at least two days of the week. Sometimes, even if not concerned with the business,... they, voluntarily and happily, should stay with us in the late hours of the sitting. It has an effect on morale quite out of proportion to the effort made'.[3]

In April 1964, halfway through Douglas-Home's year in office, the Chief wrote to him almost in despair:

> You asked me to write you a brief note about our present discontent. They are manifold: that there is no consultation with backbench members; that Ministers pay more attention to the Opposition than to their own supporters; that the Chief Whip makes no effort to represent the opinion of the Party; that the Executive of the 1992 Committee is out of touch with its members, and so forth ad nauseam.
>
> The fact is that twelve years of Conservative Government and a five-year Parliament have brought morale to a low ebb...
>
> What is to be done? The answer has two legs.
>
> As Heath said the other day, we must try to show that the Government is single-minded in its purpose.
>
> The second leg lies in trying to regain the confidence of our members; not by you, you have not lost it, but by Ministers. As I said so often to Macmillan, where as in 1951 all Ministers were, by the nature of things, the friends of those who remained on the backbenches, they have since become increasingly separated from them. They now have few friends left.

If Redmayne had stood back a little he might have seen that he was arguing the case for greater use of the whips as a go-between ministers and backbenchers. As the number of parliamentary Bills increased session by session and as the demands of the media to talk to ministers became greater, their workloads became heavier and their daily schedules more full. Complaints about lack of contact with backbenchers followed inevitably.

Margaret Thatcher entered the House of Commons in the 1959 election and in the same year won a place in the ballot for Private Member's Bills. These represent a unique opportunity for a backbencher to promote a popular cause – such as extending the opening hours of pubs – and at the same time attracting publicity and the notice of the front bench. Her whip, Harwood Harrison, toiled for a week to help her find a suitable Bill. Guardianship of Infants, Crown Privilege and Contempt of Court were among the subjects that were recommended to Margaret. She turned them all down and decided to draft her own Bill. Her whip wrote a note to Redmayne which concluded with the words: 'She has acquired a strong anti-whip complex. We have, in her own words, "turned a potentially cooperative member into an uncooperative one".'[4]

Macmillan made a point of keeping Redmayne informed about odd political developments. After Hugh Gaitskell's death, Harold Wilson and George Brown were the two contenders for the Labour leadership. Macmillan sent Redmayne a note on 7 February 1963 saying that Hartley Shawcross[5] had lunch with him that day. Shawcross had told Macmillan that George Brown 'hoped to scrape in by a few votes'. But if Wilson won, Shawcross would not serve under him or work with him. 'He was more bitter about Wilson than I expected. He regarded him as a dangerous man in every sense of the word.'[6]

Patronage passed constantly through his hands. Jackie Smyth, an MP for many years and aged sixty-nine, wished to leave the House at the next election and suggested that he should be made a hereditary peer or, if that was not possible, a life peer. However, Redmayne added in a note to the Prime Minister, 'his real resentment is the fact that he has not been made a back bench privy councillor.' The majority at Norwood was only 7,000 in a three-cornered contest. This was too close for comfort, so Redmayne suggested that Smyth was made a privy councillor immediately and that might stop him wishing to retire.[7]

In July 1963, knowing that a general election had to happen soon, Redmayne sent a long list to Macmillan detailing nineteen Conservative members who had made claims for honours but not yet received them and a further eighteen who deserved them but had not yet got them.[8] Dispensing patronage, though, was not a task that he particularly enjoyed. Six years later, on 10 April 1969, when he was in the Lords and another election was getting close, he wrote to Ted Heath, now the leader of the party and Prime Minister-in-waiting, advising strongly that Members of Parliament should be told that there was 'no automatic reward on retirement'. He continued,

'Over the years we recreated a terrible precedence in this respect – and a terrible number of baronets as a result of it.' To have a list of political honours twice a year was mistake 'and you should not return to it'. Once a year was quite enough. He added that he knew that Ted was 'against hereditaries'. He did not argue the point but commented that many people in the country did not share Ted's opinion. Ted acknowledged the letter with a typical one-sentence reply saying, 'This is extremely helpful.'

Redmayne comes over in his memos to the Prime Minister as, above all, the efficient businessman. He only comments on policy 'if I judge the political effect to be bad' and, in this context, he queried the wisdom of raising Post Office charges when, according to the clear calculations in his memo, the average return on the Post Office's net assets annually over the past five years was 7.17 per cent. Not many ministers would have bothered to make this precise calculation. As early as 9 October 1962 he suggested that there should 'a free vote on the Common Market'.[9] Britain had applied to join the European Economic Community a year earlier and de Gaulle had not yet vetoed the application. Redmayne told the Prime Minister that a free vote would put Labour into confusion and 'it would have the merit that we should not be forced into it.' His foresight was remarkable as this was precisely the tactic adopted by Ted Heath as Prime Minister and Francis Pym as Chief Whip ten years later.

Redmayne's official view was that whips were there to receive opinions, not to influence them. At times he personally found this reticence difficult. He wrote a memo to himself on the scrapping of the British-designed Skybolt missile in favour of the US-designed Polaris. He was critical of the influence of the USA and felt that we were being pushed around by the Americans. He had 'a sense of increasing political weakness in world affairs' and a worry about our ability to realise our wish to be leaders in Europe. Most obviously he resented the Bill that Ted Heath brought in in 1984 to abolish resale price maintenance. In his autobiography Heath describes RPM, its common abbreviation, as follows: 'the system whereby a manufacturer or wholesaler selling goods to a shopkeeper could compel him to sell them to customers at a fixed price.' Ted Heath went on to say, 'This was clearly absurd and archaic, punishing the ordinary consumer by keeping prices higher than they needed to be.' Redmayne, a retail shopkeeper himself, thought the existing system neither absurd or archaic. Hundreds of his friends in the retail trade agreed with him and small shopkeepers, who saw their profit margins threatened, wrote to their constituency MPs protesting and they were supported by John Morrison, chairman of the 1922 Committee. He sent a note to the Prime Minister insisting that 'unless a very different approach is adopted by Ted Heath, quite frankly, HMG will be more likely to fall than not.'[10]

Redmayne was at loggerheads with his former boss. He said at Cabinet that 'they had gone barking mad' and later commented that 'Heath showed an almost malevolent lack of interest in the problems' the Bill gave him personally and the whips' office in general.[11]

The Bill was modified before the second reading debate but got into trouble at the committee stage. The 'Chemist's amendment' would have removed any drug and surgical appliance from the ambit of the Bill. Heath strongly opposed this and won the vote on the amendment by just one vote, 203 to 204. For the next three weeks, he said in his autobiography, 'I was engaged in parliamentary guerrilla warfare with my own colleagues. Finally, my patience snapped.' He obtained Douglas-Home's agreement and 'the rebels were eventually mollified by ten carefully worded but ultimately minor amendments.' As to the part played by his colleague, the Government Chief Whip, he wrote, 'It was unfortunate that Martin Redmayne, himself a small businessman, was opposed to the policy. Instead of trying to sell a decision that had been collectively agreed by the Cabinet as I had done in my days as Chief Whip, he kept up the pressure on the Prime Minister by arguing for a number of important changes put forward by recalcitrant MPs.' To me he said of Redmayne, 'When he became Chief Whip he never said a word to me at all. I had offered him help at any time but he never came back to me with a single question.'[12]

The Bill to abolish RPM finally got royal assent in July 1964. The October election, where Douglas-Home was defeated and Labour formed a government with a majority of just four, was certainly influenced by the row over RPM. Douglas-Home accepted that it had lost them votes and Redmayne blamed it in part for the eventual loss of his seat in the 1966 election. What Tory MPs had experienced was the determination of Ted Heath to achieve his objective despite the opposition of the Chief Whip, the chairman of the 1922 Committee and the party chairman.

The first ten months of the previous year, 1963, were, however, the time of greatest trial for Redmayne. Luckily, he had by then been in the whips' office for twelve years. He knew the ropes very well but he was still capable of misjudging his colleagues. The first trouble broke out in the spring. A clerk in the private office of Tam Galbraith, a senior MP and Minister at the Admiralty, was found to have been spying for Russia and was subsequently sent to prison for eighteen years. His name was Vassall and he was known to be a homosexual. The scandal developed as it was found that Vassall had frequently delivered red boxes with government papers in them to Galbraith's home in Scotland and then had a meal with Mr and Mrs Galbraith before returning to London. Galbraith had written the occasional personal and friendly note to Vassall. The press jumped on these revelations and the impression was built up that the relationship between Galbraith and Vassall had been uncomfortably close. A rumour circulated that Galbraith and Vassall were going to flee together from Britain. Galbraith, a thoroughly honourable and steady Tory, was hugely embarrassed by the publicity and wondered what to do next.

An evening debate was scheduled in the Commons and Redmayne, as Chief Whip, implied that the Prime Minister would like to have Galbraith's resignation in his pocket before the debate began. Galbraith thought the Prime Minister was, in fact, demanding his resignation, which Prime Ministers can always do, and thus wrote a resignation letter. When it became known that the Prime Minister had accepted his resignation but had not actually asked for it, it was widely assumed that Galbraith was guilty and that was why he had resigned. Galbraith was shattered by this experience and brought libel cases against some of the newspapers involved. When he asked, though, for Macmillan to talk directly to his solicitor, Macmillan refused and told him to look forward, not backward. The inquiry, led by Lord Radcliffe, cleared Galbraith in every respect and he was re-elected six times after the Vassall affair. He was the first minister in my memory to be 'mercilessly pursued by the press'. Nuclear arms were proliferating and it was the time for spies and scandal.

The case of Jack Profumo, the Tory MP who slept with a call girl, Christine Keeler, at the same time as she was having an affair with Ivanov, a Russian embassy official, was brewing before the Vassall affair and broke immediately afterwards. Rumours about the affair caused Redmayne to summon Profumo after midnight to his Commons' office. Iain Macleod, the Attorney General John Hobson, and the Solicitor General Peter Robinson were all present, three Ministers and the Chief Whip. Profumo, who had been in bed after taking a sleeping pill, came with his solicitor. Bill Deedes followed around 2.30 a.m. and typed out the statement that Profumo made in the Commons at 11.00 a.m. the following morning. In this he swore that, though he knew Christine Keeler, he had never been to bed with her, and his colleagues believed him. Unfortunately, it was not true. Spurred on by more newspaper probing and threats from a bizarre character, Doctor Stephen Ward, who had first introduced Keeler to Profumo, to reveal everything as rumour had caused his practice as an osteopath to suffer, Profumo came to see Redmayne on 4 June and told him that he had lied. In an unpublished article that he wrote about the affair, Redmayne said, 'When Profumo came to see me and said without preamble that in respect of the girl his statement has been untrue I was tempted… to tell him to go away and spare us this appalling catastrophe which he was bringing about.'

The trouble for the government went beyond Profumo personally. It lay in persistent rumours that the Secret Services had known for some time about the Ivanov–Keeler–Profumo triangle and that Ivanov might be using Keeler to get security secrets out of Profumo. Either they had not told the ministers responsible or they had told the ministers and the latter had done nothing about it.

A full inquiry was ordered and this took place under the lead of Lord Denning.

Allegations flew around and two Tory Members of Parliament, Stoddart Scott and Dudley Williams, reported to the whips a conversation that they had had with the Labour MP, Colonel Wigg. This included the comment that Doctor Ward's hobby was the seduction of young girls of sixteen or seventeen and 'that the wives of one or two of the members of the House of Lords [he mentioned two] came from Dr Ward's stable.'[13]

Redmayne wrote to the Prime Minister saying that he 'was thought not to have kept the Prime Minister fully informed and to have failed to advise you correctly. It is suggested that I resign. Needless to say, I shall do as you please'. Macmillan's reported answer was characteristic: 'If you resign, I resign.'

An initial debate took place in the Commons on 17 June. Peter Rawlinson, the Solicitor-General, wrote to Redmayne immediately before the debate saying that they were likely to be accused of gullibility over Profumo's deceit and they would be criticised for helping to draw up Profumo's statement to the House. In the event the government majority fell to fifty-seven against their normal figure of ninety-eight and Redmayne commented, 'It was far from a famous victory.'[14] The *Stockport Express* sounded the views of their two local Tory MPs. Their comments were that 'the personal integrity of the Prime Minister was vindicated but there had been two complete breakdowns in the security service.' When it came out on 25 September, Denning's report was rougher on the politicians. It concluded: 'It was the responsibility of the Prime Minister and his colleagues, and of them only, to deal with this situation, and they did not succeed in doing so.' The thought of a debate on the Denning Report hung over Macmillan and Redmayne throughout the summer holidays. In a later article Redmayne blamed himself and asked why, in April and May, they had not perceived the real truth.

The trouble was that the stories flying around were so fantastic. Macmillan felt he had already made a mistake over Galbraith and Vassall. He was determined not to make the same mistake twice. The Attorney General had known Profumo for years and could not believe he was not telling the truth. It was easier to believe this than the contrary. Then 'on 4 June truth died.'[15] At the same time as the Profumo affair, rumours were circulating that Duncan Sandys, son-in-law of Winston Churchill, was the headless man of whom an unusual, and revealing, photograph was being circulated in the divorce case between the Duchess and the Duke of Argyll. The press invented the term 'The Kissing Ring' and a senior MP, Henry Kirby, wrote to the Chief Whip advising him that he intended to abstain on the vote on the Profumo affair. He commented, 'As you know, the day-to-day ramifying revelations with regard to the goings on of the Kissing Ring, with their multi-racial tarts, ponces, drugs, guns, ministers, stately homes, peers etc. are no news to me …' Thus 1963 became like the last years of the Major administration.

In persuading Conservative MPs to vote with the government in the censure debate of 17 June, Martin Redmayne had given the impression to some that there would be a change in the leadership of the party once the Denning Report on the Profumo affair was published.

Two days after the censure debate Margaret Thatcher was one of those reported to the Chief Whip as being in favour of a change. Bellenger, a senior and maverick MP,[16] wrote:

My Dear Martin

If I am seen speaking to you again today I shall be judged your permanent spy. Yet I must tell you that at dinner tonight Margaret Thatcher made clear that she was for the Prime Minister going at once and stuck to her guns when challenged by Julian Critchley and myself on behalf of the loyalists. So I am bound to say that a degree of loyalty from within the Government would not come amiss at this time.

Yours, Bellenger

The Denning Report's final conclusion, that the Prime Minister and his advisers had failed to deal with the matter successfully, may have been a statement of the obvious but it added to the sense of excitement and anticipation as the party conference season drew near. The parallel with the recent events at and following the 2003 Conservative Party Conference is an obvious one.

The debate on Denning was expected to take place soon after the House resumed in November. The Tory Party Conference opened on Tuesday 8 October. Macmillan was dithering as to whether he should announce his intention to resign at the conference or go on at least until January 1964 by which time he would have been Prime Minister for seven years. Redmayne, in daily conversation with him, got one impression one day, another the next. There was no easy choice of successor. Redmayne's own view was that the Cabinet would want Rab Butler, who was Home Secretary, the House of Commons would want Reggie Maudling, who was Chancellor of the Exchequer and much more of a new face, while the constituencies would want Hailsham because of his public personality and charismatic speaking powers. A further twist to the plot was the thought in Macmillan's mind that there might be deadlock between these three candidates. The end result could be that Cabinet and Tory MPs would then turn back to him and beg him to stay on.

Tim Bligh[17] records in his 'brief chronological account of the main events and developments leading up to Lord Home's appointment as Prime

Minister', that on the evening of Monday 7 October Macmillan, still at 10 Downing Street and due to go to Blackpool for the conference a day to two later, kept on going to the lavatory. He told Bligh that he could not pass water and was in acute discomfort.

At 5.00 a.m. the following morning, 8 October, a catheter was put into Macmillan in order to help him urinate. At Cabinet a few hours later, Macmillan, 'looking white and drawn', was nonetheless able to lead his ministers through a number of agenda items. At 1.00 p.m., after Cabinet had ended, a specialist visited Macmillan, 'relieved him of discomfort' but insisted that he went straight into hospital for an operation for prostatic obstruction.

This cast the die for Macmillan.

The following day, Wednesday, Martin Redmayne arrived at the conference in the evening having arranged for all the Cabinet ministers who were at the conference to meet him in Rab Butler's room. He told them that 'the Prime Minister had instructed me to put in hand the process of consultation which was to find his successor.'[18] Redmayne himself had been agonising for some weeks. When he visited the Prime Minister at Chequers at the end of September, he wrote himself copious notes as to what he should say to Macmillan regarding the advantages and disadvantages of his staying on. He wrote that

> the Chief Whip is expressly the servant of the Prime Minister, more intimately so than any other minister. He cannot be, in the same sense, the servant of the party, yet his post demands that he represents the opinion of the party however unacceptable or unpalatable that may be. In the first role his instinct may be blind support for the PM's decisions; in the second he must know and say where the decisions may lead. But overall there's a third consideration – a human one – on what is best for the man himself.

Macmillan's obstruction to the prostate solved Redmayne's immediate problem, but the actual timing was to prove disastrous for Hailsham. Hearing the news that Macmillan was definitely going to resign, Hailsham went over the top. He changed the text of the speech that he was about to deliver to the Conservative Policy Centre (the more political and thinking element in the party), threw his hat into the ring, declared that he would renounce his peerage and was willing to serve the party. His enthusiasm proved not infectious but excessive and the odds on his success immediately lengthened.

Redmayne, with his military mind and liking for order, was well prepared. Lord Lambton, an extrovert MP, had done his own poll a month earlier. He approached all Tory backbenchers and got answers from 161, or 55 per cent of them. In the light of what happened subsequently, the results were surprising.

They were: first choice: Maudling, ninety-three; Butler, twenty-eight; Hailsham, eighteen; Heath, eleven; Powell, seven. Sixty-five made a second choice: Maudling, thirty-five; Heath, twelve; Butler, nine; Hailsham, six; Powell, three.

Combining first and second choices: Maudling 56 per cent; Butler 16 per cent; Hailsham 10 per cent; Heath 10 per cent.

Lambton reported these figures to Redmayne who paid no attention to them. Before the conference was over, he made himself responsible for sounding out fifty junior ministers, and 300 MPs. He immediately issued his own instructions to his team. They were to get in touch by telephone or any other means with every Tory Member of Parliament. 'Whips are to receive opinions and not to influence them... get second choices or aversions if possible.'[19]

The Redmayne papers in the archives at the Bodleian Library include countless sheets with MPs' names on them marked in blue, green and red, showing the number of first, second and third choices and those whom individual MPs could not stand at any price; technically, those to whom 'they had an aversion'. By Wednesday 16 October, he gave his preliminary figures to Macmillan. Maudling was out of the running. Home, who had not been mentioned at all in Lambton's survey, was now at the top with a total of 176 first, second and third choices and only forty-two 'aversions', thirty of these personal, twelve because he was a peer. Hailsham had slipped badly. He had 104 first, second and third choices but seventy-nine 'aversions', sixty-eight of them personal, eleven because he was a peer.

Redmayne felt entitled to write a note to the Prime Minister[20] in which he was firmly in favour of Home. 'I have canvassed the views of 300 members of the Commons... I have carefully studied the quality of support given to these four candidates [Home, Maudling, Hailsham and Butler].' Maudling's support came, in Redmayne's view, from the younger and more junior element. 'There is very little personal objection to Maudling, but he fails to get sufficient positive support.' The quality of Hailsham's backing was 'comparatively unimpressive'. 'That given to Home and Butler is more mature but Home's covers a far wider cross section of the party. Apart from Home's actual lead, I am impressed by the general goodwill shown towards him.' Redmayne ended with the marvellously moderate sentence: 'It would be desirable to move towards an early conclusion of this difficult period.'

Maudling had been eased out of top place. In his autobiography he comments rather sadly that, during the summer of 1963 all the polls of Conservative MPs published in the *Daily Telegraph* gave him a very large majority.

> During the summer recess things appeared to change. For some reason I could not quite discern, my own position had weakened, and I could gauge this from the reactions from some of my Cabinet colleagues which, while always cordial, were somewhat less enthusiastically cordial after the recess than they had been before. But still the question remained, would Harold go or would he stay on?

All, in his judgement, depended upon how the various candidates performed at the conference. 'I had to make a speech myself fairly early in the proceedings as Chancellor. My friends told me that it was very important that I should get it right. I am afraid that I did not.' Maudling then, with a modesty most unusual in such a prominent politician, quoted an article from the *Sunday Express* of 4 October 1973, a full ten years later. This article, by Wilfred Sendall, a prominent political correspondent, praised the content of the speech.

> It was a cracker. I have read innumerable political speeches in my life but never one which seemed so right for the occasion It was eloquent, moving, wise. It merited the adjective statesmanlike. Even now, reading it again after ten years, I feel that given the delivery it deserved it would have brought the conference to its feet and swept Maudling to the front in the leadership race... If only the

delivery could have matched the words. But, alas, it fell abysmally below them. Handed to Churchill, or to Macmillan or Macleod, this text would have produced a famous speech. Maudling himself wrecked it.[21]

His delivery was flat, dull, uninspiring. Yet this did not stop Jim Prior, when called in by the Chief Whip, saying that he would vote for Maudling. As he went out of the door, Redmayne asked him, 'What about Home?' Prior told me,[22] 'I replied that I didn't know he was at the conference. And then as an afterthought I added, "Oh well, he might be persuaded to stand. I suppose he'd be all right."' Jim Prior does not know to this day whether Redmayne regarded this as a first or second choice for Home.

Maudling wrote his memoirs fifteen years after the conference. He was still mystified by the way in which he had been effectively blackballed and delisted.

And so the voices were collected. The traditional yet mysterious process continued. I am not quite sure to this day what happened... The views of the parliamentary party, their Lordships, and the party in the country were collected and sifted and presented under the guidance of the Chief Whip, Lord Redmayne,[23] to Harold Macmillan, whose fundamental duty it was to advise the Queen. It became slowly realised by some, again mysterious, process that the advice was that she should send for Alec.

On 17 October the *Daily Mail* had a strong leak that Macmillan was going to advise the Queen to call for Home. This resulted in a late night meeting at Enoch Powell's house in South Eaton Place, very like that organised by Tristan Garel-Jones two nights before Margaret Thatcher's resignation. The Chief Whip was asked to come. He arrived there to find Macleod, Maudling, Erroll (President of the Board of Trade) and possibly Lord Hailsham. He did not stay to the end but wrote, 'These ministers seemed unwilling to accept that the Conservative Party had really opted for Lord Home. They did not seem open to persuasion on that point.' The next day the deed was done. Bligh records, 'The Chief Whip and I went to see Macmillan at 8.30 in hospital.' They advised him that Home should be the man recommended to the Queen.

The following day, 18 October, Redmayne confirmed in writing his final figures to Tim Bligh.

	first choice	second and third choices where expressed	definite aversions
Home	87	89	30
Butler	86	69	48
Hailsham	65	39	78

Maudling had dropped out of the reckoning altogether. Doubtless this table was immediately passed on to Sir Michael Adeane, the Queen's private secretary, in order that the Queen might be fully convinced that, in calling for Home, she was being advised to call for the right person. Redmayne's concern was that, unless her advisers were persuaded that Home had sufficient support to form a government, the Queen might call for the Labour leader, Harold Wilson, instead and ask him to dissolve Parliament and force an election. A general election was in any case due to take place within the next twelve months and the scandals of 1963 had left Wilson and the Labour Party looking like certain winners.

Home went to the Palace and was asked to form the next government. He was sufficiently unsure of his position with his leading colleagues that he did not formally accept the appointment and kiss hands at this stage. That had to wait until the following day after he had received agreement from both Hailsham and Butler that they would serve in a government led by him.

Although Home got on immediately with the business of forming a government, rumours circulated that Redmayne was the villain who had orchestrated Macmillan's departure and his replacement by Home. He was certainly not alone in thinking that it was time for Macmillan to retire. Oliver Poole, then chairman of the party, had visited Macmillan at the beginning of the crucial fortnight, on Monday 7 October. One of Macmillan's oldest and most trusted friends, he told him that he must not stay on. If he did, the next general election would be a huge defeat for the Tory Party. 'The name of Macmillan would go down in history as one of hatred, ridicule and contempt. He did not wish to live to see this happen.'[24]

Macmillan's resignation apart, Macleod wrote in the *Spectator* of January 1964 that Redmayne had weighted the result in favour of his own candidate.

This was in answer to two interviews that Redmayne gave to the *Listener* magazine in December 1963 in which he said, 'One had to start off by getting what I would call a numerical guide – one then had to consider the shade of opinion expressed in various letters and reports.' Many in the inside circle of Westminster took the view that the Chief Whip had taken advantage of the consideration of 'shades of opinion' to favour his own candidate. Redmayne, of course, denied this. He appears not to have remembered a secret and personal letter, typewritten on three pages of foolscap, which he wrote to Home on 2 October, a week before the conference started. He noted, first, that Home was to dine with the PM on Sunday night (6 October).[25] He then stated that in his view Tory MPs were split, Maudling 35 per cent, Butler 35 per cent, Hailsham 30 per cent. Maudling he dismissed with the destructive comment, 'he shows more pressing ambition than I had thought likely or might seem wise.' He then adds,

> I have tried to keep an open mind. My loyalty as Chief Whip is primarily to the Prime Minister, but in a situation of this sort I must take a view of the interests of the party... if the Prime Minister decided to go, the process of selection of a successor is so difficult as to be almost impossible to accomplish without damage to the party... if on the other hand you are willing to step into the breach, almost all our difficulties would disappear. In my judgement, the party would give you unanimous support... I appreciate what an enormous sacrifice this would be. You would have to be Prime Minister in the Commons; that might last for a few months.

The penultimate paragraph ends, 'No man could want a more difficult assignment, and yet I do not hesitate to put it to you because I know that you will look at it squarely and will see that it has sense in itself and in a queer way honour for you.' This letter is grandiloquent and very serious. It obviously had the desired effect on Home in persuading him, after much hesitation, to stand for the leadership and, in the event, to win it. Did Redmayne delude himself into thinking that his persuasion was not a decisive factor in obtaining the result that he wanted? Whatever his later scruples, it is clear that it was he who chose the winner of the short-lived battle that began in the Conference Hall at Blackpool on 9 October 1963 when he arrived in Blackpool with Macmillan's message. It was the same day – 9 October – forty years on that Iain Duncan Smith made his last speech as a leader to a Conservative Party Conference in the same Conference Hall.

The Redmayne papers were only recently placed in the Bodleian. They might have helped me if I had had the time to read them before the events of November 1990 that led to the resignation of Margaret Thatcher. I would have liked, for example, to have had the time to take a more detailed poll of ministers and Tory MPs on the evening of the Tuesday after the first poll results were announced and on Wednesday before Margaret took her decision to resign. But time was not on my side. I only had thirty-six hours from the announcement of the results of the first ballot until the decisive Cabinet on Thursday morning. Redmayne, by contrast, had nine days, from Tuesday 8 October until 17 October, to survey the scene and, in his case, to ensure that his choice was the man summoned to the Palace.

Redmayne attached a note to the files of letters that he received from MPs giving him their preferred option for leader. He wrote,

> Letters and telephone messages from Members about the Leadership written in the few days of the Blackpool Conference or immediately after... These were part of the background of the advice given by me to Macmillan, but it must be remembered that the whips' office for the two/three days after Blackpool resembled a Mid-West cattle auction. Some years after the event Michael Hughes Young [Deputy Chief Whip] and I re-checked the 'evidence'. The result was well enough the same, but we agreed that in cold blood so long after the events, it was difficult to be *sure* – as we had been at the time.

Initially, seven members of the Cabinet said they would not serve under Home unless Butler himself agreed to serve and these seven included Macleod, a chairman of the party, Hailsham, an ex-chairman, and the Chancellor of the Exchequer, Maudling.[26] In the event only two – Macleod and Powell – refused to join the team. Lord Home gave up his title and returned to the Commons in a by-election as Sir Alec Douglas-Home.

Far from being a gentle hand on the tiller, Douglas-Home threw himself into party political activity. He appeared frequently on television and dashed round the country attending party political meetings. Slowly his face came to be recognised and liked. The mood in the Tory parliamentary party and in the country improved rapidly. Douglas-Home, aware that, setting himself on one side, the first choice of Tory MPs for Prime Minister would clearly have been Reggie Maudling, not Hailsham or Butler, kept him on as Chancellor of the Exchequer. It was in Maudling's nature to be an optimist. He followed a policy of expansion and encouraged consumer spending. Redmayne himself became the most important link between the parliamentary party and party organisation.

In May 1964 a daily committee was formed which met every morning at No. 12 Downing Street no matter whether the Commons was sitting or not. Redmayne was in the chair. Lord Blakenham, now chairman of party organisation. Lord Poole, vice-chairman of the party and Bill Deedes, MP for Ashford, were the other regular attenders, different ministers and whips being summoned as needed. Since 1962 Deedes had been the minister without portfolio responsible for 'coordination of government information services'. Deedes had been a journalist throughout the 1930s and was one of the first experts in political spinning. An information panel had started in 1962, chaired by Deedes, which was frankly propagandist. Ministers were required to be much more open in telling Members of Parliament their policies and objectives, and this was in turn to be passed round the country. Redmayne's daily committee was a further weapon in a new campaign to put over forcibly the government's message of what they were doing and why. This was 'the most noteworthy innovation of the 1959–64 Parliament'[27] and Redmayne was very much in charge.

The major irritant was Ted Heath's Bill to abolish retail price maintenance. This was seen as a serious threat to the small shopkeeper. Twenty Conservative MPs voted against it on 10 March 1964 and about twenty abstained on the second reading. Fourteen days later on 24 March the figures got worse. Thirty-one Conservatives voted against and over twenty abstained. Redmayne expressed his irritation to Douglas-Home on the timing, the haste and the lack of preparation for Ted Heath's Bill. Nonetheless, the Tories' political prospects improved. By August Redmayne felt sufficiently confident that he wrote to Douglas-Home 'a carefully argued paper on the relative merits of recasting the government immediately after the election or waiting till the Christmas recess.'[28] In the event Redmayne's optimism was not quite justified.

When the general election finally came in October 1964 Labour won with a majority of just four seats. Redmayne stayed on as Conservative Chief Whip for two months and then, in his own words, 'went off to other tasks,' including becoming a director of Harrods. He was defeated at the 1966 election, when Labour increased their majority to ninety-six.

Douglas-Home gave up the leadership of the Tory Party in July 1965, ten months after losing the general election. By then, a new electoral procedure for leadership had been adopted under which every Conservative MP had a vote. Ted Heath won the first ballot by 150 votes as opposed to Reggie Maudling with 133 votes and Enoch Powell with fifteen. Heath lacked by a large margin the 15 per cent majority that was required under the new rules. Nonetheless, Maudling and Powell both withdrew in Heath's favour and the second ballot was cancelled. The quiet way that Maudling described this in his memoirs contrasts vividly with the furore around party leadership elections that now exist:

> I went out to lunch in the City while awaiting the result, and halfway through lunch I was telephoned by Robert Carr to say that he had bad news, the figures were Ted 150, me 133, Enoch 15. That, it seemed to me, was that. The party had spoken, and although there was a provision for a second ballot on such a narrow result, there was not much point in asking people to say the same thing over again... so I rang him up, conceded defeat and said I would be glad to serve under him in his capacity as leader of the party.[29]

The ease with which Maudling abandoned the race, the fact that he was having a City lunch while waiting for the result, epitomise both the strong and the weak points of the man. He did not have the determination to win that characterised both Ted Heath and, with more languor but much guile, Harold Macmillan. Yet if Maudling had been chosen leader at the Conservative conference in 1963, this story would surely have been a different one.

Fifteen years younger than Douglas-Home, he would not have resigned after Labour's victory by only four seats in the general election of October 1984. He would have continued as leader of the Tory Party in opposition and it would have been he, not Heath, who would then have won the 1970 election and become Prime Minister. Ironically, therefore, it can be argued that, although Redmayne and Heath never got on in the whips' office, it was Redmayne's support for Home as leader in 1963 that made the job of Prime Minister available to Heath in 1970. The influence of the Chief Whip of the day had unforeseen consequences in the far future.

FOURTEEN

Today's Commons – the Black Spot

Peace did not come to the Tory Party with the departure of Margaret Thatcher. John Major had been her choice to defeat Michael Heseltine. His victory led to a truce durable enough to win the 1992 election but not thereafter. Since then there has been such a series of parliamentary rebellions, first in the Tory Party over the Maastricht Treaty and then in Labour over war on Iraq, foundation hospitals and university tuition fees, that the ability of whips to maintain unity on the government backbenches has disappeared. This has fundamental implications for the future at Westminster.

Before becoming Prime Minister, Major had been, first, Foreign Secretary and then Chancellor of the Exchequer, but for too brief a time. He was always competent but he had not gained enough experience and maturity to steer a parliamentary party that, after thirteen years in office, was self-indulgent to the point of arrogance in its approach to discipline. Richard Ryder was his Chief Whip from 1990 to 1995. Ryder had been a whip before, from 1986 to 1988, and he knew the ways of the office. He was close to Major in his approach to policy but he suffered from painfully bad health and lacked an ability to command that would have weighed more on the scales than his good brain and pleasant personality. Unfortunately, Major and Ryder inherited a bunch of malcontents led by the likes of Bill Cash.[1] It was my mistake that, when Chief Whip, I had not suggested to Margaret Thatcher that she made Cash a junior minister in the Department of Social Security. There he could have absorbed himself in the complexities of our benefits system. Instead, deprived of a ministerial red box, he became a tedious and gloomy expert on the details of the legislation that bound together the European Union.

Once again, the Common Market proved the fault line in Conservative geology. The No Turning Back Group, from twenty to thirty strong, were determined to resist any attempt to move towards ever closer European union and the vehicle for their resistance was the parliamentary approval for the Treaty of Maastricht. They revelled in defying three-line whips in order to vote against its enactment into British law and Iain Duncan-Smith, briefly to become the leader of the party, was one of those who were unrepentant in their repeated rebellion. Tested thus brutally, the power of Richard Ryder and of his successor, Alastair Goodlad, proved more shadow than substance. Eight Tory MPs had the whip taken away from them but this only confirmed them in their rebellion. Richard Body, a long-time Tory MP, resigned the whip in sympathy with the eight. Their Conservative associations shared drinks with them in the local pubs, and congratulated them on their independence.

John Major gave vent to his feelings in remarks to ITN's political editor, Michael Brunson, that were meant to be off the record but were taped by BBC technical staff. As the *Observer* of 25 July 1993 wrote:

Mr Brunson raises the problem of the three rebel Cabinet ministers who threatened resignation if Mr Major agreed to the social chapter in order to secure ratification of the Maastricht Treaty. Why, Mr Brunson asks, should he not simply sack them?

Mr Major: 'Just think it through from my perspective. You are the Prime Minister, with the majority of eighteen, a party that is still harking back to a golden age that never was and is now invented. You have three right-wing members of the Cabinet who actually resign. What happens in the parliamentary party?'

Mr Brunson observes that Tory MPs would create a lot of fuss, but that Major is Prime Minister. He could easily find three new Cabinet members.

Mr Major then bares his soul. 'I could bring in other people. But where do you think most of the poison is coming from? From the dispossessed and the never-possessed. You can think of ex-ministers who are going around causing all sorts of trouble.

'We don't want another three more of the bastards out there.'

As Ted Heath succinctly put it, 'You whips are so busy now controlling the vermin you have no time for controlling the government.'[2] This must sound like familiar music to Tony Blair, given the troubles he has had with parliamentary supporters of Gordon Brown.

Being 'anti Europe' had, as Geoffrey Howe regularly pointed out to me, become a sub-tribal culture in Britain. Fed as they are on exaggerated detail of fraud, incompetence and excessive spending in the European Commission, the more Britons go to Spain for their holidays, buy farmhouses in France and see their football clubs paying millions for Italian players, paradoxically the more they dislike the idea of a federal Europe. Labour were lucky to be in opposition at the time of the debates on the Maastricht Treaty. Although George Robertson, their leading spokesman, was personally strongly pro-European, he managed, in Parliament, to be hostile enough about the detail of the Treaty to keep votes of his own party solid while wooing and attracting the Tory rebels.

Add to this the repeated petty scandals in the Tory Party, and the inevitable result was the crushing Conservative defeat of May 1997. Labour were returned with a majority over the Conservatives of 253, and three Government Chief Whips followed in relatively quick succession, Nick Brown and then the first women Chief Whips, Ann Taylor and Hilary Armstrong. Large majorities always give Chief Whips problems – not of winning votes of confidence but, en route, of stopping a growing tendency to rebellions. Labour's first six years to 2003 were quiet. They inherited a healthy economic balance sheet and their Members of Parliament were preoccupied with a determination to win a second election. That achieved, the parliamentary situation changed rapidly. Government whips have found that they had to deal with regular rebellions on issues ranging from university tuition fees to a two-tier system of hospitals in the National Health Service. Blair's unqualified commitment to join President Bush in attacking Iraq and Saddam Hussein causes a number of his regular supporters to team up with the regular rebels.

As I write this, no one knows how the struggle for the party's leadership and philosophy between Tony Blair and Gordon Brown will eventually end. Margaret Thatcher remarked to me, after Nigel Lawson's departure, that one can only afford to lose one's Chancellor of the Exchequer once during one's time in office. It is possible that even once is too often.

19 March 2003 was the first of a number of crucial days when the Labour majority, then 165, looked threatened. At midday I joined a line of Labour peers in the front row of the Commons Strangers' Gallery. We asked each other how Blair could possibly deal with the lack of a second UN Resolution on Iraq, the openly half-hearted support of Clare Short[3] who had accused him of recklessness, and a very large number of rebellious Labour MPs on whom the whips had been leaning for several days. Iain Duncan Smith's polished head shone from the opposite side of the despatch box. As is traditional, the Prime Minister entered the Chamber only a few seconds before kick-off. There was no roar, not even a mutter, of supporting approval. A Private Bill, normally allowed ten minutes of parliamentary time, was disposed of in four minutes and, at 12.35, the Prime Minister got to his feet.

The Commons, though full, was rather quiet and, if anything, grumpy and irritated. But it was an occasion when one knew that, like Geoffrey Howe's resignation speech in November 1990, the next hour would decide history. Forty-eight minutes later, after answering a number of hostile interventions and dealing with Clare Short's precarious position so elegantly that the whole House chuckled, Blair sat down. Although the vote was not for another eight hours, he had won the day.

The message that Labour whips had tried to convey was simply that, if over half the Labour parliamentary party voted against the Prime Minister, he would resign. Tony Blair made this clear enough in the last minutes of his speech in a handwritten alteration to the printed text.

> To retreat now, I believe, would put at hazard all that we hold dearest … I will not be party to such a course. This is not the time to falter. This is the time, not just for this government – or, indeed, for this Prime Minister – but for this House to give a lead: to show that we will stand up for what we know to be right.

If Blair resigned, it would put Labour parliamentary seats at risk. The argument was just successful enough.

One hundred and thirty-nine Labour MPs out of a total of 412 voted that evening against their government on a three-line whip. Instead, they supported an amendment drafted by a Labour ex-Cabinet minister which said that 'the case for war against Iraq has not yet been established, especially given the absence of specific United Nations authorisation.' This was the largest ever rebellion of Labour MPs.

After a nerve-racking resignation speech the previous evening by the ex-Foreign Secretary, Robin Cook, and Clare Short's public comments, Blair expected a much larger rebellion. The possibility of more than 200 Labour MPs voting against him was on the cards, and the Cabinet Secretary, Andrew Turnbull, made enquiries about the constitutional position. As with the fall of Margaret Thatcher, if Blair resigned immediately, who should Turnbull advise the Queen to ask to lead the government until Blair's successor was elected? The look of relief on Blair's face when Hilary Armstrong, the Chief Whip, came in from the lobby to advise him of the size of the rebellion spoke volumes. The Tory Party had voted with the government and the majority was substantial.

Blair had spoken brilliantly, with clarity and passion. He had never before sounded so much like a Prime Minister. But it was by making the personal stakes so high that he diminished the Labour parliamentary rebellion. Nearly halfway through a Parliament and with the economy possibly going downhill, a sensible proportion of Labour MPs knew that the loss of Blair as Prime Minister was more than likely to put their own seats at risk. It is in that ability to persuade a Member of Parliament not to put his seat in jeopardy that the hidden threat still lies, but it has to be carefully used.

In May 2003 the BBC showed a much heralded drama documentary called *The Project*. It is a story of disillusionment with New Labour. A young, attractive black MP, a 'Blair babe', is especially disenchanted when the Home Office, under covert instructions from 10 Downing Street, so waters down a Freedom of Information Bill – a manifesto commitment – as to make it easier than ever for ministers to keep hidden that which they do not wish the public to know.

Bravely the MP announces that she will vote against the Bill and then, as she walks through the depths of the Commons, a threatening arm is thrown round her neck by a burly Labour whip. When she invades a palatial Westminster office to protest to the Government Chief Whip, he looks up her bulky file, tells her that she is currently booked to become Parliamentary Secretary at the Department of Transport after the next election. But, if she votes against the Freedom of Information Bill, she will in the whip's words 'become unelectable': the new hospital promised to her constituency, which has the likely West Midlands name of Wroker, will be built elsewhere; if her constituents want a bypass round a pretty village, they will find that the money is not available. The Blair babe reflects briefly and the documentary ends happily. The MP for Wroker votes as the whip requires and becomes parliamentary under-secretary to the Lord Chancellor, a job with more prestige than that at Transport.

The outside world expects this sort of thuggery from the whips and is disappointed if they do not get it. Two weeks before the release of *The Project*, the *Today* programme was talking about 'the Mafia world, the dark secrecy of the Government whips'.[4] Life was like that in the days of Bob Mellish[5] and Michael Cocks.[6] As Chief Whips, they saw the Labour government through the last years of Harold Wilson and those of Jim Callaghan as Prime Ministers. They were famously tough. Ben Whitaker[7] told me that it was never any use arguing with Mellish or trying to explain your point of view which might be somewhat different to that of the government. 'Never mind what you think, laddie,' said Mellish, 'you just go and get into the lobby.' When the Labour majority evaporated in the months up to the election of May 1979, Cocks had to be worried about every vote. He sent a junior whip up to Coventry in order to remonstrate with the elderly and senior Labour MP, Maurice Edelman. He instructed the whip to rebuke Edelman for his poor attendance in the Commons and to insist that he must turn up to vote much more regularly. The whip performed his duty, got a promise from Edelman that he would appear more frequently for crucial votes and arrived back in his London flat around midnight. He turned on the BBC news only to hear the reader announcing that Maurice Edelman had just had a severe heart attack and had been taken to hospital. Immediately afterwards, his telephone rang and he heard Cocks' voice remonstrating, 'Over the top, over the top.'

But life is not like that any longer and the BBC drama documentary was out of date before it was shown. Transparency is now the buzzword as the Commons and the Lords strive to become more available and more under-standable to the outside world. Secrecy, confidences never being leaked 'outside the office', used to be the rule of the game but that is no longer the case. If threatened by the whips in the manner of *The Project*, the first thing most MPs would do would be to run to the media, and the media would be wholly on their side, and so would their constituency officers.

Ann Taylor was the Labour Government Chief Whip from 1998 until the election of 2001. She served two years in the office in the 1970s under Cocks and his deputy, Walter Harrison. They gave her splendid training. Ann remembered pleading with the wives of difficult MPs to get their husbands back on side, agreeing that the husband's talents had not yet been fully recognised by the Prime Minister but this would certainly happen in the future. When she became a whip, foul language abounded in the whips' office. One of the senior whips got into the habit of having his chair next door to hers. Every time one of the members said the f-word, he would say, 'Sorry, Ann.' Everyone laughed and the stress disappeared.

This prepared her for becoming Chief Whip in 1998 and she regarded herself as a whip from the old school but not in terms of the physical manhandling and browbeating of *The Project*. She considered her main achievement the rebuilding of the regional system that had faded, for Labour, during eighteen years in opposition. She revived it along the lines the Tory whips had followed. Every whip was responsible not only for one or two ministerial departments but also for around twenty to thirty MPs, all from the same part of the country. The whips were expected to call everyone on their list each weekend, on some pretext or other, to make certain that their mood was all right. She remembered the truism that you had to know your clients. Each MP was different, had different problems, sometimes different ambitions. You needed to know where they were coming from and where they were trying to get to.

Those who follow this sympathetic approach are not natural bullies. Ann Taylor was not; her successor, the current Chief Whip, Hilary Armstrong, was hesitant at the start. She had not been in the whips' office before and was surprised to find herself in this role so early after the 2001 election, but claimed to have learned a lot from her father, Ernest, who was a whip during Wilson's government. A few months into her new job, she had an interview with a notable dissident MP, Paul Marsden, who is reported to have told the Chief that he would only turn up on Wednesdays. She tried to argue with him to join the mainstream of the party and to be a better attender. He leaked his version of the interview to the BBC and this included the sentence from Armstrong: 'The trouble with people like you is that you are so clever with words that us up North can't argue back.'[8] Perhaps Armstrong was trying a bit of northern self-deprecation but it did not sound well.

No Chief Whip should ever suggest that a backbencher is cleverer or knows more than they do. The essence of being a successful Chief Whip is the ability, like the Delphic oracle, to leave difficult customers in doubt as to how much you actually do know. The subtlety of the author Michael Dobbs' prototype Chief Whip, Francis Urquhart, saying 'you may think that but I could not possibly comment' is that the respondent is left uncertain whether the Chief Whip has inside knowledge or not. And doubt eats into the resolution of even the hardiest backbencher.

Media attention magnifies the problems, but they do not change in substance. 'Some MPs just don't turn up,' said Armstrong. 'The doubters are the most difficult.' As I walked away from her office in the Commons (a small office just off the Members' lobby, very different to the palatial office in *The Project*) I heard a woman MP arguing with two whips. 'Unless you give me a proper office, how can I do my work?' The whips looked harassed. She appeared to have a problem with a broken window which no one had turned up to mend.

In his record of his interview with Armstrong Paul Marsden referred to 'free votes' being allowed on issues of conscience, 'free' meaning unwhipped; the MP can vote whichever way he likes, preferably having listened to the arguments first. Recently the Tory Party leadership were cack-handed in insisting on a three-line whip in a Commons vote against the proposition that gay couples should be allowed to adopt children. This was an obvious error. The Opposition Chief Whip advised the Shadow Cabinet to have a free vote but was overruled. Eight Tory MPs, including Ken Clarke and Michael Portillo, ignored the whip and voted in the government lobby. Thirty-five abstained. These were unnecessarily high figures.

The Shadow Cabinet's decision was a mistake not just because the issue was essentially a non-party issue of conscience but also because there was no chance whatsoever of Tories winning the vote and defeating the government.

This underlines the purpose of whipping. It is to assemble your parliamentary forces so that, by winning votes, you can implement, amend or veto legislation. By contrast, on questions of high principle, there may well be no point in imposing a three-line whip because this will not win more votes. Better let principle hold sway as Francis Pym argued with Britain's accession to the European Community in 1971. The vote on starting the Iraqi war without a second UN Resolution was another case in point.

But Commons procedure is slowly changing. More Bills, especially those with technical detail in them, will be published in draft, giving the opportunity for pre-legislative scrutiny and for a degree of agreement on content. This may lead to better legislation or it may, simply, be a means of the government getting its programme of Bills through the Commons more easily. Either way, it argues against the need for so much whipping to push Bills through the House.

Ann Taylor assured me that she still felt the whips' office performed a very useful function in terms of party management and keeping in touch with MPs. That is doubtless so, but it could be achieved by a mixed bag of office managers and welfare workers. Hilary Armstrong's thinking is dominated by the knowledge that it was the break-up of the parliamentary party that so far has prevented a Labour government from ever serving two full consecutive terms in office. She herself toyed with proportional representation as a junior Member of Parliament but is now convinced of the merits of first past the post and is thus committed to a two-party system. With the inevitable conflict between the parties that this involves, she believes that whipping must continue, although obviously different in style and pressure when there is a majority of twenty as opposed to one of 170.

David Maclean, the Tory Chief Whip, takes a very practical view of the usefulness of whips. They are personnel managers, keeping their MPs informed about office and travel allowances, seeing that only the right claims are made for expenses, sending them text messages about the progress of debate and when to expect votes. Maclean told me that during a recent 'ping-pong' end of session battle with the Lords on a Home Office Bill, he kept up a running commentary throughout the night of text messages with his backbenchers who had been warned to be ready for votes at any time. He told them what discussions were going on with the Home Secretary and at what hour of the night there would be votes. Then finally, 'Blunkett has conceded,' 'there will be no more votes tonight.'

The backbenchers followed the minute-by-minute commentary with much more interest than usual; bars and tea rooms were crowded and by the next day there was more concern and more knowledge about the contents of the Bill. Modern technology had shown its worth, along with whips warning their MPs of votes in real time.

When Maclean first appeared before the post-Nolan Committee on Standards in Public Life, he was questioned as if he were the human resources director of a young company: 'What are you doing to educate and offer guidance to your MPs? Are you training them in the ways of the Commons? Do you listen to their career ambitions?' Maclean took it to heart. Conservative MPs now submit to an annual appraisal at which they are asked what talents they think they have that are not being used. Further questions follow: where do they wish to be in five years' time? What do they think of party policies and what is wrong/right with them? New Members of Parliament like this. They wish to become more professional and even two prominent grey beards approved. Sir Patrick Cormack[9] referred to the current whips' office as the most courteous he had ever known and Sir Peter Tapsell, MP for a series of remote Lincolnshire constituencies for nearly forty years, is alleged to have remarked with some charm after an interview, 'I am told I have a strange voice – I would like a smart little woman to correct it for me.'

Parliamentary parties use their websites to provide all the details of the day's business. E-mails arrive on the laptop throughout the day announcing immediate changes of business or the formation of yet another parliamentary committee to which some dignitary will be invited only to find that he has an audience of two – the chairman and the secretary. I have received e-mails from Labour MPs detailing what they are about to say in a Commons speech in opposition to their own party's policy. I expressed my surprise at this to Graham Allen[10] who had turned from being a Labour government whip into a rebel and he replied, truthfully enough, that it would not have happened in my day.

One of the essential functions of the Conservative whips' office was, at best, to choose or, at the worst, to help in the choice of the next leader of the party. William Hague changed all of this when all members of the Conservative Party, 300,000 of them throughout Britain, were given a vote on the choice of the next leader. In the Commons, and particularly in the Tory whips' office, this was regarded as a disaster. In 2001 the Tory MPs wanted Ken Clarke but the country members voted for Iain Duncan Smith. Every week of Duncan Smith's reign David Maclean was visited by parliamentary colleagues wringing their hands and saying there must be a change of leader but unable to suggest a candidate who would command a majority in both the Commons and the country.

At last, in October 2003, after a conference speech by Duncan Smith the content of which was reasonable but the presentation of which was, like Maudling's speech to the conference in 1963, appalling, the 165 remaining Tory MPs stared into the abyss and realised that they had no chance of winning the next election unless they had a change of leadership. Under the new rules, fifteen per cent of their number had to write not to the Chief Whip but to the chairman of the 1922 Committee, Sir Michael Spicer,[11] asking for a vote of confidence in the leader. Spicer thus had to receive letters from twenty-five Tory MPs in order to activate the vote of confidence. For two weeks after the beginning of the new parliamentary term there was intense speculation whether the vote of confidence would be triggered or not. A number of MPs sucked their thumbs, told friends they would write, but lacked the steel to do so. Then three Tories declared publicly that they had sent their Black Spot letters to Spicer and within two days he announced that he had received 'an appropriate number' of letters for the vote of confidence to take place. The informed guessing was that he had by then received some fifty letters rather than twenty-five. He had been alarmed at the possibility of a judicial review of any decision that there should be an election but was now on clearly safe ground.

On Wednesday 29 October, I listened to Duncan Smith making his last, hopeful speech to the 1922 Committee. The long, panelled Committee Room 14 on the first floor of the Commons is the traditional setting for these meetings. It was packed and when Duncan Smith came into the room the same desks were banged as they were when Ted Heath, Margaret Thatcher or John Major addressed us. Duncan Smith was listened to in silence for twenty minutes; it was only when he attacked the Labour government for the collapse in the economy that hands appreciatively banged again on the desk-tops. It was a brave but humble speech. He made clear that, like William Hague, he had not known enough about the difficulties ahead when he took on the task of leading a Conservative Party two years earlier, but by now he had learned the hard way and thought that he had mastered the handling of Blair. Inevitably, he called on Tory backbenchers to support him; he could take the party forward and win the next general election if the party united behind him. Otherwise, a leadership election would lead to bitter warfare. As he finished and left the room, the public relations expert next to me, Charles Hendry,[12] commented, 'brave but it won't have won him any votes'.

Four hours later Spicer announced that, in the vote of confidence, Duncan Smith had seventy-five votes for him, ninety against. He resigned immediately. This was by far the best support from his backbenchers that he had ever received; in the three ballots for leadership in 2001, out of 166 possible votes, he first won thirty-four, then forty-two, then fifty-four – never more than a third of the parliamentary party. It was only the votes of the members of the party outside Parliament that had given Duncan Smith his leadership post in preference to the MPs' choice, Ken Clarke.

Throughout Duncan Smith's speech in Committee Room 14, David Maclean sat, looking amiable and unmoved, in the Chief Whip's traditional seat at 1922 Committee meetings – on the platform nearest the window overlooking the Thames. That evening he circulated a surprising letter to Tory MPs and peers:

Dear Colleague

Now that Iain has resigned as leader of the party, I feel that it is the honourable thing for me to step down also. In defending Iain's leadership in recent weeks, I have had to take a higher public profile than is customary for Chief Whips. Now that we have a leadership election it is vital that the whole whips' office is, and is seen to be, neutral and impartial. I cannot let my past commitment to the leader give rise to any suggestion that the office will not operate with the highest standards of neutrality and my departure will make that abundantly clear. It will also give the new leader a completely free hand to appoint a new Chief Whip.

I am grateful to all colleagues for the support they have given me over the last two years. My excellent deputy, Patrick McLoughlin, has assumed the responsibilities of Acting Chief Whip and I am certain that you will give him your full support also.

Maclean, a sensible and approachable Chief Whip, was referring to the fact that, at the Conservative Party Conference he had openly declared his support for Duncan Smith and all twelve members of the whips' office were reported as backing his view. Factually, this was incorrect. A number of the whips – and Maclean himself – believed that Duncan Smith should go. Their official attitude – reflected by the Chief Whip – was born of loyalty and a belief that they should discipline those who were 'playing around'.

Privately, McLoughlin, a tough deputy who had been in the office since 1995, trawled a number of colleagues with small majorities and asked about their chances at a general election. When he got the answer that they could not possibly hold their seats with Duncan Smith as their leader, his typical reply was, 'May I tell that to the Chief Whip?' Maclean himself had been a Minister of State in the Home Office when Howard was Home Secretary. He had been part of Howard's team when he ran for the leadership in 1997. From his past experience, it would be surprising if he did not consider Howard a more likely election winner than Duncan Smith.

Maclean's public letter was a splendid example of a Chief Whip reading the tea leaves correctly. He did the right thing and was rewarded accordingly. Howard succeeded to the leadership without any contest that would have required voting by the party members outside Parliament, and within the week Maclean was reinstated as Chief Whip. Howard's first tussle with Blair at Prime Minister's Questions saw Maclean back in the Chief Whip's traditional seat at the gangway end of the Treasury front bench. His long crook in his hands (he suffers from multiple sclerosis), he shouted his approval of Howard's retorts and abandoned the traditional inscrutability of a Chief Whip in favour of enthusiastic support. Howard's decision to put him back in the office was received with doubt by some but approval by the majority.

But the river runs deeper than that. If there is a Conservative leadership contest, the two MPs with the most votes are put before the 'country' members and it is they who have the final say about who should lead the party. The will of MPs is subordinated and the paramount influence of the Chief Whip disappears. Ironically, under this system he retains power in regicide but not in king-making.

The heading to a *New Statesman* article of 3 November 2003 was 'Doomed from the start. Unlike Labour, the Tories democratised their party before they modernised it. So MPs were saddled with a leader they never wanted.' The author of the article then wrote, 'It is worth remembering that no political party serious about taking power has ever given its ordinary members the final say about who should lead it.' In the autumn of 2003, overwhelmed by dread of a countrywide election that could take six weeks, Tory MPs decided to have no election at all. The only solution was to award the prize on this occasion to one person, Michael Howard. Obviously, this is unlikely to happen again. At some stage, whether or not the Tories win the next general election, Howard will resign and a leadership contest will follow. By then, there must be a change in the rules.

Ian Gilmour,[13] writing in the *Daily Telegraph*,[14] said, 'The Magic Circle, or men in grey suits, call it what you will, can never be revived, and the Hague process is fatally flawed. From now on, MPs alone should elect their leader.'

In reality, it is impossible to take away the vote entirely from those who were only given it six years ago. The more practical route is to create an electoral college in which the National Union – the party organisation – will have no more than 25 per cent of the votes, the balance staying with Members of Parliament. The majority must lie with those who are in the cockpit of the Commons and who know from daily experience which of their colleagues has the wisdom, the fight, the personality and the philosophy that are most likely to take them into government and to keep them there.

Despite this whittling down of the power and influence of the whips, Hilary Armstrong and David Maclean both assured me that backbench MPs still want to be whips. In their eyes, the whips' office remains important as an organiser, in the modern jargon a facilitator. As before, the whips' office arrives at collective judgements on who are to be trusted and who not, and their judgement is scarcely ever wrong. They enjoy being on the inside track. The 'Office' is a remarkable club and, noticeably more in the Conservative Party than in Labour, for the newcomers to the Commons it is a first step on the ladder of promotion. After David Maclean resumed being the Opposition Chief Whip, four of his whips were promoted to shadow ministerial posts; they were on their way upwards.

Nonetheless, my judgement is that, beneath the daily gathering of information and the ordering of parliamentary business, there is a fundamental shift of influence away from the whips, and this is for two particular reasons: first, the absence of secrecy – everyone now leaks to the press, an MP regards his media exposure as more important than his parliamentary exposure – and, second, the process started by the Nolan Committee on Standards in Public Life.

After the strictures of Lord Nolan about failures to declare outside interests, it is much harder for MPs to have a second, outside job. While Leader of the Commons, Robin Cook said in the debate on the Modernisation of the Commons on 29 October 2002 that he expected his MPs to be full-time professionals. But the aim of a full-time professional is, in almost every case, to climb up the executive ladder and to increase salary, reputation and job satisfaction by becoming a minister.

Gone are the Knights of the Shires, the Sir Derek Walker-Smiths and the Sir Donald Kaberrys, or the elderly trade union officials who came to the Commons out of an unemotional but pervasive sense of duty. They were often in the second or third bloom of life, they had had a satisfactory career in their profession or in the Services. The Commons was a good club. The whips told them what the business was, they listened, usually followed suit and occasionally rebelled by absenting themselves. They are replaced by younger political animals, fresh from a Whitehall research company, a parliamentary consultancy, a public relations firm or a local authority, and very anxious to progress on the Westminster escalator. Excepting the votes on a matter of principle, they barely need to be told how to vote. Their instinct for survival is too great, the longing for executive power too much of an obsession.

Pairing is rarely officially countenanced, but there are substantial benefits coming with the job. By April 2003, an MP's annual salary was in excess of £55,000, his staffing allowance for his office was between £63,000 and £72,000 (and it was perfectly permissible to employ a partner as a secretary provided hours were properly invoiced). Incidental expenses allowance was £18,000, additional costs £19,000, car mileage 54p for the first 20,000 miles and a bicycle allowance 7p for unlimited miles. On top of this, there have been handsome increases to retirement pensions. Many, particularly on the Labour benches, are now earning a higher salary, and better expenses for their offices and accommodation, than ever before in their lives. At a time of increasing insecurity in employment for the middle-aged, the Commons look a good bet, provided your seat is reasonably safe and party officials, either centrally or locally, do not judge that you should be replaced by a more pliant or more newsworthy supporter. This is where the patronage now lies.

When the government has a large majority the purpose of whipping for the opposition almost disappears. Keeping up morale is more important than the size of your minority vote. As James Arbuthnot, the Opposition Chief Whip from 1997 to 2001, pointed out to me, the small number of Conservative Members elected in the 1997 general election – 165 – banded together like a Mid-West herd of cattle protecting themselves against the wolves. They needed distraction, away days and morale-boosting parties more than three-line whips. Their number only increased by one, to 166, in the 2001 election. It is better to be generous, as a Chief Whip, in letting your Members off for the evening than to earn their wrath by heavy whipping for votes you have no chance of winning.

Of course, this will change when a government is again elected with a small majority, but the fact remains that there is a mixture of public discontent, apathy and cynicism with regard to Parliament that has reached levels not seen since the eighteenth century. This is reflected in the high numbers of the electorate who forget those who fought to get them a vote and do not go near the polling booths on election day. These abstainers would not be impressed by stories going round Westminster that some Labour MPs were recently offering their whips a deal: support for the government on variable tuition fees provided the government committed itself to total banning of fox-hunting. Whipping is increasingly seen as undemocratic and, in light of the demand for openness and transparency, out of date.

The tussle over the Higher Education Bill at the end of January 2004 showed the degree to which the whips had been sidelined by the government and by the parliamentary Labour Party. Seventy-two Labour MPs voted against their party and nineteen abstained. An overall majority in the Commons of 161 was reduced to the paltry figure of five. If all Tory MPs had voted with their party, the majority would have been one.

What was noticeable on the day of the vote, and in the newspaper accounts afterwards, was the almost total absence of any reference to the Labour Chief Whip, Hilary Armstrong. John Prescott, the Deputy Prime Minister, was on the *Today* programme that morning saying, 'We are still twenty short.' No. 10 commented throughout the day that the result was 'far too close to call'. Afterwards, the Chancellor's spokesman claimed credit for the Chancellor winning over four named rebels. That in turn was pooh-poohed by No. 10 who insisted that it was conversations held by Tony Blair and John Prescott that had been the decisive influence on the conversions.

What of Hilary Armstrong? She walked into the Chamber to show the final voting figures to the Prime Minister, she wore a russet suit, and after-wards Blair went to the whips' office to have a drink. That was the media coverage of the whips' influence. Blair had once again taken the limelight, had put his personal reputation on the line and had given the impression that he might leave the job if defeated.

This prime ministerial involvement was necessary in March 2003 when Britain was being taken to war against Iraq without a second UN Resolution. It was totally unnecessary ten months later on an issue as detailed and, for most people, as remote as variable university tuition fees that will not commence until 2006. The persuasion of rebels should have been left to the Labour whips' office. No announcement should have been made to the press or to television on the size of the rebellion. An air of quiet confidence, however false, should have permeated for days before the vote. Details of concessions should have been kept secret until announced in the speech of the Secretary of State, Charles Clarke, opening the debate. The Prime Minister should not have staked his own position on the result. If defeated on the second reading, he should have called for a vote of confi-dence immediately, as John Major did after a defeat on the Maastricht Treaty, and this he would have won by a massive amount. Those would have been the tactics of Conservative Chief Whips.

Charles Clarke later said that mistakes were made. They certainly were, and they increased the chances of a Black Spot being handed to Tony Blair by those who wanted to see him replaced by Gordon Brown.

The day of the vote started with seventy-eight potential rebels having their picture on the front page of the *Independent*. That is the sort of publicity that goes to the heads of backbenchers, wins the support of their constituency associations and makes it much harder for a rebel quietly to change his stance. Why was all the publicity grabbed by senior ministers from Tony Blair onwards? Simply because No. 10 wished to be like the

White House, with a controlling finger in every pie, and did not have the confidence or the common sense to leave dealings with difficult backbenchers to the whips' office.

When I told Margaret Thatcher that I thought we would lose a vote on the Poll Tax – a far more basic issue than tuition fees – she never asked for the likely figures nor did I give them to her. She told me to get on with the job of winning the vote. On the crucial day I asked her to see a handful of rebels to whom I felt she could usefully talk. We never released their names to the press, nor did I ever tell the press the likely size of a rebellion. Michael Jopling, Government Chief Whip from 1979 to 1983, told me that his practice was exactly the same.

I realise it is easy to be, in an acronym used by Denis Healey[15], an LTA – Laudator temporis acti – someone who praises the past. But the Parliamentary Secretary to the Treasury still has under him a deputy and fourteen other government whips. It is senseless not to use and have confidence in them, and let them take the flak if things go wrong.

The ability of the whips to change the minds of their colleagues lies in the fact that they wheedle and cajole quietly and behind the scenes. Every MP is an individual, with individual likes, dislikes, problems and ambitions. It is the business of the whips to know exactly how the land lies and what particular inducement may win over that individual. This may vary from a genuine concern to help parents on low wages get their children into further education through to a demand for more cash from the Department of Health to save an Accident and Emergency Unit at the local hospital. But it is a whip's task to know the details, and this is a knowledge that a busy minister will not possess. The more senior a minister is, the more likely he is to be ignorant of the true qualities of his backbenchers.

Labour whips have been sidetracked and they are not helped by the fact that they have lost their few remaining powers of patronage. Of course, there are no governorships of Indian cities or Australian states to be allotted to a friendly and loyal supporter. But junior ministerial appointments are very important to the ambitious backbencher and they are now decided not by advice directly from the Chief Whip to the Prime Minister but at No. 10. Janet Morgan, the Prime Minister's 'Head of Political and Government Relations', and made a baroness in 2001, is held particularly responsible. In the *Spectator* of 17 January 2004 Peter Oborne wrote, 'Since returning to Downing Street from the Cabinet Office, Morgan has borne the burden of responsibility for the summer reshuffle – universally recognised as the most incompetently handled event of its kind in living memory – then foundation hospitals, and now the top-up fees shambles. No. 10 has lost its political touch.'

Elderly Labour MPs still enjoy being sent to the Lords, and they are good company as we sit at dinner at a long communal table. But the future of appointed peers is yet unresolved, as I discuss in the final chapter. One suggestion is that the number of politically appointed peers should be related to the number of votes received by the different parties at a general election. If Labour are now seen as on an electoral downslide, then the chance of a Labour MP becoming a Labour baron rapidly diminishes.

There are select committees in the Commons which attract candidates for membership. Treasury and Home Affairs have prestige, Defence and the All Party NATO committees provide interesting travel. But even here the whips have to be cautious after No. 10's ill-fated attempt to remove the chairmanship of the transport committee from Gwyneth Dunwoody, a powerful character who has not only been an MP for most of the years since 1966 but is also a daughter of Morgan Phillips, some time General Secretary of the Labour Party.

The most obvious downgrading of Hilary Armstrong and her whips lies in the loss of No. 12 Downing Street as their quarters. This is a prestige building, slightly grander in its façade than either No. 10 or No. 11. Here the Chief Whip reigned, invitations to parties there were treasured, and the so-called secret passage hid the Chief Whip from the eyes of the press outside as he went to call on the Prime Minister. Alastair Campbell, Blair's renowned Director of Communications, took the house over in 2001, and Armstrong had to search for offices, elegant enough but out of sight, in the area that lies between No. 10 and Whitehall. The downgrading was obvious. I found this a surprising mistake until I remembered that, immediately after Blair won the 1997 election, the story went round Westminster that he intended to govern without appointing any whips at all.

Then there is the sad question of where the Government Chief Whip sits in the Commons. Tradition dictates that this is on the right-hand side of the Prime Minister, next to the gangway on the Treasury front bench. The Prime Minister's parliamentary private secretary sits in the row immediately behind and is within easy reach of either the Prime Minister or the Chief Whip for the purpose of passing messages and keeping in touch with other ministers on the front bench. In the same article in the *Spectator* Peter Oborne wrote, 'After 2001 it was pathetic to watch Armstrong squeezed out of this position, and often forced to crouch alongside all the parliamentary aides and other rabble and detritus on the gangway itself.'

In opposition the Tories have promised that, once back in government, they will restore No. 12 to the whips. This will be a first step in their reinstatement. A year or two in the whips' office must again be seen as a useful step on the way to a junior ministerial post and, of course, a dominant figure, known to be close to the Prime Minister, needs to be appointed as Chief Whip. But will all of this be enough to restore the whips to their former position of influence? I very much doubt it. The craze for openness now runs against old-fashioned, quiet whipping. More than half of the current Labour MPs have rebelled at least once, and this is a habit that grows with acquaintance. The rebels have found themselves being organised by an ex-Government Chief Whip of their own party, Nick Brown. This is like finding General Eisenhower undermining Field Marshal Montgomery. It underlines how, in one respect at least, parliamentary practice is changing.

In his biography of Lord George Bentinck, Disraeli said that the Chief Whip must have 'consummate knowledge of human nature, the most amiable flexibility and complete self-control'.[16] These are still admirable qualities in any Chief Whip but they did not stop seventy-two Labour MPs rebelling against their government on tuition fees or 139 rebelling on the war against Iraq.

Governments have to get their business through and whipping will, especially in times of small majorities, remain a useful way of organising a programme of legislation. MPs, who have not listened to the debate will run into the Chamber, will ask the whip on duty, 'Which way do we go?' and will walk blindly into whichever lobby the whip indicates. Tony Blair or his successor may come to see the dangers of taking too much patronage and influence away from the whips and may once again ask the Chief Whip for some advice on who to promote from backbencher to parliamentary under-secretary to Minister of State.

But the present Parliamentary system with an over-powerful executive and an ineffectual and resented Upper House cannot continue. The lack of trust in politicians is dangerously prevalent. Change must come, change that will lead to better legislation and to Westminster again becoming the focus of interest, respect and even of good government. The changes I suggest in the next chapter are intended to contribute to that effect.

FIFTEEN

The Second Chamber – a Call for More Powers

Those who regard the House of Lords as out of date and ready for abolition will not be surprised to know that the full title of the Lords' Government Chief Whip is Captain of the Honourable Corps of the Gentlemen-at-Arms, and that of the Deputy Chief Whip Captain of the Queen's Bodyguard of the Yeomen of the Guard. The first of these titles goes back to 1509, preceding the historic origins of the Commons' Chief Whip by at least a century. The establishment of the band of gentlemen pensioners, as they were first called, took place in the first year of the reign of Henry VIII. Henry, with his love of splendour and grand paraphernalia, was determined to have around him a 'new and sumptuous troop of gentlemen to attend his person and service'.[1] Needless to say, he was copying the French king, Louis XI, who in 1474 had instituted La Grande Garde de Corps consisting of one hundred gentlemen of 'rank and consequence.'[2]

The first important event in which the Gentlemen-at-Arms were active was in 1553 when

on the insurrection of Sir Thomas Wyat, they were very active in defending the Palace at Westminster, which was beset by a party of the rebels from Westminster... After marching up and down in front of the Palace, to keep off the rebels, for the space of an hour, news was brought that Wyat was taken.

Edward Underhill, one of those present on the occasion, then tells a little story:

Anon after, the Guard of Pensioners were all brought into the Queen's presence, and everyone kissed her hand; and of whom they had great thanks and large promises, how good she would be unto them. But few or none of us got anything although she was very liberal to others that were enemies to God's word, as few of us were.[3]

This has resonance 450 years later. If Edward Underhill found Queen Elizabeth difficult, Lord Denham had the same problem with Margaret Thatcher.

Denham, always known as Bertie, was the archetypal House of Lords Chief Whip. He occupied this post from 1978 to 1991, and for all of these years bar the first in opposition he was Captain of the Gentlemen-at-Arms. On appointment he received a gold stick of office from the sovereign and, while in office, he had the right of direct approach to the sovereign on any matter dealing with the Corps.[4] The taxpayer gave Bertie a handsome military uniform which he wore at state visits and the Opening of Parliament.

The Deputy Chief Whip is appropriately one rank lower in the Order of Gentry, being Captain of the Queen's Bodyguard of the Yeoman of the Guard. This body was, however, formed twenty-four years earlier than the Gentlemen-at-Arms by Henry VII at his coronation in 1485. The pretext given was to add additional splendour to that ceremony but in reality it was to give greater security to the monarch's person.

The Crown upon the King's head, having put perils into his thoughts... wherefore, for the safeguard and preservation of his own body, he constituted and ordained a certain number, as well of good archers, as of divers other persons, being hardy, strong, and of agility, to give daily attendance on his person, whom he named Yeomen of the Guarde.

The present Deputy Chief Whip is Lord Davies of Oldham. He was briefly president of the Royal Society for the Prevention of Accidents, so he might well be considered an appropriate heir to this illustrious post.

'Margaret Thatcher thought the House of Lords a nuisance,' I recently said to Bertie Denham. 'You, Tim, also thought the Lords a nuisance,' Bertie replied. 'So did all the other six Government Chief Whips in the Commons that I had to deal with. But the purpose of the Lords is to be a nuisance to the Commons.' Bertie's view centred round the fact that he saw the first loyalty of the Leader of the House of Lords – currently the Labour Baroness Amos but with such stalwart recent predecessors as Lords Carrington and Whitelaw – being to the Lords. Duty to his party came second. The same was true of the Chief Whip. Their objective was to see that the House of Lords 'as a whole gets a fair deal from the government of the day'.[5] They had to fight for the rights, as they saw them, of their House. Technically, this means that if the opposition in the Lords defeats the government on an amendment at the committee stage of a Bill in the Lords, the government should not try to reverse this at the two later stages, the report stage and the third reading, before the Bill goes back to the Commons. It is up to the Commons to change the Bill back to what the government wanted and then send it back again to the Lords where it will be reviewed afresh. Bertie told me that, early in his career as Government Chief Whip, he got his colleagues to reverse during the final stage of a Bill a decision that the opposition had won at committee a week or two earlier. He was subsequently buttonholed by four elderly and vastly senior peers who told him that this was not the right thing to do. The Lords' decision had to be taken into account in the Commons and the Commons had to decide whether they rejected or accepted the Lords' amendment.

Bertie quoted two examples to me of what he meant by the Lords getting a fair deal from the government of the day. The first was when the Lords, with a very large Tory majority, passed an amendment that would have required public companies to declare in their annual accounts any contributions that they had made to political parties. This was in the days when such transparency was not legally necessary and when the Tories benefited far more from company contributions than Labour. It was evident that this required openness would be much more damaging to the finances of the Tory Party than to any other party, and Margaret Thatcher was 'speechless' when Bertie said that he could not immediately reverse it in the Lords. She turned to David Waddington, her Chief Whip in the Commons, who replied that he could, of course, reverse it in the Lower House. Margaret turned to Bertie. 'You are lucky to have such friends,' she said. Bertie accepted that.

Similarly, when the Lords voted down the Commons and decided against parents paying for school transport, Bertie refused to put a three-line whip on a vote to reverse this decision. 'I had far too many friends who felt very strongly on this issue. I knew they would not support such a change whatever the whipping was, so there was no point in having such a strong whip.' Bertie was always of the opinion that one three-line whip a year was enough for the Lords. When supporters are all part-time and voluntary, friendship, gentle persuasion and the occasional telephone call are the only means of getting them to the Lords to vote. This was certainly my impression when I, as Chief Whip in the Commons, negotiated with Bertie on the likely business of our two Houses the following week. I knew that Bertie wanted the Lords to be allowed periodically to show its muscle and this must not be immediately reversed by Tory Members in the Lords. We alternated for our meetings between his office one week and mine the next. With courtesy, he took the view that he was the junior member of the team but the quality of the drinks in his office was greatly superior. He was, and remains, an expert in mixing Bloody Marys.

If Bertie, with slightly raised eyebrows and the beginnings of a smile, seemed typically calm in 1990 when I persuaded him that a piece of legislation, the Dangerous Dogs Bill, should not be amended at its final stages in the Lords, that good humour disappeared in 2004 when he talked about the ill-conceived, final removal of the hereditaries from the Lords without any clear decision as to who or what would be their replacement. 'I will go to the stake fighting this,' he said. That is not just because he would like the remaining ninety-two, of which he is one, to stay. It is because he feels that the Lord Chancellor, Lord Falconer, has broken the agreement that was given 'on Privy Council terms' that the ninety-two would not be removed until the government came forward with their proposals for the other side of the equation: who is to replace the hereditaries and are they to be all elected, all appointed or a mixture of the two?

When Labour was elected to government in 1997 and discussions began about reform of the membership of the House of Lords, the intention of Lord Cranborne, the then Leader of the House, was that this should all be completed in one comprehensive Bill. In this the hereditaries would leave the House and legislation would be enacted that would decide the composition of the successors, be they elected or appointed. But theory did not meet practice. There was so much discussion, and lack of agreement about the future membership of the Upper House, that a compromise was reached in the House of Lords Act of 1999 under which all the hereditaries bar ninety-two were removed and these ninety-two were to stay – and this is where the Privy Council Oath came in – until the government had decided and put forward their plans on the future membership.

A Royal Commission was set up to examine this 'Stage 2' of reform. In the intervening years the number of appointed life peers increased and no single party now has an overall majority in the Lords. No one can force through an amendment to a Bill without support from members of another party. But the government has again lost patience. Saying that too much time has elapsed without any recommendations being agreed by majorities in either House, the government is now committed to introducing a Bill that will do away with the remaining ninety-two hereditaries and rely, for the time being at least, on an independent commission to appoint new life peers. Knowing that this will be fought tooth and nail in the Lords, they have delayed introducing the Bill until after the next election. The hereditaries' grandfathers, those who were there in 1910 and 1911 and took part in the battles between a Liberal majority in the Commons and a Tory majority in the Lords, would recognise the scene. Those who accept the government's wishes and remain active but unobstructive in the debates are likely to be offered life peerages. The ones who raise substantial uproar will disappear from Westminster for ever.

Oliver Henley, another of the ninety-two hereditary survivors, sees the issue with less passion than Bertie Denham. He took over as Opposition Chief Whip at the end of 1998 when Robert Cranborne, who had engineered the deal about the hereditaries against the wishes and without the knowledge of his leader, William Hague, was removed from the post of Opposition Leader. Tom Strathclyde moved up from Chief Whip to take his place. Henley accepts the inevitability of the last hereditaries disappearing but believes that a majority of elected members are necessary if the Upper House is ever again to have real power in revising the work of the Commons. I share this view. What Henley had to deal with from 1999 onwards was the disappearance of a permanent Tory majority in the Lords and the appearance of many more ex-MP Labour peers.

The atmosphere changed, particularly at Question Time. This became sharper, more antagonistic. The questions were, and are, longer and more political, though it is still a rebuke to say that a speech is of 'the House of Commons variety'. From having only seventy to eighty regular supporters in 1997, the Labour Chief Whip found himself with 120 rising to 140 while the Tories were reduced by four-fifths from 470 to around the same number as Labour. But Henley had no new weapons with which to persuade the Tory peers to come and vote. He twice quoted Bertie Denham's saying to me: 'In the Commons the Chief Whip has patronage. I only have a bottle of whisky.' When Henley took over as Chief Whip, he found the cupboard in the Chief Whip's room full of bottles of Grouse whisky and only half a bottle of gin. He agreed that using three-line whips in the Lords would have no effect. He tried two-line whips of varying thickness, the wider lines indicating more seriousness than the slimmer. He soon found that most of us who take the Tory whip and receive the list of next week's business did not notice the difference between the heavy two-line whip and the light one. Whisky apart, he had few inducements to offer. Invitations to join select committees, with the exception of a new Economic Affairs Committee, were not widely sought. Invitations to become shadow spokesmen on the opposition front bench were attractive only to those who were industrious, had time on their hands and enjoyed speaking.

For Lord Carter, the practical and experienced Labour Government's Chief Whip from 1997 to 2002, working behind the scenes with the opposition party was the key to the smooth running of the Lords. The European Parliamentary Elections Bill was a case in point. This was the Bill that introduced the proposed and very unpopular list system for the European parliamentary elections of June 1999 under which all the candidates and the order of priority in which they would be elected were chosen by political parties. This was known as the closed list system. The Labour majority in the Commons allowed it through but at third reading the Lords passed an amendment to introduce an open list system on a model practised in Finland. The Commons disagreed, the Lords refused to give way and Baroness Jay, as Leader of the Lords, announced that the Bill would be immediately reintroduced in the next session under the Parliament Acts which recognise the right of the Lords to veto a Commons Bill for one session only.

The difficulty was that, by November and the end of the first session, time had nearly run out for the organising of the new regional list system, whether open or closed, whether a Finnish model or a British model. Lady Jay announced that in the new session the complete Bill would have to go through all its stages and achieve royal assent by mid-January 1999 if there were to be enough time for the regulations governing nomination of candidates, counting procedures and expense limits to be passed before the election on 10 June. The Tories in the Lords realised that, however much they were opposed to the closed list, they had neither the time nor the funds to insist on a satisfactory alternative. The two opposing Chief Whips hatched a quiet plot despite William Hague, the then leader of the Conservative Party, continuing his opposition to the Bill. The second version, the European Parliamentary Elections Bill 1998–99, was presented in the Commons on 27 November, at the beginning of the new session, and taken through all its Commons stages by 2 December.

Normally, Commons Bills in the Lords pass their second reading without a vote, and hostile amendments are not proposed until the committee stage two or three weeks later. There was no time for that. The Tories put down an amendment at second reading stating

> this House declines to give the European Parliamentary Elections Bill a Second Reading on the grounds that it includes an undemocratic 'closed list' system providing for the selection of MEPs by party choice, an approach which would end the historic right of the British people to choose the candidates they wish to be elected, a step for which the House notes with great concern no mandate was sought or given at the last general election.

These were fine words but the whips' tactics were designed to achieve the contrary result. We Tories were encouraged to vote for the amendment in the Aye lobby and 167 of us did. 'We are trying very hard,' one Conservative whip reported to *The Times*,[6] but Denis Carter was counting the votes that went into the Aye lobby and making certain that those going into the No lobby were fewer. The Liberals wondered which way to turn and were persuaded to abstain. The result was that only ninety-three voted against the Tory amendment. The Lords refused to give the Bill a second reading with the result that the Bill failed for a second session running. The Parliament

Acts procedure came into force immediately and the Bill was presented for royal assent and passed into law just a month later on 14 January, precisely in line with Labour's timetable. This was a remarkable example of two opposing Chief Whips working quietly together. Denis Carter told me that, when he explained to Cabinet what had happened, 'they thought it was a miracle.'

In many ways the long survival of the hereditaries from the Parliament Act of 1911 until the disappearance of most of them in 1999 was also a miracle. This was partly due to the fact that, outside the Lords' Chamber where we debate, there is little sign of political parties. The Commons' dining room is clearly divided into the Tories', Labour's and the Liberals' tables. The Tory Chief Whip in the Commons has his own little table. In the Lords, for lunch, tea or dinner, we sit at a long common table which will take up to sixty members. On a busy day it will have a sprinkling from all the parties, plus cross-benchers, bishops and law lords. This friendly, collegiate approach is due to a formidable Labour life peer, Baroness Llewellyn-Davies, who was Government Chief Whip from 1974 to 1979. She was the first lady to hold the office of Captain of the Gentlemen-at-Arms and it was the Queen's personal decision that she should not be required to wear a uniform. More importantly, it was she who introduced the idea that, if we all regularly ate together, outside the Chamber we would not be active politicians. And that, in a strange way, has worked. Denis Carter told me that Tony Blair, like Margaret Thatcher, really regards the Lords as trouble. We are viewed as a lot of grumpy, difficult septuagenarians. But nonetheless, there is a surprising amount of agreement between the official channels, as the whips are called, regarding the number of defeats that should be inflicted on the government. Forty government defeats a year were acceptable. In the 2002–03 session the figure was nearer seventy, and that was getting awkward. The question now is whether the lack of party hostility in the Lords can be built on to create a constructive Upper House that will be more active in restraining the executive government that now dominates the Commons.

As I described in Chapter 10, since 1909 the powers and membership of the Lords have been actively debated. The 1911 Parliament Act starts with the preamble:

Whereas it is expedient that provision should be made for regulating the relations between the two Houses of Parliament: and whereas it is intended to substitute for the House of Lords as it at present exists a Second Chamber constituted on a popular instead of hereditary basis, but such substitution cannot be immediately brought into operation, and whereas provision will require work hereafter to be made by Parliament in a measure effecting such substitution for limiting and defining the powers of the new Second Chamber, but it is expedient to make such provision as in this Act appears for restricting the existing powers of the House of Lords...

The subsequent ninety years have seen a steady erosion in the powers of the Lords, but until the Blair government took office in 1997 no legislation was brought forward for reform along the lines proposed in 1911.

In the 1911 Act the Lords lost their veto powers over any Public Bill which the Speaker judges to be a Money Bill. The most obvious of these is the Finance Bill. This governs the amount of 'supply', to use the old-fashioned word, to the government. It incorporates the measures in the Budget, and is by far the most important measure in the Westminster annual round. The Lords continued to have a right to veto Bills that extended the duration of Parliament between general elections to more than five years but for all other Public Bills their right to veto or to delay was limited to two parliamentary sessions. In 1949 the power of delay was reduced to one session as the Prime Minister, Attlee, wished to get a Bill nationalising the steel industry on to the statute book before the 1950 election. This can in practice mean a delay of as little as thirteen months and two days between the Commons' first examination of a Bill and its receiving Royal Assent. To complete the history, in 1958 life peers were created by the Conservatives – the only change to the composition or powers of the Upper House ever made by a Conservative government – and, in 1999, the Labour government removed from the Lords all but ninety-two of the hereditary peers. The government announced their intention of sacking these ninety-two in the 2003–04 session.

Throughout the past century, the cry from the Commons was that the Lords lacked legitimacy because, first, so many were there only because they had inherited a title and, second, because no one in the Upper Chamber was elected. For that reason, whenever the Lords exercised their limited powers to amend, revise and delay, they were contemptuously told by ministers and querulous MPs that they were thwarting the will of the people, expressed via the elected majority in the Commons. No regard was paid to the fact that only 44 per cent of the electorate voted for Labour in the election of 2001 but that was sufficient to give them a majority of 189 seats. As a result, the Lords have always been timid in the amount of revision or amendment that they felt they could impose on an elected government. There is a good deal of bluster towards the end of the parliamentary session when the time is running out during which the government must obtain parliamentary sanction to its Bills. At the last moment, the Lords will cave in, obtaining only a few minor changes that are just sufficient to enable each side to claim a victory. A hereditary Conservative peer described this to me as 'Toy Town politics', an unkind description that is, sadly, merited.

Now the government, after inconclusive debates in both Commons and Lords as to who should replace the hereditary peers, has decided that new peers should be appointed by 'an independent commission'. Who appoints the commissioners who, in turn, will appoint the members of the Upper House? Who, in turn, will suggest most names to the commission as suitable candidates for appointment? The answer to both questions, is, of course, the government. Because it is not elected, an all-appointed Second Chamber will be no more legitimate, no more seriously able to act as a reforming brake on the Commons than the ineffective House of Lords of the twentieth century. The reason why the Commons does not wish to have elected members in the Upper House is that they know that the argument about legitimacy would then be reversed. It is they, the Commons, who would then have to give back some of the powers that were taken away in the 1911 and 1949 Parliament Acts.

Putting this the other way round, for the Upper House to have sufficient legitimacy to rein in the Commons effectively and to require them to think again before rushing ahead with unnecessary or badly drafted legislation, it must be at least partly elected. Without a portion of its members being representative of the electorate, the Second Chamber will never exercise its delaying and reforming powers with strength and conviction. 'Fifty per cent elected' could be a reasonable starting point, with the percentage rising over the next twenty years as existing life peers die. The argument that a hybrid Second Chamber, part elected, part nominated, could not work properly holds no water; there is no reason why the elected members should regard themselves as senior to those nominated or vice versa. A Member of Parliament pointed out to me that the Commons is itself hybrid, the two different classes being those who have safe seats which they can hold for life and those who have marginal seats which they may well lose at the next election. Inevitably, this causes some differences in attitude and judgement.

But the further argument needs answering that the Upper House, if it has elected members slavishly following the whip, will become a pale shadow, a mere clone, of the Commons. Coming from twenty-three years in the Commons, what I have found in the Lords is an ability to work together from all sides of the House for the improvement of legislation. This may consume a great deal of time but the ethos is still primarily a non-political one. Our surroundings are absurdly grand, the average age is too high, but much of the discussion is led by experts in their field, speaking from a lifetime of experience. This is a benefit that should not be lost.

A possible, radical solution is that potential members of the Upper House should be nominated by local supporters to stand on a county or borough list with no political label attached; they would be elected once only, for a period of ten or fifteen years, and not be permitted to stand again. With no personal concern about re-election a genuine independence is ensured. A 'front bench' of ministers would be chosen by the government of the day but no one else would formally take a party whip. There would be no 'government' sitting on one side of the House and 'opposition' sitting on the other. All bar the ministers would sit where they chose.

Alternatively, only the members of the Upper Chamber who had avowed political attachments would be the ones who stood for election. The cross-benchers, without political history and labels, would be those nominated by a non-government commission, or by various professional bodies representing teachers, doctors, accountants, businessmen, trade unions, charitable bodies and so forth. They would become the truly independent party of the Second Chamber. If one-third of the Second Chamber were thus cross-benchers, independent and drawn from a wide range of professions and expertise, this should be sufficient to see that the

Second Chamber does not simply become an elderly replica of the Commons. With the advantages of websites, e-mail and instant communication, this should not mean a return to the chaos of Walpole's day. Rather, it could lead to a revising Second Chamber where elected and appointed members genuinely follow Burkean principles and pursue what they, as individuals, consider the best solutions for the country and the common good.

The previous Lord Chancellor, Lord Irvine, who appeared to have the papal gift of regarding himself as infallible but was nonetheless sacked by Blair, said in a debate on constitutional reform in the Lords on 18 December 2002, 'for this House to be efficient it must add value to Parliament. That primarily must be through its composition – the kind of people that it attracts.'[7] That goes to the heart of the matter. The revised and reformed Second Chamber has to be sufficiently independent and have enough powers to persuade good candidates, men and women, who are successful and experienced in other walks of life, to stand either for election or for nomination. They would be paid at a salary of, say, half that of Members of Parliament and would retire at an 'appropriate' age.

It has often been said that there is little point in reforming the Upper House simply because the elected Commons are no longer doing their job of checking the executive. I agree with that. The point of having a reformed Second Chamber is that it should be more effective in itself and should offer genuine checks on the executive. *The power to delay* is the essential element of an effective Second Chamber. Reform of the Upper House must be married to a limited increase in its delaying powers along with the election of a proportion of its members.

The opportunity for this may come very soon. Peter Hain, Leader of the House of Commons and Lord Privy Seal, recently responded to the Lords delaying at Second Reading the Bill to abolish the Lord Chancellor's office. He threatened: 'I think instead of just looking at the composition we will also seek to curtail the powers of the Lords and seek to get manageable procedure into the Lords ... We need to bring down the period that it can frustrate the will of the Commons from a year to under a year, and we need to get procedures in place that allow legislation to go through.' These are formidable words and they have been followed by Blair's instruction to the

Lord Chancellor, Lord Falconer, to produce a Government paper outlining proposals for a reduction in the powers of the Upper House.

This is the first time the Government has talked of reducing the powers of the Lords and this will involve formal revision of the Parliament Acts. Those who think the Government's executive power in the Commons is now excessive should seize this historic opportunity to do the opposite of what Tony Blair seeks.

I have two suggestions to make for the reform of the Upper House. First, from the day the Second Chamber has elected members, a joint Commons/Lords Select Committee should be set up, with equal membership from either House, to look at current economic affairs. This will re-establish at a modest level the interest of the Second Chamber in the supply of finance to the Government that was abolished in the 1911 Act. Secondly, the power to delay Bills for two consecutive sessions should be returned. With a Second Chamber whose membership is partly non-politically aligned, and which has the power to delay legislation for a significant part of a parliament, Government would be obliged to have more regard as to how it could get the support of that Chamber.

There is no prospect of a written constitution for the United Kingdom, nor should there be. Disillusionment with Parliament and apathy among voters are reflected in the historically low turn-out at elections. This therefore is the right moment to grasp the opportunity for change and to create a Second Chamber that revives interest in and respect for the Parliamentary process. As Disraeli remarked, 'finality is not the language of politics'. We should not be frightened of seeking to interest voters in Westminster again.

APPENDIX

'Personal and Private' note dated 5 October 1971 and sent by Francis Pym, Government Chief Whip, to Edward Heath in advance of the Division on the European Community, 28 October 1971. (See page 290.)

Government Chief Whip
12 Downing Street, London SW1

PERSONAL AND PRIVATE

PRIME MINISTER

The Division on the European Community
28th October 1971

1. I attach my up-to-date assessment of the position of individual Members, on the assumption that the fishing interest is satisfied. This shows:-

    (a) Hard Line antis......................26

    (b) Likely to vote against us with an outside chance of abstention.........6

    (c) Uncertain, with a good chance of voting pro......................13

    (d) Remainder in favour.................281

                         326

The absolute blackest picture is therefore 45 defectors. A more likely figure is 38, and it could conceivably be as low as 30.

I am, of course, working - by various indirect means - on every Member in categories (b) and (c).

2. On this analysis the division cannot be won without some Labour votes and/or abstentions.

3. The Labour Party position is impossible to assess with accuracy. The morale of their pro-Europeans has been high, and they claim that 40-60 will vote with us in _any_ circumstances. But their estimates have varied as widely as 20-80 and we cannot tell their true strength yet. If Labour imposes a 3-line Whip, the pressures will be such that only some 20 will come into our lobby, while a further 20 might abstain. It could be even worse than that, in which case the division could only be won by some of our hardliners voting pro on a straight Party basis.

4. The Liberals it seems are 5 : 1 in favour.

/Contd

353

5. On this speculative basis, the outcome would be:-

	AYES	NOES
Con.	281	45
Lab.	20	249
Lib.	5	1
Indep.	-	6
	306	301

Majority: 5

This allows for 20 Labour abstentions, plus the Speaker, Chairman and Deputy Chairman.

If the Conservative antis were reduced to the more realistic 38, and everything else was the same, the majority would be 19.

If reduced to 35 – which is quite likely – the resultant majority would be 25, which is our current overall majority.

Obviously the position in the Labour Party is critical. If my assumption in paragraph 3 is too optimistic and our hardliners remain obdurate in all circumstances, the outcome of the vote is at risk.

6. In the past two months there has been one crucial change in the situation, which gives us the opportunity to build a bigger majority.

With the constituencies swinging firmly and sharply behind your leadership, all the pressures on Members have been to support the Government. Such a strong and favourable reaction was not expected originally, but it has happened. The result is that whether you have a 3-line Whip or a free vote, the result will be almost exactly the same.

My assessment is that upon a free vote there are now no additional names to add to the list attached. If they all take advantage of the opportunity and vote against, the total is still 45. Members have made their position clear, and the imposition of the Whip itself will help us only at the very edge of the margin. If the Labour Party follow suit, it is difficult to believe their pros would vote in less strength than 45, and more likely 75.

7. In my minute of 18th August I said that a free vote might yield the best result but it was then too soon to judge.

My conclusion now is that it will yield the best result, provided we play it right.

8. **Other advantages:**

(a) Extremely popular in the country.

(b) Legislation will be easier for us to handle and more difficult for the Opposition to oppose officially.

(c) The larger the majority the better do you fulfil your undertaking that you would only take us in with the 'full-hearted support of Parliament and people'.

(d) Relationships within the Party will remain harmonious.

9. **The snags:**

(a) Impossible to justify in theory or logic.
I think the answer is that so many Members are going to defy this 3-line Whip anyway that the currency is devalued.

(b) On what basis does one impose any 3-line Whip hereafter?
This long-term aspect disturbs me, but one answer is that there is little point in imposing a 3-line Whip when it is going to be flouted by more Members than our Parliamentary majority.

(c) The pressure of the constituencies on our antis will be nullified.
But the effect has been achieved already and there is little left to gain here. In any case the constituencies will not weaken their support and, indeed, many want a free vote and will work harder because of it.

(d) A certain loss of control.
But when I try to quantify this I find it negligible owing to the unusual nature of the issue.

(e) How do we know we shall not be let down by Labour Members?
We don't, but the evidence does not suggest we shall be. Public pressure on Labour also to have a free vote will be immense and the range of our contacts with their pro-Europeans is such as to give confidence that in these circumstances at least 50 will support us. In the event of Labour issuing a 3-line Whip in the end, it would of course be possible for you to do the same thing on the same basis.

(f) Our antis will claim a victory.
But they could not obtain any worthwhile advantage out of that and most of our pros will be equally pleased.

(g) It will be said that you have done this because you could not win otherwise.
This is true to the extent that the majority on a Whipped vote is likely to be small. But what does that matter if you obtain a reasonable majority by means of a free vote? The popularity of it could even bring a small favourable tide of its own.

10.   It has been clear to us all along that, if you decide to take this course, you could only depart from the normal expected practice of a 3-line Whip by holding rigidly to it from the very outset to the very end. This you have succeeded in achieving - to the extent that the press largely regard the issue as closed.

There exists therefore the precise opportunity you need - to spring a surprise that will, in my judgment, serve your Parliamentary end, please the people, and raise the whole level of the final stages of the debate to a new plain.

11.   One factor as yet unknown is the outcome of the Conference debate next week. We confidently expect a substantial vote of support. If so, your Saturday speech would seem the ideal moment to announce a free vote, possibly with the condition that the Opposition did the same.

This would be in time for the P.L.P. meeting when Parliament meets in the following week. There is a risk that it would be too late to bear upon the Shadow Cabinet discussion on whipping which appears, from the press, likely to take place next week. You may think it worth taking that risk, because in all other respects the 16th seems the right timing.

A further problem is how to handle the clamour for a free vote that will be repeated and repeated throughout the Conference debate. We should have to give consideration to what AD-H should say to hold the position. I think it would be a mistake for him to make the announcement because it might be said that we won the vote by this means and not on the merit of the argument. In any case, it is such an important decision that you yourself should certainly make it.

It is vitally important that this decision, if you take it, is kept top secret. The slightest whisper in the bars at Brighton would blow the story.

<u>5th October, 1971</u>

NOTES

Chapter Six

1. British Library, additional MSS 34324, Folio 290.
2. The quotations that follow are from *The Letters of Horace Walpole, Fourth Earl of Orford*, vol. I, 1732–1743, edited by Mrs Paget Toynbee and published by Clarendon Press, Oxford, 1903.
3. One of the Lords of the Treasury who had been chairman of the Committees of the House of Commons from 1727 to the date of this letter.
4. Sir Lewis Namier, *Crossroads of Power, Essays on 18th Century England*.
5. D.M. Clark, *American Historical Review*, vol. XLIII.
6. Stanhope, *The Life of William Pitt*, p. 103.
7. Ibid, Appendix, p. iii.
8. Ibid, p. 116.
9. Ibid, p. 138.
10. Notes by Horace Walpole, 17 March 1783, quoted in Stanhope, p. 146.
11. Stanhope, op cit, p. 146.
12. Ibid, p. 148.
13. Ibid, p. 152.
14. Gurowich, *Party and Independence in the early and mid-Victorian House of Commons*, p. 109.
15. *Encyclopedia Britannica*, 11th edition, Essay on Edmund Burke, p. 833.
16. Ibid, p. 833.
17. Gurowich, op cit p. 112.
18. Sir John Sainty, in a letter to me of 19 February 1997 quoting from Strachey and Fulford (eds) *Greville Memoirs*, 1938, vol. IV, p. 207.
19. Gurowich, op cit p. 295.
20. *English Historical Review*, vol. 91, July 1976.
21. Public Records Office, T.165/1, p. 209.
22. Hanham, Professor, *English Historical Review*, vol. 91, July 1976, p. 581 – quotation from the diary and correspondence of Charles Abbot, Lord Colchester.
23. Ibid, p. 580.

Chapter Seven

1. Halevy, *The Triumph of Reform 1830–1841*, p. 27, note 5.
2. Briggs, Asa, *The Age of Improvement 1783–1867*, p. 294.
3. These letters appear in *Henry and Eliza*, written and published privately by the present Lord Hampden, great-great-grandson of Henry Brand.
4. The letters, from which quotations follow, are in the private collection and library of the present Lord Hampden.
5. First volume, *Brand's letters* in House of Lords' Records Office, B59/1866.
6. Briggs, *The Age of Improvement*, p. 501.
7. Ibid p. 509.
8. Ibid, p. 509.
9. Ibid, p. 513.

Chapter Eight

1   Shannon, R., *The Age of Salisbury*, p. 123.
2   Chilston, E.A., *Chief Whip*, p. 89.
3   Shannon, op cit, p. 519.
4   Chilston, op cit, p. 44.
5   Shannon, op cit, p. 521.
6   Ibid, p.193
7   Churchill, Winston, *Lord Randolph Churchill*, p. 446.
8   Chilston, op cit, p. 69.
9   Ibid, p. 83.
10 Shannon, op cit, p. 210.
11 Douglas to Salisbury, 17 July 1886, Salisbury 3M; Chilston, *Chief Whip*, p. 84.
12 Chilston, op cit, p. 146.
13 Shannon, op cit, p. 429.
14 Chilston, op cit, p. 95.
15 Ibid, p. 95.
16 Ibid, p. 98.
17 Salisbury MSS. Chilston, op cit, p. 101.
18 Chilston, op cit, pp. 102–103.
19 Shannon, op cit, p. 235.
20 Chilston, op cit, p. 117.
21 Ibid, p. 121.
22 Ibid, p. 127.
23 Ibid, pp. 128–9.
24 Ibid, p. 222.
25 Ibid, p. 225.
26 Fergusson of Kilkerran archives, Sections 11/102 and 11/108.
27 Chilston, op cit, p. 173.
28 Ibid, pp. 275–6.
29 Ibid, p. 328.
30 Ibid, p. 310.
31 Ibid, pp. 329–30.

Chapter Nine

1   Shannon, R., *The Crisis of Imperialism 1865–1915*, p. 64.
2   Ibid, p. 185.
3   Pinto-Duschinsky, M., *British Political Finance*, Table 7, p. 29.
4   Ibid, p. 34.
5   Ibid, pp. 57 and 58.
6   Ibid, p. 43.
7   Ensor, R.C.K., *England 1870–1914*, p. 386.
8   Hazlehurst and Woodland, *A Liberal Chronicle*.
9   Lehmann MSS, quoted in Hazlehurst and Woodland, *A Liberal Chronicle*, p. 13.
10 Arthur Ponsonby's diary, 3 July and 5 June 1907, quoted in Hazlehurst and Woodland, op cit, p. 14.
11 Hazlehurst and Woodland, op cit, p. 19.

12   Whiteley to Asquith, 29 May 1908, Asquith MSS, quoted in Hazlehurst and Woodland, op cit, p. 21.

13   The car was a 14-16 HP Darracq; it had a top speed of 40mph and cost £375.

14   Hazlehurst and Woodland, op cit, p. 33.

15   Ibid, pp. 33–34.

16   Ibid, p. 40.

17   Harris, Jose, *Private Lives, Public Spirit*, p. 103.

18   Ensor, *England 1870–1914*, p. 408.

19   Ibid, p. 409.

20   Koss, Stephen, *Asquith*, p. 109.

21   Ibid, p. 106.

22   Ensor, *England 1870–1914*, p. 414.

23   Ilbert's diary, 29 July 1909, quoted in Hazlehurst and Woodland, *A Liberal Chronicle*, p. 128.

24   Ibid, p. 128.

25   Ibid, p. 139.

26   Ibid, p. 139.

27   Ibid, p. 157.

Chapter Ten

1   Vincent, J. (ed.) *The Crawford Papers*, p. 146.

2   Murray, A.C., *Master and Brother*, pp. 39–41.

3   Ibid, p. 35.

4   *Elibank Papers*, MS8802, National Library of Scotland.

5   Murray, *Master and Brother*, p. 44.

6   Vincent, op cit, p. 150.

7   Ibid, p. 168.

8   *Elibank Papers*, MS8802.

9   Ibid, MS 8802.

10   Murray, *Master and Brother*, p. 49.

11   Vincent, op cit, 19 March and 23 March 1911, pp. 180–182.

12   Ibid, p. 186.

13   Ibid, p. 188.

14   Ibid, p. 191.

15   Ibid, p. 195.

16   Ibid, p. 205 et seq.

17   *Arthur C Murray's Diary*, 1911, National Library of Scotland.

18   Foreign Secretary and a determined supporter of Votes for Women.

19   *Elibank Papers*, MS8803.

20   Secretary of State at the Board of Education.

21   Donaldson, F., *The Marconi Scandal*, pp. 21–23.

22   Chancellor of the Exchequer, 1903–5 and 1919–21; Foreign Secretary, 1924–9; Nobel Peace Prize, 1925.

23   President, Local Government Board, 1900–5 and 1915–16.

24   Chancellor of the Exchequer, 1916–18; Leader of the House of Commons, 1916–21; Prime Minister, 1922–3.

25   Vincent, op cit, p. 243.

26   Ibid, pp. 249–51.

Chapter Eleven

1   The notes, family letters and newspaper cuttings from which I quote in this chapter are in the collection of Gay, Lady Charteris, David Margesson's daughter.
2   Now in the library of Lord Crathorne, Tommy Dugdale's son.
3   Long-time Scottish MP, Minister of Agriculture and of Health in Second World War, married to a sister of Nancy Dugdale.
4   He held every senior ministerial post, including Home Office, Foreign Office and the Exchequer. Challenged unsuccessfully for the leadership in 1957 and 1963.
5   Sir Thomas Inskip MP, Minister for Co-ordination of Defence, 1936–39.
6   Colville, J., *The Fringes of Power, Downing Street Diaries 1939–1955*. Colville became Assistant Private Secretary to the Prime Minister October 1939.

Chapter Twelve

1   Hutchinson, G., *Edward Heath: a personal and political biography*, p. 83.
2   Eden, A., *Full Circle*.
3   Lord Wright of Richmond, Head of the Diplomatic Service, 1986–91.
4   Heath, E., *The Course of My Life*, p. 58.
5   Ibid, p. 58.
6   Sir Paul Bryan DSO MC, MP for Howden Division of East Riding, Yorkshire, 1955–83.
7   Bryan, P., *Wool, War and Westminster*.
8   Ibid, p. 230.
9   Lord Carr of Hadley, MP for Mitcham 1950–74, Sutton Carshalton 1974–76; Home Secretary 1972–74.
10 MP for East Toxteth 1931–50, Beckenham 1950–57, Government Chief Whip 1951–55.
11 Quoted in Campbell's *Edward Heath, a biography*, p. 83.
12 Stuart, J., *Within The Fringe*, pp. 145–7.
13 Heath, op cit, pp. 163–4.
14 Ibid, p. 169.
15 Ibid, p. 175.
16 MP for Rushcliffe since 1970, Chancellor of the Exchequer 1993–97.
17 The Earl of Kilmuir, *Memoirs: Political Adventure*, p. 285.
18 Heath, op cit, p. 179.
19 Ibid, p. 181.
20 Ibid, p. 188.
21 *The Times*, 12 October 1971, quoted in Campbell's *Edward Heath, a biography*, p. 401.
22 Campbell, J., *Edward Heath, a biography*, p. 402.
23 Labour MP for Farnworth and the unofficial whip for his party's pro-Europeans.
24 MP for Westmorland 1964–83 and for Westmorland and Lonsdale 1983–97; Minister of Agriculture 1983–87.
25 Campbell, J., *Edward Heath, a biography*, p. 103.

Chapter Thirteen

1   Bodleian Archives, Box 6791, Folio 112.
2   Lord Renton, MP for Huntingdonshire 1945–79; Minister of State at the Home Office 1961–62.
3   Bodleian Archives, Box 6787, Folio 3.
4   Sir Nicholas Redmayne's papers as shown to the BBC.

5   Ex-Labour MP and ex-Attorney General.
6   Bodleian Archives, Box 6787, Folio 17.
7   Ibid, Folio 13.
8   Ibid, Folio 19.
9   Ibid, Folio 32.
10 Heath, E., *The Course of My Life*, pp. 259–61.
11 Sir Nicholas Redmayne's papers as shown to the BBC.
12 Conversation with Ted Heath, 17 June 1998.
13 Bodleian Archives, Box 6787, Folios 208–211.
14 Ibid, Folio 132.
15 Ibid, Folio 132.
16 Conservative Councillor. Then Labour MP for Bassetlaw, 1935–68.
17 Bodleian Archives, Box 6790, Folios 131–50; Sir T J Bligh DSO, DSC and bar; Macmillan's principal private secretary since 1959.
18 Bodleian Archives, Box 6791.
19 Ibid, Folio 149.
20 Ibid, Folios 58–69.
21 Maudling, R., *Memoirs*, pp 125–28.
22 Conversation on 6 November 2003.
23 Redmayne was made a peer in 1966.
24 Bodleian Archives, Box 6791, Folio 137.
25 Bodleian Archives, Box 6787, Folios 49–51.
26 Seldon, A. and Ball, S. (eds) *Conservative Century*, p. 78.
27 Lord Windlesham, *Political Quarterly*, vol. 36, no. 2, April–June 1965.
28 Bodleian Archives, Box 6791.
29 Maudling, *Memoirs*, p. 127.
30 Ibid, p. 136.

Chapter Fourteen

1   MP for Stafford 1984–97; MP for Stone since May 1997.
2   Brandreth, Gyles, *Breaking the Code*, p. 472.
3   MP and ex-Secretary of State for Overseas Development.
4   *Today* programme, 25 October 2002.
5   Labour MP for Bermondsey 1945–82; Government Chief Whip 1969–70, 1974–76.
6   Labour MP for Bristol South 1970–87; Government Chief Whip 1976–79.
7   Labour MP for Hampstead 1966–70.
8   BBC, 22 October 2001.
9   Conservative MP since 1970.
10 MP for Nottingham North since 1987.
11 MP for South Worcestershire 1974–97; MP for West Worcestershire since 1997.
12 MP for High Peak 1992–97; MP for Wealden since June 2001.
13 MP for Norfolk Central 1962–74; MP for Chesham and Amersham 1974–92; Lord Privy Seal 1979–81; now a Conservative peer.
14 *Daily Telegraph*, 31 October 2003.
15 Labour Secretary of State for Defence 1964–70; Chancellor of the Exchequer 1974–79.
16 Quoted by Martin Redmayne in the Home Service Broadcast recorded 10 October 1966.

Chapter Fifteen

1   Thoms, W.J., *The Book of the Court*, p. 352.
2   Ibid, p. 353.
3   Ibid, p. 354.
4   Allison, R. and Riddell, S. (eds) *The Royal Encyclopedia*, p. 214.
5   Conversation with Lord Denham 17 December 2003.
6   *The Times*, 15 December 1998.
7   Hansard, column 695, Wednesday 18 December 2002.

BIBLIOGRAPHY

Allison, R. and Riddell, S. (eds) *The Royal Encyclopedia* (Macmillan Press)

Blacker, J. (ed.) *Have You Forgotten Yet?* (Leo Cooper, 2000)

Bodleian Archives, Boxes 6787, 6790 and 6791

Brandreth, Gyles, *Breaking the Code, Westminster Diaries May 1990–May 1997* (Weidenfeld & Nicolson, London 1999)

Briggs, Asa, *The Age of Improvement 1783-1867* (Longman Inc., New York, 1959)

Brivati, B. and Heffernan, R. (eds) *The Labour Party* (Macmillan Press Ltd, 2000)

Bryan, Paul, *Wool, War and Westminster* (Tom Donovan Publishers Ltd, 1993)

Campbell, John, *Edward Heath: a biography* (Jonathan Cape, London, 1993)

Chilston, Viscount, *W.H. Smith* (Routledge & Kegan Paul, London, 1965)

Chilston, E.A., *Chief Whip. The Political Life and Times of Aretas Akers-Douglas, 1st Viscount Chilston* (Routledge & Kegan Paul, London, 1961)

Churchill, Winston, *Lord Randolph Churchill* (Odhams, 1951)

Clark, Alan, *Diaries* (Weidenfeld & Nicolson, 1993)

Clark, D.M. *American Historical Review*, vol. XLIII

Colville, John, *The Fringes of Power, Downing Street Diaries 1939–1955* (Hodder & Stoughton, London, 1985)

Cradock, Percy, *Know Your Enemy* (John Murray (Publishers) Ltd, 2002)

Donaldson, Frances, *The Marconi Scandal* (Rupert Hart-Davis, 1962)

Dugdale, Blanche, E.C., *Arthur James Balfour, First Earl of Balfour, vol. I* (Hutchinson & Co., London, 1936)

Dugdale, Blanche, E.C., *Arthur James Balfour, First Earl of Balfour 1906–1930* (Hutchinson & Co., London, 1936)

Eden, Anthony, *Memoirs, Full Circle*

Ensor, R.C.K., *England 1870–1914* (Clarendon Press, Oxford, 1936)

Evans, E.J., *The Great Reform Act of 1832* (Methuen, London, 1983)

Gascoigne, Bamber, *Encyclopedia of Britain* (Macmillan Press, 1993)

Gurowich, P.M., *Party and Independence in the early and mid-Victorian House of Commons* (Doctorate thesis, 1986)

Halevy, Elie, *The Rule of Democracy 1905–1914* (Ernest Benn Ltd, 1932)

Halevy, Elie, *The Triumph of Reform 1830–1841* (Ernest Benn Ltd, 1923)

Halevy, Elie, *Victorian Years 1841–1895* (Ernest Benn Ltd, 1951)

Hampden, Lord, *Henry and Eliza* (privately printed)

Hanham, Professor, *English Historical Review*, vol. 91

Harris, Jose, *Private Lives, Public Spirit* (Oxford University Press, 1993)

Hazelhurst, C. and Woodland, C. (eds) *A Liberal Chronicle J.A.Pease 1908–1910* (Historians' Press, 1994)

Heath, Edward, *The Course of My Life, My Autobiography* (Hodder & Stoughton, London, 1998)

House of Commons, Official Report, *Parliamentary Debates, Fifth Series – vol. 365* (H.M. Stationery Office, London, 1940)

House of Lords Records Office, *Brand's letters vol. 1 B59/1866*

Howe, Geoffrey, *Conflict of Loyalty* (Macmillan, London, 1994)

Hurd, Douglas, *Memoirs* (Little, Brown, 2003)

Hutchinson, George, *Edward Heath, a personal and political biography* (Longman, 1970)

James, R.R. (ed.) *Chips, The Diaries of Sir Henry Channon* (Weidenfeld & Nicolson, London, 1967)

Jenkins, R., *Asquith* (Collins, 1978)

Johnson, Nancy E. (ed.) *The Diary of Gathorne Hardy* (Clarendon Press, Oxford, 1981)

Kilmuir, The Earl of, *Memoirs: Political Adventure*

Koss, Stephen, *Asquith* (Allen Lane, London, 1976)

Macmillan, Gerald, *Honours For Sale* (The Richards Press, 1954)

Macmillan, Harold, *Riding The Storm 1956–1959* (Macmillan & Co Ltd, 1971)

Maudling, Reginald, *Memoirs* (Sidgwick & Jackson Ltd, 1978)

Murray, Arthur C., *Master and Brother* (John Murray, 1945)

Namier, Sir Lewis, *Crossroads of Power, Essays on 18th century England* (London, 1962)

National Library of Scotland, *Elibank Papers*

National Library of Scotland, *Arthur C. Murray's Diary 1911*

Pinto-Duschinsky, Michael, *British Political Finance 1830–1980* (AEI Studies, 1981)

Ridley, J. and Percy, C. (eds) *The Letters of Arthur Balfour and Lady Elcho 1885–1917* (Hamish Hamilton Ltd, 1992)

Rothschild, Robert, *Peace for our Time* (Brassey's Defence Publishers Ltd, 1988)

Seldon, Anthony, *Major, A Political Life* (Phoenix, 1997)

Seldon, A. and Ball, S. (eds) *Conservative Century* (Oxford University Press Inc., 1994)

Shannon, R., *The Age of Salisbury, 1881–1902: Unionism and Empire* (Longman Group Ltd, 1996)

Shannon, R., *The Crisis of Imperialism 1865–1915* (Hart-Davis, MacGibbon Ltd, 1974)

Stanhope, Earl, *The Life of William Pitt, vol. I* (John Murray, 1861)

Stuart, James, *Within the Fringe: An Autobiography* (The Bodley Head, 1967)

Tennant, Ernest W.D., *True Account* (Max Parrish & Co Ltd, 1957)

Thoms, W.J. *The Book of the Court* (Henry G. Bohn, 1854)

Toynbee, Mrs Paget (edited and arranged by) *The Letters of Horace Walpole, Fourth Earl of Orford, vol. I* (Clarendon Press, Oxford, 1903)

Vincent, J., (ed.) *The Crawford Papers. The Journals of David Lindsay 27th Earl of Crawford and 10th Earl of Balcarres 1871–1940 during the years 1892 to 1940* (Manchester University Press, 1984)

Windlesham, Lord, *Political Quarterly*, vol. 36, no. 2, April–June 1965

Wright, D.G., *Democracy and Reform 1815–1885* (Longman Group Ltd, 1970)

INDEX